THE ORIGINS AND CHARACTER OF THE ANCIENT CHINESE CITY

THE ORIGINS AND CHARACTER OF THE ANCIENT CHINESE CITY

VOLUME I

THE CITY IN ANCIENT CHINA

PAUL WHEATLEY

ALDINETRANSACTION
A DIVISION OF TRANSACTION PUBLISHERS
NEW BRUNSWICK (U.S.A.) AND LONDON (U.K.)

First paperback printing 2008

This book is printed on acid-free paper that meets the American National Standard for Permanence of Paper for Printed Library Materials.

Library of Congress Catalog Number: 2008018010
ISBN: 978-0-202-36202-1
Printed in the United States of America

Library of Congress Cataloging-in-Publication Data

Wheatley, Paul.
    [Pivot of the four quarters]
    The origins and character of the Chinese city / Paul Wheatley.
        p. cm.
    Originally published under title: The pivot of the four quarters: a preliminary enquiry into the origins and character of the ancient Chinese city. Chicago: Aldine Pub. Co., 1971.
    Includes bibliographical references and index.
    ISBN 978-0-202-36202-1 (volume 1 : alk. paper) -- ISBN 978-0-202-36203-8 (volume 2 : alk. paper)
        1. Cities and towns--China--History. 2. Cities and towns, Ancient--China. 3. China--History--221 B.C.-960 A.D. I. Title.

HT147.C48W5 2008
307.760951--dc22

                                                        2008018010

Dedicated to the Memory of

NUMA DENIS
FUSTEL DE COULANGES

VOLUME ONE
THE CITY IN ANCIENT CHINA

Contents

List of Figures

Preface

This volume seeks in small measure to help redress the current imbalance between our knowledge of the contemporary Western-style city on the one hand, and of the urbanism characteristic of the traditional world on the other. Specifically, it is an attempt to elucidate the manner in which there emerged on one part of the North China plain during the second millennium BC hierarchically structured, functionally specialized social institutions organized on a political and territorial basis, and to describe the way in which, during subsequent centuries, they were diffused through much of the rest of north and central China. The exigent question as to whether all the multifarious groupings of population past and present that are conventionally designated as 'urban' do indeed constitute a unitary field of study is discussed but not assumed; and those aspects of urban theory which, though relevant to our topic, have been derived predominantly from the investigation of Western urbanism, are tested against, rather than applied to, the society of ancient China. Moreover, whereas the majority of previous investigations into the nature of the Chinese city have been undertaken from the standpoint of the humanist, in the following pages I have adopted a point of view closer to that of the social scientist. In other words, I have espoused a generalizing and comparative approach in contrast to the hitherto more commonly essayed discussion of the formal and specifically Sinic features of Shang and Chou cities. Instead of seeking to distil from the totality of their characteristics the uniqueness of the earliest Chinese cities, I have tried to isolate and analyze those cross-cultural regularities which they shared with urban forms in other cultures. In practice this has meant that I have measured a fragment of the Chinese urban experience against a generalized model of urban genesis, a procedure which has posed problems of both a conceptual and a technical nature. So far as the conceptual aspect is concerned, the construction of a model has been the logical outcome of a commitment to a broadly hypothetico-deductive methodology, a belief that advances in our understanding of urban genesis will result in the first instance from the generation of testable hypotheses, rather than from a Baconian inductivist approach which, in my opinion, is concerned more with proof than with discovery. Whatever the inadequacies of the model discussed in Chapter Three, it is at least testable against both existing evidence and that which is likely to become available in the future. In this way not only do theoretical considerations act as a check on the validity of historical reconstructions, but the empirical substantiation of particular sequences and circumstances is capable of inducing revision and qualification of even the most cherished generalizations. Furthermore, the comparative method would seem particularly appropriate to an examination of the emergence, in widely separated regions and at widely different times, of such an intricately interrelated set of institutions as the city, and this conclusion must surely be reinforced when the whole problem is bedevilled by appalling lacunae in the evidence. At the same time, I am aware that my analysis is conducted at such a broad level of conceptualization that it does little more than identify gross criteria for assigning the early Chinese city a role in the infinitely complex pattern of urban evolution, without specifying those idiomorphic features that made it distinctively Chinese. It goes without saying that a more truly explanatory schema would consider differences as well as similarities between urban forms in diverse cultures. However, this is perhaps the appropriate point at which to draw attention to the sub-title of this work, the purpose of which is to affirm the partial nature of the inquiry, the incipient stage of the investigation, and the proleptical character of the conclusions.

At the level of technique, the single tool indispensable for a study of this nature is that assemblage of cognizances and crafts which constitutes the discipline of Sinology. It is not, as participants in a recent symposium have been at pains to emphasize, an end in itself, but it is a prerequisite for any worthwhile comparative study involving ancient China, and I regret that my own technical competence in this field has not permitted me to pursue my arguments in greater depth and with greater subtlety. My excuse is the old one adduced by Hippocrates.

The evidence bearing on urban genesis, in China as elsewhere, is both direct and indirect in character. Direct evidence is almost entirely the product of archeological research, for only in the Western tracts of that realm of secondary urban generation (this term is defined on p. 9) which has recently come to be known as Southeast Asia *sensu stricto* is the process even partially documented in written records (as opposed to archetyped in literary tradition). That region is virtually unique in that divers Chinese histories, encyclopedias, and topographies preserve observations, both informal and official, relating to the period of city generation. Although fragmentary and ambivalent, these records are still capable of affording some degree of control over the more hypothetical constructs derived from investigations in other cultural realms. In China such contemporary literary evidence is entirely lacking.

PREFACE

Indirect or circumstantial evidence, by contrast, is of a more diversified character, comprising inferences from the morphology, symbolism, and functioning of later cities, especially the great capitals, urban archetypes *par excellence*, as well as information derived from folklore and mythology. This latter genre of source material always proves especially difficult to handle. The collective memory of traditional society is by no means unresponsive to happenings in the past but, unable to retain individual persons and specific events, transforms them respectively into archetypes and categories, heroes and heroic situations. And because myth is the ultimate, not the primal stage, in the creation of these archetypes, it is often hazardous to attempt to reverse the process and to isolate the paradigm at the core of the legend. Evaluating such evidence is rather like trying to grasp a fish at the bottom of a deep pool. As the intruding hand shatters the shadowy image, so the irruption of a 20th-century mind into the conceptual framework of the ancient world inevitably induces cultural refractions of such magnitude that the image of the quarry at best undergoes distortion, at worst is wholly lost from sight. But recognition of the limitations imposed by this anamorphosis is a condition of entry into the traditional world, and the social scientist who would concern himself with urban genesis must be resigned for the present to seeing his elusive fish disintegrate into a thousand glittering fragments as he reaches towards the bottom of what is a very deep pool indeed. It is not to be doubted that in the future the social scientist and the historian will be able to probe the nature of the traditional world with subtler instruments less destructive of its value systems than those at present available, but meanwhile the present study should be regarded as no more than a distant glimpse, refracted almost to unintelligibility, of one early cultural manifestation of the most complex artifact yet devised by man. On finishing this volume the reader will need no reminder of the manner in which that image, so comprehensible and definite at a distance of three thousand and more years, disintegrated when we sought to examine it more closely.

University of California, Berkeley
and University College London
February 1968

NOTE

Orthographical matters

The exact manner in which the Shang people pronounced their words is probably beyond recall, but it is generally presumed that they spoke an early version of what later became the Chinese language. They certainly wrote in a script which was subsequently recognized as distinctively Chinese. In any case, of one thing we can be certain: the Chou scholars who composed the few literary analecta purporting to relate to Shang times, and which may indeed have preserved some authentic Shang values, rendered personal names, place names, and technical terms in early Chinese forms. The phonetic garb of this Chou Chinese as it was pronounced in about 800 BC (technically known as Archaic Chinese) has been reconstructed largely by the labors of Bernhard Karlgren, and is employed in the present work for the transcription of names and terms prior to the Han. This expedient provides only imperfect renderings of words from the later part of the Chou period, but is even less satisfactory in the discussions of the Shang city in Chapter One. However, there is every reason to suppose that the versions of names and terms that result (signified in the text by a brace of asterisks) are a good deal closer to the Shang vocalizations than are the phonologically reduced forms of Modern Standard Chinese. The inelegance of the phonetic symbols, which may even appear forbidding to some readers, is in my opinion not too high a price to pay for the enhanced awareness of the richness of ancient Chinese culture that they reveal. By disclosing the more diversified sound structure of the so-called Archaic language, they help us to recover some of the sensuous texture of that ancient world, and enable us to give the ancient names something approaching, however imperfectly, their original sound. Nevertheless, had Professor Schafer published his simplified version of the Karlgren reconstructions before I had written this book, I should have been happy to have used it. As it is, so that readers accustomed to Modern Standard Chinese pronunciation may the more easily recognize the words in their Archaic dress, I have always added the standard Wade-Giles version in parenthesis when the word is first mentioned. Occasionally, when dealing with names as familiar as those of, say, the culture heroes Yao, Shun, Huang-Ti, and Yü the Great I have relied primarily on the Modern Standard Chinese forms, and relegated the Archaic reconstructions to parenthesis. Certain Han and T'ang names have been transcribed according to Karlgren's reconstruction of Ancient Chinese (denoted by a single asterisk), the dialect of *Ḍ'i̯ang-·ân (Ch'ang-an) in about AD 600. In the case of a few names which are so well known outside China that they have a claim to be regarded as a part of world, rather than Chinese, culture, I have retained the Modern Standard Chinese transcription alone. Such, for example, were the style of the founder of the Ch'in dynasty, Shih Huang-ti, and the names both of the historian Ssŭ-ma Ch'ien and of his great work, the *Shih-Chi*. The names of dynasties and provinces have usually been rendered in their Modern Standard Chinese form (e.g. Shang, Chou, T'ang, etc.), although the names of the individual Chou states have been Archaized. The conventional orthographic distinction between Shen-hsi and Shan-hsi has been retained for the sake of convenience, even though, as the pronunciations of the two characters differ only in tone, it has no basis in the Wade-Giles system.

The system of transcription employed by Bernhard Karlgren and followed in the present work is as follows.

Voiceless consonants		*Voiced consonants*
Gutturals	k, k', χ [X]	$g, g',$ ng, γ
Palatals	$\hat{t}, \hat{t}', \acute{s}, t\acute{s}, t\acute{s}'$	$\hat{d}, \hat{d}', \acute{n}, j, \acute{z}, d\acute{z}', \acute{n}\acute{z}$
Dentals	t, t', s, ts, ts'	$d, d', n, l, r, z, dz, dz'$
Supradentals	$ş, tş, tş'$	$dẓ'$
Labials	p, p'	b, b', m, w
Laryngals	$\cdot(\cdot iu)$	$O\ (iu)$

K', g', etc. are aspirates; χ = German *ach*, γ = North German *g* in *wagen* (fricative); $\hat{t}$ etc. are formed like the Italian *c* in *città* with the predorsum against the alveoli; the laryngal $\cdot$ ($\cdot iu$) is the 'Knacklaut' in German *Ecke*; no initial letter : O (iu) is a smooth vocalic ingress as in English *aim*.

> *Vowels*
> $\hat{a}$ as in French *pâte*
> a as in French *patte*
> $\hat{a}$ = short $\hat{a}$
> $ə$ as *e* in German *Knabe*
> e as in French *été*
> $\ddot{a}$ as in German *Bär*
> ε = a still more open, slack $\ddot{a}$-sound (English *man*)
> v as in English *but*
> i as *ee* in English *bee*
> o as in German *Sommer*
> $\hat{o}$ as in French *beau*
> $\hat{o}$ = short $\hat{o}$
> $\mathring{a}$ = an open *o* as in English *law*
> $\breve{u}$ as in English *value*
> u as in English *rude*
> $\breve{a}, \breve{e}, \breve{o}$ = short *a, e, o*
> $i, e, ə$ = subordinate vowels in diphthongs or triphthongs

Reproduced from 'Grammata Serica Recensa,' *Bulletin of the Museum of Far Eastern Antiquities*, no.29 (Stockholm, 1957), pp.3–4.

Bibliographical matters

As a very high proportion of the sources and scholarly expositions consulted in the preparation of this volume are mentioned only once and have no continuing relevance to the work as a whole, a bibliography has not been considered necessary. However, full references are provided in the *Notes and References*

NOTE

which follow each chapter. On those occasions when references are repeated, they are usually given in abbreviated form. Some Chinese authors writing in Western languages adopt transcriptions other than those of the Wade-Giles system and, moreover, not infrequently transpose the order of their family (*hsing*) and personal (*ming*) names, while yet retaining the Chinese sequence when writing in that language. In such cases the author's preferred Western form has been preserved, with the Wade-Giles orthography and the Chinese order appended in parenthesis, e.g., Kwang-chih Chang (Chang Kuang-chih); Tjan Tjoe Som (Tseng Chu-sen). In citations of contemporary Chinese works in the Glossary the simplified (and sometimes unauthorized) characters now or recently in use in the People's Republic of China are reproduced exactly as in the original books and articles.

Matters of definition

City in this volume is used generically to denote any urban form, and carries none of the ancillary connotations of size, status, or origin implicit in contemporary, everyday American or English usage. *Urbanism* is used to denote that particular set of functionally integrated institutions which were first devised some five thousand years ago to mediate the transformation of relatively egalitarian, ascriptive, kin-structured groups into socially stratified, politically organized, territorially based societies, and which have since progressively extended both the scope and autonomy of their institutional spheres, so that today they mould the actions and aspirations of vastly the larger proportion of mankind. *Urbanization* refers to the ratio of urban dwellers to total population, and can be expressed algebraically as

$$u = \frac{Pc}{Pt}$$

where u = degree of urbanization,
Pc = the number of urban dwellers,
Pt = the total population.

It follows that the distribution of urbanization is not necessarily (and today is still a long way from) the same thing as the distribution of urbanism (number and spatial arrangement of cities) or the distribution of urban dwellers.

Acknowledgments

In constructing the model of urban genesis which constitutes Chapter Three I benefited greatly from reading Robert McC. Adams's *Lewis Henry Morgan Lectures* for 1965 under the title *The Evolution of urban society: early Mesopotamia and Prehispanic Mexico* (Aldine Publishing Company, Chicago 1966). In this imaginative comparison of structural change in 'two territorially extensive, complex, long-lived, innovative, characteristically "civilized" societies', Professor Adams has carried forward the methodology of cross-

NOTE

cultural analysis to a point where he can be said, in Thomas Kuhn's phrase, to have inaugurated a new paradigm of knowledge. I am grateful to Professor Adams for allowing me to read his book before publication. I am also indebted to Mrs T'ung Huang Yih of University College London not only for a great deal of meticulous assistance during the later stages in the preparation of this book, but also for the calligraphy which graces the *Glossary*. Finally, I would like to express my thanks to Mr A.R.Turnbull and his colleagues at the University of Edinburgh Press for the skill and care that they have brought to bear on the production of this book, and to Mr Peter McIntyre for the discernment with which he has compiled the analytical index.

References

The notes and references are printed at the end of each chapter, and the appropriate page-number for each note is printed at the top of each text page.

Part One

THE CITY IN ANCIENT CHINA

●

1

The Genesis of the City in China

INTRODUCTION

Writers on the general topic of urban origins have not usually given much consideration to the Chinese experience. With very few exceptions they have confined their attention to the climacteric events that took place at various times in Lower Mesopotamia, Egypt and Nuclear America.[1] Some, while acknowledging the essentially independent character of the earliest Chinese urban configurations, have excluded them from consideration on the grounds that the available evidence is both exiguous and unrepresentative. It is true that, in comparison with the archeological evidence that has accumulated over the span of a century or so in relation to the cities of Sumer, or over a somewhat shorter period in relation to those of Mesoamerica, the Chinese materials are meager in quantity. They are also fragmented and both spatially and temporally discontinuous, while the stages immediately prior to the emergence of urban forms are but poorly elucidated. However, only a small proportion of the total finds from Sumer and Mesoamerica bear directly on urban generation, so that the abundance of archeological materials should not be taken to imply vast resources for the study of city origins. Moreover, as has frequently been pointed out, excavation has been confined almost exclusively to the environs of monumental complexes at the expense of the territory which supported them, as well as to the levels of the monumental complexes at the expense of the antecedent formative phases in their development.

In China the foundations for the study of urban origins were laid during fifteen seasons of excavation at An-yang, undertaken by the Archeological Section of the former National Research Institute of History and Philology of the Academia Sinica between 1928 and 1937.[2] It is true that these excavations were concerned solely with a single city, and were performed under conditions of great difficulty, but they did reveal a fairly detailed and reliable plan of part of the last Shang capital, as well as bringing to light a considerable number of ancillary and other contemporary settlements and an oracular archive of more than 17,000 pieces of inscribed bones and shells. Almost equally important was the fact that these excavations established beyond doubt the

3

historicity of the Shang dynasty, hitherto known only from literary sources, at the very moment when a new school of critical historians was questioning the authenticity of virtually all pre-Han texts, and by implication the existence of the early dynasties.[3] By revealing on oracle inscriptions the names of no less than twenty-three of the thirty Shang kings mentioned in literary sources, Tung Tso-pin and others reaffirmed the potential worth, though not necessarily the factual accuracy, of the literary tradition so far as the Shang was concerned.

After the end of World War II field work was resumed at An-yang by members of the Chung-Kuo K'e-hsüeh Yüan, but more recently interest has tended to focus on a group of sites in the neighborhood of the city of Cheng-Chou in northern Ho-nan.[4] Discovered in 1950, these remains have provided an uninterrupted chronological sequence beginning with the phase of Developed Village Farming and culminating in a clearly defined example of Shang urbanism. Subsequently, other urban and proto-urban Shang sites have been located in an arcuate zone curving across the North China Plain from Shan-Hsien in the southwest to Ch'ü-yang in the northeast. The four fully fledged ceremonial cities and half dozen or so proto-cities, incompletely excavated as they are, still provide information in considerably more detail than is available for, say, Archaic Egypt or the central Andes.

The reaffirmation of the latent value of certain literary sources which is a corollary of these excavations of Shang urban sites has significant implications in view of the limitations of archeological evidence for the purpose in hand. As Robert Adams has recently been at pains to point out, archeological interpretation tends, from the nature of the tools and techniques that it employs, as well as by reason of other disciplinary proclivities, to overweight the integrative purport of its cultural assemblages. 'Emphasis is given,' as he says, 'to objects and institutions evoking consensual patterns of behavior – art styles, cult objects, rituals – rather than to those which might suggest incipient patterns of differentiation and stratification.'[5] Moreover, the nature of the raw materials of archeology has not infrequently predisposed its scholars to pay greater attention to technological matters than to social and institutional change, a tendency that is clearly apparent in the theories of urban genesis proposed by the archeologists of a generation or two ago. And as the processes of urban development brought a great increase in the complexity of social, economic, and intellectual institutions, so archeological techniques have proved progressively less capable of elucidating these relationships in their entirety.

It is in this context that the written word becomes a useful adjunct to archeological materials in the achievement of a balanced interpretation. As we shall see subsequently, the earliest Chinese records, inscribed on bone and shell, were of restricted import, being concerned only with certain activities of a small, though influential, group of people. They are probably comparable in their utility to the so-called Protoliterate texts of Mesopotamia from the end of the fourth millennium B C, but are of much less use than the wealth of varied and detailed cuneiform documents available by the end of the Early Dynastic period (c. 2500 B C), selective and in other ways inadequate though these latter are as a basis for the reconstruction of contemporary urban life. However, although the oracle records are unsatisfactory for present purposes, they afford a good deal more information than, say, the Mayan inscriptions of the Classic period, of which only the calendrical information has so far been deciphered. In the New World the handful of documents that survived the Spanish conquest of Mesoamerica are largely irrelevant to the study of urban origins in either the Aztec or Mayan realms, but there are post-Conquest Spanish records which do provide accounts of contemporary indigenous urban life refracted through the prism of an alien culture, as well as traditional genealogies, recollections, and pseudo-annals compiled in a Spanish idiom by native authors soon after the Conquest. In some respects these last are analogous to the 'classical' litera-ture of China that was reconstituted in Han times but which may preserve pheno-crysts of Shang history embedded in a matrix of later material. The nature of these early Chinese literary sources will be discussed in subsequent sections.

It is, of course, true that in no region of nuclear urbanism does the evidence, whether archeological, literary, or mythological, afford an adequate base on which to erect a definitive account of urban origins. It is all a matter of degree. Few scholars would deny that early Mesopotamia and Prehispanic Mexico offer the most ample and most diversified documentation of this momentous transformation, but even there the source material falls far short of adequacy. In Archaic Egypt, on the other hand, direct evidence for the crucial trans-formation from village to city appears to be lost for ever, buried far below the surface of the Nile alluvium. As far as archeological exposures are concerned, the situation of the Indus valley is not too dissimilar from that of China. Both exhibit two or three partially excavated cities and a constellation of lesser sites, but in the case of Harappā and Mohenjo-daro the earlier excavations were subject to only poor stratigraphic controls, so that we are left with a picture of powerful and flourishing cities but with little idea as to their mode of origin, while the inscriptional resources, which are apparently of a restricted functional range in any case, have not yet been deciphered. In the central Andes relevant archeological investigation has, with very few exceptions, been little better than superficial, there are no Prehispanic literary sources, and between us and the origin of urban forms is interposed the screen of Inca domination which, even when it did not obliterate earlier cities, transformed them into its own cultural image. It is true that the Inca screen is not entirely opaque, but it is a much more powerful distorting instrument than are the reconstituted Han texts. Adams has also made the point that the territories in this culture realm which have received the most attention from archeologists have not been those about which Spanish ethnohistories have the most to say.[6]

In this ecumenical context the case for undertaking a study of urban origins in China appears not to be wholly devoid of merit. Several urban and proto-urban sites partially excavated, one of which provides a complete chronological sequence from a level of Developed Village Farming through to the emergence of a ceremonial city, coupled with a vast archive of 100,000 inscribed oracle bones and shells, a handful of texts that may preserve memories of actual Shang events, and a corpus of later mythology which may reflect authentic Shang values is an inadequate, but not negligible, basis on which to found an argument. This is even more to the point when the evidence available in each of the other realms of nuclear urbanism is so meager, fragmented, and ambiguous that a comparative approach alone appears likely to provide fruitful insights into the dynamics of urban genesis. The Chinese evidence alone would prove inconclusive even were it very much more abundant than is in fact the case, but it assumes a completely new significance when viewed in the light of the totality of materials available for a study of the early history of urbanism.

There is, however, another set of objections which seem to have weighed heavily against the Chinese experience with students of urban origins. Mindful of the fact that the earliest Chinese cities post-dated those of Sumer and Egypt by about a millennium and a half, and those of the Indus valley by approximately a thousand years, some scholars have regarded the process of city formation in China as in some way secondary, contaminated as it were by the presence of cultural traits diffused from Southwest Asia. It is certainly possible for primary diffusion of the set of integrated institutions that is the city to occur through the migration of a people into new territories, as happened so notably when the Spanish-style city was carried to Latin America, when the English-style city was transported to North America, Australasia and elsewhere, or when Russian-style cities were founded in Siberia. This mode of urban diffusion is virtually inseparable from the extension of empire and was, in fact, a necessary concomitant of such happenings in ancient days, no less than of European colonial expansion from the sixteenth to the nineteenth century. The foundation of such cities is usually associated with (1) the creation of an administrative organization moulded according to, and designed to sustain, the value system of the colonial homeland, (2) the imposition on the simpler society of the legal definitions of property current in the colonists' homeland, and (3) not infrequently the extension to embrace the newly colonized territories of certain sectors of the metropolitan economy. But since the time of Joseph de Guignes no one has seriously contended that the Chinese people themselves derived from the Middle East.[7] So-called secondary diffusion, the direct borrowing of culture traits, is out of the question in the second millennium BC so far as such a complicated artifact as the city is concerned. So, indeed, is stimulus diffusion, which is held to occur when the *idea* of some technical process proves sufficient to induce its reinvention. It is, of course, obvious that the likelihood of diffusion of a complex invention depends very greatly on the general level of technological attainment of the societies concerned. While it is possible that some of the more fundamental inventions may have emanated from one or more hearths, the contemporary world affords abundant evidence that even the most complex technological achievements can now spread from continent to continent virtually instantaneously through the media of secondary or stimulus diffusion. In the sphere of urban forms, for example, the contemporary planned city, originally devised according to Western values, can be found in one form or another on five of the six continents. But in ancient times, at the lower end of the scale of technological competence, it is inconceivable that any form of city could have spread by either secondary or stimulus diffusion. Consequently, I am at a loss to understand what Sir Mortimer Wheeler had in mind when he declared, 'So also, we may suppose, in the third millennium BC India (Pakistan) received from Mesopotamia the already-established *idea* of city-life or civilization, but transmuted that idea into a mode substantially new and congenial to her'.[8] Apart from the imposition by an already established political authority of urban foundations – usually for administrative or military purposes – in tributary or uninhabited territories (primary diffusion), cities formerly could come into being only where an appropriate conjunction of internal forces induced spontaneous readjustments of social, political and economic relationships. Mere knowledge of city life diffusing through a folk society could, and can, never be sufficient to induce the generation of urban forms.

Of course, this is not to deny that in numerous instances cities have arisen as a result of the secondary diffusion of nexuses of cultural traits which have stimulated the evolution of society towards the point where cities were generated. Just such a process seems to have preceded the emergence of urban forms on the peripheries of the core regions of urban genesis, especially in those sectors where political jurisdiction lagged behind cultural imperialism. In particular it would seem to have been characteristic of parts of the Levant, the shores of the Ægean, Etruria, the Sudan, Central Asia, South China and Southeast Asia. This last region is of especial interest from the point of view of urban origins and I shall examine it in detail in a separate publication. Suffice it here to point out that the adoption in the western territories of Southeast Asia of certain political institutions on the Indian model induced a sequence of socio-economic changes that culminated in the emergence of ceremonial cities on an impressive scale. By no stretching of terms could this process be characterized as primary, secondary or stimulus diffusion of urban forms. It is clearly *generation* of urban life with which we are concerned in this corner of Asia, and I think it must have been a process of this nature that Bronislaw Malinowski had in mind when he wrote, 'Diffusion . . . is not an act, but a process closely akin in its working to the evolutionary process. For evolution

7

deals above all with the influence of any type of 'origins'; and origins do not differ fundamentally whether they occur by invention or by diffusion.'[9] More recently Julian Steward, presumably thinking along similar lines, has asked whether, '. . . each time a society accepts diffused culture, it is not an independent recurrence of cause and effect?'[10] Subsequently, Morton Fried has distinguished between what he calls pristine and secondary states,[11] the former denoting 'a state that has developed *sui generis* out of purely local conditions,' the latter 'dependent upon pressures, direct or indirect, from existing states.' Where such pressures exist, he notes correctly that the process of development may be accelerated, condensed or warped. The relationship of the formation of the state to the emergence of civilization on the one hand and to the generation of urban life on the other is not easily defined, and will be the subject of comment in a later chapter, but whatever form that relationship may prove to take, if 'city' is substituted for 'state' in the sentences quoted above, Fried's distinction between pristine and secondary remains valid. There are cities which are (1) pristine or, in our terminology, of primary generation, and there are those which are induced directly or indirectly by the presence and activities of other urban forms. Those which are (2) inspired directly are the result of the extension of empire, those (3) induced indirectly are of secondary generation. Of these classes both (1) and (3) exemplify processes of generation, as opposed to imposition, of urban forms.

The problem of genetic interconnection between the primary realms of nuclear urbanism is by no means completely resolved. Secondary diffusion of culture traits between Protoliterate Mesopotamia and Gerzean Egypt has been established beyond doubt, and Mesopotamian cultural influence was certainly not absent in the Indus valley during the third millennium BC. The civilization of the Huang valley would appear at this stage of archeological investigation to have absorbed relatively few traits directly from Southwest Asia, and virtually none of a specifically urban character, but the role of stimulus diffusion, though at the moment not easily evaluated, may nevertheless have been considerable. However, among the civilizational nuclei of the Old World, the Chinese seems to have been the one most effectively insulated from contact with other foci of high civilization, and despite the lateness of its flowering, to have enjoyed an unusual degree of autonomy in its development.

The major discontinuity in the continuum of culture is obviously that between the Old and New Worlds, but the rapidly accumulating body of literature relating to trans-Pacific cultural contacts bears eloquent testimony to the fact that secondary or stimulus diffusion cannot be completely excluded from any study of sociocultural change in Nuclear America. However, even the most ardent proponents of cultural diffusion between these realms have not claimed to discern any direct borrowings of specifically urban traits, and Gordon Willey spoke for the majority of American prehistorians when he characterized

8

the higher civilizations of the pre-Columbian New World as standing, 'To the best of our knowledge . . . clearly apart and essentially independent from the comparable culture core of the Old World.'[12] Within Nuclear America the Andean civilizations apparently owed little to the cultures of Mesoamerica, but this latter realm itself constituted one great web of culturally interrelated developments.

In these circumstances, and with a measure of diffidence appropriate to the current fragmentary state of the archeological record, I am proposing to treat Mesopotamia, Egypt, the Indus valley, the North China Plain, Mesoamerica, the central Andes, and the Yoruba territories of southwestern Nigeria as regions of primary urban generation. Whether or no this is justified as an operational expedient, empirical field research alone will ultimately decide. Cases such as that of western Southeast Asia, on the other hand, or the Sudan, Etruria, the shores of the Ægean and so forth, I shall consider as instances of secondary urban generation. Investigation of urban genesis on the North China plain, particularly at the present stage of its archeological exploration, will probably not yield conceptual tools of a calibre equal to those forged in the study of Mesopotamian or Nuclear American urban origins, but such an undertaking will be bound to provide materials for the comparative study on which will eventually be based a generalized hypothesis of city origins and, ultimately, a comprehensive theory of urbanism.

THE HISTORICITY OF THE SHANG DYNASTY

It is usually asserted that cities first appeared on the North China plain during the Shang dynasty, which flourished during the second half of the second millennium BC. This is certainly the impression to be derived from those literary sources which purport to recount the history of Shang, where we read of 'cities' being founded, prospering, being besieged, and being captured. Precisely what was implied by the term which we translate as 'city' will be discussed at a later stage.

According to the traditional version of Chinese history as preserved in the ancient literature of that country, the creation of the universe was followed by the rule of a series of culture heroes who devised the basic elements of civilized living. They in turn were succeeded by a line of dynasts who styled themselves the Hsia (**G'å), and who were eventually deposed by the founder of the Shang dynasty. The precise dates of this latter dynasty have not yet been settled to the satisfaction of all concerned. Until the beginning of this century, Chinese scholars accepted the chronology set forth in historical works written long after the events which they purported to describe, and placed the beginning of the dynasty at 1766 BC and the end at 1122 BC. More recently Bernhard Karlgren[13] and Homer Dubs,[14] founding their opinions on analyses of the *Chu-shu Chi-nien* and of astronomical data respectively, have proposed a time span from 1523 to

9

1028 BC. Members of the Academia Sinica (as reconstituted on T'ai-wan), however, have adopted the estimates, based on a study of oracle bones, of Tung Tso-piṇ, namely 1751 to 1111 BC.[15] This in fact accords with Dr Noel Barnard's conclusion, based on a re-evaluation of the implications of the chronological information in the *Chu-shu Chi-nien* and *Han-Shu*, that the Chou dynasty could not – even on the evidence of traditional texts – have been inaugurated later than 1100 BC.[16] If this were so, then for the present study, which is concerned with developmental trends rather than with precise chronology, there is little advantage to be gained by departing from the traditional dating of the Shang dynasty. Perhaps it should be remarked parenthetically that traditional Chinese historiography has tended to reserve the style Shang (**Śị*ang*) for the dynasty prior to the founding of the last capital at Yin (**·*Ị̣ən*), after which this latter term has normally been used. This is also, generally speaking, the practice of members of the Academia Sinica at the present time, but some contemporary scholars have sought a compromise in adoption of the term Shang-Yin.[17] However, the Shang never referred to themselves by any term other than Shang, and Noel Barnard is inclined to believe that the Western Chou followed suit,[18] so that, outside quotations and titles where it is necessary to preserve the style Yin, in this work the dynasty which witnessed the earliest development of urban forms in China will be known as the Shang.

In the classical canon the Shang were accorded a supernatural origin, tracing their descent back, according to one account, to the legendary Yellow Emperor. They owed their emergence as an effective political organization to one of their culture heroes, **Sị̣at (Hsieh), who allegedly served the emperors Yao (**Ngiog), Shun (**Śị̣wən) and Yü (**Gị̣wo) with such devotion that he was granted the benefice of Shang, a territory which Chinese commentators have usually assigned, on no very strong grounds, to the neighborhood of Shang-Chou in Shan-hsi.[19] During a span of fourteen generations, with the aid of a succession of culture heroes who introduced, among other innovations, the concept of animal traction, invented the chariot, and devised new modes of economic organization, the clansmen of Shang consolidated their power to such a degree that, when the misconduct and oppressive rule of the emperor of Hsia, the first recorded Chinese dynasty, became insupportable, they were able, under the leadership of **T'âng (T'ang) the Successful, to overthrow the old dynasty and establish themselves as rulers of the Central State, the core region of higher culture which, together with peripherally located tribal groupings, constituted the Chinese ecumene.[20] The dynasty thus established endured for seventeen generations, not without vicissitudes, it is true, but nevertheless maintaining hegemony over a unified state which occupied the whole of the North China plain, together with a fringe of highland to the north, west and south.[21] Finally, towards the close of the second millennium BC, when early

Shang paternalism had degenerated into tyrannical oppression, the dynasty was itself overthrown by the Chou (**Tjôg), one of its own feudatories.

This version of Shang history was substantially that accepted by all scholars of early Chinese culture, whether Chinese, Japanese or Western, until the second decade of the present century. Then a new school of critical historians arose to challenge the veracity of the canonical texts, which alone at that time underpinned the traditional interpretation of Chinese history. Not only did these iconoclasts succeed in showing that the classical histories had been moulded in response to disputes and theorizings of a much later period, but they were also able to demonstrate that the chronological order of the Culture-heroes, Sages and Ancestors was the reverse of the sequence in which their descendants came to power.[22] Early in the Chou period, for instance, Yü the Great featured as a god who, at an unspecified but remote time in the past, had conjured the dry land from out of the waters. By the end of the Chou he had assumed the role of a human king, and during the Chan-Kuo era he came to be regarded as the founder of the Hsia dynasty. The sage rulers Yao and Shun are both completely absent in the earliest extant Chinese literature and are but shadowy figures in the *Analects*, yet in the traditional chronology they precede Yü. Among the last to join the august circle, probably under Taoist patronage, was Huang-Ti (**Gʻwâng-Tieg), the Yellow Emperor, for whom there was no historical niche available later than the 27th century BC. And so he was, in the late Arthur Waley's words, 'put into this remote period by the chronologists merely in just the same way as someone arriving late at a crowded concert is put at the back of the room.'[23] Pʻan-ku (**Bʻwân-ko), from whom the universe was born, first appeared in Chinese literature at an even later date, although the nexus of ideas of which he is the focus certainly existed unrecorded at an earlier period. Furthermore, Ku Chieh-kang has pointed out that each school of thought in ancient China modified these legends so as to ensure that its own central doctrine was clearly exemplified in the Golden Age.[24] The Mohists, for example, in the interests of good government emphasized the abdication legends and the accession of virtuous and competent commoners,[25] the Taoists praised Huang-Ti for conforming to the cosmic process and not transgressing against the course of Nature, and so on. Not infrequently downright emendation of a text might take place for illustrative and didactic purposes, as when Shun persists in the *Tso-Chuan* as a descendant of Chuan-Hsü (**Tʻjwan-Sju), that is a member of an aristocratic lineage, whereas in every other source he has been ascribed a humble birth in accordance with the Confucian principle that moral qualities, not right of birth, should qualify for kingship.[26] Of course, this imaginative reconstruction of allegedly defective or deficient texts should not be judged by present-day standards of historiographical conduct, for in ancient China the annals were recorded predominantly for didactic and moralistic, not for analytical, purposes.

11

So destructive did textual criticism of this sort appear to be that for a time all records relating to the period prior to the Chou were considered spurious. In the last forty years, however, archeological excavation has amply confirmed the historicity of *a* Shang culture (even though politically it may not have been organized in the unitary state implied by the classical canon), and in so doing has raised again the issue of the still earlier Hsia dynasty. As Ssŭ-ma Ch'ien could rely on sources of sufficient accuracy for him to record the styles of Shang kings, some two-thirds of which have been verified on oracle bones, may he not also have had access to authentic historical records relating to the Hsia? So far no archeological finds have been connected with this dynasty, but the classical histories picture it as an era of high culture. This would certainly be possible if it had existed contemporaneously with the Shang and the dynastic annals of the two states had subsequently been fused into a unified tradition. Or possibly the Hsia was no more than a proto-Shang tribe whose memory was preserved in the official Shang records. I do not think it very likely that it can have been a purely preliterate, pre-urban, folk society existing wholly *prior* to the advent of the Shang, as Andersson suggested,[27] for in that case it would have lacked an instrument for perpetuating its past and would have been history-less. There would have been no written tradition to incorporate in a Shang, and later in a Chou, version of events. Recently Professor Kwang-chih Chang has shown that the genealogy of the Hsia kings, as preserved by Ssŭ-ma Ch'ien in the *Shih-Chi*, exemplifies the same alternation between two prominent lineage groups with the posthumous ritual designations of **tieng* (*ting*) and **·i̯ɛt*(*i*) as characterized the Shang royal house; and moreover, according to the same source, at the change of dynasty the throne would have passed from a Hsia monarch of the *tieng* group to a Shang king of the *·i̯ɛt* group.[28] This observation provides support for a suggestion put forward as long ago as 1936 by Ch'en Meng-chia, whose researches into ancient mythology led him to the conclusion that the Hsia and Shang were chronologically successive segments of a single royal lineage.[29] The succession from **Li̯ər-ki̯wɛr (Lü-kuei) of Hsia to **T'âd-·i̯ɛt (T'ai-i) of Shang would then have had no more significance than any of the other transfers of power between the two politically dominant lineage groups beyond the fact that it subsequently became enshrined in the canonical texts as a change of dynasty. The reasons why such significance should have been ascribed to this particular articulation in the dualistic organization of the ruling lineage are unknown, but would almost certainly have concerned matters of political prestige. The four books in the *Shu-Ching* which were traditionally held to be of Hsia date, in the form in which we now know them, are Chou compilations, though certain of their astronomical data may have derived ultimately from the Shang period or even earlier.[30] Creel has proposed that the concept of the Hsia state as it has come down to us may have been a fiction devised by the Chou to provide a precedent for the doctrine by which they legitimized their overthrow of the Shang.[31] Chang's tentative interpretation, even if confirmed subsequently, need not necessarily invalidate the suggestion for, had the Chou indeed fabricated the dynastic genealogy of the Hsia, they would surely have constructed it on the dualistic principles with which they were familiar. My own view is that, while there is no room to doubt that the form in which the traditional account of the Hsia dynasty is cast owes a great deal to editorial moralizing, the hazy divide between mythology and history should be drawn so as to include that dynasty in the latter category.

SOURCES FOR THE STUDY OF SHANG URBANISM

Apart from oracle archives, whose significance will be discussed in a subsequent section, there are no contemporary Shang records still extant. There are, however, a few sections in early texts which may preserve, in edited form, either authentic Shang materials or, perhaps more probably, faint echoes of Shang happenings. In handling such records it is clearly of first importance – but also often very difficult – to distinguish genuine transmissions from those events and cultural features which later generations wished upon the Shang, either because they were incapable of piercing the screen of cultural relativity and so assumed that the Shang had espoused the cultural values and mores of, say, the Chou or Han, or perhaps from a conscious desire to enhance the prestige of particular ancestors. And always, between us and the reality of pre-Ch'in events, is interposed the murky screen that was drawn across the course of Chinese history by Han scholars in their reconstitution of the ancient texts, a screen sometimes rendered yet more opaque by the exegetes of Sung Neo-Confucianism.

Among the classical texts which have traditionally been supposed to record events under the Shang dynasty are five of the books of the *Shu-Ching* or *Book of Documents*, one of the Five Classics of Chinese literature. This work has been the subject of interminable philosophical and philological controversy ever since the emergence of two variant versions of the text in the 2nd century B C. The extant version preserves the essence of this distinction and, although it is now agreed that chapters deriving from the antique-script (*ku-wen*) text include post-Han forgeries, the status of all sections of the 'modern' [that is Han]-script (*chin-wen*) text has not been evaluated precisely.[32] Of the sections which purport to preserve Shang material only that entitled * *B'wân-kǎng (P'an-keng)* is of direct interest in connection with Shang urbanism. It consists of a collection of speeches allegedly made by B'wân-kǎng, nineteenth ruler of the dynasty, in connection with the founding of a new capital, that one, in fact, which has been partially excavated at An-yang. This particular chapter is certainly not pre-Chou in date and at best can only be a rifacimento of fragments from earlier times. Creel has even charged that it was composed in the cause of Chou propaganda.[33]

13

B'wân-kăng reigned during the middle years of the Shang. This is of some importance because Edouard Chavannes has demonstrated that the relatively detailed accounts of the first and last rulers of each dynasty as related in the *Shu-Ching* are late accretions to a basically genealogical text.[34] Even so it should be borne in mind that B'wân-kăng was the founder of the last capital of the dynasty, which, even without the attentions of Chou editors, would probably have accounted for the fact that his actions bear not a few of the archetypal imprints inseparable from the culture hero. All in all, I think it must be concluded that even the *B'wân-kăng* chapter reflects Chou conceptions of urbanism rather than those of Shang times. In fact, it has been suggested that it was concocted to provide a precedent for the transference of the capital to the east at the end of the Western Chou period.[35]

Another account of Shang times occurs in the *Chu-shu Chi-nien*, popularly rendered in English as the *Bamboo Annals*. This work purports to be an official chronicle of the state of Wei (****Ngįwǝr*) from high antiquity to the end of the 3rd century B C. It was found in an early Wei tomb in A D 281, by which time the bamboo slips on which it was written were sufficiently unfamiliar to give rise to the name by which this work has been known ever since.[36] The extant text is demonstrably corrupt but Wang Kuo-wei has partially reconstructed the original from early quotations.[37] The chronology of this text agrees with orthodox dating subsequent to 827 B C, but prior to that date the two systems diverge considerably, and some scholars have seen reason to prefer that of the *Bamboo Annals*.

The third historical work to devote a substantial section to the Shang period is that which, since the 2nd century A D, has been known as *Shih-Chi*, that is *Records of the [Grand-]'Historian'*. Compiled by Ssŭ-ma Ch'ien under the inspiration of his father, Ssŭ-ma T'an, just after the beginning of the 1st century B C, this work was originally entitled *T'ai-shih Kung Shu*, which might be translated as *The writings of his Honor the Grand Historian*. Chapter III of this work preserves an outline of Shang history under the rubric *Yin Pen-chi*, which, together with a genealogy of the ruling house in another part of the same work, has provided the basis for the received view of Shang history until the present century. Closely associated with the *Shih-Chi* are three commentaries on it, by P'ei-Yin (5th century A D), Ssŭ-ma Cheng, and Chang Shou-chieh (both 8th century) respectively, which in most modern editions are combined with the text of the *Shih-Chi* itself. Ssŭ-ma Ch'ien is often held, by virtue of his analytical treatment of events, to have been the founder of Chinese historiography. Independent in his judgment, critical and prudent he certainly was within the framework of Han thought, but he was no more capable than any of his contemporaries of transcending the limits of Han culture, so that his chapter on the Shang transmits a distinctly Han view of events under that dynasty. Nevertheless, as mentioned above, the fact that he was able to compile

14

a genealogy of Shang rulers which has since been in great measure verified proves that he must have had access to early records since lost.[38] Perhaps his account of Shang times may be characterized most aptly as echoes of Shang themes absorbed into the conceptual framework of the Han *Weltanschauung*.[39]

The last of the ancient texts which may preserve some genuine Shang materials of importance is the *Shih-Ching* or *Book of Odes*, which, since the 2nd century BC, has been considered one of the Five Classics. In its present form it consists of 305 early songs of varied origins. Some are folk songs in the broadest sense of the term, but strict patterns of meter, rhythm and rhyme betray the fact that even these have been transformed within the ambience of a sophisticated literary tradition. Others of the songs are ceremonial odes of one sort or another, some of which are important for present purposes because they incorporate legends of dynastic origins and exploits, including the founding of capital cities. Among these are the *Shang-Sung* (**Śiang-Dz'i̯ung*), which were traditionally supposed to date from Shang times, even though Ssŭ-ma Ch'ien had ascribed them to a minister of the state of Sung (**Sông*) living during the Eastern Chou. It now seems unlikely that even the earliest of the *Odes* can antedate the Chou dynasty, and the later parts of the *Shang-Sung* may be but little earlier than Confucius. However, the rulers of Sung were lineal descendants of the Shang royal house, so that the odes used at the Sung court may possibly have preserved authentic attitudes espoused in times past by ancestors of that house.[40] If we may believe a colophon to the *Yin Pen-chi*, Ssŭ-ma Ch'ien himself took his account of the early Shang from the *Shang-Sung*.[41] In the present work occasional recourse will be made to the *Shang-Sung* not for factual information but for material illustrative of an ancient value system.[42] Other items of Chou literature also include incidental references to allegedly Shang customs, but they are mostly of dubious authenticity and, in any case, do little to forward the study of urban origins in China. Some of these sources will be discussed subsequently in connection with Chou cities.

When literary sources are as exiguous as those mentioned above, to say nothing of the fact that they are ill-adapted to the purpose in hand, it is obvious that the burden of sustaining any hypothesis of urban origins will fall on archeology. The progress of this discipline in China since World War I has already been touched on, and it only remains to set the excavations of Shang cities in their historical context. The first Shang site to be explored was situated some two and a half miles northwest of the *hsien* city of An-yang, on the western edge of the North China plain at the foot of the T'ai-hang mountains. Actually it lay in a meander of the Huan river on the northern edge of the village of Hsiao-T'un (Fig. 2), in a locality known to both the compiler of the *Tso-Chuan* late in the Chou and Ssŭ-ma Ch'ien early in the 1st century BC as *Yin-hsü* or the Ruins of Yin, the location traditionally associated with the last Shang capital.[43] Oracle bones and scapulae had been turned up by the plough and eroded from the bank of the Huan river regularly since the closing decades of the 19th century and had already been the subject of study by Chinese scholars, one of whom, Tung Tso-pin [44], began excavations at Hsiao-T'un in the autumn of 1928, under the auspices of the Archeological Section of the Research Institute of History and Philology of the Academia Sinica (*Kuo-li Chung-yang Yen-chiu-yüan Li-shih Yü-yen Yen-chiu-so*). By reason of the hot summers and bitterly cold winters, digging was restricted virtually to the spring and autumn, but between 1928 and 1937 no less than fifteen seasons of field work were undertaken in and around Hsiao-T'un. Excavation had to be abandoned prematurely at the time of the Japanese invasion, but was resumed in 1949.

This was the first large-scale controlled excavation to be undertaken by Chinese (or for that matter in China, if one excludes the primarily paleontological investigations, excellent of their kind, at Chou-k'ou Tien in the early twenties), and it served as a training ground for virtually a whole generation of Chinese archeologists. The site at Hsiao-T'un had been greatly disturbed, 'more or less thoroughly dug up' in the words of Cheng Te-k'un,[45] before the archeologists from the Academia Sinica began their work, and the local folk subsequently continued to plunder oracle bones and bronzes illicitly between seasons. Moreover, the character and emphasis of the excavations underwent considerable change during the fifteen seasons of work. The excavators themselves discerned five stages in the development of their investigation.[46] During the first stage, which comprised three seasons' work, digging was exploratory and unsystematic, but the discovery of some 4,000 pieces of oracle bones and shells, in addition to the usual miscellaneous archeological bric-à-brac associated with a major site, served to emphasize the importance of Hsiao-T'un in the early history of China. The second stage (seasons four to seven) saw the development of systematic excavation and the division of the site into the sectors which have provided the framework for all subsequent digging. A start was also made on the investigation of architectural remains, and the significance of the distinction between the pit dwelling and the surface structure raised on a stamped-earth platform was recognized. The third stage (seasons eight to ten) was characterized by greater mastery of working techniques and the extension of the investigations to other sites in the vicinity of An-yang, notably the royal cemetery at Hsi-pei Kang to the northwest. The royal mausolea on this site also provided the main focus of interest during the fourth stage (seasons eleven and twelve), but in the fifth and final period (seasons thirteen to fifteen) excavation was again directed to the architectural features at Hsiao-T'un. When in 1937 work had to be discontinued owing to the Japanese invasion of North China, it had already become apparent that the archeological complex at An-yang was a magnificent representative of the urban sector of ancient Shang culture, a culture which already incorporated many of the traits which are customarily recognized as being distinctively

Chinese. How far that high culture had diffused through the countryside by the end of the second millennium BC is still a matter for debate, as indeed is the precise relation of the city to preceding cultures, though we do know that the site was inhabited before T'âng the Successful founded his new ceremonial center there.[47] During the period of hostilities the bulk of the archeological collections from An-yang was transported to southwest China for safe keeping, after which it was returned to Nan-ching at the end of the Sino-Japanese war, and finally brought to T'ai-wan in 1949. Under these circumstances it is not altogether surprising that the materials have, even at this time, not been published in their entirety, and currently there are two streams of information relating to An-yang to be tapped, one emanating from Pei-ching and reflecting the contemporary activities of the Chung-Kuo K'e-hsüeh-yüan, the other flowing out of T'ai-wan and bringing detailed reports on the work of the old Academia Sinica, now some thirty years in the past. Both of these, of course, are additional to the plethora of journal articles which, particularly during the interwar years, constituted a veritable An-yang genre of archeological literature. Since World War II, when An-yang has functioned as a training camp for young field archeologists, investigations have been mainly concerned with outlying sites such as Hsüeh-chia Chuang, whose exploration has brought an added awareness of the extent and complexity of this ancient center.

In the same period the investigation of Shang sites has spread far beyond the vicinity of An-yang, so that it is now possible to define a nuclear hearth of Shang urbanism within the broad zone of Shang culture, and to distinguish this latter from a peripheral belt of territory into which individual Shang culture traits had diffused in somewhat irregular fashion. The most important of the specifically Shang sites discovered since World War II, especially from our present point of view, is probably that at Cheng-Chou in northern Ho-nan. Excavations are still in progress, but enough has been published to show that this was another Shang urban complex comparable to that at An-yang. In fact, most students of ancient China are inclined to agree with the excavators that the remains at Cheng-Chou are probably those of **Ngog (Ao),[48] a Shang capital of earlier date than dynastic An-yang, which, according to literary sources, was founded by **D'i̯ông-tieng (Chung-ting), tenth king of the dynasty (1562–1549 BC in the traditional reckoning, about a century later in Tung Tso-pin's chronology). An extensive city wall has been traced, and some degree of social and economic differentiation is already apparent in the areal distribution of finds, but perhaps most important of all is the reasonably complete stratification from Yang-shao times to the period of high Shang culture. Unfortunately, this is so far the only example of such a chronological sequence that has come to light and there is no assurance that it is of general application to Shang urban development.

The immense energy and devotion with which the Chinese have tackled the problems of national reconstruction, coupled with the need to forge an historical identity in strong contrast to the deplorable self-image of the colonial period, have had repercussions in the field of archeology. Field surveyors move ahead of the developers and, whenever possible, archeological teams salvage remains which would otherwise be destroyed in the process of economic development. Needless to say, much of this rescue work is done hurriedly and occupies a great deal of skill that might otherwise be engaged in planned excavations directed towards the solution of specific problems in Chinese prehistory, but nevertheless the quantitative increase in archeological materials during the last two decades has been enormous.

The Shang period has received its share of attention, so that it will be possible later in this chapter to provide some account of two other ceremonial cities as well as of a number of proto-urban centers in northern and western Ho-nan and in southern Ho-pei. Altogether there are now more than 150 excavations of so-called Shang sites for which reports are available, but on examination not a few of these turn out to be concerned not so much with Shang culture *sensu stricto* as with isolated Shang traits in a primarily Neolithic context.

The deficiencies of archeological research in China have been the subject of frequent comment by scholars in that field and there is no call, especially for one who is not an archeologist, to repeat them here – though, of course, any evaluation of the implications of the archeological record must take account of the methods by which the record was obtained. Suffice it to point out that, as late as 1959, an American scholar could write that, 'In the whole of China there is simply *not one dependable stratigraphic excavation* of a site.'[49] Today, when field techniques have been greatly improved, Chinese archeology has still not freed itself entirely from the inheritance of its past. There is still a tendency among some scholars to use archeological materials to verify preconceived interpretations of the classical literary sources, and, despite the publication of a few interpretative studies in recent years, the typological classification of artifacts, often on the basis of single elements of form or composition, appears to be the primary concern of many authors. Refinement of the systematics of space and time distributions is receiving fairly continuous attention, but so far there has been virtually no attempt to apply the concept of developmental trends in the manner both advocated and demonstrated by, among others, Robert J. Braidwood in Southwest Asia, Gordon R. Willey in Nuclear America and Robert McC. Adams in his recent comparative study of urban origins in the Old and New Worlds.[50] There has been no sustained endeavor to reconstruct the culture and society of ancient China, to use the typologies and classifications proposed as tools for an examination of the direction of sociocultural change, or to deduce the interplay of forces contributing to such change. In short Chinese archeology still awaits its first syncretistic evaluation of the secular trends in the nexus of institutional, social, political and economic change of which the archeological record is the material manifestation. From this generalization it is necessary to exclude one outstanding scholar, a Chinese working outside China, namely, Professor Chang Kuang-chih of Yale University. In a series of prescient publications [51] over the past decade, this author has essayed single-handedly to chart the configurations of cultural growth in pre-Ch'in China in terms of developmental trends transforming levels of sociocultural complexity, and the conceptual framework of this present chapter owes much to his labors.

There is one further category of evidence of importance for the present investigation which is archeological in the sense that it is usually acquired from the earth by means of the specialist skills of the trained excavator, but which constitutes a medium sufficiently recondite to have given rise to a discrete branch of study. This is the oracle archive, the link between mute archeological evidence *sensu stricto*, whose implications must be elucidated by a trained interpreter, and the literary record which to a much higher degree is capable of speaking for itself. [52] The earlier scholars in the field of Chinese epigraphy put great faith in the potentialities of the oracle bones, often believing that they would ultimately provide the basis for a definitive history of the Shang dynasty, but, as more and more of them were deciphered, it became increasingly obvious that their information was not of the anticipated level of comprehensiveness. Discussion of the nature of the information inscribed on the oracle bones and of the role of scapulimancy will be reserved for subsequent sections : here we shall concern ourselves only with the limitations of this corpus of evidence.

In the first place, the oracle records contain a vast body of information relating both directly and indirectly to the ceremonial rituals and religious beliefs of the royal lineage, but they disclose relatively little about other aspects of the activities of the royal house, either public or private. A little can be gleaned by the diligent student concerning the political and administrative structure of the Shang state [53], but virtually nothing about the peasantry and artisanry who constituted the broad base of the social pyramid. Even within this contextual framework, which is oriented exclusively towards élite status, and which within that focuses overwhelmingly on the royal house, the information is spread very unevenly. The vast bulk of the oracle bones have come from An-yang, either directly through excavation or indirectly from the hands of dealers in 'dragon-bones', while those from Cheng-Chou have seldom been deciphered. This means that, apart from questions concerning remote ancestors, they relate to only twelve of the thirty kings who are recorded in the *Shih-Chi* as comprising the Shang dynasty, which in turn implies that they relate to a period of city *founding* rather than to the earlier and climacteric phase of city generation. And not all Shang kings were equally committed to the ordering of

19

their personal and public lives according to the principles of scapulimancy. Under **Tso-kap (Tsu-chia), for instance, divination was restricted almost entirely to routine enquiries concerning sacrifice, military campaigns, hunting, royal itineraries, and the king's safety during ritual periods, whereas **Mjwo-tieng (Wu-ting) was given to consulting the oracle on a host of personal and public problems, ranging from his own toothache and the illness of the crown prince to the choice of crops and the possibility of rain. Finally, of the 100,000 or so oracle bones, mostly fragmentary but occasionally complete, which have so far been discovered, less than 15,000 have been deciphered.[54] The rest are either in such poor condition that there is little or no hope of eliciting their information or else the characters have not been identified. It is not surprising, then, that Tung Tso-pin, one of the pioneer interpreters of these records, after a lifetime's study should have been led regretfully to conclude that no more than a hundredth part of the total spectrum of Shang culture could be deduced from the oracle bones.[55]

This is the negative aspect of the oracle archives. Possibly some of the vigor with which some scholars have stated this case reflects disappointment at the nonfulfilment of earlier hopes. Imperfect though the oracle record be, it is still a much more valuable resource than any that exists for a comparable phase of development in most of the other areas of primary – or of secondary, for that matter – urban generation. As remarked above, these inscribed bones have a utility for present purposes at least comparable to that of the Protoliterate texts of Mesopotamia, are superior to the inscriptions of Archaic Egypt and the glyptic materials of the Indus valley in that a much higher proportion can be deciphered, and have no analogues at all comparable in the New World. The following pages will make frequent reference to information from this source.

The Genesis and Morphology of Shang Cities

Urban forms first developed in China on the great northern plain, a vast embayment of alluvial deposits, enclosed by peripheral uplands on north, west, and south but open to the sea at two points on its eastern rim. Structurally this plain comprises an enormous composite alluvial fan to the west and a composite subaerial delta to the east, both built up by the Huang river, its distributaries, and other streams flowing from the western mountains. The hearth of Shang culture occupied the higher parts of the fan, stretching in an arc from the neighborhood of present-day Ch'ing-yüan in central Ho-pei to the vicinity of Po-Hsien in northern An-hui, and comprising the territory known to the Chinese in later times as the Chung-yüan or Middle Plain. The physiographic history of the plain has not been elucidated with any degree of precision, but it seems likely that the lower northern and southern fringes were still extensive marshlands in Shang times. At present the Huang river flows obliquely across the plain from southwest to northeast, but in the past it has followed a variety of other courses, some passing to the north and others to the south, of the Shan-tung peninsula. In Shang times there is evidence that it bifurcated soon after entering the plain, one channel reaching the sea in the vicinity of modern T'ien-chin, the other at a point where the ancient coastline intersected the course of the present Huang river.[56] I have been forced into using this last periphrasis by the existence of a great deal of doubt as to the precise run of the coast in Shang times. It is certain that the leading edge of the Huang delta then lay to the west of its present position, but in the absence of reliable literary records, archeological distributions, and certainty that the rate of advance of the delta front has been constant over the past three thousand years, it is impossible to locate the Shang coastline precisely.

Today the climate of the plain is extreme : hot in summer, bitterly cold in winter, with summer monthly rainfall means up to five or six times those of winter, and a mean annual variability of 20 to 30 per cent (extreme variations are, of course, much more severe). More will be said about some aspects of the environment in a later chapter, but the thorny question of climatic change must be raised forthwith. And equally early in our investigation it must be stated that no definite conclusion is at present possible. In the absence of that type of problem-oriented research which is beginning to yield important results in Mesopotamia and Mesoamerica, it is impossible in China to apply the strictly scientific tools of the paleoclimatologist, so that it becomes necessary to rely on inferences from conditions in Asia generally during the second millennium BC, on the ecological implications of faunal assemblages from the An-yang excavations, and especially on the evidence of the oracle archives.[57]

When the An-yang faunal remains were analyzed it became clear that certain species such as the elephant, water deer, tapir, and bamboo rat had since become extinct or were now found only in more southerly latitudes. This led Father Teilhard de Chardin and C. C. Young to suggest the possibility of a deterioration in climatic conditions since Shang times.[58] However, the argument is not quite that simple. Present knowledge of the ecological history of the North China plain is insufficient to enable us to distinguish the possible effects of climatic change from those of human occupance. As man came to mould the environment to suit his own needs, so he must inevitably have eliminated certain ecological niches and the animals that occupied them, and part of the discrepancy between the ancient and modern faunas may stem from this cause.[59] Dr J. G. Andersson, the pioneer investigator of the Chinese Stone Ages, after an ingenious attempt to combine both genres of evidence with later literary sources, hesitantly speculated that the climate of ancient China might have been slightly warmer than at present.[60] But he concluded with a caution that millennia of human occupance had gone far towards an irreparable obliteration of the evidence.

Subsequently Hu Hou-hsüan,[61] relying on an impressive corpus of data culled from ancient texts, was able to reinforce the idea that there were marked differences in the patterns of ecological adaptation in ancient and modern China, but he made virtually no attempt to distinguish between the effects of natural and human agency. Hu also touched on the evidence of oracle bones, but this was exploited more fully by Karl Wittfogel.[62] Analysis of 108 queries concerning the weather abstracted from some 14,500 pieces of bone and shell led this author to confirm Andersson's suggestion that during the later Shang the climate was somewhat warmer than at present. Almost immediately, Tung Tso-pin, excavator of some of the largest oracle archives at An-yang, denied that these records could at present be used to furnish reliable evidence of climatic change, though they might possibly be made to do so after more intensive research.[63] He was particularly critical of Wittfogel's techniques of analysis, especially in so far as they related to the structure of the archaic language. According to Tung, the oracle records, as they can be evaluated by presently available methods, do no more than confirm the existence of two seasons : a cold, drier (but not completely rainless) winter and spring (from the tenth to the third month), followed by a wetter, warm summer and autumn (from the fourth to the ninth month). This dichotomy was reflected in the form of the enquiries submitted to the oracle. During the drier season the questions relating to precipitation were usually cast in some such form as, 'Will there be rain [or snow or hail] ?' Sometimes the query was tied to a particular time period such as a month or five days. During the wetter season, however, the questions were usually framed on the lines of, 'Will the rain stop ?', 'Will the rain continue ?' or, perhaps, 'Will there be a fine day ?'. It is, of course, true that the weather sequence of the North China plain is not this simple, but, nevertheless, the oracle records on this interpretation afford no support for any theory of climatic change. However, it may be pointed out that Tung's interpretation is qualitative and leaves open the possibility of quantitative variation. The amount of rainfall and the relative warmth of the seasons may have been modified, even though the regimen of the seasons remained essentially unchanged.

In these circumstances we can take the enquiry no further at present, and it will be necessary to await the resolution of this problem by the paleoclimatologists of the People's Republic of China.

PRE-URBAN NORTH CHINA

The Yang-shao stage. It is necessary at this point to sketch in briefly the cultural and social milieu within which Shang cities were generated. Fortunately there is no need to carry our discussion back before the appearance of food production in North China. I say fortunately, for evidence of even the terminal food-gathering phase is exiguous, and there is no shred of evidence bearing on either the period or the place at which farming was initiated. In these circumstances

22

no intellectual profit would accrue from our reopening the controversy as to the relative contributions of external versus indigenous stimuli, a debate which, in the context of China's search for a national identity, has recently been pursued with especial vigor.

As no modern dating techniques have been applied in Chinese archeological work, it is not possible to propose an absolute chronology for the sequence of pre-urban societies which is, nevertheless, clearly evident in the archeological record. Suffice it to say that, at some undetermined time in the past, the western sectors of the Chung-yüan witnessed a series of ecological adaptations which eventuated in the achievement of what Robert Braidwood has called Primary Village Farming Efficiency.[64] In China, a late phase of this level of development is known as the Yang-shao stage, after a village of that name in Mien-ch'ih Hsien in western Ho-nan, which was considered until recently to provide the type-site for this culture.[65] Now it has become evident that the Yang-shao excavations revealed a transition phase between representative Yang-shao and a succeeding culture, but the name has become securely attached to the former, and will be used as such in this work. The earlier phases of Yang-shao culture, on present evidence, appear to have developed in and around the middle Huang valley, specifically in the vicinity of the confluences with the Fen and Wei rivers. Subsequently the culture diffused eastward on to the western edge of the plain proper, and northward and westward along the valleys leading into central Shan-hsi and eastern Kan-su.

All our knowledge of North Chinese prehistory has been acquired in little more than three decades of investigation, and during the first half of this period – from 1920 when Andersson discovered the site at Yang-shao Ts'un until 1937 when Japanese armies overran the plain – excavation was sporadic and uncoordinated. During the war years it was virtually non-existent. Only since about 1950 has the tempo of archeological exploration and investigation quickened as a result of the salvage operations already referred to, but these have been by no means sufficient to resolve all the problems outstanding in any evaluation of Yang-shao culture. However, enough has been laid bare to provide the basis for a general discussion of this stage, and we are fortunate in being able to draw on the masterly synthesis of all currently available information by Professor Chang which has been mentioned above.[66]

There can be no doubt but that the Yang-shao culture was based on a fairly advanced paleotechnic ecotype which, dimly discernible though it is by reason of a paucity of evidence, appears to have taken the form of some sort of long-term fallowing system. At least this seems to be the implication of the discontinuity of occupation at most of the sites. The implements of cultivation, namely hoes, spades, possibly digging sticks,[67] and semi-lunar stone sickles, are not inconsistent with this interpretation, while the prevalence of stone axes of a round or lentoid cross section and symmetrical edge adapted for forest clearance would tend to confirm it. The staple crops of the Yang-shao farmers were millets (*Setaria italica*, Beauv. var. *germanica* Trin. and *Panicum miliaceum*, L.), supplemented by wheat and an alleged sorghum usually identified by Chinese authors as *kao-liang* (*Andropogon sorghum*, Brot.). However, this crop was unknown in China until Sung times and there is, indeed, some likelihood that this grain, which was indubitably of African origin,[68] was popularized by the Mongol conquerors late in the 13th century A D.[69] As sorghums were by all accounts relatively late introductions into China, presumably the grain discovered in Yang-shao excavations was one of the larger millets. Another attribution that is almost certainly erroneous, but which has become firmly established in the relevant literature, is the inclusion of rice (*Oryza sativa*, Linn.) in the Yang-shao crop inventory. This seems to have arisen when the site at Yang-shao Ts'un itself was considered to be representative of that stage, whereas it is now known to have derived from a late or even transitional phase of the culture. There is, however, a strong likelihood that hemp was cultivated.[70] Dogs and pigs were the most common of the domestic animals, with cattle and sheep rather less prominent in the economy. A half-cut cocoon (*Bombyx mori*, Linn.) found at Hsi-yin Ts'un proves that silkworms were raised at this time.[71] There is also abundant evidence that hunting and fishing contributed important supplements to the Yang-shao diet, and the preservation of a foxtail weed (*Setaria lutescens*, Beauv.) at Ching-Ts'un probably implies the gathering of wild grains.[72] Crafts were well developed and included, in addition to the manufacture of stone, bone and antler implements, a mature tradition of handmade and moulded domestic pottery, the red and grey wares that became famous almost from the moment when Andersson discovered the first presumed Yang-shao site in 1920. Silk may have been spun on stone and pottery spindle whorls, which are common on Yang-shao sites, and hemp was probably used with the eyed bone needles which have also been found fairly frequently.

Settlements took the form of compact, self-contained, economically autonomous villages comprising a dozen or so semi-subterranean dwellings often grouped around a communal long-house. The planned and segmented layout of some of these settlements has been held to suggest that they functioned on a lineage or clan basis. Areal differentiation within the village was often manifested not only in the distinction between individual dwelling and long-house but also in the presence of an incorporated or annexed sector occupied by pottery kilns, and in a cemetery adjacent to the settlement.[73] In fact the disposition of some settlements excavated in the Pan-Shan in eastern Kan-su,[74] coupled with the evidence of similar relationships discovered among a group of settlements in Hua-Hsien in eastern Shen-hsi, indicate that during later phases of the Yang-shao stage several neighboring villages sometimes shared a common cemetery. This conclusion in turn has led to the further inference that population pressure had already induced the fission of parent villages into smaller clusters which were engaged in the colonization of cultivable lands interstitial and peripheral to the nuclear hearth.[75] That some process of expansion such as this was at work is also implicit in the very marked stylistic uniformity of the Yang-shao horizon over a wide extent of territory. To Professor Chang's scholarly acumen we owe the observation that these settlements were characterized by discontinuous but repetitive occupance, a conclusion hitherto obscured by the preliminary and sometimes unsystematic character of the investigations at most of the larger Yang-shao sites. Presumably at least some of the Yang-shao farmers moved their residences as they rotated their fields on a selectively repetitive pattern.

Professor Chang believes, on the basis of the occurrence of deer burials, the frequency of female symbols in ceramic decoration, and on the evidence of two stylized heads wearing fish-shaped headdresses depicted on p'an-basins from Pan-p'o Ts'un, that the Yang-shao villagers probably performed some kind of fertility rites to ensure the growth of their crops and the success of their hunting and fishing.[76] It is not unlikely, moreover, that some of the more carefully executed pottery bowls and miniature vessels may have been employed in the same rites. Whether or not the shamans – if that is indeed what they were – depicted on the p'an-bowls were full- or part-time specialists cannot be determined at this point, but it is certainly significant that the decorative arts were concerned only with domestic activities to the exclusion of the preoccupations of a ritual or secular élite. Certainly the coarse mesh of our archeological sieve has retained no evidence of social distinctions other than those based upon age, sex and personal achievement; but the still incipient state of Chinese archeology makes it difficult to be sure whether Yang-shao society should be categorized as an egalitarian or as a rank society. The first of these is defined, in the terms of Morton Fried,[77] as a society in which there are as many positions of prestige in any given age-sex grade as there are persons capable of filling them. In a rank society, on the other hand, differences in prestige are structured in another way. Additional limitations having nothing to do with sex, age or personal attributes are placed on access to prestige, so that there are fewer positions of valued status than individuals capable of achieving them. Neither in egalitarian nor in rank society is there developed exploitative economic power or genuine political power. In typical rank societies only two kinds of authority can be invoked, familial and sacred, and there is no access to the privileged use of force in support of either. Yet despite the equalitarian character of their economic and political sectors, rank societies do exhibit certain status differences, manifested in sumptuary specialization and ceremonial function. Such differentiation appears on present evidence not to have progressed far in Yang-shao society, but it may have been already initiated in rudimentary form.

The Lung-shan stage. In 1928, at Ch'eng-tzǔ Yai near Lung-shan Chen in Shan-tung, Wu Gin-ding (Wu Chin-ting) brought to light a culture which has since been proved to be a successor to the Yang-shao stage.[78] For almost thirty years these two cultures were regarded as contemporary, the Yang-shao adapted to the environment of the western uplands, the Lung-shan to that of the eastern plains. The *renversement* of this interpretation came with the recognition, during excavations in 1956 and 1957 at Miao-ti Kou, near Shan-Hsien,[79] of a proto-Lung-shan cultural assemblage overlying remains of the Yang-shao stage. Subsequently, this transitional stage has been identified at several other sites, including some, among them Yang-shao Ts'un itself, which had been excavated previous to 1956. Even more recently the Lung-shan culture has been found to extend into the western uplands, a final reason for abandoning the mutually exclusive two-culture theory.

Lung-shan culture seems to have developed in the nuclear area about the zone of contact of the provinces of Ho-nan, Shan-hsi and Shen-hsi, in which the Yang-shao culture had previously emerged. From there it spread through all eastern and southeastern China, where strongly marked regional traditions evolved that have been characterized by Professor Chang as 'Lungshanoid'. [80] Here we shall be concerned only with those traditions which developed in the nuclear area and on the North China plain, that is with the classical Lung-shan culture.

It is clear from even a cursory inspection of the available evidence that between the Yang-shao and the Lung-shan there had supervened considerable structural readjustments within society, in the ecotype on which it was based, and in political organization.[81] In the first place, for reasons that can at present only be speculated about, selectively repetitive occupance had been replaced by relatively permanent, certainly long-term, settlement. On the other hand, the invention of the well now allowed a wider choice in the selection of settlement sites. Villages were on the whole larger than in Yang-shao times and frequently surrounded by permanent ramparts of stamped earth. Within these walls there can be discerned the same contrast between semi-subterranean dwellings and communal long-houses as was found in Yang-shao villages, with added importance accorded to pit granaries, a symbol of the greater degree of permanence of Lung-shan settlement.[82] As Lung-shan farmers gradually colonized the still swampy plains to the east of their cultural hearth, so they developed a tendency either to seek or to build earthen mounds on which to locate their villages.

This increased permanence of village life reflected a change from shifting to permanent cultivation. Presumably some system of short-term fallowing, that is a rotation of crops, had replaced the Yang-shao swidden system or rotation of fields. The crop staples in the nuclear area were still millets, possibly supplemented at this time by wheat, though this has so far been archeologically attested only in the Huai valley.[83] Rice had also been incorporated into the crop inventory of the eastern plains, and cattle and sheep now seem to have played a more important role, although pigs and dogs remained the most numerous of the domestic animals. Possibly the domesticated horse may also have had some significance at this time, and poultry had certainly gained in importance. But the remains of wild game and the presence of fishing gear on the archeological sites leave no doubt that both hunting and fishing made substantial contributions to the Lung-shan way of life.

Although farming methods had been improved, the actual tools of the farmer seem not to have changed significantly since Yang-shao times, and the principal implements were still the hoe, spade, digging stick, and sickle. It should be noted though that Chang has discerned in the stone assemblages of Lung-shan a shift in emphasis from cutting tools suitable for skinning to those better adapted to harvesting.[84] There had, however, been considerable advances in industrial technology. Stone tools were mostly polished and were characteristically of asymmetrical edge and rectangular cross-section, that is they were of the adze family and adapted to the needs of carpentry, in contrast to the wood-felling axes of the Yang-shao stage. Moreover, although tools and implements of bone, antler, and mollusc persisted into the Lung-shan stage, there are certain indications that bronze working may have begun at this time. It is claimed that traces of a metal saw can be discerned on some fragments of antler, and metal objects have allegedly come to light on Lung-shan sites in Kan-su and Ho-pei, but these records are not beyond dispute.[85] However, it is a fact that the abrupt curves of a good deal of Lungshanoid pottery give the impression of being skeuomorphs inspired by metallic prototypes. If such did exist it is virtually certain that they were used for ritual purposes, and there is no evidence at all (in fact there is a good deal to the contrary) that either implements or tools were made of metal. In the field of ceramics the potter's wheel had been introduced (although hand-made pieces still predominated), pastes had been standardized, and the old Yang-shao tradition had been enriched by a distinctive style and a great variety of forms, notably tripods (*li, ting, chia,* and *kuei*) and ring-footed vessels (*tsun, p'ou,* and *tou*) which are usually ascribed ritual associations. The evidence for textile manufacture is wholly inferential but the frequent finds of spindle whorls, bodkins and eyed needles would seem to indicate that, though there may have been no major advances since Yang-shao times, this complex of crafts was not ignored.

In the sphere of religion the Lung-shan remains are less equivocal than are those from Yang-shao sites, and there is a close association between religious activities and status differentiation among the villagers. For the first time there is unambiguous evidence, in the form of phallic images, ceremonial vessels, bird motifs and scapulimancy, of an institutionalized ancestor cult[86] which may, however, have originated in Yang-shao times, and which probably provided the stimulus for a shift in the application of the decorative arts from domestic utensils to ceremonial crafts. This shift is signally evident, as is remarked above, in the pottery tradition. It was almost certainly as a response to the need to communicate with ancestors who, after making their contribution to the life of the settlement, had returned to the bosom of the earth, that there arose the practice of scapulimancy, which is attested in excavations and surveys almost throughout the extent of the Lung-shan culture realm, from Kan-su to Shan-tung and from Liao-ning to An-hui.[87] It is difficult to avoid the conclusion, particularly in view of the subsequent status of this ritual pseudo-science, that it must have been the prerogative of a specialized priesthood. Another indication of status differentiation within the community comes from an excavation at Liang-ch'eng Chen in Jih-chao in Shang-tung, where a hoard of finely worked jade objects is presumed to represent very considerable private wealth. That such differences in status did in fact exist is confirmed by variations in burial postures and inequalities in the quantities and qualities of accompanying grave furniture.

Nor was societal differentiation only hierarchical. There are also clear indications of occupational specialization. In addition to the skills of the ritual experts mentioned above, pottery manufacture, making use of the wheel and producing some wares of extreme delicacy and refinement, was almost certainly in the hands of specialists, as was metal working if it was in fact in existence in Lung-shan times. It has often been pointed out that the massive walls which surrounded at least some Lung-shan settlements, together with the presence of a variety of offensive weapons in Lung-shan villages, and the fact that some of the skeletons unearthed at a site near Han-tan had obviously encountered violent deaths,[88] imply the development of organized warfare and the emergence of incipient political consciousness consequent upon a more precise definition of political groupings. This conclusion is in agreement with the integral character of the functional network of village life and institutions so far as they can be reconstructed from the archeological evidence. Each settlement constituted an essentially self-contained unit.

If Professor Chang Kuang-chih is correct in his contention that in the Lungshanoid settlements there were specialized craftsmen, full-time administrators, and priest-shamans, and that there were also a theocratic art and a theocratically vested ceremonial pattern, which, no longer the common property of the entire village, were the prerogatives of a selected portion of the villagers[89] – and this is certainly the direction in which the available evidence points and is a conclusion consonant with the overall Lung-shan cultural configuration – then this society must surely be classed as a stratified society in the strict sense in which that term is used by Morton Fried.[90] Like the rank society defined above, a stratified society has fewer positions of valued status than individuals capable of filling them, but it goes further than the rank society in associating various degrees of status with differentials in the means of access to strategic resources.[91] In a fully developed stratified society, high status persons are privileged to enjoy almost unimpeded access, low status folk have only impaired access, to the community resources and are hedged about by socially sanctioned restraints which can often be circumvented only by the payment of dues, rents, or taxes either in labor or in kind. In my reading of Chinese prehistory the Lung-shan society was of this type.

Although Lung-shan society may be classed as stratified in this specialized sense, and although the Lung-shan ecotype was probably a paleotechnic sectional fallowing system pursued at the level of (in Braidwood's phrase) Developed Village Farming Efficiency,[92] nevertheless the Lung-shan community was still to a very large extent a society based on kinship. In fact, to judge from conditions in the immediately succeeding Shang period, kinship probably provided the basis for the differential access to resources which we have remarked above as implicit in Lung-shan archeological assemblages. In the over-generalized terminology of a decade ago, it was still a folk society. I am using this term broadly in the sense in which Robert Redfield first introduced it: 'The folk society may be conceived as that imagined combination of societal elements which would characterize a long-established, homogeneous, isolated and non-literate integral (self-contained) community.'[93] Redfield was interested primarily in processes of social change, and it has been pointed out, by George Foster among others,[94] that the categories which he devised for this purpose are unsatisfactory tools for the classification of societies, subcultures or communities in terms of structure. This is probably true (though in his later works Redfield did modify his scheme to some extent to meet the desiderata of his critics[95]), but it is not a complete disqualification in a study such as this, which is concerned pre-eminently with a period of climacteric social change. Different problems demand the formulation of different categories as research tools. Moreover, in the following pages, I shall endeavor to take some account of the deficiencies in Redfield's formulations, in particular his failure to demonstrate adequately the relationship between folk society and social class.

As far as the archeological evidence allows us to visualize Lung-shan society, it appears to accord closely with the anthropologist's generalized model of the more advanced form of folk society. Small, relatively isolated communities of proliterate agriculturalists were engaged in sedentary subsistence farming in the context of an economy that was structured around status relationships rather than some form of exchange. At the Yang-shao stage the division of labor, apart from that necessitated by and appropriate to differences in sex and age, was restricted to the recognition that certain individuals were especially skilful at certain crafts which were, nevertheless, practised by all men, at the same time as a few members of the community devoted a proportion of their labor to the perfection of a specialized accomplishment not attainable by the majority of their fellows, namely the keeping open of channels of communication between the group and the realm of the supernatural. By the Lung-shan stage, both occupational and sacral distinctions had become more clearly defined, but social relationships were still essentially familial, with kinship as the basis of all groupings and the whole of society permeated by common understandings as to the nature and purpose of life.

Some scholars,[96] considering that Redfield placed too much emphasis on the isolation of folk societies and ignored the systematic economic and ritual exchanges into which most of them enter, have pointed out that it is not the degree of involvement with other groups but rather the nature of that involvement which is the distinguishing feature of folk societies. One of the most succinct of the characterizations of the social and economic aspects of such societies that take account of these relationships is that provided by Marshall Sahlins:

'In primitive economies, most production is geared to the use of the producers or to discharge of kinship obligations, rather than to exchange and gain. A corollary is that *de facto* control of the means of production is decentralized, local, and familial in primitive society. The following propositions are then implied : (1) economic relations of coercion and exploitation and the corresponding social relations of dependence and mastery are not created in the system of production; (2) in the absence of the incentive given by exchange of the product against a great quantity of goods on a market, there is a tendency to limit production to goods that can be directly utilized by the producers.'[97]

It will be our task in the next section to relate the manner in which the instruments of economic coercion and exploitation and the concomitant relations of dependency emerged on the North China plain, and in a subsequent chapter some effort will be made to elucidate the dynamics underlying these changes.

THE EARLIEST URBAN FORMS

It was in the social and cultural milieu just described that, probably early in the second millennium BC, there was initiated a series of structural changes which transformed the whole configuration of society. Professor Chang has justly termed this a quantum change,[98] for it not only established North China in the roster of civilizations, but also thrust it into the secular cycle of world urbanization whose consummation is only now to be anticipated. That the earliest Chinese urban forms arose in the Chung-yüan is clear enough, but the precise location in which the event first occurred still eludes us. The tacit assumption of some authors that Shang urbanism was generated by the Ho-nan phase of the Lungshanoid horizon is extremely probable but still unproven. So far, the earliest evidence of this transition derives from excavations in the vicinity of Cheng-Chou in northern Ho-nan. Although the investigations are still incomplete, they have already laid bare a long stratigraphical sequence from a lower phase on the very border between Lungshanoid and Shang to the floruit of that dynasty, and they reveal explicitly and unequivocally that, at Cheng-Chou at any rate, Shang urbanism developed directly out of the cultures of the North Chinese Neolithic. It is, nevertheless, still possible that this may have been a local phenomenon, and we must be wary of generalizing from the sole instance of such evidence so far uncovered.

Cheng-Chou.[99] The archeological investigations conducted in the vicinity of Cheng-Chou more or less continuously since the discovery of the site in 1950 have extended over an area of some forty square kilometers from Hsi-ch'eng Chuang in the west to Feng-huang T'ai in the east and from Tzŭ-ching Shan in the north to Erh-li Kang in the south. Altogether nearly thirty sites have been explored, of which about half a dozen lie within or close under the walls of an ancient ceremonial center.

Both Yang-shao and Lung-shan remains have been excavated at sites in the vicinity of Cheng-Chou such as Lin-shan Chai, Niu-Chai and Ko-ta-wang, and the earliest Shang phases stratigraphically attested appear to have evolved out of these stages. The following table summarizes Chang Kuang-chih's systematization of the five stratigraphical phases that have been discerned in the Cheng-Chou excavations.[100]

v	Jen-min Kung-yüan phase	Jen-min Kung-yüan III
		Ko-ta-wang III
iv	Upper Erh-li Kang phase	Erh-li Kang II
		Jen-min Kung-yüan II
		Pai-chia Chuang II
		Nan-kuan-wai III
		Tung-Chai III
iii	Lower Erh-li Kang phase	Erh-li Kang I
		Jen-min Kung-yüan I
		Pai-chia Chuang I
		Nan-kuan-wai II
		Tung-Chai II
		Ko-ta-wang II
ii	Lo-ta Miao phase	Lo-ta Miao
		Nan-kuan-wai I
		Tung-Chai I
		Ko-ta-wang I
i	Shang-chieh phase	Shang-chieh

The site at Shang-chieh appears to have been a Lungshanoid settlement on the threshold of the transformation to urban form. Nine floors of dwelling houses were excavated, together with fifteen subterranean storage chambers exhibiting the typically Lungshanoid pocket shape. The inventory of the stone industry is particularly Lungshanoid in expression but some of the ceramic forms, particularly the *li* tripods, *tou* ring-footed vessels, jugs, bowls, and wide-mouthed jars are characteristically Shang. No metal artifacts have been found. Pig bones which had been used for divination have come to light,[101] but none bears evidence of the elaborate preparation which was associated with later phases of the Shang. The Shang-chieh stratigraphy is not continued upward and at the moment the value of the site rests solely on its very evident transitional character between Lungshanoid and Shang proper.

At Ko-ta-wang an early Shang phase lies directly above and was presumably continuous with a Lungshanoid stratum. Grouped with this phase are others of similar configuration at Nan-kuan-wai, Lo-ta Miao, and Tung-Chai. At each site the remains of apparently permanent villages were found, together with pottery kilns at Ko-ta-wang. The large quantity of shell artifacts, the bone hairpins with awl-shaped heads, and the unprepared oracle bones were still strongly Lungshanoid, but pocket-shaped storage chambers were less prominent, and Shang-style traits were increasingly evident in the ceramic assemblages.[102]

It is with the Lower Erh-li Kang phase that a distinctively urban nucleus first appears in the archeological record,[103] and it persists through the two succeeding phases. No one feature can be diagnostic of urban life, but at Cheng-Chou the configuration of the total assemblage of remains is decidedly urban in the sense in which that term is defined in Chapter Four. The most impressive single feature, though not one necessarily indicative of urbanism,[104] is the trace of a massive earthen wall enclosing a rectangular, presumably ceremonial, enclave some 2 kilometers from north to south by 1·7 from east to west. It thus occupies approximately 3·2 square kilometers, an area more than twice as large as that of the present-day walled city of Cheng-Chou (Fig. 1). The fact that this modern city is located directly above the ancient enclave may be symbolic, though not necessarily illustrative, of the extreme permanence of some site values in traditional China, but it has seriously hampered archeological investigation of the Shang city. So far two sections of the wall have been investigated, one of 1,720 meters at Tzŭ-ching Shan to the north of the present-day city, the other of 2,217 meters at Erh-li Kang to the southeast. Both sections show that the wall was built by the *hang-t'u* or stamped-earth technique. *Hang-t'u* was the term applied by the pioneer field archeologists at Hsiao-T'un to the layers of rammed earth[105] of which the Shang builders had made their foundations and city walls. The technique consisted of piling earth into a caisson of wooden planks, and then pounding it until it was sufficiently compact to withstand the ramming of another layer above it. Successive layers were added in this manner, one above the other, until the desired height was attained. The

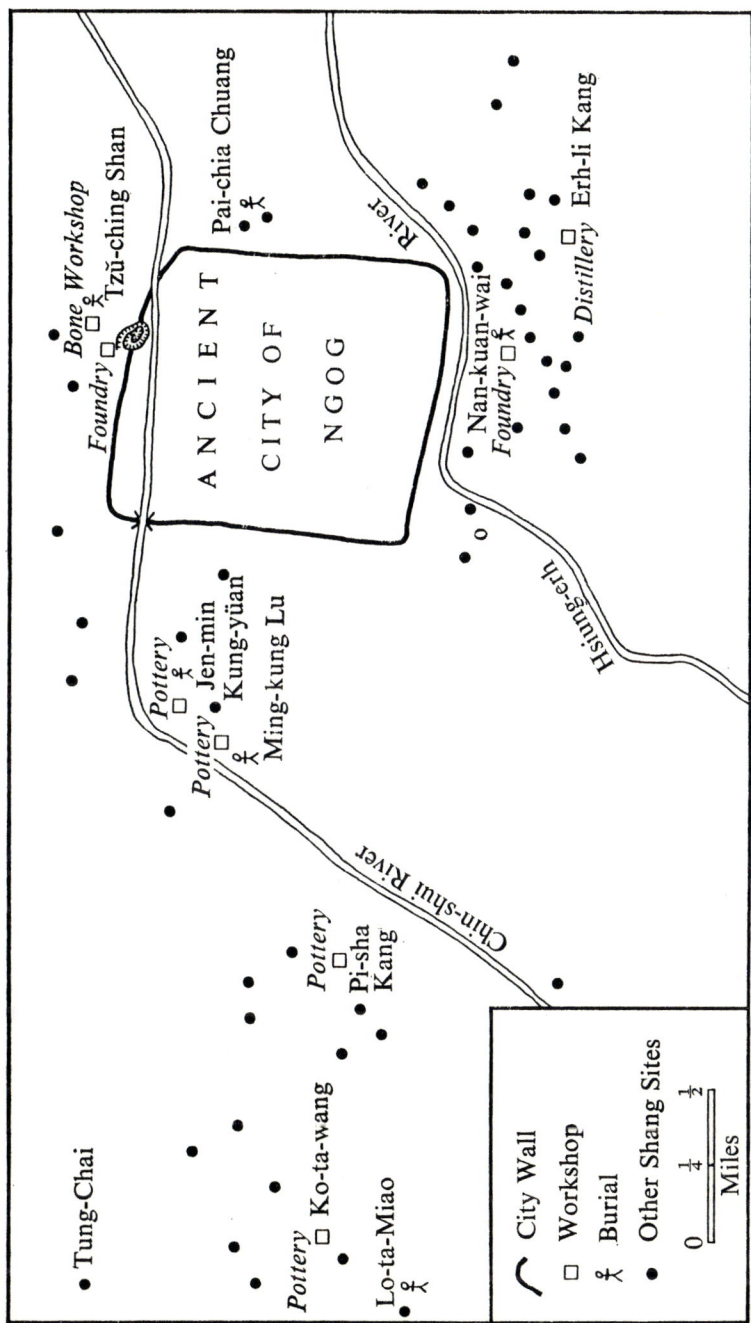

[1] The walled ceremonial precinct at Cheng-Chou which, together with its dependent settlements, may have constituted the city of **Ngog (Ao). Based on a plan in An Chin-huai, 'Shih-lun Cheng-Chou Shang-tai ch'eng—chih—Ao[**Ngog]-tu', Wen-wu, nos. 4 and 5 (1961), p. 73.

process, which was employed widely in China in subsequent ages and is used even today, was depicted vividly, not to say onomatopoeically, in the Ode **Mįan* in *Shih-Ching* [Mao CCXXXVII]:

And so [Duke **Tan-B'įwo : Tan-Fu] summoned the Master of Works,
And so he summoned the Master of the Multitudes [that is the farmers called for corvée],
And charged them with the construction of dwellings.
They set their plumb-lines vertical,
They lashed the boards to hold [the earth],
And raised the Temple [of the Ancestors] on the cosmic pattern.[106]

They collected [the earth] **ńįəng-ńįəng*,
They measured it out **Xmwəng-Xmwəng*,
They rammed it down **təng-təng*,
They scraped repeatedly **b'įəng-b'įəng*;
As the hundred **to*-lengths [of wall] all rose upward
The [rhythm-giving] drums could not keep pace.[107]

In The Ode **Sįĕg-kân* [*Szŭ-kan* : Mao CLXXXIX] the same process is again depicted onomatopoeically:

They are lashing [the frames for the earth] **klâk-klâk*,
They are ramming [the earth in them] **t'âk-t'âk*.

Although, as noted already, the presence of the modern city has allowed only sporadic excavation within the enceinte delimited by the ancient wall so that its function can only be speculated about, the general configuration of the settlement and comparison with the apparently analogous sector at Hsiao-T'un (pp. 39–43 below), together with such remains as have been revealed in this central core, would seem to indicate that it constituted a ceremonial and administrative focus for a group of surrounding villages and hamlets. At least one of the buildings within the enceinte, even though incompletely excavated, was larger than any building so far discovered outside, and has been interpreted as a public edifice of some description. To the north of it was a large platform of rammed earth, which invites comparison with an altar in the center of the settlement at Hsiao-T'un, while from the northern edge of the enclave came a hoard of finely worked jade hairpins, which must establish beyond doubt the élite occupancy of the site.[108]

At distances ranging from a few hundred yards or less up to four or five miles from the enceinte there were located a variety of apparently ancillary settlements, a high proportion of which contained dwellings, both semi-subterranean and surface, often with a door in the southern wall. Subterranean storage chambers were distributed virtually throughout the settlement. At Erh-li Kang,

Pai-chia Chuang, Nan-kuan-wai, and to the west of the Ming-kung Lu drainage channels were interspersed among the dwelling sites.[109] One of these at Pai-chia Chuang still preserves the impressions of rounded posts which impliedly supported the sidewalls of the drain. The excavators concluded that these channels formed part of a drainage system, though whether it was designed merely to lead off rain water or functioned in the disposal of sewage as well is unknown. Burials have been unearthed at Erh-li Kang, Nan-kuan-wai, Pai-chia Chuang, Tzǔ-ching Shan, Lo-ta Miao, in the Jen-min Kung-yüan, and along the Ming-kung Lu, but the greater numbers, as well as the larger and more elaborate interments, have been found either within or close to the central enceinte, notably in the Jen-min Kung-yüan and at Pai-chia Chuang.[110] Full details have not yet been published but the excavators at this latter site refer to 'large tombs' with elaborate furnishings and, in two cases, to human sacrifices. These large tombs at Pai-chia Chuang apparently belong to the Upper Erh-li Kang phase, and similar graves in the Jen-min Kung-yüan to the final phase of that name. It is worth noting in connection with the development of the ceremonial enclave that, whereas the oracle archives associated with the Lower and Upper Erh-li Kang phases were largely unprepared bones, in the Jen-min Kung-yüan phase they consisted predominantly of elaborately prepared turtle carapaces.

Handicraft workshops appear to have been scattered through the settlements surrounding the ceremonial and administrative enclave. All those discovered so far have been assigned to the two Erh-li Kang phases. Nearly all the old Lungshanoid industrial traditions were still in existence, although some had undergone stylistic modifications. About 150 meters north of the enceinte, for example, there was a bone workshop from which has been recovered more than a thousand pieces of bone in all stages of preparation. The raw materials consisted mainly of bones of ox, pig, and deer, supplemented, somewhat surprisingly, by a proportion of human bones. The finished products comprised mainly arrow heads and hairpins.[111]

Somewhat farther afield, about 1,200 meters to the west of the central enclave, there was a pottery comprising no less than fourteen kilns, together with storage pits containing both fired and unfired pottery and tools of the trade, and the houses of the potters. It is noticeable that this particular site yielded only pottery of a fine clay texture, mainly *p'en* basins, *tseng* steamers, *kuei* bowls, and *kuan* jars, so that it could be argued that other kilns must have existed to manufacture both the sand-tempered domestic wares, such as *li*, *ting*, and *hsien* tripods, and the hard, glazed and white pottery which are attested at numerous sites throughout the city and its environs.

Other kilns have, in fact, been located, notably in the Jen-min Kung-yüan[112] and at Ko-ta-wang,[113] though none has yet provided evidence of such extensive operations as that just mentioned. Close to the Jen-min Kung-yüan were more potters' dwellings, still housing their tools and gear. Kilns dating from late in the Shang-chieh phase have been discovered at Pi-sha Kang and again at Ko-ta-wang.

Bone carving, ceramics, and jade working were already traditional crafts in Shang China, and there is abundant evidence that the lithic industry persisted to supply a wide range of tools and implements. What was wholly new and at the same time distinctively Shang in style and conception was bronze foundry, which first appeared in the Lower Erh-li Kang phase. Two foundries have been discovered so far, the one approximately 100 meters north of the ceremonial enclave, close to the Tzŭ-ching Shan,[114] and the other some 500 meters south of the enceinte, at Nan-kuan-wai.[115] The southern foundry was the larger, occupying 1,050 square meters, and was also the earlier, having been assigned to the Lower Erh-li Kang phase. The northern foundry was of Upper Erh-li Kang date and was associated with a residential sector for the craftsmen. It is significant that, both at the large kiln site described above and at the Tzŭ-ching Shan bronze foundry, the workmen's houses were provided with stamped-earth foundations, which presumably reflected a status somewhat above that of the common folk, who had to be content with semi-subterranean dwellings.

The last indication of spatial specialization in the technological complex of Cheng-Chou is provided by the tentative identification of a distillery at Erh-li Kang. It has been suggested that a white deposit on the inner surface of a collection of large, coarse-textured jars may have resulted from their having been used as containers for some sort of alcoholic drink.[116]

An-yang.† The stratigraphy of the Shang excavations northwest of An-yang has been much less fully elucidated than that at Cheng-Chou, partly because of the disturbance of the site by looters,[117] partly because of interruptions in the progress of excavation, and not least because this was the site where Chinese archeologists to a large extent effected their own training. Moreover, even today the results of the excavations undertaken between 1928 and 1937 have still not been published in their entirety. The absence from the published reports of Fascicle 1 of Volume I,[118] which will presumably deal with general considerations relating to the location and excavations, makes it especially difficult for anyone who has not been fortunate enough to visit An-yang to get a clear idea of the nature of the site and the work performed there, and forces all students of this aspect of Shang culture to rely on small-scale sketch maps in journals, such, for example, as that often reproduced from *K'ao-ku Hsüeh-pao* for 1947.[119] However, these disadvantages are to some degree mitigated by the greater intensity of excavation in the central sector of the city as compared with Cheng-

† An-yang is strictly the name of a *hsien*, the chief city of which is Chang-te Fu. However, like many other cities in similar positions, this *hsien* capital is often called by the name of its *hsien*.

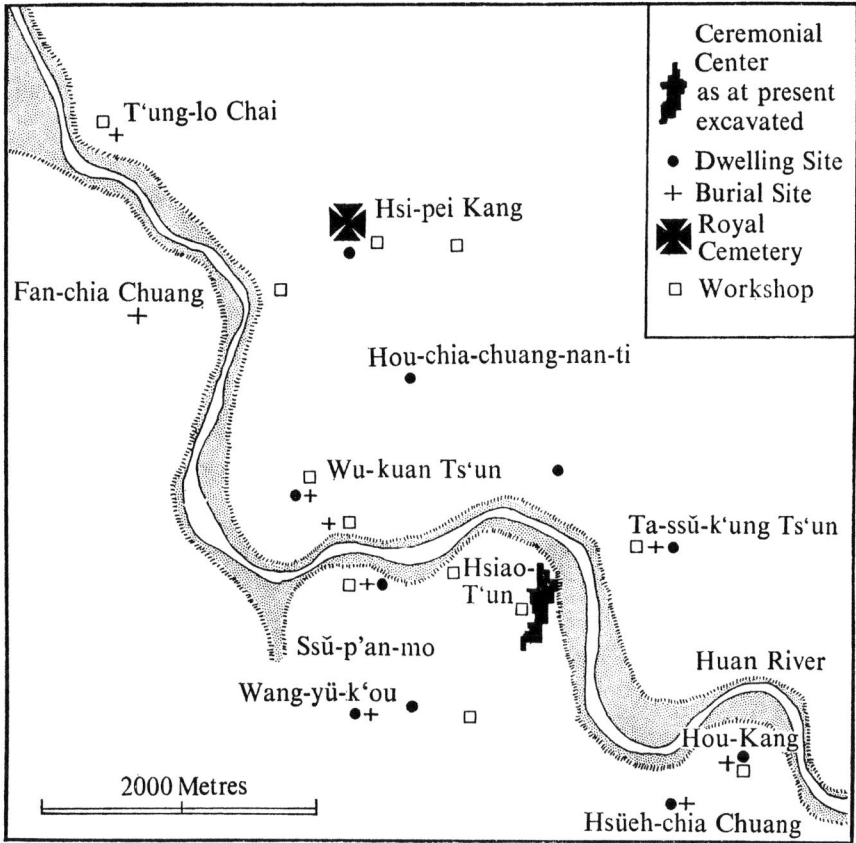

↟	Ceremonial Center as at present excavated
•	Dwelling Site
+	Burial Site
✖	Royal Cemetery
□	Workshop

T'ung-lo Chai

Hsi-pei Kang

Fan-chia Chuang

Hou-chia-chuang-nan-ti

Wu-kuan Ts'un

Ta-ssŭ-k'ung Ts'un

Hsiao-T'un

Ssŭ-p'an-mo

Wang-yü-k'ou

Huan River

Hou-Kang

2000 Metres

Hsüeh-chia Chuang

[2] The ceremonial precinct at Hsiao-T'un which, together with its dependent settlements, constituted the Great City Shang. Based on sketch maps in Shih Chang-ju, 'Yin-hsü tsui-chin-chih chung-yao fa-hsien; Fu: Lun Hsiao-T'un ti-ts'eng', *Chung-Kuo K'ao-ku Hsüeh-pao*, no 2 (1947), pp. 4 and 76.

37

Chou. It is clear from the evidence published to date that, as at Cheng-Chou, the settlement at An-yang consisted of a centrally situated ceremonial and administrative focus surrounded at varying distances by smaller dependent villages and hamlets. In this instance the core enclave was located in a loop of the Huan river immediately north of the village of Hsiao-T'un, and the attached settlements stretched along both sides of the river for a distance of some five kilometers (Fig. 2).

As soon as the stratigraphy of the Cheng-Chou site was published it became clear that the city at An-yang represented a somewhat later phase of Shang development. At Hsiao-T'un itself the excavators had already recognized three Shang levels, separated by a stratigraphical break from a Lungshanoid cultural stratum below.[120] The middle level, characterized by the adoption of the *hang-t'u* technique in the construction of architectural foundations, was held to have been initiated when B'wân-kăng established his capital at An-yang – in 1384 BC according to Tung Tso-pin's reckoning. The lower level, which consisted mainly of semi-subterranean dwellings and storage pits, would then have represented a pre-dynastic, but still Shang, occupation of the site, and the upper level could be considered to indicate a post-dynastic occupance, subsequent to 1111 BC in Tung's chronology. More recently Tsou Heng has claimed to distinguish two sub-stages in the dynastic phase, an initial one, presumably dating from the founding of the capital by B'wân-kăng, which was characterized by *hang-t'u* foundations in association with a system of drains, and a subsequent one in which *hang-t'u* structures were no longer accompanied by drainage channels.[121] The published evidence does not inevitably entail Tsou Heng's interpretation, but it is clearly prudent to refrain from dogmatic judgments until the reports of the excavations have been published in their entirety. In any case what is more relevant to present purposes is Tsou Heng's correlation of the *hang-t'u* phase at Hsiao-T'un with the Jen-min Kung-yüan phase at Cheng-Chou. The Hsiao-T'un phase prior to the *hang-t'u* he assigned a position earlier than the Jen-min Kung-yüan but later than the Upper Erh-li Kang. Subsequently more elaborate syntheses have been proposed, notably that of Cheng Te-k'un, who attempts a grand correlation of all Shang sites in five phases : Proto-Shang, Early Shang, Middle Shang, Late Shang, and Post Shang.[122] The present author is inclined to agree with Chang Kuang-chih that such syntheses are premature,[123] and in the following discussions archeologically based subdivisions in the progress of Shang urbanism will be restricted to the recognition of a distinctively earlier sequence of stages represented by the evolutionary forms at Cheng-Chou, followed, whether conformably or not, by a Late Shang floruit at An-yang. For practical purposes it will be accepted that the earlier phases of dynastic settlement at Hsiao-T'un were roughly contemporaneous with the decline and abandonment of Cheng-Chou (Fig. 7).

So much for the stratigraphical underpinnings of the two main expressions of Shang urbanism. It is appropriate, however, to mention here a periodization devised by Tung Tso-pin which was based on information from the oracle archives.[124] Some 30,000 of these inscribed bones and shells were recovered *in situ* at Hsiao-T'un, of which 13,041 inscriptions have been published to date, and Tung used the style by which the court diviners addressed the royal ancestors to discriminate five periods in the dynastic occupancy of that site. In terms of his own chronology these were as follows:

v 1209–1111 BC. Under the rule of two kings, **Tieg-·i̯ɛt (Ti-i) and **Tieg-si̯ĕn (Ti-hsin).

iv 1226–1210 BC. Under the rule of two kings, **Mi̯wo-·i̯ɛt (Wu-i) and **T'âd-tieng (T'ai-ting).

iii 1240–1227 BC. Under the rule of two kings, **Bli̯əm-si̯ĕn (Lin-hsin) and **Kăng-tieng (Keng-ting).

ii 1280–1241 BC. Under the rule of two kings, **Tso-kăng (Tsu-keng) and **Tso-kap (Tsu-chia).

i 1384–1281 BC. Under the rule of four kings, **B'wân-kăng (P'an-keng), **Si̯og-si̯ĕn (Hsiao-hsin), **Si̯og-·i̯ɛt (Hsiao-i), and **Mi̯wo-tieng (Wu-ting).

Subsequently this schema has been modified to include only four periods of alternating conservatism and innovation.[125] Tso-kăng is then incorporated in period i and Tso-kap is assigned to the former period iii, which has now been redesignated as period ii. Tung also claimed to be able substantially to validate the objective reality of these periods by content analysis of the oracle archives. Using such categories as foreign ethnonyms and toponyms, personal names, and the special preoccupations of individual monarchs, combined with grammatical constructions, forms of the characters, and styles of calligraphy, he demonstrated a remarkable consistency in several aspects of the cultural morphology of each phase in his scheme. To a large extent, too, Tung's proposed periodization has been reflected in the changing spatial emphases brought to light by the field archeologists at An-yang. Oracle records from Tung's first phase (1384–1281 BC), for example, have come predominantly from the northern sectors of Hsiao-T'un, those from phase ii (1280–1241) from the west-central sectors, those from phase iii (1240–1227) from the southwest, those from phase iv (1226–1210) from the southeast, while those deriving from the last phase (1209–1111) have been found concentrated in a small sector of the northeast.

So far no wall has come to light to delimit the extent of the ceremonial and administrative enclave at Hsiao-T'un but, in view of the fact that *hang-t'u* ramparts featured in the earlier Cheng-Chou phase and in the Lungshanoid stage even before that, and continued into historical times long subsequent to the Shang, it is not unlikely that their absence is only apparent, a temporary consequence of the incompleteness of the excavations, perhaps helped by the unauthorized disturbances of the site. In any case, even if a wall had enclosed the eastern flank of the ceremonial center, it is doubtful if it would have survived the encroachment of the Huan river which has eroded away the edge of the settlement on that side. The surviving sectors of the ceremonial focus occupy about 10,000 square meters (Fig. 3).

On reading some of the earlier accounts of the excavations at Hsiao-T'un, one was left with the impression of a maze of *hang-t'u* foundations, semi-subterranean dwellings, storage pits, and burials of both men and animals in a wide range of attitudes and circumstances (Fig. 4). The Chinese archeologists expended a great deal of effort in fitting these various features into elaborate classifications, usually on a morphological basis,[126] but few of these schemes seemed to throw much light on the way in which the settlement as a whole functioned. More helpful for our present investigation are the spatial distinctions observed by Shih Chang-ju.[127] Although nothing has survived of the architecture of the city above foundation level Shih was able to distinguish a tripartite division into:

1. A northern sector containing fifteen rectangular, cardinally oriented structures raised on *hang-t'u* foundations. This he interpreted as the residential preserve of the ruling élite (A in Fig. 3 : cf. also Fig. 5).

2. A central sector, now partly eroded by the Huan river, but still containing twenty-one large halls, arranged in two longitudinally oriented rows on the south side of a square platform of *hang-t'u* construction (B in Fig. 3). These halls, also supported on *hang-t'u* foundations above a complicated system of underground drainage channels, and associated with a large number of human burials, are believed to have been the ancestral temples of the royal lineages, in which case Ling Ch'un-sheng may well be correct in his identification of the square *hang-t'u* platform (Y on Fig. 3) as the foundation of a *t'an* for the worship of ancestors.[128]

3. A southwestern sector, consisting of seventeen carefully ordered *hang-t'u* foundations, which Shih considers to have been the ceremonial heart of the central enclave (C in Fig. 3). A stepped *hang-t'u* structure (Z on Fig. 3) was almost certainly the foundation of a sacrificial altar.[129]

That this enclave at Hsiao-T'un was indeed the ceremonial and administrative focus of the (or a) Shang state is attested not only by mutilated and archetyped fragments of information preserved in the literature discussed in a previous section, by the presence of sacrificial and consecratory victims, both

---

[3] Plan of the ceremonial precinct at Hsiao-T'un. Based on a plan in Shih Chang-ju, *Hsiao-T'un: I-chih-ti Fa-hsien yü Fa-chüeh: Chien-chu I-ts'un* (T'ai-pei, 1959), fig. 4. For details of this complex see pp. 39–43 of the text.

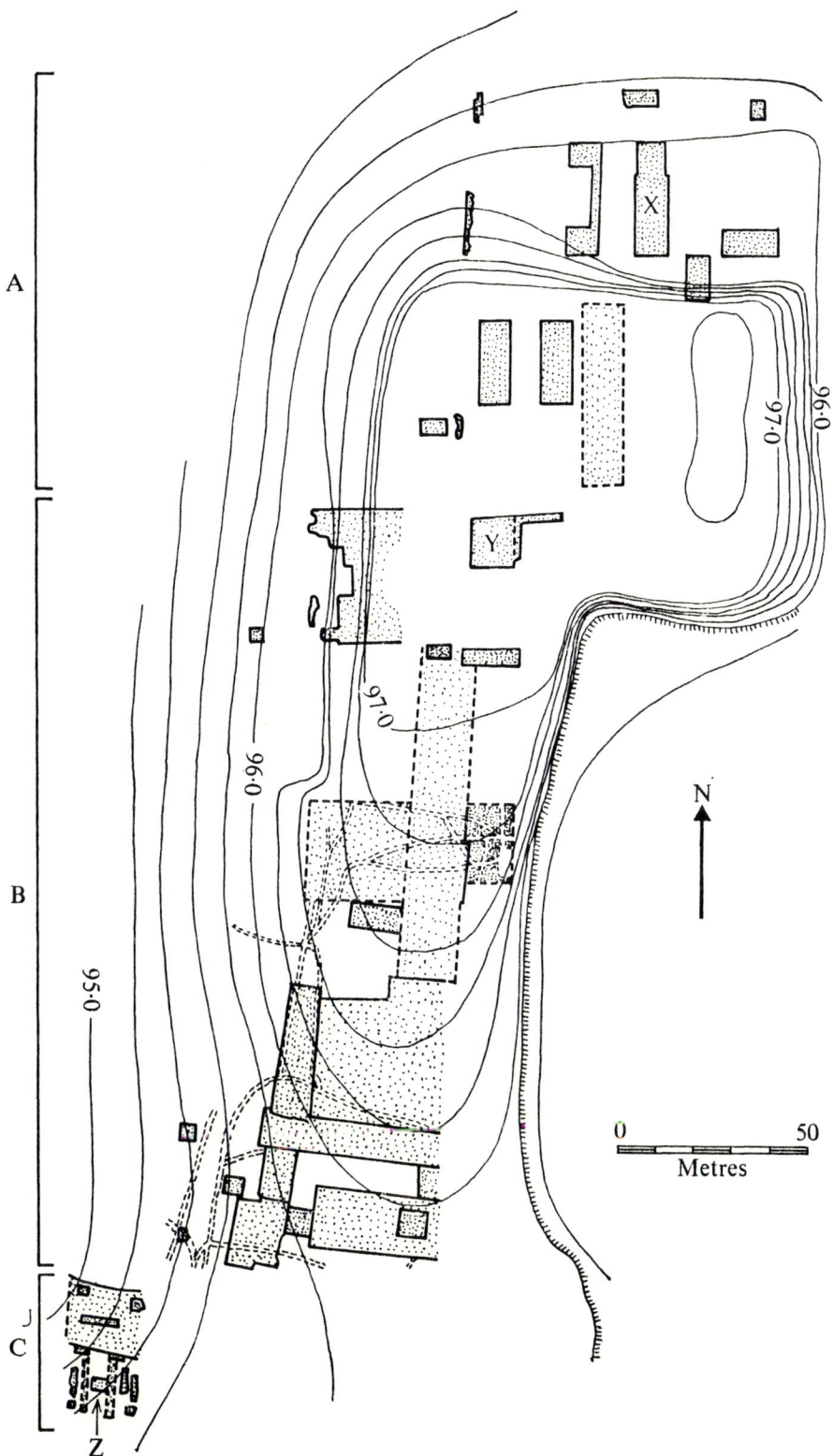

A

B

C

J

Z

X

Y

N

97·0

96·0

97·0

96·0

95·0

0   50

Metres

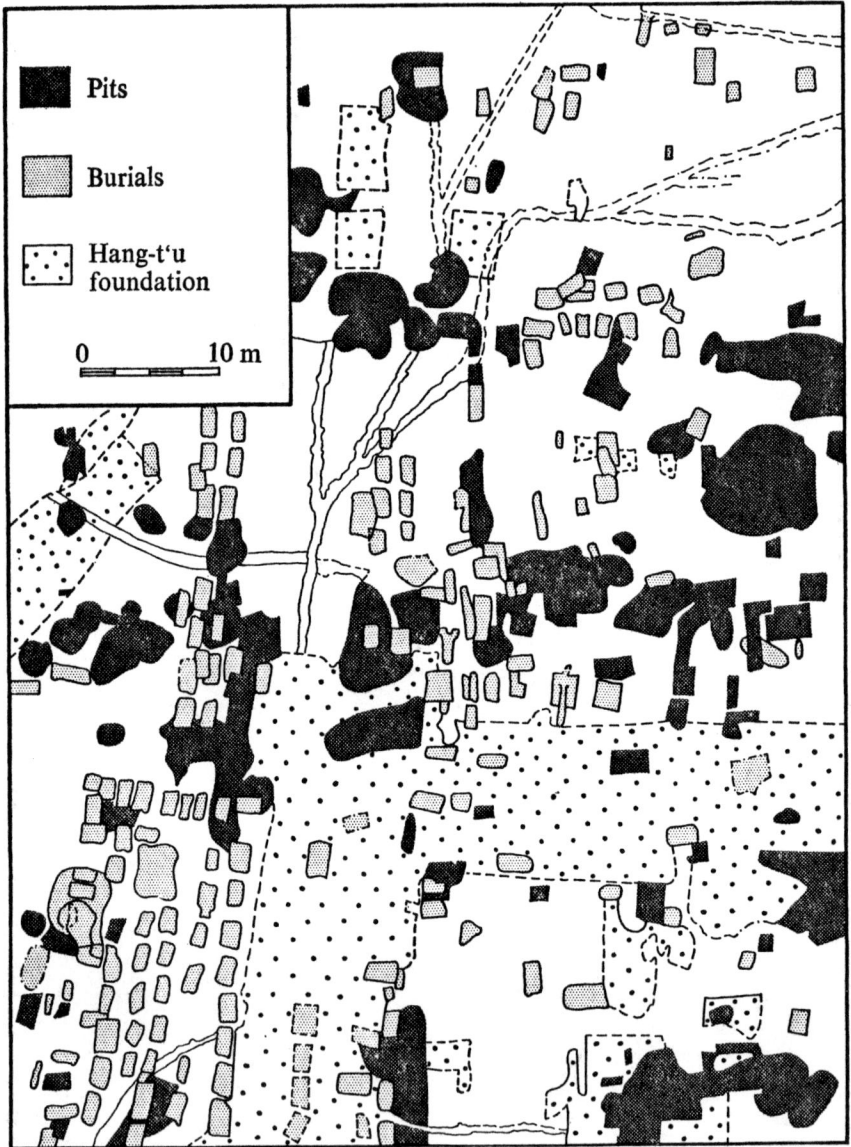

[4] Land use in part of the southwestern sector of the ceremonial enclave of the Great City Shang so far as it can be reconstructed from archeological excavation. Based on a plan in Shih Chang-ju, 'Yin-hsü tsui-chin-chih chung-yao fa-hsien; Fu: Lun Hsiao-T'un ti-ts'eng', *Chung-Kuo K'ao-ku Hsüeh-pao*, no. 2 (1947), fig. 20.

human and animal, which accompanied the construction of temple and altar, and by the finding (not always by archeologists) of an enormous number of bronze ritual vessels, but also by the huge quantity of oracle bones unearthed at the site. As these bones were associated exclusively with the royal court and the priesthood, their very numbers afford impressive testimony to the importance of Hsiao-T'un in the ceremonial organization of the state.

In one of the *hang-t'u* foundations excavated in the northern residential sector (X on Fig. 3) the pillar bases were still in their original positions, so that the archeologists of the Academia Sinica were able to reconstruct the general appearance of the building (Fig. 6).[130] The framework was of wood with outer walls of *hang-t'u* and a thatched gable roof, but with dimensions of twenty-four meters by eight, and an estimated overall height of six meters, it must have appeared as a reasonably imposing edifice. The position of a low platform, which has been interpreted as part of a flight of steps leading up to foundation level, suggests that the building faced the east. Shih Chang-ju has compared this structure to the royal palace allegedly erected by the first ruler of the Hsia dynasty, and described in the ancient Chou text *K'ao kung Chi*,[131] which was subsequently incorporated in the *Chou-Li* (*Chou Ritual*). Like so many other Chou texts, this latter work was given its present form in Han times, although it certainly incorporates materials from earlier periods.[132] The *K'ao-kung Chi* (*Record of Artificers*), which was substituted for a lost sixth book of the *Chou-Li* after that text had been recovered in Han times, is usually considered to be a work of considerable antiquity. In fact, it has been suggested that it may have been an official document of the state of **Dz'iar (*Ch'i*). Whatever its pedigree may be, it is not impossible that it preserved an architectural prescription from very ancient times which may have devolved ultimately from just such a building as that which we have been discussing. The fact of the preservation of this architectural prescription is itself a strong indication of the ceremonial purpose of its structural prototype. Its internal disposition is, in fact, consonant with habitation by just such an extended family as characterized the royal and aristocratic lineages of Shang.

In and around the more imposing dwellings of gods and their earthly mediators were what Tung Tso-pin has called service areas.[133] These included more than 600 semi-subterranean dwellings of servitors and menials, storage pits, some provided with round or rectangular bins, stone and bone workshops, pottery kilns, and bronze foundries (Fig. 4).

As at Cheng-Chou, the ceremonial enclave at Hsiao-T'un had its constellation of associated settlements. Among the most important of these was the cemetery at Hsi-pei Kang, near Hou-chia Chuang and some three kilometers to the northwest of Hsiao-T'un.[134] The report of the excavators of this site is scheduled for another of the volumes which is still unpublished, but from sundry information contained in papers oriented primarily to other topics, and from an early discussion by Paul Pelliot,[135] it can be ascertained that eleven massive mausolea were brought to light. Ten of these were excavated by Professor Kao Ch'ü-hsün and his associates in the nineteen-thirties, and one by the Chung-Kuo K'e-hsüeh Yüan in 1950. Apparently these mausolea were arranged in two lines, one of seven tombs and one of four, running from north to south and separated by an unoccupied strip of land about 100 meters wide. All were accompanied by sacrificial human burials. They have usually been interpreted as the resting places of the eleven Shang monarchs from B'wân-kǎng, who established the capital at An-yang, to Tieg--jɛt, penultimate ruler of the dynasty, and thus reflected a time span of nearly two and a half centuries. Strictly speaking, it has not been proven that these tombs were those of the royal lineages. The field archeologists who excavated them called them simply 'large tombs' in 'a cemetery area', and it was Pelliot who, in a lecture at the Harvard Tercentenary Celebrations in 1937, first voiced the assumption that they were royal graves. However, it is unlikely that any group other than the royal clan would have commanded sufficient social power to undertake the excavation of these enormous pits, or have been able to muster sufficient wealth to furnish them with mortuary articles of the quantity and quality evidenced at Hsi-pei Kang. Professor Chang's elucidation of the dualistic arrangement of these tombs (to be discussed in a later section) is a powerful confirmation of Pelliot's assumption. This vast burial ground also contains, in addition to workshops and pit dwellings, literally thousands of humbler burials and sacrificial pits. Presumably some of these represented ordinary burials, but it is abundantly evident that many were of a sacrificial nature. From the records so far published it is impossible to distinguish the two types, but it is evident that the construction of the great mausolea at Hsi-pei Kang was accompanied by the same type of consecratory sacrifice as that which sanctified the palaces and temples at Hsiao-T'un. Cheng Te-k'un makes the pertinent point that, as elsewhere in East Asia, the residences of both the living and the dead were constructed on the same principles.[136] Two other large and richly furnished tombs (although on a smaller scale than those at Hsi-pei Kang) have been excavated at Hou-Kang,[137] about 1,500 meters downriver from Hsiao-T'un, and at Wu-kuan Ts'un, about the same distance to the northwest,[138] respectively. If these are to be described as royal tombs, then they are presumably those of the collateral, not of the main, lineages.

Other settlements associated with the ceremonial enclave at Hsiao-T'un

---

[5] A reconstruction of the ceremonial enclave of the Great City Shang at Hsiao-T'un as seen from the northeast. The workshops and semi-subterranean dwellings of the ţjông-ńjĕn (chung-jen) are interspersed among the more important structures raised on *hang-t'u* foundations only impressionistically.

44

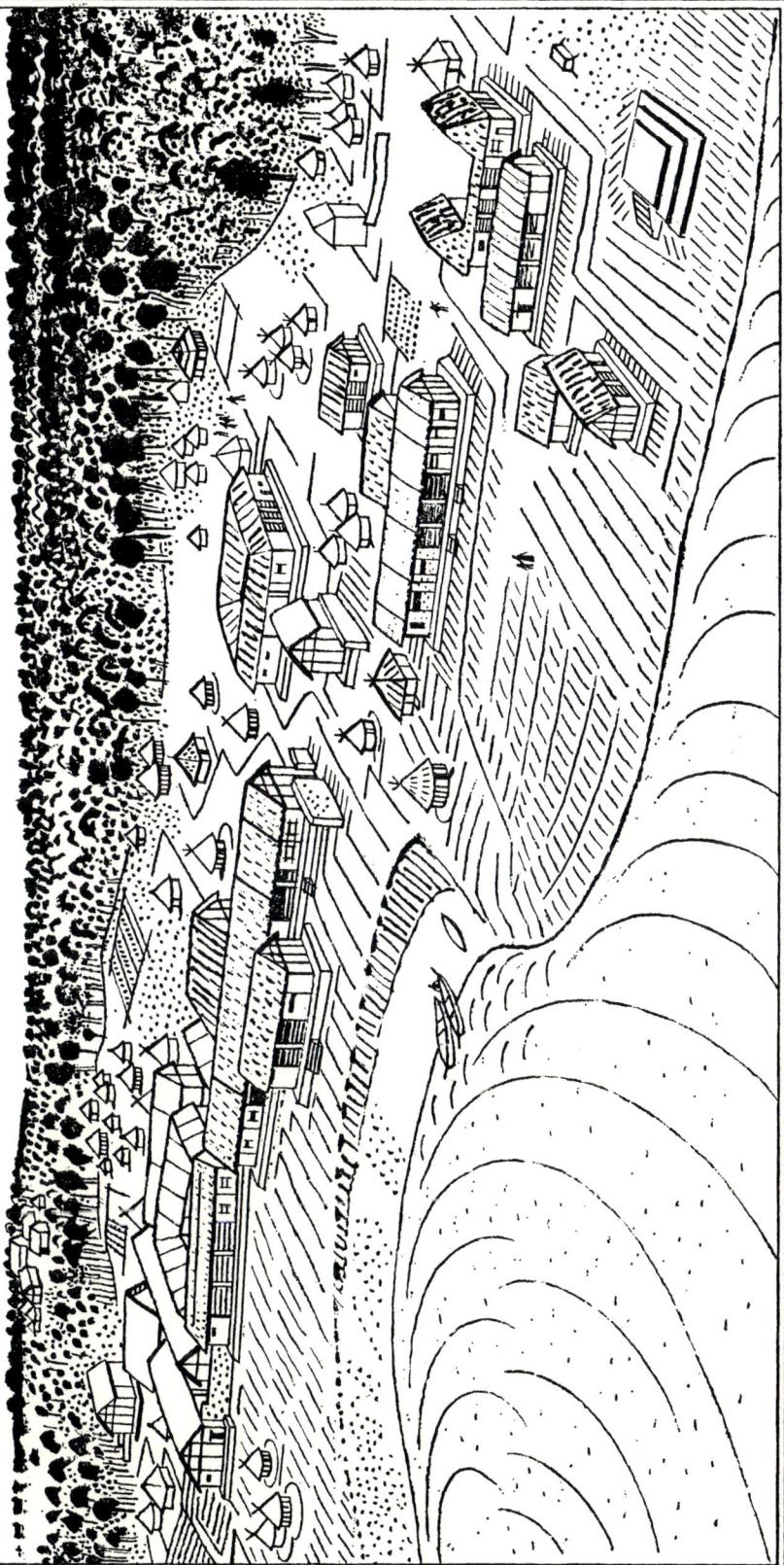

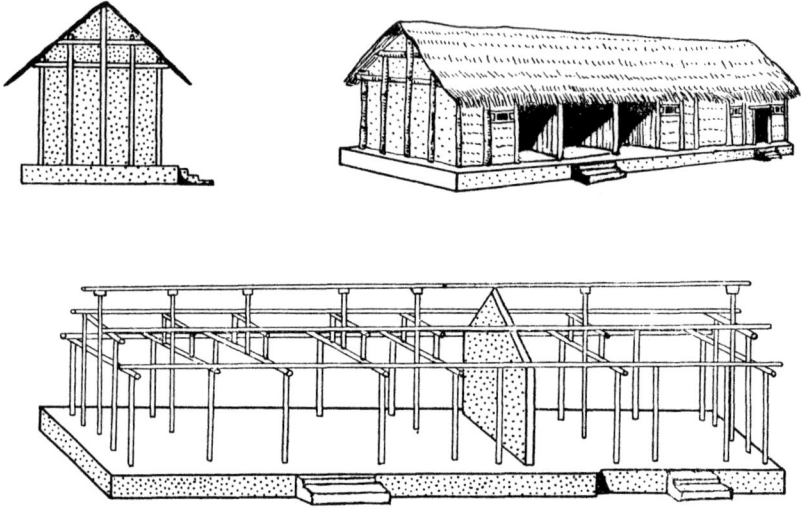

[6] Reconstruction of building A4 (X on fig. 3) in the northern sector of the ceremonial enclave of the Great City Shang. Redrawn from Shih Chang-ju, 'Yin-tai ti-shang-chien-chu fu-yüan-chih i-li', *Kuo-li Chung-Yang Yen-chiu-yüan Yüan-k'an*, vol. 1 (1954), p. 276.

have been discovered (but not fully reported on) at Hou-chia-chuang-nan-ti, Ta-ssŭ-k'ung Ts'un and Hsüeh-chia Chuang, as well as at a number of minor sites. Hou-chia-chuang-nan-ti, located midway between Hsiao-T'un and Hsi-pei Kang, appears to have been of special importance for, in addition to two foundations of *hang-t'u* construction (itself diagnostic of élite status), each furnished with subterranean storage chambers, there have also come to light caches of oracle bones.[139] As the enquiries inscribed on these particular bones were concerned primarily with the welfare of the royal family, the ordering of evening rituals, the weather and schedules for royal itineraries, it has been proposed that Hou-chia-chuang-nan-ti was the site of a resort palace of the Shang kings.[140]

At Ta-ssŭ-k'ung Ts'un both tombs and dwellings have been excavated. The former are of considerable interest in that, despite their relatively small size compared with those at Hsi-pei Kang and Hou-Kang, they were each provided with one or two human sacrifices, together with artifacts of bronze and jade.[141] The site at Hsüeh-chia Chuang is basically similar to that at Ta-ssŭ-k'ung Ts'un in that it has yielded dwellings, storage pits and graves, but human sacrifice appears to have been absent, being replaced in some of the larger tombs by dog sacrifices. There was also a fairly well-developed industrial aspect to the settlement, manifested in the presence of bone workshops, pottery kilns, and bronze foundries.[142]

Other Shang cities. Morphologically the ancient settlements at Cheng-Chou and An-yang appear to have had much in common. Each comprised a centrally situated ceremonial and administrative enclave, which can be safely presumed to have afforded a habitation only for members of the royal lineages, for a priesthood, and for a few selected craftsmen, together with, perhaps, something in the nature of a praetorian guard. Both the peasantry, who provided the material subsistence on which the ceremonial center depended, and the majority of the artisans who supplied it with ritual furniture, lived in villages dispersed through the surrounding countryside. Although the evidence is even more fragmentary than in these two instances, a similar settlement morphology, in which tributary villages surrounded a centrally located cult center, seems to be implied by Shang remains in the vicinity of both Lo-yang and Hui-Hsien.

In historical times Lo-yang was a prominent nodal center in the heart of the Chung-yüan, at a point where latitudinal routes across the North China plain were combined into a single strand prior to entering the passes through the western uplands, so that it is not altogether surprising to find it featuring among the more important Shang settlements so far discovered. Investigations at this site have been of a reconnaissance nature and the reports published so far have been preliminary in character,[143] but no less than twenty mausolea, complete with human and animal sacrifices, have been excavated in the neighborhood, together with, significantly, bronze foundries. The remains, which occur above Yang-shao and Lung-shan levels, apparently derive from all stages of Shang development, and it is possible that some of the tombs may date from a settlement of Shang survivors in the years after the Chou conquest.

For Hui-Hsien we are fortunate in being able to draw on the report of large-scale excavations undertaken by members of the Chung-Kuo K'e-hsüeh Yüan in 1950–51.[144] It is Kuo Pao-chün's conclusion that the settlement here was more or less contemporaneous with that at An-yang. Once again tombs with human and animal sacrifices occur, together with a bronze foundry, and Kuo has discerned a chronological sequence in the evolution of the burial customs as exemplified in the northern and southern sectors of the site.

The predominantly typological and classificatory point of view which pervades the reports of excavations at Lo-yang and Hui-Hsien is not particularly helpful in a study of more broadly conceived developmental trends, but the total cultural configurations of these two settlements would seem to indicate that their congeners are to be sought in the urbanized communities of Cheng-Chou and An-yang rather than in the population nuclei of pre-urbanized society. Chang Kuang-chih has, however, drawn attention to a possible variant

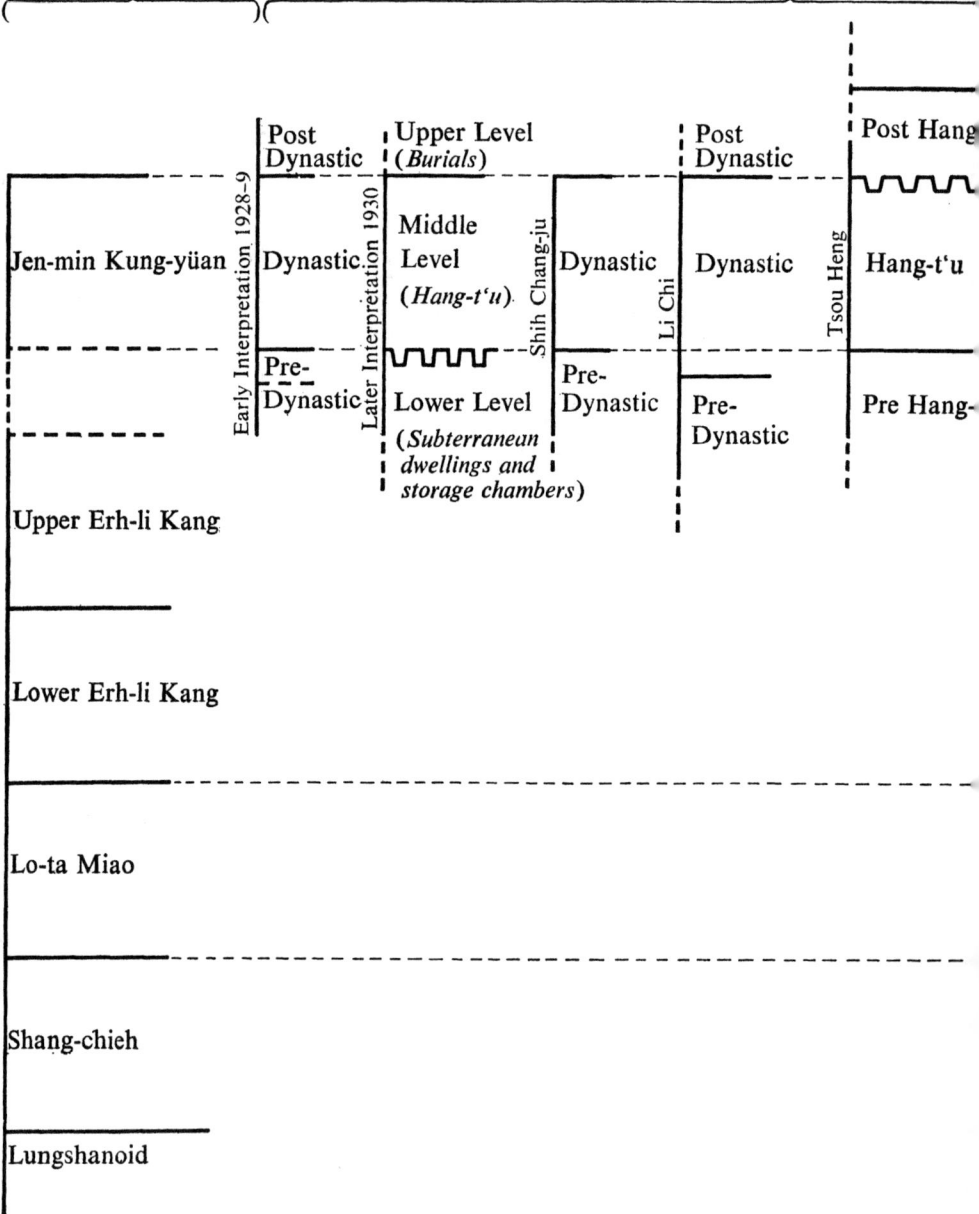

CHENG-CHOU   AN-YANG

| Jen-min Kung-yüan | Early Interpretation 1928-9 | Post Dynastic | Later Interpretation 1930 | Upper Level (*Burials*) | Shih Chang-ju | | Li Chi | Post Dynastic | Tsou Heng | Post Hang |

Jen-min Kung-yüan — Early Interpretation 1928-9 — Dynastic — Later Interpretation 1930 — Middle Level (*Hang-t'u*) — Shih Chang-ju — Dynastic — Li Chi — Dynastic — Tsou Heng — Hang-t'u

Pre-Dynastic — Lower Level (*Subterranean dwellings and storage chambers*) — Pre-Dynastic — Pre-Dynastic — Pre Hang-

Upper Erh-li Kang

Lower Erh-li Kang

Lo-ta Miao

Shang-chieh

Lungshanoid

[7] A tentative systematization of the archeological evidence for the earlier phases of the urbanization process in North China.

48

	HSING-T'AI	LO-YANG	HUI-HSIEN
		Chung-Chou Lu III (*Post Shang*)	
Tung Tso-pin 1209–1111 1226–1210 1240–1227 1280–1241 1384–1281	Upper Yin-kuo Ts'un (*Late Shang*)	Hsi-chiao II (*Late Shang*)	Liu-li-ke II (*Late Shang*)
		Hsi-chiao I (*Middle Shang*)	Liu-li-ke I (*Middle Shang*)
	Middle Yin-kuo Ts'un (*Early Shang*)	Chung-Chou Lu II (*Early Shang*)	
	Lower Yin-kuo Ts'un (*Proto-Shang*)	Chung-Chou Lu I (*Proto-Shang*)	
	Lungshanoid	Lungshanoid	

49

of this type of settlement pattern in which similar administratively and cere-
monially interdependent congeries of economically distinct settlements seem
to have existed without benefit of centrally situated cult centers.[145] Such, for
example, would appear to have existed in the vicinity of Shih-li Miao in Nan-
yang Hsien,[146] Lu-wang Fen in Hsin-Hsiang,[147] Ch'ao-ko in T'ang-yin Hsien,[148]
Shih-li P'u in Nan-yang Hsien,[149] Ta-hsin Chuang in Chi-nan Hsien,[150] Feng-
chia An in Ch'ü-yang Hsien[151] and at Hsing-T'ai in southern Ho-pei. Most
of these sites have received only cursory attention and have been inadequately
reported for present purposes, but at Hsing-T'ai excavation has been of a
somewhat more intensive, though still preliminary, character.[152] The lowest
stratum revealed in any of the ten sites investigated, and found only at Yin-kuo
Ts'un, has been correlated with the urban-threshold stage of Lo-ta Miao at
Cheng-Chou, but other sites have yielded evidence of later Shang phases distinguished by such diagnostic horizon markers as oracle records, bone hairpins, and characteristic pottery forms. Pottery kilns occurred at several locations and a bone workshop at one, but *hang-t'u* foundations were completely
absent and bronze artifacts were almost equally rare. At Ts'ao-yen Chuang
only eight small bronzes (arrow heads, awls and ornaments) were found among
some hundreds of bone and pottery objects. It is not impossible that the interdependence of the Hsing-T'ai settlements, which is implied by the irregular distribution of handicraft workshops, was organized from an administrative center
as yet undiscovered. Alternatively, the cultural configuration of the network of
settlements might be explained as the result of the secondary diffusion of
culture traits from a Shang culture hearth, so that Hsing-T'ai, together with the
other apparently proto-urban nexuses enumerated above, may have constituted examples of secondary urban generation (cf. p. 9 above) actually in
progress during Shang times. In this connection it is pertinent to recall Chang
Kuang-chih's attachment of a spatial significance to the typological classification of Shang sites that we have been discussing. An urbanized Shang society
would appear to have been restricted to a zone in northern Ho-nan, running
from the neighborhood of Lo-yang in the west (if the interpretation of this site
proposed above should prove acceptable), through Cheng-Chou to An-yang
in the north (Fig. 8). Round this core area there could then be said to exist a
halo of territories, extending from Shan-Hsien in the southwest to Ch'ü-yang
in the north and Chi-nan in the east, where diffusion of Shang culture traits had
prepared the way for the initiation of the process of secondary urban generation
as described above. Beyond that lay a much wider zone, reaching into northern
Ho-pei, central Shan-hsi, Shen-hsi, Hu-pei, northern An-hui and eastern Shan-

---

[8] The nuclear region of Chinese urbanism. Sites plotted beyond the limits
of developed Shang culture have yielded Shang culture traits only in
primarily Lungshanoid contexts.

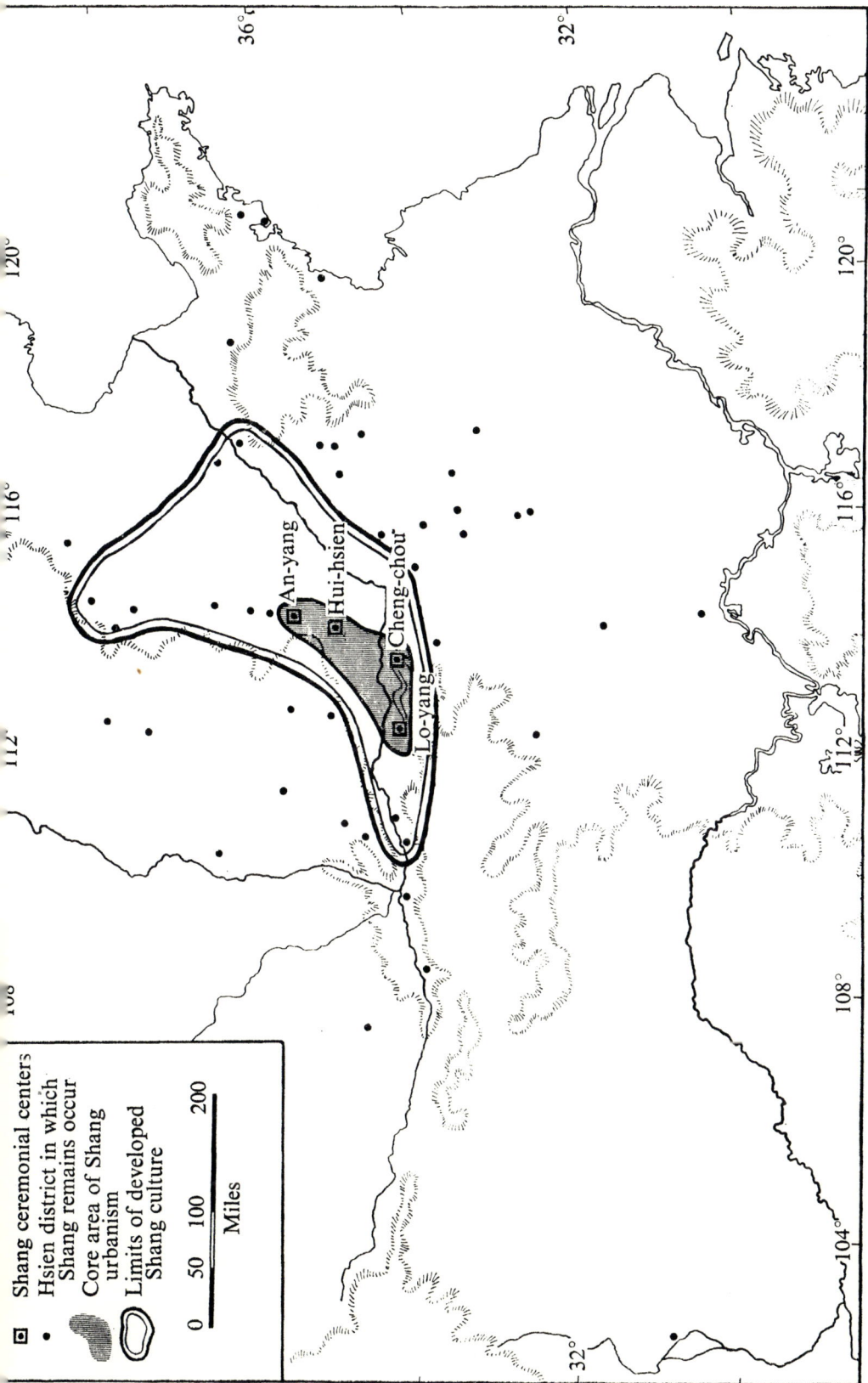

Shang ceremonial centers

□ Shang ceremonial centers

● Hsien district in which Shang remains occur

Core area of Shang urbanism

Limits of developed Shang culture

An-yang
Hui-hsien
Cheng-chou
Lo-yang

0 50 100 200
Miles

tung, in which selected Shang culture traits had diffused among pre-urban societies in a still predominantly Neolithic context.

THE POLITICAL STRUCTURE OF THE SHANG STATE

The political entity in Late Shang times appears to have partaken of the nature of patrimonial domain, a form of traditional rule which operates through a pervasive combination of traditionalism and arbitrariness.[153] It is characteristic of patrimonialism that the ruler treats all political administration as his personal affair, while the officials, appointed by the ruler on the basis of his personal confidence in them, in turn regard their administrative operations as a personal service to their ruler in a context of duty and respect. Provided they do not violate tradition or the interests of the ruler, their control over their subject populations is absolute, and as arbitrary as the ruler's is towards them. In Shang China this type of domain is not only implied by Chou writings of later times but is also attested directly by the oracle archives. At the pinnacle of the Shang political hierarchy was the king, referred to as **giwang (wang) during his lifetime but posthumously as **tieg (ti). As the earthly instrument for the accomplishment of Heaven's (**Djang-Tieg : Shang-Ti) designs, the king was responsible for all government policies, and all decisions were officially attributed to him under his style of **Djo jět-ńjěn (Yü i-jen), 'I, the Unique Person'. The affairs of the state were termed the king's affairs in official records, and appointments to government posts were reported, in the king's words, as 'to assist my affairs'.

THE GRAND LINEAGE OF SHANG

The royal branch of the ruling clan of the Shang was designated **Tsjəg (Tzŭ) in Shih-Chi, and its founding ancestor was accorded a miraculous birth in Chinese mythology. In the words of Ssŭ-ma Ch'ien,

'The mother of **Sjat (Hsieh), [founder] of the Yin [dynasty], was called **Kăn-d'iek (Chien-ti). She was a daughter of the **Ńjông (Sung) lineage and second consort of **Tieg-K'ôk (Ti-K'u). When, as with two companions she was going to bathe, she saw a dark bird let fall its egg, Kăn-d'iek picked it up and ate it. As a result she conceived and gave birth to Sjat.'[154]

It is evident that the grand lineage occupied a position of supreme importance not only in the ceremonial activities of the state but also in its political structure, but the precise manner in which it functioned has been obscure. Recently Chang Kuang-chih has suggested that the ten Heavenly Stems which appeared in the posthumous styles of the Shang kings represented ten lineages which together formed the ruling branch.[155] He further concludes that the throne customarily alternated between two of the more important lineages, but occasionally passed to certain less politically influential affiliates. Royal marriages, according to Chang's hypothesis, were characterized by a patrisib endogamy after the manner of patrilateral cross-cousin marriage, and the throne passed from maternal uncles to sororal nephews in two generations, or from grandfathers to grandsons in three generations. When it was first published this hypothesis appeared to activate a good deal of hitherto latent speculation among Chinese litterateurs and anthropologists, some of whom were extremely critical of Chang's proposal.[156] However, in a later paper he was able to neutralize most of the adverse criticisms, and went on to amplify his theory by linking the dualism operative in the succession to the Shang throne with the well known but incompletely understood **$d\underset{.}{i}og$-$m\underset{.}{i}\hat{o}k$ (chao-mu) system that obtained during the earlier years of the Western Chou dynasty.[157] At the same time he suggested that the Shang lineages may have had something in common with the ramage system elucidated by Raymond Firth[158] and Marshall Sahlins,[159] or with the stratified lineages described by Morton Fried.[160] Subsequently Liu Pin-hsiung has used Chang's work as a basis for his own hypothesis that the kinship organization of the royal house of Shang was based on a ten-section double-descent system.[161] Characteristically such systems consist of five patrilineal descent groups which cross with two matrilineal moieties to produce ten marriage sections.[162] In the case of the royal house of Shang it appears that the rule was bilateral cross-cousin marriage between a man or woman and his or her second cousin once removed. Liu claims that the rearrangement of the genealogy of the Shang dynasts on this basis reveals the significance of certain classificatory characters in the posthumous styles. For instance, **$d\underset{.}{i}ang$ (shang) was a style restricted to the founding ancestor of the grand lineage; **$d'\hat{a}d$ (ta) was assumed only by the founder of the dynasty and by the first king to be provided by each of the patrilineal descent groups; **$s\underset{.}{i}og$ (hsiao) denoted the last king of a particular branch or one who had no successor within his branch; **$ngw\hat{a}d$ (wai) signified a king with no successor within his section; and **$t\underset{.}{i}\hat{o}ng$ (chung) occurred both in sections which contained a $d'\hat{a}d$ ruler but no $s\underset{.}{i}og$ and in the style of the middle ruler in a section of three.

The evaluation of hypotheses such as these must remain a matter for the necessarily restricted number of scholars who are specialists in both Shang records and kinship organization, and even then their conclusions will be applicable only to the élite strata of society. About the kinship systems obtaining among the ordinary folk we know practically nothing. But even to the layman it is evident that the Shang lineages incorporated features of both kin and class. Power and authority always lay in close consanguineal proximity to the alleged main line of descent. In this respect the Shang kinship units would seem to have had much in common with the groups which Paul Kirchhoff has called conical clans,[163] that is 'kinship units which bind their members with common familial ties but which distribute wealth, social standing, and power most unequally among the members of the pseudo-family. Such kin units trace

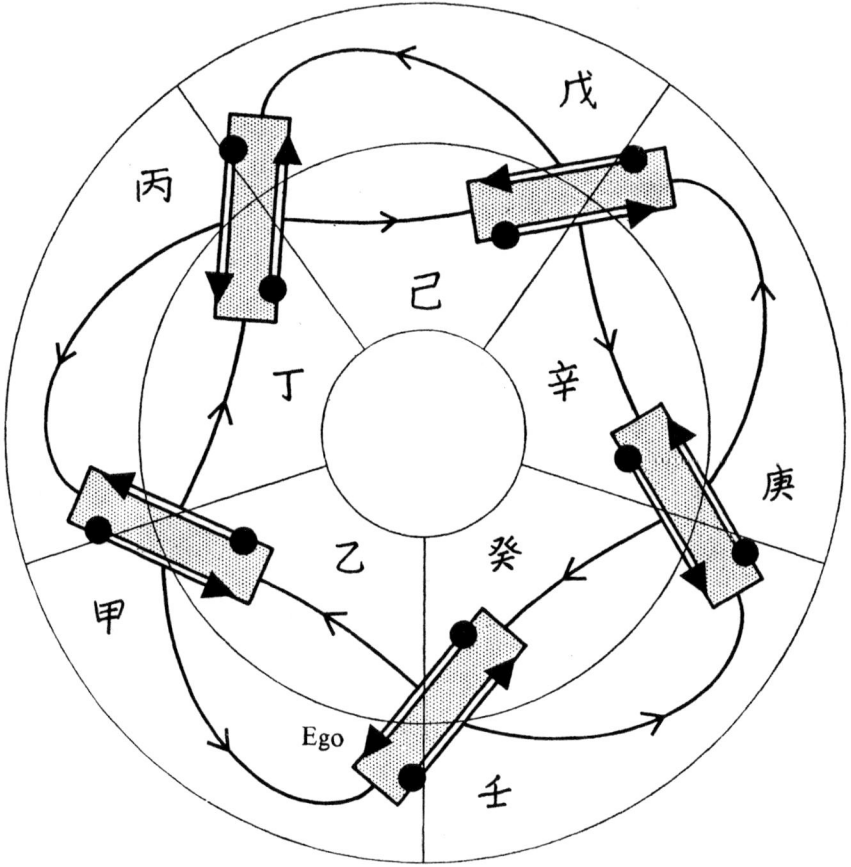

[9] Functional diagram of the ten-section system of the royal house of the Shang dynasty as reconstructed by Liu Pin-hsiung, 'Yin-Shang Wang-shih shih-fen-tsu-chih shih-lun', *Chung-yang Yen-chiu-yüan: Min-ts'u-hsüeh Yen-chiu-so Chi-k'an*, no. 19 (1965) p. 107.

their descent back to an original ancestor, real or fictitious; but, at the same time, they regularly favor his lineal descendants over the junior or "cadet" lines in regulating access to social, economic, or political prerogatives.' Such conical units of fictional kin would have produced just such a close correlation of political status with kinship descent as does characterize the Shang socio-political system.

Presumably at Hsiao-T'un the palace was one among the cardinally oriented structures in the northernmost sector of the ceremonial enclave (cf. p. 40 above). Political custom, though, makes it unlikely that one building served as the palace of the monarch continuously for more than a single reign. Under the descent system described above it is probable that the architectural foundations which have been exposed in the northern sector at Hsiao-T'un represent a series of royal dwellings, at least one for each change in the ruling lineage. In this connection it is instructive to recall Chang Kuang-chih's suggestion that the arrangement of the supposedly royal tombs at Hsi-pei Kang, with seven mausolea in the western row and four in the eastern, may have reflected the dualism already evident in the posthumous styles of the dynasty.[164] Moreover, while it might be a coincidence that there were eleven mausolea and also eleven kings buried during the An-yang period,[165] other correspondences adduced by Professor Chang are less easily disposed of. In the first place he has made a strong case for regarding the **$tieng$ ($ting$) and **·iet (i) groups within the Shang lineage system as the equivalents of the $d\!iog$ and $mi\hat{o}k$ generations of Chou times.[166] On this basis it can be said that, of the eleven Shang kings from B'wân-kăng to Tieg-·iet, four were $d\!iog$ ($tieng$) and seven were $mi\hat{o}k$ (·iet); and – what would be an even more extraordinary coincidence – of the eleven mausolea at Hsi-pei Kang, four were in the $d\!iog$ row (east) and seven in the $mi\hat{o}k$ row (west) as those distinctions were set out in the Li-Chi.[167] Shih Chang-ju had already speculated on the resemblance between the layout of the cemetery at Hsi-pei Kang and that of the ancestral temples of the royal house in the central sector at Hsiao-T'un,[168] both of which were arranged in two rows running from north to south, and he also pointed to the human burials associated with both sites. This is in accord with the prescription for the arrangement of shrines within ancestral temples as described in the Li-Chi.[169]

THE PRACTICE OF GOVERNMENT[170]

Some authors have regarded the Shang state as virtually a theocracy. Wolfram Eberhard, for example, refers to the Shang ruler as the 'supreme lord and religious leader' and as 'a high priest'.[171] L. Carrington Goodrich speaks of the king as having 'a kind of priestly function',[172] and William Watson characterizes the Shang government as 'to some extent a theocracy'.[173] There is certainly considerable validity in this point of view, for the ruling monarch was a member of a lineage which coexisted ontologically on earth and in the heavens above, and was the pivotal figure in all ritual procedures. The royal ancestors themselves were credited with supernatural power, and divination of their wishes was in the hands of a group of priestly augurs, experts in scapulimancy (**tiĕng-ńiĕn : chen-jen or **puk : pu), who were sufficiently important in the administrative hierarchy to have had their names recorded on the oracle scapulae and plastra.[174] So far no less than 117 of these tiĕng-ńiĕn have been counted, but this number certainly does not include all those who practised the art of divination during the two and a half centuries of dynastic An-yang.[175] The calendar of rituals for the glorification of, and communication with, the ancestors was elaborate and strictly controlled. Its performance was in the hands of specialists in ceremonial known as **ngio-sliəg (yü-shih), who might on occasion serve as envoys to neighboring territories.

It is characteristic of patrimonial domain that governmental and court administration coincide. Patrimonial rule is simply an extension to political subjects of the ruler's patriarchal control over his family. As Reinhard Bendix succinctly puts it, 'All political transactions that do not involve the [ruler's] household directly are nevertheless amalgamated with the corresponding function of the court.'[176] He goes on to cite the European instance of the supervision of cavalry, which might be put in the hands of the 'marshal' who supervised the royal stables.[177] Although the oracle records do not afford a comprehensive overview of all aspects of Shang government, this particular facet is clearly evident. A score or so official titles have been recognized so far, which may be functionally discriminated as secretarial, civil and military. The secretarial officials were closest to the seat of power and consequently highest in the hierarchy. Most important were the **·iĕn (yin) councillors, among whom was numbered the great minister **·ɟɛr-ɟuĕn (I-Yin). It seems that there were at any one time several court officers of ·iĕn rank, who were in charge of agriculture, the management of palace affairs, the organization of feasts, and numerous similar matters. Collectively the corps was known as the **Tâ-·iĕn (To-yin), and some of its members enjoyed great prestige. In fact Professor Chang Kuang-chih has suggested that some of the most influential among them may have been the heads of prominent lineages temporarily excluded from supreme power by the operation of a diôg-miôk style order of succession.[178] In this connection the position of ·ɟɛr-ɟuĕn, chief minister under T'âng the Successful (posthumous style **T'âd-·iɛt : T'ai-i) and several succeeding kings, is particularly interesting. In the ritual cycle of the Tsiəg grand lineage he was accorded the same respect as were the ancestors of T'âd-·iɛt himself. Moreover, his cult was especially prominent during the reign of Miwo-tieng, the most powerful of all the tieng group of kings of the An-yang dynasty, which suggests to Professor Chang that ·ɟɛr-ɟuĕn may have been the head of the tieng group of lineages during the reign of T'âd-·iɛt of the ·iɛt group.

Other offices within the secretariat were those of the diviners and ceremonial

specialists mentioned previously, the court chroniclers (**tsâk-tsʻĕk : tso-tsʻe)
who were entrusted with the drafting of the royal edicts and the superintendence
of the court archives, the **kung (kung) or master artificers (whose province
included the provision of music as well as the supervision of artisan crafts and
welfare), and the **li̯əg (li) or general duties officials.

Further removed from the source of power, but still personal servants and
personal representatives of the king, were the civil officers, known in the oracle
records as **di̯ĕn (chʻen) or **t̪i̯ĕng (cheng). Collectively they were called the
**tâ-di̯ĕn (to-chʻen) or corps of officials, but the use of such epithets as
**ngi̯wăn-di̯ĕn (yüan-chʻen : principal official), **si̯og-di̯ĕn (hsiao-chʻen : sub-
ordinate official) and **pi̯ĕk-di̯ĕn (pʻi-chʻen : appointed official) would seem to
imply that the various offices carried distinct differences in rank. Similar titles
and offices occur subsequently both on bronzes and in literature dating from
the Chou period.[179]

The third order of officials, the military, is also well represented in the
oracle inscriptions. Those most frequently mentioned include the **mâ (ma)
officers, possibly those charged with the responsibility of assembling, pro-
visioning or equipping mounted warriors, the **bʻi̯ŭk (fu) and the **d̪ʻi̯ŏg
(she) who were presumably connected in some way with archery, the **·ăg
(ya), **gi̯wad (wei), and **s̪i̯u (shu) who appear to have functioned as various
sorts of guards and garrison troops.

The extension of patrimonial authority. The situation described above approximates closely to the model of patrimonial rule as conceived by Max Weber,
but it is also clear that by the Late Shang the acquisition of large extrapatrimonial territories which could not be governed on the basis of the ruler's
personal resources and household management had induced an extension of
the administrative staff, as well as the elaboration of a military force, to perform
public duties beyond the scope of the royal household. There is abundant
evidence that the Shang kings had been forced to delegate authority by granting
benefices in return for services rendered to the throne. These benefices, which
were often referred to as **kwək (kuo), [180] took several forms. A relatively small
proportion were granted either to princes of the Shang, under the title tsi̯əg, or
to queens (**bʻi̯ŭg : fu) who were no longer required to attend at court. Those
in the vicinity of the ceremonial and administrative center were often designated
·ăg (ya) or **ńźi̯uĕn (jun); others, mainly on the fringes of the Shang polity,
were known as **păk (po), a title usually rendered into English as 'earl'.
Together with the **gʻu (hou), or marquisate, the păk was a benefice customarily bestowed on members of the court who had, by meritorious service, given
proof of both their loyalty and their administrative or military ability. **Nəm
(nan) and **dʻien (tʻien) appear to have been benefices connected in some way
with agricultural matters, possibly with reclamation of land : to judge from

the oracle records they were conferred only infrequently. The total number of benefices in the gift of the Shang king is unknown, and doubtless it fluctuated from time to time, but merely incidental references in the oracle records of Mịwo-tieng (1339–1281 BC in Tung Tso-pin's chronology) and Tieg-sịĕn (1174–1111 BC) attest the existence of four *tsịag*, three *b'ịŭg*, fifteen *păk*, twenty-seven *g'u*, two *nəm* and one *d'ien*. There is no reason to believe that these constituted more than a proportion of the total number of benefices during the periods concerned. From oracle and literary sources the more important benefices would appear to have included **B'âk* (*Po*), a former ceremonial center of the Shang dynasty,[181] and **D'ịĕng* (*Cheng*), both in the **Tịông-Śịang* (*Chung-Shang*) or metropolitan area; **Dz'ịər* (*Ch'i*) in the east; **Ts'ịam* (*Ch'ien*), **K'ịang* (*Ch'iang*), **Tịôg* (*Chou*) and **Djuk* (*Shu*) in the west; **Tsịĕng* (*Ching*) and **G'wân* (*Huan*) in the north; and **G'wɛr* (*Huai*) and **Ñịak* (*Jo*) in the south.[182] It appears that the organization and government of the individual benefices was patterned on that of the central government.

The chief duties of the benefice holders seem to have been concerned with the defence of the frontiers of Shang territory,[183] the supply of man-power for both military and construction purposes, and the collection of tribute for the court. Beneficed women assumed these obligations in the same way and on the same scale as their male counterparts, and the oracle archives record military expeditions under the command of two of Mịwo-tieng's superannuated queens against the K'ịang and **Lịung-pịwang* (Lung-fang) barbarians respectively. The nature of the liturgical obligations[184] prescribed for each benefice not unexpectedly varied according to the natural resources of the territory, and ranged from, for example, 250 tortoise plastra from the marquisate of **Tsịok* (Ch'üeh) in the west, to sacrificial cattle from the benefice of Prince **G'wĕk* (Hua) in the east.[184a] Especially meritorious service by a landholder was sometimes rewarded by a grant of the liturgical proceeds from his benefice for a period of years. Records of numerous such endowments have been found in the form of inscriptions on bronze ritual vessels cast specially for the occasion.

In addition to the benefices within the ambit of established and permanent Shang authority, there was an outer zone of **pịwang* (*fang*) territories. These were mostly the territories of tribal chieftains friendly to the Shang ruler whose authority over their own people had been confirmed by investiture according to Shang political theory. Such territories were sometimes known as **pŭng* (*pang*). That the process of proto-sinicization had already begun is attested by the fact that some of these chieftains figured in the oracle records as *păk* and *g'u*, presumably an indication of at least some adherence to Shang cultural norms and values on the part of the *pịwang*. The analysis of the oracle records of Mịwo-tieng and Tieg-sịĕn referred to above revealed the existence of at least twenty-six such *pịwang*. Among the more important of these territories were the **T'o-pịwang* (*T'u-fang*), **Kôg-pịwang* (*Kao-fang*), and **Kịwər-pịwang*

(*Kuei-fang*) on the northern margins of the Shang culture realm, and the *Ńi̯ĕn-pi̯wang* (*Jen-fang*) on the south.

The extension of the Shang patrimonial domain and the concomitant attenuation of the duties of the personal dependents of the monarch rendered necessary the maintenance of a military force competent to compel recalcitrant benefice holders to meet their obligations. The core of this force was the household guard, which was almost certainly accommodated close to the royal apartments in the ceremonial enclave. This was probably a carry-over from the early days of Shang patrimonialism when the polity had taken the form of a city-state, but by the later years of the dynasty such a praetorian guard had become wholly inadequate as an instrument for the enforcement of the royal will, so that a larger force had to be raised by conscription. According to the oracle records the numbers conscripted might range from 1,000 to 30,000 – although this last figure must be suspect when we read that the military expeditions conducted against some of the *pŭng* territories required only from 3,000 to 5,000 troops. On the other hand it is recorded that **B'i̯ŭg-Xôg (Fu-Hao), a queen of Mi̯wo-tieng with a benefice in the northwest, alone contributed no less than 10,000 troops to an expedition against a northern tribe, and on another occasion it was claimed that as many as 2,656 enemy soldiers were slain. The term used for conscription was **tang-ńi̯ĕn (*teng-jen*) or **tang-t̮i̯ông-ńi̯ĕn (*teng-chung-jen*), and recruits were known variously as **ńi̯ĕn (*jen* : men), **si̯og-ńi̯ĕn (*hsiao-jen* : common folk), **gi̯wang-ńi̯ĕn (*wang-jen* : king's men) and **t̮i̯ông-ńi̯ĕn (*chung-jen* : mustered men). The army seems to have comprised two main corps, one of infantry and one of chariots, each sub-divided into three sections that fought on the left, in the center, and on the right respectively. Shih Chang-ju believes that the war chariots constituted the spearhead of all attacks.[185] From the oracle records it would appear that, in later Shang times at least, the army was employed predominantly against *pi̯wang* raiders. Particularly was this true of the reigns of Mi̯wo-tieng, Tieg-·i̯ɛt and Tieg-si̯ĕn. Concerning one such punitive expedition directed against the *Ńi̯ĕn-pi̯wang* to the south of the Huai river during the reign of the last of these kings, no less than seventy-eight entries have been counted on the oracle bones, and the extant information is sufficiently complete to allow the route of the army to be reconstructed in detail. On this particular occasion the troops were under arms for at least 260 days.

The nature of Shang patrimonialism. Whereas I have been describing the Shang polity as a patrimonial domain, not infrequently other scholars from both East and West have categorized it as a feudal system. Certainly both types of domain revolve about rulers who grant rights in return for military and administrative services, but beyond that the contractual character, social and legal aspects, and ideologies of the two systems are analytically distinct.

Whereas patrimonial government is an extension of the principles of paternal authority and filial dependence that obtain within the extended household of the royal family, feudal government is founded on a contractually ordered fealty, structured upon a basis of knightly militarism. 'Feudalism', in the words of one of Max Weber's American expositors, 'is domination by the few who are skilled in war; patrimonialism is domination by one who requires officials for the exercise of his authority.' [186] This having been said, it must be admitted that at the institutional level the two systems are not always entirely distinct. The extension of patrimonial rule over extrapatrimonial territories may induce the emergence of political structures which appear morphologically similar to, or even occasionally merge with, others arising from the centripetal orientation of independent status groups under stress of external factors, such as war. It may then be difficult to distinguish the personal obedience of a dependent from the public duties of a political subject. Patrimonial governments exhibit feudal aspects whenever such a ruler grants territorially based benefices on an hereditary basis, and feudal régimes equally exhibit patrimonial aspects whenever fiefs are subject to a strong central administration. In fact, Weber himself was constrained to admit that the differences between patrimonial and feudal governments were often distinct only after the personal positions of patrimonial officials and landed notables had been traced historically.[187] Whereas a patrimonial retainer is essentially a personal dependent, a knight entering the service of his ruler preserves his independence.

Although the materials available are inadequate for a complete analysis of the Shang system of government, it would seem clear enough that we are dealing with a matter of personal benefices granted to retainers rather than with an impersonal contractual relationship between ruler and vassal.[187a] It was the 'good king' of patrimonial ideology, the mediator on behalf of his people between heaven and earth, who occupied the position of supreme ruler, rather than a warrior-hero at the head of a free camaraderie of warriors of pledged loyalty to their leader. The patrimonial king legitimates his rule in terms of the welfare of his subjects and dependents, from among whom his servants and representatives are usually chosen. Their chances of preferment are almost entirely dependent on the confidence of the ruler in their abilities, and precipitate translations from the lowest to the highest orders of society and back again, often for wholly personal reasons, are a characteristic feature of patrimonial government. Under such a régime the ruler is by no means committed to maintaining a fixed distribution of property, and new landowners are usually not unwelcome as long as they do not assume the leadership of social groups capable of exercising authority independently of the arbitrary will of the supreme ruler. Royal favorites and rags-to-riches stories are characteristic of patrimonial domain. The tradition that ·Ɪɛr-Ɪuɛ̌n, who held high office under the first four kings of the An-yang dynasty, had ingratiated himself with T'ầng the Successful by skilfully exploiting his knowledge of the culinary arts [188] is probably apocryphal, but it is nonetheless true to the patrimonial mode. Moreover, Professor Chang has tentatively suggested that the conservative and innovative periods which Tung Tso-pin believes to have alternated during the An-yang period (p. 39 above) *may* have witnessed parallel changes in the personnel of the administration.[189] If so, such changes would have been wholly consonant with a patrimonial régime.

It is not difficult to define analytically other discrepancies between patrimonialism and feudalism : the social distinction between benefice holder and feudal vassal, even when the former has divested himself of much of his patrimonial dependence; the contrasting attitudes to property rights, to education, and particularly to legal matters, the patrimonial ethic tending to transform questions of law and adjudication into questions of administration, while the feudal order, concerned principally with contractual negotiation about rights and privileges, tends to transform problems of administration into problems of law and adjudication.[190] But the evidence for conditions relating to Shang times is too meager to permit of profitable discussion of these points. Suffice it to say that what evidence is available points to a patrimonial rather than a feudal style of government. The heavy reliance on military force towards the end of the dynasty, however, implies that some dependents at least were beginning to appropriate their benefices, though whether in response to a decline in central authority or as a result of the extension of Shang government beyond the limits imposed by distance and the communications media of the time is uncertain.

THE EXTENT OF SHANG DOMINION

We have spoken above of the areal extent of Shang culture but, despite the fact that more than 500 place-names have so far been identified in the oracle records, the boundaries of the territory subject to Shang dominion can only be a matter of speculation. A late gloss on a passage in the *Chu-shu Chi-nien* depicts the state under Mịwo-tieng, twenty-second of the Shang rulers and fourth in the An-yang period, as stretching far into west and south China. Under the rubric Mịwo-tieng we read:

'In his time the oecumene (*sc.* territory under Shang control) did not extend eastwards beyond the **Kŭng (*Chiang :* the Lower Yang-tzŭ) and the **G'wâng (the [Lower] Huang) [rivers], westwards beyond the **Tiǝr (*Ti*) and **K'ịang (*Ch'iang* [tribes]) (usually located near the Wei-Huang confluence), southwards beyond the **Kịĕng (*Ching*) and **Mlwan (*Man* [tribes] : referred vaguely to South China),[191] and northwards beyond **Sâk-pịwang (*Shuo-fang :* in Han times this was the name of a city on the Huang river in present-day Kan-su, but in this earlier context the graphs should certainly be read as "the northern regions generally").'

Despite the fact that this passage, or others of similar import, have formed the basis for most reconstructions of the Shang empire, the extent of territory it depicts is certainly an exaggeration, born no doubt of the anhistoricity of Han – or later – perceptions of the past. We have seen in a previous section (p. 50) that a fully urbanized Shang society (in the sense defined in Chapter Four) on present evidence existed only in northwest Ho-nan. Surrounding this core area in all directions but broadening to the east and north was a zone of territories that would seem to have been fully acculturated to Shang values, and, beyond that, occupying most of the rest of the North China plain, stretched the peripheral lands where individual Shang culture traits were only just beginning to penetrate.[192] It is tempting to see in this archeologically attested cultural zonation a reflection of the ternary world view of the Shang themselves. A metropolitan district on this view contained a royal seat and ceremonial-administrative center, known in the records as a **$d'\hat{a}d$-$i\hat{e}p$ (ta-i), and probably some of the chief settlements of the dependent benefices, for which the term $\cdot i\hat{e}p$ (i) seems to have been used.[193] These would doubtless have boasted less imposing ceremonial complexes than that associated with the central government. This central area was surrounded by the benefices of $p\breve{a}k$ and $g'u$, these in turn being succeeded by an outer circle of incompletely assimilated $p\breve{u}ng$ territories.

Even if this interpretation were to prove correct in principle, the extent of the individual zones could be modified at any time – in fact, they certainly will be – by new archeological discoveries. More importantly, this view of the Shang ecumene raises again the problem of the nature of the literary records relating to the Shang state. How many states, and concomitant ceremonial centers, existed in the Shang culture realm at any one time is uncertain. The memory of one such polity has survived in the reconstituted literature of ancient China, and there is little reason to doubt that its last capital is represented by the ruins at Hsiao-T'un. But whether there were other similarly constituted polities within the ambit of developed Shang culture, and if so how many, cannot be known at this stage. The frequency with which the recorded Shang government was either at war with far from remote neighbors or repelling tribal raids at no great distance from the ceremonial center affords some indication that the effective political unit for which records survive was not large. In this case the inscribed oracle bones which have been brought to light outside the presumed capitals at Cheng-Chou and Hsiao-T'un may represent either earlier ceremonial foci of the recorded Shang state or, perhaps not less probably, rival capitals whose annals have been lost or suppressed. In this connection it is instructive to note that bone-text *Chia* 3510 (12) sought guidance as to whether a $\acute{s}i\dot{u}$ (possibly a **$\acute{s}i\dot{u}$-$dzi\dot{e}g$ $tsi\dot{e}g$: cf. Note 183) should join forces with the king (**$gi\dot{w}ang$) of a neighboring state, the name of which cannot be deciphered.[194] Moreover, it is no longer possible to overlook Noel Barnard's discrimination of two epigraphic traditions associated respectively with Shang and Chou polities. The former was identified with short and predominantly divinatory bronze inscriptions, the latter with longer secular texts designed for the instruction of posterity. It may well turn out, as Dr Barnard has indeed tentatively speculated, that the Chou, far from being the rude barbarians of traditional annalists, were in fact possessors of a more advanced culture than that of the Shang, and possibly therefore of a more complex political organization.[195] In any case, it is not at all impossible that the idea, which is implicit in later texts, of a unitary, maturely structured state dominating more or less the whole of the North China plain during Shang times was a Chou invention. If not, then it is unlikely to have materialized before the latter part of the so-called Shang period. In earlier times the Shang culture area probably comprised a number of competing ceremonial centers, each of which exercised direct control over a limited terrain in its immediate vicinity, and exacted tribute from other centers and surrounding tracts of territory to the extent that its ruler was powerful enough to do so.

CLASS DIFFERENTIATION IN SHANG SOCIETY[196]

On the stratified character of Shang society archeology, oracle bones, and later literary records are in agreement. Although the kinship oriented groupings of a folk-type society had not, as we have seen, been entirely eliminated, nevertheless a social system founded upon the physical expansion of a kin group within an established context of felt rights and obligations had been to a very large extent replaced by a politized social order. The incipient status differentiation that was already discernible in Lung-shan cultural assemblages had, by middle Shang times at latest, crystallized into a pyramidal society with the king and the royal lineages at the apex, a corps of officials, secretarial, civil and military, below and a broad stratum of *ţiông-ńi̯ĕn* or peasantry at the base. We have already had a good deal to say about the upper echelons of this society and there is no need to recapitulate those remarks here. Suffice it to recall that political and social roles were related to ceremonial status through the medium of kinship, and that, through the real or fictional relationship of a proportion of benefice holders to the grand lineage of Shang, the settlement and tenurial hierarchies of the kingdom also received ritual sanction and were articulated with the central government.

The gulf between the peasant at one end of the social scale and the noble at the other, besides permeating the whole of later literature relating to the Shang, is only too apparent in the character of the dwellings inhabited by each. Whereas the peasant in the countryside and the servitor in the royal or aristocratic ceremonial enclave each lived in a semi-subterranean dwelling, normally some four meters or so in depth and about as wide, the noble occupied an imposing structure raised on a *hang-t'u* foundation at ground level. It is scarcely an exaggeration to equate nobility with *hang-t'u,* and commonalty with pit, dwellings.[197] It is true that neither order used stone in the superstructure of its dwellings, but the gabled, pillar-supported roof and non-structural, screen-type walls of the aristocratic residence contrasted strongly with the wattle and daub lean-to of the peasantry.

The same disparity in degree of access to strategic resources is also apparent in the unequal treatment accorded to members of the two orders in death. So far at least 2,300 Shang graves have been excavated, of which more than 2,000 were in the vicinity of An-yang. The great majority of these have naturally been of a simple character. The extremely meager and simple grave goods associated with this type of burial are a world away from the 1,878 funerary articles, many of jade, bronze and marble, which remained in a supposedly royal tomb at Hou-Kang, despite it having been rifled twice.[198] Customarily the peasant or mechanic was consigned to a grave that was little more than a hole in the ground and furnished with a few pottery vessels. Occasionally a jade or stone artifact was added but, on the other hand, burials with no trace of a pit and no grave furniture whatsoever were not rare. At the other end of the social scale were the royal mausolea at Hsi-pei Kang and some tombs of the nobility that were hardly less impressive. The excavators have detected an evolutionary sequence in élite burials from the simple interments of Proto-Shang times, through the somewhat larger and more elaborate tombs of the Cheng-Chou phase, to the massive mausolea of dynastic An-yang, a sequence that is accompanied by an ever greater disparity in the mortuary practices of the two main orders of society. By Middle and Late Shang times even a medium-sized tomb of the type which the excavators call 'regular', and which presumably was the grave of a member of one of the politically less prominent lineages comprising the royal branch of the ruling clan or of some non-royal member of the aristocracy, bears witness to the expenditure of considerable labor and skill, as well as to the pre-emption of personal service on a far from modest scale. The tomb itself usually took the form of a rectangular pit, in the floor of which a smaller *yao-k'eng* [199] was excavated. Over this latter was raised a wooden structure in the shape of a *kuo* or coffin chamber, and the space between this and the walls of the tomb was then filled with grey earth [200] or, in some cases, with pebbles and stone chips (presumably to minimize the ravages of damp), so as to form a platform surrounding the *kuo*.[201] Both coffin and chamber were often painted with designs in black, white, red, and yellow, and mortuary objects, often in considerable quantity, were arranged on the platform. These included pottery vessels, especially *ting* and *li* tripods, *kuei*, *p'en*, *tou*, *kuan*, *chüeh* and *ku*, and, in the more elaborate burials, bronze vessels and weapons, and jade artifacts. Most such tombs also contained sacrificial victims, mainly animal but in a handful of cases human. Among the 166 tombs excavated at Ta-ssŭ-k'ung Ts'un, for example, five contained human victims.[202] In one (Tomb 175) a chariot, complete with horses and charioteer, was brought to light. It is not unlikely that an earth tumulus was raised over the finished grave, but if so none has survived to the present.

The royal mausolea at Hsi-pei Kang were conceived on an even grander scale.[203] These great cruciform pits, some with ramps on all four sides, and with all the features of the 'regular' tomb incorporated in more elaborate form, were the scene of veritable holocausts of men and animals, and there is evidence that before they were rifled they contained enormous wealth in the form of mortuary furnishings. The largest of these royal tombs occupies an area of no less than 380 square meters. Similar large-scale immolations of men and animals, apparently a prerogative of the ruling lineage, were also associated with the ancestral temples in the central sector at Hsiao-T'un, though it is often impossible to be sure whether these had been sacrificed at the consecration of the buildings or during subsequent ceremonies of ancestral worship. Oracle records from the same site contain numerous references to the sacrifice to the ancestors of the royal lineage of prisoners obtained on raids among the tribal peoples of the west, notably the K'iang pastoralists. But Professor Shih Chang-ju has also shown that some of the burials exhibited a sequential arrangement consonant with the several stages of building construction, such as the consecration, chronologically, of hang-t'u foundations, of pillar bases, of entrances and, finally, of the completed building.[204] Seven of the structures in the central sector at Hsiao-T'un were apparently consecrated in this manner. As many as 852 human beings, 15 horses, 10 oxen, 18 sheep, 35 dogs, and 5 fully equipped chariots and charioteers were entombed at the dedication of these buildings, and 187 sacrificial pits excavated. In the southernmost or ceremonial sector at the same site a single building claimed 35 human sacrifices, and on another occasion some 300 animals constituted a single offering to the ancestors. Although disparities in quantity and quality of mortuary furniture do not necessarily reflect correlative distinctions in social status, ceremonial and ritual on a scale such as this cannot but have reflected a remarkable concentration of social power.

Such activities were a prerogative of the élite in their ceremonial centers, but the bulk of the Shang populace was made up of a peasantry living in villages and hamlets scattered through the countryside. Some of these rural folk could be described as free farmers, others should perhaps be more accurately designated serfs, defined in this context by Wolfram Eberhard as 'families in hereditary group dependence upon some noble families and working on land which the noble families regarded as theirs.'[205] One of the great controversies in recent Chinese historiography has concerned the precise nature of this rural component in Shang society, and the answers given to this problem have accorded closely with ideological conviction. In China the prevalent practice, derived largely from the writings of Kuo Mo-jo,[206] has been to designate it a slave society, thus bringing the Chinese experience within the schematic formularies of Engels, Morgan, and Marx. Most Western historians have rejected this interpretation in favor of a free or serf society. In actual fact the disagreement is really a matter of semantics. Both Kuo Mo-jo and his disciples on the one hand, and Western historians such as Eberhard on the other,[207] are substantially in agreement as to the implications of the evidence, but Kuo and his colleagues, holding preconceptions which predispose them to ascribe social change to economic factors rather than to internally generated fluctuations in the loci of power, use the term 'slave' with a broad connotation unacceptable to their opponents. It is certain that a small slave class – using this term in the restricted sense of Roman law as a creature virtually without rights – did exist in Shang China but, as it were, outside the structural dimensions of society, and it seems probably not to have been self-perpetuating. Although its numbers were continually being replenished by the raiding of peripherally situated tribes, no inconsiderable proportion of its total complement was expended in ritual and dedicatory immolations. Mao Hsieh-chün and Yen Yen have drawn attention to the fact that some of the sacrifices offered during the dedication ceremonies of important buildings were live slaves (or, the same thing, prisoners of war) suffering from malnutrition.[208] It would seem also that their bones were sometimes used in the manufacture of artifacts.

It has been the custom to group the craftsmen of Shang society together with the *t̬i̯ông-ńi̯ĕn* in a single class, but this may have had the effect of obscuring certain significant social distinctions between these two groups. It is true that, apart from a small number who resided within the precincts of the ceremonial centers, the craftsmen lived and worked in predominantly agricultural villages, but there is evidence that at least some of them enjoyed a status somewhat above that of the peasantry. Among the kilns of the pottery on the Ming-kung Lu near Cheng-Chou, for example, were found the houses of the potters, which were much superior to the semi-subterranean dwellings of the farming community in the vicinity.[209] Like those of the nobility, though on a smaller scale, these homes were surface houses erected on a foundation of *hang-t'u*, were furnished with a south-facing door and sometimes a window, and contained both a low platform at the rear and a corner fireplace with a chimney in the wall. The dwellings associated with the bronze foundry at Tzŭ-ching Shan, immediately north of Cheng-Chou,[210] indicate a standard of living comparable to, if not higher than, that of the potters, so there is ground for suggesting that craftsmen and artisans were sometimes socially distinguishable from the *t̬i̯ông-ńi̯ĕn*.

Both literary records and the disposition of archeological remains tend to imply that particular handicrafts were probably the prerogatives of individual kin groups, and possibly that certain branches of a particular handicraft were wholly within the hands of specific lineages. In the *Tso-Chuan*, under the fourth year of Duke **D'ieng (Ting : 505 B C) it is related that, when King **Ḓi̯ĕng (Ch'eng) was consolidating the Chou kingdom after the conquest of Shang,

Duke **T̂i̯ôg (Chou) bestowed on **K'âng-śi̯ôk (K'ang-shu), the first Marquis of **Gi̯wad (*Wei*), seven lineages of **·*Jən* (*Yin*) people, five of which bore the name of products, presumably those which they themselves manufactured, namely the **D'ôg (*t'ao*=kiln) lineage, the **Śia (*shih* :?= trappers) lineage, the **B'wân (*fan* : horse accoutrements) lineage, the **G'ia (*Ch'i* : cooking pot) lineage and the **B'wân (*fan* : harness) lineage.[211] Although this passage was not written down in its present form until relatively late in the Chou dynasty, has been subject to editing in later times, and relates to the last decade of the 6th century BC, yet there is a general consensus among classical scholars that some of the *Tso-Chuan* material is of considerable antiquity, so that it is not impossible that we have here a genuine recollection of a close relationship between kin groupings and handicraft organizations in the Late Shang. We have already noticed the fact that one of the potteries at Cheng-Chou appears to have specialized in a limited range of wares (p. 35), which implies that at least some of the other potteries in the area were equally specialized. There is no evidence that I know of to support the notion that these specialisms were expressions of kin affiliations, but it is not impossible that such was the case. The retention of specialist techniques as the prerogatives of particular kin groups is a phenomenon well known in other social and cultural contexts. Moreover, Professor Chang has drawn attention to the partitioned plan and regular arrangement of the houses of the bronzesmiths at Tzŭ-ching Shan, which may be held to indicate not only that these craftsmen's families were of the extended type, but that they all belonged to the same patrilineage.[212] This interpretation would tend to confirm the authenticity of the information contained in the *Tso-Chuan*. All in all, the implications of a close relationship between kin and craft in Shang times are not negligible, particularly when it is remembered that the archeological evidence, all of which derives from the Cheng-Chou complex, relates to the Middle Shang (Lower and Upper Erh-li Kang), while the literary record, if indeed it is of Shang provenance at all, throws light on the very last years of the An-yang dynasty.

TECHNOLOGICAL CHANGE

Although the basis of life in the Shang state (or states) was agriculture, and although one of the chief preoccupations of the Shang kings was the promotion of agricultural prosperity through ritual intercession, it is noteworthy for the present study that this period saw no significant advance in field technology. There is no reason to believe that the short-term fallowing system practised in Lung-shan times had been improved upon to any degree, nor that the crop assemblages had been radically changed. The staples were still millets, with barley, wheat and rice (probably grown as a dry-field crop) somewhat less important.[213] Hu Hou-hsüan has stated that two crops of millet and rice were harvested each year,[214] but this would have been a virtual impossibility on the

North China plain in the absence of irrigation, and of this there is no evidence. Hu has claimed that it was probably practised in Shang times on the grounds that double-cropping would not have been feasible without it,[215] but this is a circular argument, whose conclusions are not compatible with what we know of Chou farming practice in subsequent centuries or can infer of Shang technological achievement. The water channels which have come to light at both Cheng-Chou and Hsiao-T'un, needless to say, were installed for purposes of urban and domestic drainage and, on all the evidence at present available, had nothing to do with irrigation. Much more credible is the evidence of the oracle bones that millet was grown in the first half of the year and wheat in the second, that is a summer crop was succeeded by a winter one, though, of course, they need not have been grown in the same field.[216]

Field preparation was still undertaken with the aid only of thick and heavy stone hoes hafted to wooden handles, and with a double-pronged levering instrument not dissimilar in principle to the *fumisuki* of later Japan, the cas-chrom of the Hebrides or the Irish *loy*. This implement seems to have developed out of the digging stick of Lung-shan times and to have been the forerunner of the **lįwər-dzįəg (lei-szŭ) of Chou times,[217] but it marked no new technological stage in the history of Chinese agriculture. At the end of the season the crops were harvested either with the semi-lunar knife which had been the common tool in the Lung-shan period or, increasingly frequently, with the *lien*-sickle.[218] This, an invention of the Shang period, was certainly a more efficient harvesting tool than the old semi-lunar knife, particularly on the North China plain where harvesting had to be fitted either into fine intervals during a rainy summer or into a short period between the end of that season and the onset of winter, but it signified no great change in the organization of the basic Sinic ecotype. The domestic animals that were raised were those of Lung-shan times, with the possible addition of the water buffalo, but there may have been some elaboration of the stock-breeding aspects of the economy in response to an augmented demand for cattle, sheep and dogs for sacrificial purposes.[219]

The remains of wild animals on archeological sites bear sufficient testimony to the importance of game as a supplement to agricultural produce in the Shang diet, but this subsistence activity should not be confused with the aristocratic pastime of the conventionalized hunt, which featured prominently in the oracle inscriptions, and which served the several purposes of simulating military training, inculcating qualities of character, and providing an acceptable outlet for the physical energies of the élite.[220] Possibly these two modes of hunting are reflected respectively in the finds of both stone and bronze arrow heads which have turned up in some quantity on archeological sites. The importance of fishing in Shang times is also revealed by the presence of fish bones and tackle of all sorts, ranging from hooks to tangles.

Among the handicrafts attested by, or inferred from, archeology, oracle bones, and literature, are shaping and carving in stone, jade, bone, shell and wood, bronze foundry, pottery manufacture, textile weaving and tailoring, and construction in earth and wood. Most of these crafts had their roots deep in the Neolithic past of North China. Carpentry and weaving, for example, had been practised by the earliest farmers of the Chung-yüan, lithic and bone industries at an even earlier date, and *hang-t'u* construction had been a Lungshanoid innovation; and in none of these crafts did the Shang period witness any radical improvement in technique, as opposed to elaboration of ornament, immediately prior to, or concomitantly with, the emergence of maturely developed ceremonial complexes.[221] The lithic assemblages, for instance, were all produced by the techniques of prehistoric times, namely sawing, chipping, pressure-flaking, hammering, pecking, polishing, and perforation, and, generally speaking, the tools manufactured in this way were of traditional patterns.[222] One innovation was the *lien*-sickle mentioned above. Another was the much less common *ch'i*-axe, a flat, more or less rectangular tool, with a straight or slightly curved cutting edge and with a series of tooth-shaped projections along each of the longer sides. Some of the more elaborate examples in jade were probably designed for ceremonial use, but striations on some stone specimens would seem to indicate that they at least had served a practical purpose. The primary use of the early stone prototype of the *ch'i*-axe is unknown, but it can hardly be regarded as marking a radical change in Shang technology.

A characteristic feature of the Late Shang stone industry is the unmistakable signs of decline in both the standard of craftsmanship and the use of many tool types, presumably as they were replaced by bone or, perhaps more probably, by wooden models. If this were so, though, none of the wooden forms has survived three millennia of inhumation. However, this apparent decline in the role of stone in technology was paralleled by a rise in the employment of more elaborate lithic artifacts for mortuary and ceremonial use. Associated with this trend was the carving of marble and jade, both in the Late Shang employed exclusively for ornamental purposes. We have already had occasion to notice the caches of jade artifacts accumulated in certain localities within Lungshanoid villages, and apparently implying some degree of status differentiation among the inhabitants, but Shang jades attained a much higher degree of sophistication in regard to both style and execution, particularly towards the close of the period.[223] Much of this advance appears to have derived from the application of some rotary apparatus, nothing of which has survived, needless to say, to the disk-knife, tube, and point which formed the essential items in the Shang jadesmith's technological equipment. Not only are jades from the earlier Shang occupational levels conceived and executed in a relatively crude fashion, but they are also directed preponderantly towards utilitarian purposes, whereas in the later period the vast majority of the articles produced by the jadesmith fall within the categories of ceremonial or mortuary objects (including *pi* disks, *tsung* squares and *kuei* scepters), ornaments of one sort or another and including numerous forms of pendants, and various types of decorative fittings for weapons and furniture.

Documentation for an account of the changes in Shang pottery technology is more adequate than for any of the other industrial traditions.[224] In addition to the quarter of a million sherds accumulated from the pre-World War II excavations in and around An-yang, substantial hoards have also subsequently been brought to light at Cheng-Chou, Lo-yang, Hui-Hsien, Hsing-T'ai, Ch'ü-yang and elsewhere, while evolutionary sequences of form and technology have been reconstructed without much difficulty. Although the wheel had been employed extensively in the manufacture of Lung-shan pottery, it appears to have been used, if anything, rather less frequently in Shang times.[225] Wheel marks tend to occur especially infrequently in the collections from Hsiao-T'un, that is, from Late Shang times, but are somewhat more common in sherds from Cheng-Chou, earlier Lo-yang (which has yielded a complete sequence from Late Neolithic to post-Shang), Hui-Hsien and Hsing-T'ai. In other words, it is the lateness of the Hsiao-T'un levels to which the paucity of wheel-turned pottery should be attributed. Why the Middle and Late Shang potters should have tended to reject wheel-shaping in favor of ring-building and beating and, to some extent, mould-building is unknown.

While the wheel-shaping of pottery was failing to advance in popularity or efficiency, it is clear that marked improvements were being introduced into the design of kilns. In fact Ma Ch'üan has been able to demonstrate an evolutionary typology in the remains of kilns from the potteries in the neighborhood of Cheng-Chou.[226] The earliest type was represented by two kilns which have been assigned to a proto-Shang level at Lo-ta Miao. Basically they preserved the Lung-shan traditions of firing. By the Middle Shang, however, several kilns in the potteries near the Ming-kung Lu, in the Jen-min Kung-yüan, and at Kang-tu and Ko-ta-wang Ts'un exhibited evidence of considerable improvement. The provision of heat vents in the floor of the baking chamber, for example, ensured better control of the fire in the Ming-kung Lu kilns, and some of those in the Jen-min Kung-yüan incorporated chimneys in the form of cylindrical tubes of baked clay. At Pi-sha Kang and Ko-ta-wang Ts'un a series of Late Shang kilns exhibited larger baking chambers, which necessitated more sophisticated systems of heat vents, together with thicker baking floors which obviated the need for supporting pillars in the fire pits. Berthold Laufer has suggested that contemporary developments in bronze foundry may not have been without influence in stimulating the more efficient application of heat in the pottery kilns of Shang.[227]

The effectiveness of the Late Shang kilns is evident in certain aspects of the pottery assemblages collected at Hsiao-T'un. There, in addition to the Grey and Red Wares, common on all Shang sites, which had devolved in the ceramic tradition of the North China plain, were invented two new types, a White Ware containing a high percentage of alumina,[228] and a Stoneware, sometimes glazed, which contained a high proportion of silica. The paste and glaze of this latter ware approached very closely indeed to what has been called the 'proto-porcelain' of the Han.[229] Only by means of a highly efficient kiln could the potters have ensured the constant hardness of 5 which characterizes this ware, as well as a porosity never in excess of 1 per cent for all sherds tested from Hsiao-T'un.[230] Such standardization of product suggests that this ware was designed to meet a specific demand, and it has been suggested that it may have served for the storage of water and wine, a function for which the porous Grey Ware was obviously unsuitable.[231] If such was the case, then it is not unrealistic to view the Stoneware as a response to the emergence of the great ceremonial centers of Shang, the palaces and temples of which would have posed problems of liquid storage never encountered in the agricultural villages of earlier times.

Shang ceramics, particularly the assemblage from Hsiao-T'un, exhibit great variety and richness of form. Li Chi has categorized six main classes, sub-divided into no less than 143 types and 359 subtypes.[232] Many represented the continuation of Lung-shan traditions, but no inconsiderable proportion are Shang innovations. Among these latter are the cord-marked grey *li* tripods with short feet, round-bottomed cord-marked jugs with in-turned rims, large-mouthed beakers with exaggeratedly out-turned rims, flat-bottomed small-mouthed jars with rounded shoulders (*lui*), and ring-footed, round-bottomed, small-mouthed jars (*p'ou*). In addition Shang potters produced musical instruments in the form of ocarinas (*hsün*) and bells (*nao*), as well as industrial articles such as spindle whorls, pestles, net-sinkers, *k'an-kuo* crucibles and various types of moulds, and *tsu* figures and figurines.

The most dramatic advance in all the fields of Shang industrial technology was the development of bronze foundry, which provided us with what has become the most characteristic class of Shang artifacts.[233] It is just possible that the practice of metallurgy had been initiated at the very end of the Lung-shanoid phase (cf. p. 27 above), but in the earliest (Shang-chieh) phase of Shang culture at Cheng-Chou metal artifacts are completely lacking. The succeeding Lo-ta Miao phase has been only imperfectly explored, so that the absence of metal finds in these levels *may* imply no more than rarity. However, with the Erh-li Kang phase – which saw the building of the city wall of Cheng-Chou – there is revealed a vigorous, mature, bronze industry, adapting metal-lurgical techniques to pre-existing forms both of stone, bone, and horn implements, and of pottery and wooden vessels. By Late Shang times this industry had evolved into one of the world's great technological and artistic traditions.

If the term 'bronze' be restricted in connotation, as is customary, to an alloy with from 5 to 20 per cent of tin in copper, then the majority of Shang so-called bronzes are technically misnamed, for they do not conform to this chemical composition.[234] Moreover, in Late Shang times lead played an unusually large part in their composition, sometimes alloyed with both copper and tin, but occasionally in earlier times with copper alone. This was not because the foundrymen were intentionally seeking to produce a ternary alloy, but simply because they had no means of removing such impurities. Nor was this the only respect in which the Shang bronze founder's technical repertoire was severely limited. Whereas the Western (*au sens large*) founder had mastered annealing, smithy methods, and *cire-perdue*, the Shang craftsman was acquainted only with direct casting in piece-mould assemblies and the casting-on to the vessel body of pre-cast members such as handles and lugs. He knew nothing of sheet-metal working, riveting, annealing, tracing, engraving, stamping, or repoussé, and lacked anvils, fullers, swagers, tongs, flatters, and chisels. The Western craftsman, by contrast, was capable only of the most rudimentary achievements in direct casting. It is the distinctiveness of this metallurgical technology which has convinced Dr Noel Barnard, in the course of an intensive investigation of ancient Chinese bronze foundry,[235] that Shang foundrymen owed nothing directly to West Asian achievements in this field, even though these latter were long prior in time. The fact that the Shang bronzesmiths, in developing their new medium, drew on traditional artifactual forms affords confirmation of the independent development of the industry. But that Chinese bronze foundry was *sui generis*, both as regards industrial technology, plastic form, and ornamentation, there can be no doubt.

Once it had been initiated in North China the technology of bronze casting advanced with great rapidity. All three processes which came to constitute the casting repertoire of the Shang bronze founder were in use at Cheng-Chou, that is by Middle Shang times, namely single-mould casting, valve-mould casting, and multi-mould casting.[236] The composite valve-mould for the simultaneous casting of up to eight knives or arrow heads was also in use by this time, and the principle of the *k'an-kuo* crucible was known, although this instrument was considerably refined in later periods.[237] At first merely a pot adapted for the purpose by the addition of a layer of straw-tempered clay, then a specially designed vessel wholly of straw-tempered clay, the *k'an-kuo* finally evolved into a crucible in the shape of an inverted bell, but with a rod-like projection at the bottom to hold it upright in a charcoal fire. Made of a coarse gritty ware and with double-layered sand-filled walls, it was able both to withstand very high temperatures, and also the better to conserve heat when it was removed from the fire. Dr Barnard has pointed out that these crucibles, unlike those of the early West, show the effect of firing on the outside, and thus imply the use of a true reverberatory type of furnace. In fact, such a furnace would have developed naturally from the potter's kiln of Proto-Shang times, which illustrates another important difference between Western and Shang bronze technologies. Whereas the former exhibited little affinity with ceramic manufacture, the Shang bronze founder almost certainly derived not only the majority of his forms but also his furnace and, probably, the very principle of casting in moulds, from the pre-existing pottery industry.[238]

Although the basic technique of bronze foundry had been standardized by the Middle Shang, the skills of the smiths subsequently underwent noticeable changes in respect of both technology and esthetics. Bronze vessels from the lower levels at Cheng-Chou and Hui-Hsien, for example, are inferior on both counts to most of those from Hsiao-T'un. The plastic form of the earlier vessels was often cramped and inelegant, and set off with relatively ill-proportioned accessories, at the same time that the ornamentation tended to be crudely conceived and executed either in a single plane or in low relief. With the mastery of casting technique that characterized the later periods of the Shang, however, there came greater assurance and self-confidence in artistic matters, manifested in a series of new forms and styles. In addition to the traditional forms with which we are already familiar, the Late Shang offers a wide range of new types, including several versions of *yu* and *kuei* bowls, *chih* and *tsun* cups, *i* ewers and *yu* wine decanters, together with a suite of square (*fang*) vessels (*fang-i, fang-ch'i, fang-yu, fang-lei,* and so on), musical instruments, ceremonial apparatus, and fittings of all kinds. Few of these bronze artifacts, however, were designed for anything other than ceremonial use and the non-productive pursuits of the élite strata of society.[239]

It is important for our present investigation to notice that virtually all advances in Shang technology were directed towards conspicuous consumption. The three chief classes of demand stimulating this production were the ritual requirements of the ceremonial centers, the luxury and prestige items commissioned by the royal lineages and aristocracy, and the weapons needed to arm the corps of military retainers associated with both. The tradition of Shang bronze foundry, for example, attained its apogee in a varied array of vessels for ceremonial purposes, but also produced chariot fittings – though the bronze parts were decorative rather than functional – and a fairly wide range of weapons for both warfare and hunting.[240] Among these last, some items are certain to have been ceremonial weapons and tools used only in ritual. Such, for example, was the white-jade *lien*-sickle, inlaid with turquoise and hafted to a bronze handle, which is now in the Freer Gallery of Art in Washington. Clearly this weapon was too fragile, as well as too costly, for practical use. Moreover, the symbolism incorporated in its design is itself strong evidence of its ritual purpose. At the distal end of the shaft a *t'ao-t'ieh*, symbolizing the earth, spews forth the larva of a cricket, above which is a snake disgorging a bird into the air, its natural element, together with another *t'ao-t'ieh*. The famous *mao* spear-head, fitted into a socket of bronze inlaid with

73

turquoise mosaic, which is now in the Fogg Museum of Art of Harvard University, was no less certainly designed for a ritual purpose, as indeed were numerous other highly ornate weapons and tools displayed in the museums and galleries of China, Japan and the Western world.

There was undoubtedly also a not inconsiderable private demand for bronzes, pottery, and carvings in several media to grace both the homes and the tombs of the nobility, and to a lesser extent those of minor functionaries as well. A *tao*-knife with tooth-shaped projections, an elongated adze with a minute perforation, and a thin-bladed axe with double perforation were probably all mortuary furniture. A high proportion of the rings and beads, head-dress ornaments, and figurines produced by the jade carvers were obviously destined for personal use by the more privileged sectors of the community, and numerous other jade artifacts were employed as funerary furnishings. Marble sculptures were commissioned for domestic and public architectural and ornamental purposes, and the same stone was used on a smaller scale for sacrificial vessels (apparently inspired by bronze prototypes),[241] furniture decoration and personal adornment. As for the ceramic industries, there can be no doubt that they made their contribution to both private and public display in the form of musical instruments and a wide range of containers.

In short, the overwhelming impression left by a survey of Shang technology is that its progress was a response to, not a determinant of, the emergence of a social class whose primary concerns were with ritual and ceremony, and with conspicuous display in the interests of political and social prestige. Contemporary farm implements and handicraft tools, by contrast, were almost exclusively of stone, shell, bone and, presumably, wood, and they exhibited no radical change in design or material throughout the Shang period. Writing in 1957, Huang Chan-yüeh pointed out that up to that time only three bronze spades and not more than ten bronze axes and adzes had come to light on Shang-dynasty sites.[242]

One further point is of interest for our present study, and that concerns the spatial distribution of the workshops in relation to the ceremonial centers. This has already been touched upon, so that it is only necessary to summarize the situation here. Some craftsmen certainly worked, at least temporarily, within the precincts of the sacred enclaves. At An-yang, for instance, bronze foundries, pottery kilns, and workshops engaging in the preparation of bone and stone artifacts occurred in close proximity to the palaces and temples of Hsiao-T'un, and more workshops were associated with the royal cemetery at Hsi-pei Kang. But the bulk of handicraft production was the work of artisans living in basically agricultural villages dispersed through the countryside. In the Cheng-Chou complex, for example, bronze foundries were located at Tzŭ-ching Shan and outside the south gate of the present-day city; a bone workshop had been established at Tzŭ-ching Shan; a pottery was sited about three-quarters of a mile to the west of the sacred enceinte; and what appears to have been a distillery at Erh-li Kang in the southeast. In the vicinity of An-yang, a bronze foundry, in addition to the one within the ceremonial precinct at Hsiao-T'un, was discovered among a group of dwellings at Hsüeh-chia Chuang. The site at Hsing-T'ai has so far been only partially excavated, but the same generally dispersed pattern of handicraft activity seems to be emerging, with pottery kilns located in several village clusters, and a bone workshop at another. Other Shang complexes where available archeological reports point towards the same conclusion have been mentioned on pp. 47 and 50 above.

The Economic Organization of the Shang Territories

There is a good deal of direct evidence which can be used to reconstruct the nexus of ecological adaptations and energy transfers that underpinned the evolving structure of Shang society, and its implications were summarized at the beginning of the previous section. For information about the precise manner in which the economy was organized, by contrast, we are dependent almost wholly on inference. It has already been emphasized that, although the Shang state (or perhaps states) was raised on an agricultural base, and although farming constituted one of the two major concerns of the Shang monarch, this period witnessed no significant improvements in agricultural practice. In the absence of any such technical advances, the ability of the Shang states to sustain a non-cultivating élite, at least a skeletal bureaucracy, a corps of military guards and functionaries, and a stratum of craftsmen and artisans must have derived from a reorganization of the forms of economic integration.

All that we know and have been able to infer about the village economy of North China during the Yang-shao and earlier Lung-shan phases indicates that it exhibited predominantly those 'movements between correlative points of symmetrical groupings' which have been succinctly categorized by Karl Polanyi as constituting an ideal-type system of reciprocity.[243] By Shang times, however, it is evident that an increasingly powerful centripetal force is remoulding the economy, with the allocative pressures of a ceremonial center generating appropriational movements primarily towards itself, though subsequently and secondarily centrifugally outwards. Testimony to this all-important transformation in the form of economic integration is inferential but, to my mind, conclusive. In the first place, the morphology of Shang settlements, in which agricultural villages and industrial quarters were dispersed through the countryside surrounding an elaborate ceremonial and administrative complex, is not easily explained on any other assumption. The implications of the irregular distribution of handicraft workshops are especially clear. By no means every settlement boasted one of each type, or even one at all, so that production could not have been solely for consumption within a particular village. In any case, we have already seen that the manufacture of bronze articles was almost entirely for the benefit of the élite who resided in the ceremonial centers, and it was this same class who created the demand for the more elaborate and finely executed products of the lithic, jade, and ceramic industries. Furthermore, the caches of stone sickles, often in large quantities, which are characteristic of Shang settlement sites have usually been held to indicate at least a degree of centralization in the management of agricultural labor. In one storage pit at Hsiao-T'un no less than 3,500 semi-lunar stone sickles, both used and unused, were found, and in another at the same site some 400, all of which bore signs of use. It is true that such sickles are not uncommon in Lungshanoid excavations, but it is only in the Shang period that they make up such a high proportion of the stone artifacts on any particular site. The presence of numerous storage pits in and about the ceremonial enclaves would seem to carry similar implications of centralized management. It is to be inferred that the harvest was stored in centrally located granaries, whence it was presumably distributed as required.[244] In fact, it has been suggested that it may have been such a centralization of activities as is here described, with a concomitant reliance on accurate timing and close regulation of field work, which stimulated the elaboration of the Shang calendar.[245]

Of course, centrally domiciled labor may not have been employed on all the royal domains and benefices. On particular fields controlled directly by the central administration some work may have been performed by slaves, or even by free men working for a specified number of days during the year. We know, for instance, that war captives were employed in this way, probably in many cases prior to their execution. This is, in effect, the contention of Amano Motonosuke,[246] who has suggested that the territory under the direct control of a cult center may have comprised two classes of land : a royal demesne cultivated by slaves under centralized management, and so-called clan fields farmed by a peasantry which consisted essentially of the less prestigious members of the great clans.

In any case, there can be little doubt that control of labor in one way or another had become highly centralized by Shang times: the massive constructions undertaken in the ceremonial centers are sufficient evidence of that. The wall encircling the ritual complex at Cheng-Chou affords an instructive illustration. An Chin-huai has calculated that this rampart, with a total length of 7,195 meters and an original height of 10 meters on a base 20 meters wide, could not have been raised by 10,000 workmen laboring for 330 days a year in less than 18 years.[247] How and in what quantities the labor force was disposed in time and place we cannot know, but the order of magnitude of the task is powerful testimony to the concentration of social and political power achieved by one group in North China no later than the Middle Shang. No wall has been discovered so far in connection with the An-yang complex, but Li Chi has estimated that the excavation of each of the eleven allegedly royal tombs at

Hsi-pei Kang would have required at least 7,000 man-days.[248] In a second calculation Professor Li has estimated that merely to dig the pit in Tomb HPKM 1001 at Hou-chia Chuang would have required 'no less than 4,200 day-labor units, if one labor unit at that time could have removed one cubic meter of dirt in a day, as the best of farm hands nowadays, with a much superior tool and better incentive, might occasionally be able to do.'[249]

The form of economic integration manifested in the organization implicit in the preceding paragraphs approximates closely to that which Polanyi has designated as redistribution *sensu stricto*.[250] Of course, reciprocity and redistribution are not mutually exclusive forms of economic integration. In fact, in non-market economies they customarily supplement one another.[251] Used in relation to the economy of the Shang state, the term redistribution signifies that the dominant and institutionalized movement of surplus products was away from the villages scattered through the countryside towards the ceremonial foci. In the case of some products this doubtless involved a physical relocation of goods, followed perhaps by storage and ultimately a partial return to the countryside; in other instances it was probably merely appropriational, involving only rights of disposal over the products. Side by side with this institutionalized integration of the, as it were, superordinate economy, the old forms of reciprocity persisted among villagers and nobility alike.

It is clear from what has been said above that, although Shang civilization had evolved uninterruptedly from the matrix of Lungshan culture, there had supervened between these two phases a major economic transformation, in which a predominantly reciprocal integration occurring spontaneously at village level had been subsumed into a superordinate, politically institutionalized, dominantly redistributive pattern. In Chapter Three we shall examine the possible relationships between this transformation and the emergence of urban life, and also attempt to isolate some of the factors which may have been involved in this change.

77

cNotes and References

1. This term, which will appear frequently in subsequent sections of this book, has both a geographical and a cultural connotation. It was coined by Alfred L. Kroeber [*Anthropology.* Harcourt, Brace & Co., New York 1948, p.779] to designate the axis of aboriginal complex societies in the pre-Columbian Americas, namely central and southern Mexico, Central America, the northern Andes and Peru.

2. Summaries of the successive stages of these excavations are to be found in, *int. al.*, Li Chi *et al.*, *An-yang Fa-chüeh Pao-kao*, 4 vols. Peking 1929–33; Shih Chang-ju, 'Yin-hsü tsui-chin-chih chung-yao fa-hsien. Fu : Lun Hsiao-T'un ti-ts'eng', *Chung-Kuo K'ao-ku Hsüeh-pao*, no.2 (1947), pp.1–81, and 'Hsiao-T'un C-ch'ü-ti mu-tsang ch'ün' *Kuo-li Chung-Yang Yen-chiu-yüan Li-shih Yü-yen Yen-chiu-so Chi-k'an*, vol.23 (1952), pp.447–87; Hu Hou-hsüan, *Yin-hsü Fa-chüeh.* Shanghai 1955; Tung Tso-pin, 'Chung-Kuo wen-tzŭ-ti ch'i-yüan', *Ta-lu Tsa-chih*, vol.5, no.10. T'ai-pei 1952; and *Chia-ku-hsüeh Wu-shih-nien.* T'ai-pei 1955; Ch'en Meng-chia, *Yin-hsü Pu-tz'ŭ Tsung-shu.* Peking 1956; Kuo Pao-chün, 'I-chiu-wu-ling-nien-ch'un Yin-hsü fa-chüeh pao-kao', *K'ao-ku Hsüeh-pao*, no.5 (1951), pp.1–61; Liu Hsiao-ch'un, 'I-chiu-wu-wu-nien-ch'iu An-yang Hsiao-T'un Yin-hsü-ti fa-chüeh' *K'ao-ku Hsüeh-pao*, no.3 (1958), pp.63–72; Ma Te-chih, Chou Yung-chen, Chang Yün-p'eng, 'I-chiu-wu-san-nien An-yang Ta-ssŭ-k'ung Ts'un fa-chüeh pao-kao', *K'ao-ku Hsüeh-pao*, no.9 (1955), pp.25–90; Chao Ch'ing-yün *et al.*, '1958-nien-ch'un Ho-nan An-yang Shih Ta-ssŭ-k'ung Ts'un Yin-tai mu-tsang fa-chüeh chien-pao', *K'ao-ku T'ung-hsün*, no.10 (1958), pp.51–62; An Chih-min, Chiang Ping-hsin and Ch'en Chih-ta, '1958–1959-nien Yin-hsü fa-chüeh chien-pao', *K'ao-ku*, no.2 (1961), pp.63–76; and in definitive versions in the formal reports of the excavations issued under the auspices of the old Academia Sinica of the mainland and as reconstituted in T'ai-pei. The seriation of these last items is likely to be confusing to anyone who has not seen the volumes, so it may be as well to summarize the present situation. The reports were intended to be the second publication in the *Archeologia Sinica* series (of which the first was that dealing with the excavations at Ch'eng-tzŭ Yai : *vide* note 81 below). Of the first of the An-yang volumes, which was to include a general account of the excavations, only the fascicule dealing with architectural remains has so far been published. Vol.2, which constitutes a massive report on the oracle archives of An-yang, has appeared in four parts, the titles of which are as

follows : Tung-Tso-pin, *Hsiao-T'un : Yin-hsü Wen-tzŭ*, vol.2, fasc.2. Shanghai and T'ai-pei 1948–54; Li Chi, *Hsiao-T'un*, vol.3 : *Ch'i-wu (Artifacts)* fasc.1 : *T'ao-ch'i (Pottery)*, pt.1. T'ai-pei 1956; Shih Chang-ju, *Hsiao-T'un : I-chih-ti Fa-hsien yü Fa-chüeh*, vol.1, fasc.2 : *Chien-chu i-ts'un (Architectural remains)*. T'ai-pei 1959. In addition there is a valuable book by Tung Tso-pin, *Yin Li P'u*. Li-chuang 1945; and a paper (one among many on the same subject) by the same author, 'Yin Li P'u hou-chi', *Kuo-li Chung-yang Yen-chiu-yüan Li-shih Yü-yen Yen-chiu-so Chi-k'an*, vol.13 (1948). Finally there are succinct but compendious accounts of the An-yang excavations in English in Cheng Te-k'un, *Archaeology in China*, vol.2 : *Shang China*. W. Heffer & Sons, Cambridge 1960; William Watson, *Archaeology in China*. Parrish, London 1960; and *China before the Han dynasty*. Ancient Peoples and Places Series, no.23. Thames and Hudson, London 1961; and Kwang-chih Chang [Chang Kuang-chih], *The archaeology of ancient China*. Yale University Press 1963, pp.154–62.

    3. The views of this school of historical iconoclasts, led by Ku Chieh-kang, were set out in the volumes of *Ku-Shih Pien*, vols.1–7, 1926–41. All were edited by Ku Chieh-kang except vol.4 (1933) and vol.6 (1938) which were edited by Lo Ken-tse, and vol.7 which was edited by Lü Ssŭ-mien and T'ung Shu-yeh. Similar views were expressed at this time in the pages of *Shih-Huo* and *Yü-Kung*, both of which journals were published under Marxist auspices, and also informed the work of Kuo Mo-jo [e.g. *Chung-Kuo Ku-tai She-hui Yen-chiu*. Shanghai 1927] and T'ao Hsi-sheng [e.g. *Chung-Kuo She-hui-chih Shih-ti Fen-hsi*. Shanghai 1929]. There is a useful summary in English of the work of this school in Lin Mou-sheng, 'The revolution in the history of Chinese history', *China Institute Bulletin*, vol.3 (1938), New York. For a general account of Chinese historiography in this century see J. Gray, 'Historical writing in twentieth-century China : notes on its background and development', in W. G. Beasley and E. G. Pulleyblank (eds.), *Historians of China and Japan*. Oxford University Press 1961, pp.186–212. Ku Chieh-kang, in the autobiography (*tzŭ-hsü*) with which he prefaced the *Ku-Shih Pien* series, traced the origin of the new critical school of history to two works of K'ang Yu-wei (1856–1927): cf. A. W. Hummel (transl.), *The autobiography of a Chinese historian*. Sinica Leidensia edidit Institutum Sinologicum Lugduno-Batavum, vol. 1. E. J. Brill, Leyden 1931, p.152.

    4. *Vide* An Chin-huai, 'Cheng-Chou ti-ch'ü-ti ku-tai i-ts'un chieh-shao', *Wen-wu Ts'an-k'ao Tzŭ-liao*, no.8. Peking 1957, pp.16–20 and 'Shih-lun Cheng-Chou Shang-tai ch'eng-chih – Ao-tu', *Wen-wu*, nos.4–5. (1961), pp.73–80; Tsou Heng, 'Shih-lun Cheng-Chou hsin-fa-hsien-ti Yin-Shang wen-hua i-chih', *K'ao-ku Hsüeh-pao*, no.3. Peking 1956, pp.77–103; An Chih-min, 'I-chiu-wu-erh-nien ch'iu-chi Cheng-Chou Erh-li Kang fa-chüeh chi', *K'ao-ku Hsüeh-pao*, no.8. (1954), pp.65–107, and 'Cheng-Chou Shih Jen-Min Kung-Yüan fu-chin-ti Yin-tai i-ts'un', *Wen-wu Ts'an-k'ao Tzŭ-liao*, no.6. (1954), pp.32–7; Chao

THE GENESIS OF THE CITY IN CHINA

Ch'üan-ku *et al.*, 'Cheng-Chou Shang-tai i-chih-ti fa-chüeh', *K'ao-ku Hsüeh-pao*, no.1. (1957), pp.53–73; Ch'en Chia-hsiang, 'Cheng-Chou Lo-ta Miao Shang-tai i-chih shih-chüeh chien-pao', *Wen-wu Ts'an-k'ao Tzŭ-liao*, no.10. (1957), pp.48–51; Chao Ch'ing-yün, '1957-nien Cheng-Chou hsi-chiao fa-chüeh chi-yao', *K'ao-ku T'ung-hsün*, no.9. (1958), pp.54–6; Chao Ch'ing-yün and Liu Tung-ya, 'Cheng-Chou Ko-ta-wang Ts'un i-chih fa-chüeh pao-k'ao', *K'ao-ku Hsüeh-pao*, no.3. (1958), pp.41–62; Chang Chien-chung, 'Cheng-Chou Shih Pai-chia Chuang Shang-tai mu-tsang fa-chüeh chien-pao', *Wen-wu Ts'an-k'ao Tzŭ-liao*, no.10. (1955), pp.24–42; Ma Ch'üan, 'Cheng-Chou Shih Ming-kung Lu hsi-ts'e-ti Shang-tai i-ts'un', *Wen-wu Ts'an-k'ao Tzŭ-liao*, no.10. (1956), pp.39 and 50–1; Ma Ch'üan and Mao Pao-liang, 'Cheng-Chou fa-hsien-ti chi-ko-shih-ch'i-ti ku-tai yao-chih', *Wen-wu Ts'an-k'ao Tzŭ-liao*, no.10. (1957), pp.58–9; Chao Hsia-kuang, 'Cheng-Chou Nan-kuan-wai Shang-tai i-chih fa-chüeh chien-pao', *K'ao-ku T'ung-hsün*, no.2. (1958), pp.6–9; Cheng-Chou Shih Wen-wu Kung-tso-tsu, 'Cheng-Chou Shih Jen-Min Kung-Yüan ti-erh-shih-wu-hao Shang-tai mu-tsang ch'ing-li chien-pao', *Wen-wu Ts'an-k'ao Tzŭ-liao*, no.12. (1954), pp.83–5, and Tung Hung, 'Cheng-Chou Pai-chia Chuang i-chih fa-chüeh chien-pao', *Wen-wu Ts'an-k'ao Tzŭ-liao*, no.4. (1956), pp.3–8; Yang Ch'i-ch'eng, 'Cheng-Chou ti-5-wen-wu-ch'ü ti-1-hsiao-ch'ü fa-chüeh chien-pao', *Wen-wu Ts'an-k'ao Tzŭ-liao*, no.5. (1956), pp.33–40; Yin Huan-chang, 'Pa-ko-yüeh-lai-ti Cheng-Chou wen-wu kung-tso kai-k'uang', *Wen-wu Ts'an-k'ao Tzŭ-liao*, no.9. (1955), pp.56–8. Cf. also the English-language works mentioned in footnote 2.

5. Robert McC. Adams, *The evolution of urban society. Early Mesopotamia and Prehispanic Mexico*. Aldine Publishing Company, Chicago 1966, p.28.

6. Adams, *Evolution*, pp.23–4.

7. Joseph de Guignes, *Mémoire dans lequel on prouve, que les Chinois sont une colonie égyptienne*. Desaint et Saillant, Paris 1760. Much the same idea had been propounded a century previously by Athanasius Kircher in his *Oedipus Ægyptiacus*. Romae, ex typographia V. Mascardi 1652–4. Colophon of vol.3 dated 1655.

8. R. E. M. (later Sir Mortimer) Wheeler, *Five thousand years of Pakistan. An archaeological outline*. Royal India and Pakistan Society, London 1950, p.30. Still less am I disposed to accept Hasmukh D. Sankalia's statement relating to the Indus cities : 'Some genius, who, it is believed, was under Meso-potamian influence where earlier cities existed, turned these rich agricultural villages into fine brick-built towns and cities' ['India', in Robert J. Braidwood and Gordon R. Willey, *Courses toward urban life*. Aldine Publishing Company. Chicago 1962, p.70].

9. Bronislaw Malinowski, *A scientific theory of culture*. University of North Carolina Press, Chapel Hill, 1944, pp.14–15.

10. Julian H. Steward, 'Cultural causality and law : a trial formulation of

the development of early civilizations', *American Anthropologist*, vol.51, no.1. (1951), p.4; reprinted in the same author's *Theory of culture change*. University of Illinois Press, Urbana 1955, where the reference is to p.182. In this same connection the words of Leslie White are also worth quoting: 'To the evolutionist it made no difference whether a given people obtained a trait by diffusion or developed it indigenously; it was the evolution of the culture that they were concerned with, not the cultural experiences of this or that tribe. There is thus no incompatibility between diffusion and evolution of culture . . .' [Leslie A. White, 'Evolution and diffusion', *Antiquity*, no.124. (1957), p.218]. Nor is Robert F. Murphey's thesis that the acculturative situation is not only empirically the condition of, but is also structurally necessary to, almost all human societies, irrelevant to this discussion : 'Social change and acculturation', *Transactions of the New York Academy of Sciences*, series II, vol.26 (1963–4), pp.845–54.

11. Morton H. Fried, 'On the evolution of social stratification and the state', in Stanley Diamond [ed.], *Culture in History : essays in honor of Paul Radin*. Columbia University Press, New York 1960, pp.713 and 729–30.

12. Gordon R. Willey, 'The prehistoric civilizations of nuclear America', *American Anthropologist*, vol.57 (1955), p.571.

13. Bernhard Karlgren, 'Some weapons and tools of the Yin dynasty', *Bulletin of the Museum of Far Eastern Antiquities*, vol.17. Stockholm 1945, pp.114–21.

14. Homer H. Dubs, 'The date of the Shang period', *T'oung Pao*, vol.40. Leiden 1951, pp. 322–35.

15. Tung Tso-pin, *Yin Li P'u*. Academia Sinica, Li-chuang, 1945; 'Wu-Wang fa Chou nien-yüeh-jih chin-k'ao', *Kuo-li T'ai-wan Ta-hsüeh Wen-shih-che hsüeh-pao*, vol.3. T'ai-pei 1951, pp.177–212; 'Kuan-yü ku-shih nien-tai-hsüeh-ti wen-t'i', *Ta-lu Tsa-chih*, vol.13, no.6. T'aipei 1956, pp.1–4; 'Chung-Kuo shang-ku-shih nien-tai', *Kuo-li T'ai-wan Ta-hsüeh K'ao-ku Jen-lei Hsüeh-k'an*, no.11. T'ai-pei 1958, pp.1–4. For a recent succinct statement of the current status of the question of Shang chronology see Noel Barnard's review of recent works on pre-Han archeology in *Monumenta Serica*, vol.22, fasc.1. Monumenta Serica Institute at the University of California at Los Angeles, Sumptibus Societatis Verbi Divini 1963, pp.213–55.

16. Noel Barnard, review (with postscript) of Chou Hung-hsiang's *Shang-Yin ti-wang pen-chi* in *Monumenta Serica*, vol.19 (1960), pp.486–515, especially p.515. It is interesting to recall that Herrlee Glessner Creel had come to much the same conclusion in 1937 [*Studies in early Chinese culture*. Waverly Press, Baltimore 1937, pp.xvi–xxii].

17. *Vide*, for example, the discussion of this question in Chou Hung-hsiang, *Shang-Yin Ti-wang Pen-chi*. Hong Kong 1958.

18. So far *Yin* has not been observed in *attested* (that is scientifically excav-

ated) Western Chou epigraphy, though this is not to deny the possibility that some Western Chou presently unattested inscriptions incorporating the term may eventually be validated or, perhaps more likely, materials scientifically excavated in the future may use the form *Yin*. Cf. also Creel, *Studies in early Chinese culture*, p.1, note 1, and pp.65–6.

19. I have been able to trace this tradition back to the *Kua-ti Chih* by Wei-Wang[Li] T'ai in the 7th century AD, where this original benefice of Shang is identified with the former sub-prefecture of Shang-lo, some 85 *li* east of present-day Shang-Chou; but the fact that this tradition was older even than the T'ang affords no guarantee of its authenticity.

20. This is substantially the story as related in *Shih-Chi*, chüan 3, ff.1–2. Other versions assembled in the *T'ung-chien Kang-mu* vary somewhat in detail but agree in the general tenor of their accounts.

21. This is the conception of the Shang state which is depicted, for example, in Albert Herrmann's *Historical and Commercial Atlas of China* [Harvard-Yenching Institute Monograph Series, vol.1. Harvard University Press 1935, Plate 9, II] and which has been reproduced in one form or another in numerous subsequent works.

22. Cf., e.g., Ku Chieh-kang, 'Yü Ch'ien Hsüan-t'ung hsien-sheng lun ku-shih-shu', *Ku-Shih Pien*, vol.1 (1926). As early as the 18th century the scholar Ts'ui Shu had remarked on the discrepancy between the alleged historical age of the culture-heroes and their actual literary age, but his work was virtually forgotten from that time until it was resurrected by Hu Shih in 1921.

23. Arthur Waley, *The way and its power. A study of the Tao Te Ching and its place in Chinese thought.* Evergreen Book E-84, Grove Press Reprint, New York, n.d., p.134.

24. Ku Chieh-kang, *Han-tai Hsüeh-shu Shih-lüeh*. Tung-fang, Ch'ung-ch'ing, 1944.

25. According to all Confucian sources and some Taoist texts, Yao abdicated and delivered the empire not to his son but to Shun, a virtuous farmer and fisherman. On the other hand the *Bamboo Annals* (*Kuang Hung-ming-chi*, chüan 11, f.13 verso) which, if the report of their late discovery is to be believed, presumably escaped the reconstructive efforts of Han scholars (see p. 14), relate that Shun deposed Yao by force. Implications to the same effect are to be found in *Po-wu Chih* by Chang-Hua (*c.*AD 290), chüan 2, f.1 recto and in *Han-Fei-tzŭ*, chüan 13 (probably from early in the 3rd century BC).

26. As pointed out by Wolfram Eberhard, *Artibus Asiae*, vol.11, no.4 (1946), p.359 : review of Bernhard Karlgren's *Legends and cults in ancient China*.

27. J.G.Andersson, 'Researches into the prehistory of the Chinese', *Bulletin of the Museum of Far Eastern Antiquities*, vol.15 (1943), Stockholm, p.7.

28. Kwang-chih Chang [Chang Kuang-chih], 'Some dualistic phenomena in Shang society', *The Journal of Asian Studies*, vol.24, no.1 (1964), p.51.

29. Ch'en Meng-chia, 'Shang-tai-ti shen-hua yü wu-shu', *Yen-ching Hsüeh-pao*, vol.20 (1936), pp.485–576.

30. Joseph Needham, *Science and civilisation in China*, vol.3. Cambridge 1959, pp.245–6.

31. H.G.Creel, *Studies in early Chinese culture*, p.105. Some thirty years after it was written, Creel's chapter entitled 'Was there a Hsia dynasty?' is still the most thorough and lucid analysis of the Hsia problem.

32. See Paul Pelliot, 'Le Chou King en caractères anciens et le Chang chou che wen', *Mémoires concernant l'Asie Orientale, Académie des Inscriptions et Belles-Lettres*, vol.2. Paris 1916, pp.123–77. Cf. also K.Nagasawa, *Geschichte der Chinesischen Literatur, und ihrer gedanklichen Grundlage*. Transl. from the Japanese by E.Feifel. Fu-jen University Press, Pei-p'ing 1945, p.120.

33. H.G.Creel, *The birth of China*. London 1936, pp.55–95, and *Studies in early Chinese culture*, pp.64–9.

34. Edouard Chavannes, *Les mémoires historiques de Se-ma Ts'ien*, vol.1. Leroux, Paris 1895, pp.cxl–cxli.

35. Arthur Waley, *The Analects of Confucius*. George Allen and Unwin Ltd, London 1938, p.53.

36. *Vide* Chavannes, *Les mémoires historiques*, vol.5 (1905), pp.446–79, and Kanda Kiichirō, *Shinagaku setsurin* (1933), p.1039.

37. Wang Kuo-wei, 'Ku-pen Chu-shu Chi-nien chi-chiao, part III', in *Hai-ning Wang Chung-ch'io Kung I-shu*. Commercial Press, Ch'angsha, 1940. See also Fan Hsiang-yung, *Ku-pen Chu-shu Chi-nien Chi-chiao Ting-pu*. Shanghai 1957; and Henri Maspero, 'La chronologie des rois de Ts'i au IVᵉ siècle avant notre ère', *T'oung Pao*, vol.25 (1927–8), pp.367–386.

38. Other indications that Ssŭ-ma Ch'ien had access to sources no longer extant occur from time to time in the *Shih-Chi*. A good example is afforded by the reference to a short quotation from the **T'âng t̤i̤ĕng (*T'ang cheng : T'âng's subjugation* [of the Count of **K'ât : Ko]). This is reputedly the title of a lost section of the *Shu-Ching*, but one which is to be found in neither the *chin-wen* text of Fu-Sheng nor in the *ku-wen* version provided by K'ung An-kuo. We can only conclude, therefore, that Ssŭ-ma Ch'ien obtained it from a source completely unknown at the present time. Cf. Chou Hung-hsiang, *Shang-Yin Ti-wang Pen-chi*. Hong Kong 1959.

39. On Han historiography in general see A.F.P.Hulsewé, 'Notes on the historiography of the Han period', in Beasley and Pulleyblank, *Historians*, pp. 31–43. For a summary of opinions on the date and subsequent fate of the text of the *Shih-Chi* see F.Jäger, 'Der heutige Stand der Shi-ki-Forschung', *Asia Major* vol.9 (1933), pp.21–37.

40. Cf. Wang Kuo-wei, 'Yin pu-tz'ŭ-chung so-chien hsien-kung hsien-wang k'ao' in *Hai-ning Wang Chung-ch'io Kung I-shu*. Ch'angsha 1940. Creel [*Studies in early Chinese culture*, pp.49–54] regards these poems as giving us 'a most interesting picture of the people of the State of Sung when they were as yet only half assimilated to the Chou philosophy of history'.

41. *Shih-Chi*, chüan 3, f.13 recto.

42. During the Former Han dynasty at least four recensions of the *Odes*, each with its corpus of commentary, were all taught at the capital, but from the beginning of the Later Han a collation by Mao-Heng, perhaps with some assistance from Mao-Ch'ang, gradually displaced the other versions which are now known only through early citations. Cf. Bernhard Karlgren, 'The early history of the Chou li and Tso Chuan texts', *Bulletin of the Museum of Far Eastern Antiquities*, vol.3 (1931), pp.12–33. See also Fu Ssŭ-nien, 'Shih-Ching Chiang-i-kao', in *Fu Meng-chen Hsien-sheng Chi*, vol.2B. T'ai-wan University, T'ai-pei 1952, especially pp.94–5.

43. For references to the site in Chinese literature see Tung Tso-pin, ' *Yin-hsü yen-ke*', *Kuo-li Chung-yang Yen-chiu-yüan Li-shih Yü-yen Yen-chiu-so Chi-k'an*, vol.2, pt.2. Nan-ching 1930, pp.224–40.

44. The pioneer collectors of oracle bones were Wang I-yung and Liu E, the latter of whom published the first collection of oracle inscriptions in 1903. Subsequently Wang Kuo-wei and Lo Chen-yü took the lead in deciphering the inscriptions.

45. Cheng Te-k'un, *Archaeology in China*, vol.2, p.4.

46. *loc. cit.*, pp.4–16.

47. Liang Ssŭ-yung, 'Hsiao-T'un, Lung-shan yü Yang-shao', *Kuo-li Chung-yang Yen-chiu-yüan Li-shih Yü-yen Yen-chiu-so Ch'ing-chu Ts'ai Yüan-p'ei Hsien-sheng Liu-shih-wu-sui Lun-wen Chi*, pt.2. Peking 1933, pp.555–68.

48. In P'ei Yin's commentary on *Shih-Chi* (T'ai-pei reprint of the Ch'ien-lung edition, 1964, chüan 3, f.8a) this name occurs under the orthography **Ngog* : compare the *Shih-Chi Cheng-i* of the 8th-century commentator Chang Shou-chieh, *ibid.*; but in *Chu-shu Chi-nien*, under **D'iông-tieng (Chung-ting), in *Shu-Ching*, preface, and in the 12th-century *T'ung-Chien Kang-mu* the form **χiog (*Ao*) is used.

For the identification of the Cheng-Chou sites with ancient *Ngog* see Mizuno Seiichi, *Sekai Kōkogaku Taikei*, vol.6, pt.2. Tōkyō, 1958 edition, p.9; and An Chin-huai, 'Shih-lun Cheng-Chou Shang-tai ch'eng chih – Ao-tu', *Wen-wu*, nos.4–5. Peking 1961, p.73. However, Liu Chi-i has voiced reservations about this identification: '"Ao-tu" chih-i', *Wen-wu*, no.10 (1961), pp.39–40. It was traditionally believed that *Ngog* had been located in the vicinity of present-day Ying-che but reasonably thorough reconnaissances of this district during the 1950s revealed no evidence of Shang settlement. Cheng-Chou lies about 15 kilometres to the southwest.

49. Walter A. Fairservis, Jr, *The origins of oriental civilization*. Mentor Book 251, the New American Library, New York 1959, p.133.

50. Robert J. Braidwood, 'Means towards an understanding of human behavior before the present', in Walter W. Taylor (ed.), *The identification of non-artifactual archaeological materials*. National Research Council Publication no.565. Washington, DC, 1957, pp.14–16, and 'Levels in prehistory : a model for the consideration of the evidence', in Sol Tax (ed.), *Evolution after Darwin: the evolution of man*, vol.2. University of Chicago Press 1960, pp.143–151; Robert M. Adams, 'Some hypotheses on the development of early civilizations', *American Antiquity*, vol.21, no.3 (1956), pp.227–32, 'The evolutionary process in early civilizations', in Tax, *op. cit.*, and *The evolution of urban society. Early Mesopotamia and Prehispanic Mexico*. Aldine Publishing Company, Chicago 1966; Gordon R. Willey, 'Growth trends in New World culture', in E. K. Reed and D. S. King (eds.), *For the Dean*. Santa Fe 1950, pp.223–47, 'The prehistoric civilizations of Nuclear America', *American Anthropologist*, vol.57 (1955), pp.571–93, and 'Historical patterns and evolution in native New World cultures', in Tax, *op. cit.*, pp.111–41; Carl H. Kraeling and Robert M. Adams (eds.), *City Invincible. A symposium on urbanization and cultural development in the ancient Near East*. University of Chicago Press 1960; Robert J. Braidwood and Gordon R. Willey, *Courses toward urban life*. Aldine Publishing Company, Chicago 1962.

51. Cf. especially Kwang-chih Chang [Chang Kuang-chih], 'China', in Braidwood and Willey, *Courses toward urban life*, pp.179–82, and *The archaeology of ancient China*. Yale University Press, New Haven and London 1963.

52. The study of *chia-ku hsüeh* has now attained the status of a sub-discipline, with its own nexus of distinctive skills and its own technical literature, within the general field of sinology. Since Liu E published his pioneering work *T'ieh-yün Ts'ang-kuei*, containing 1,058 rubbings, in October 1903 a vast mass of epigraphic material has become available in the form of dictionaries, catalogues and reports. Among the classics of the formative period of *chia-ku hsüeh* was *Ch'i-wen Chü-li*. Shanghai 1904, in which Sun I-jang formulated the basic principles of oracle-bone interpretation. By the time that Hu Hou-hsüan came to publish his quinquagenary summary of the achievements of the new discipline (*Wu-shih-nien Chia-ku-hsüeh Lun-chu-mu*) in 1952 he was able to include in it no less than 875 descriptive and expository works. Among these were several which could justifiably be described as landmarks in the progress of *chia-ku hsüeh*, notably Wang Kuo-wei's *Yin pu-tz'ŭ chung so-chien hsien-kung hsien-wang k'ao*, in *Kuan-T'ang Chi-Lin*, and reprinted in *Hai-ning Wang Ching-an Hsien-sheng I-shu*. Ch'ang-sha 1940; Wang Hsiang's *Fu-shih Yin-ch'i lei-tsuan*; Shang Ch'eng-ts'o's *Yin-hsü Wen-tzŭ Lei-pien*; Tung Tso-pin's *Chia-ku-wen tuan-tai yen-chiu-li, Kuo-li Chung-yang Yen-chiu Yüan Li-shih Yü-yen Yen-chiu-so Ch'ing-chu Ts'ai Yüan-p'ei Hsien-sheng Liu-shih-wu-sui Lun-wen*

Chi, Kuo Mo-jo's *Pu-tz'ǔ t'ung-tsuan,* and Sun Hai-po's *Chia-ku-wen Pien.*
More recently some 9,000 attested oracle records from Hsiao-T'un, both complete and fragmentary, have been made available in four volumes by the
Academia Sinica (cf. note 2 above) and scholars in China, Japan and the
Western world have begun to treat this immense corpus of evidence not merely
as an adjunct to the study of literary and archeological evidence but as a powerful tool in its own right. Notable among such scholars are Ch'en Meng-chia
(*Yin-hsü Pu-tz'ǔ Tsung-shu* 1956), Jao Tsung-i (*Yin-tai Chen-pu Jen-wu T'ung-
k'ao,* 2 vols. Hong Kong University Press 1959, Shima Kunio (*In-kyo bokuji
kenkyū*), and Noel Barnard, who is the first oracle specialist to face squarely
the problem of forgeries. In a series of papers and reviews in *Monumenta Serica*
and elsewhere he has sought to establish the interpretation of both bone and
bronze epigraphy on a scientific basis, making use only of rigorously attested
(i.e. scientifically excavated) primary materials, and eschewing modern *character equivalents* in transcription in favor of *modern character forms,* which preserve the original structural combination of character elements.

53. When the titles of benefice holders appear in the oracle records there is
reason to believe that they were usually members of the royal lineage.

54. Tung Tso-pin, 'Yin-tai-ti niao-shu', *Ta-lu Tsa-chih,* vol.6, no.11 (1953),
pp.9–11.

55. Tung-Tso-pin, *An interpretation of the ancient Chinese civilization,*
Chinese Association for the United Nations, T'ai-pei, T'ai-wan 1952, p.6.

56. Cf. Henri Maspero, 'Contribution à l'étude de la société chinoise à la fin
des Chang et au début des Tcheou', *Bulletin de l'Ecole Française d'Extrême-
Orient,* vol.46, no.2 (1954), pp.336–41. On the morphological evolution of the
North China plain see Ting Su (William S.Ting), 'Hua-pei ti-hsing-shih yü
Shang-Yin-ti li-shih', *Chung-yang Yen-Chiu-Yüan : Min-ts'u-hsüeh Yen-chiu-so
Chi-k'an* no.20 (1965) pp.155–62.

57. There is a summary statement of the position in Cheng Te-k'un, *Shang
China,* pp.83–7.

58. Pierre Teilhard de Chardin and C.C.Young, 'On the mammalian
remains from the archaeological site of An-yang', *Palaeontologia Sinica,*
C47. Peking 1936; C.C.Young *et al,* 'Further notes on the mammalian remains of Yin-hsü, An-yang,' *Chung-Kuo K'ao-ku Hsüeh-pao,* no.4 (1949),
pp.145–52.

59. It is not impossible, for example, that the disappearance from North
China of such animals as the racoon, tiger and sika deer might have been caused
by human agency.

60. J.G.Andersson, 'Researches into the prehistory of the Chinese, *Bulletin
of the Museum of Far Eastern Antiquities,* vol.15 (1943), pp.32–41. This conclusion has been repeated in numerous subsequent papers : cf. for example,
Ting Su, 'Hua-pei ti-hsing shih', p. 158.

61. Hu Hou-hsüan, *Chia-ku-hsüeh Shang-shih Lun-ts'ung*, series I and II. Ch'eng-tu 1944, 1945.

62. Karl A. Wittfogel, 'Meteorological records from the divination inscriptions of Shang', *The Geographical Review*, vol.30. New York 1940, pp.110–33.

63. Tung Tso-pin, Review of Wittfogel's 'Meteorological records' in *Hua-hsi Hsieh-ho Ta-hsüeh Chung-Kuo Wen-hua Yen-chiu-so Chi-k'an*, vol.3. Ch'eng-tu 1942, pp.81–8; and 'Tsai-t'an Yin-tai ch'i-hou', *Hua-hsi Hsieh-ho Ta-hsüeh Chung-kuo Wen-hua Yen-chiu-so Chi-k'an*, vol.5. Ch'eng-tu 1946, pp. 1–17.

64. Robert J. Braidwood, 'Levels in prehistory', in Sol Tax (ed.), *Evolution of Man after Darwin*, vol.2. University of Chicago Press 1960, p. 149. For the application of this concept to Chinese prehistory see Chang Kwang [Kuang]-chih, 'Major problems in the culture history of Southeast Asia', *Chung-yang Yen-chiu-yüan : Min-ts'u-hsüeh Yen-chiu-so Chi-k'an*, no.13 (1962), pp.1–26.

65. J. G. Andersson, *An early Chinese culture*. Peking 1923.

66. The same material is treated descriptively and typologically in Cheng Te-k'un, *Archaeology in China* : vol.1, *Prehistoric China*. W. Heffer and Sons, Cambridge 1959, Chapter 7. Earlier attempts at synthesis in both Chinese and Western languages were vitiated by a misunderstanding of the stratigraphical position of the Yang-shao stage. Such, for example, were the works of J. Gunnar Andersson, *Children of the Yellow Earth*. Kegan Paul, Trench, Trübner & Co., London 1934; and 'Researches'; P. Teilhard de Chardin and Pei Wen-chung, *Le Néolithique de la Chine*. Institut de Géo-Biologie, Peking 1944; Li Chi *The beginnings of Chinese civilization*. University of Washington Press, Seattle 1957; P'ei Wen-chung, *Chung-Kuo Shih-ch'ien-shih-ch'i-chih Yen-chiu*. Shanghai, 1948; Max Loehr, 'Zur Ur- und Vorgeschichte Chinas', *Saeculum*, vol.3 (1952), pp.15–55; Yin Ta, *Chung-Kuo Hsin-shih-ch'i Shih-tai*. Pei-ching 1955; Hsia Nai, 'Our Neolithic ancestors', *Archaeology*, vol. 10 (1957), pp.181–7; An Chih-min, 'Shih-lun Huang-ho liu-yü Hsin-shih-ch'i shih-tai wen-hua', *K'ao-ku*, no.10 (1959), pp.559–65. Yet even though the conceptual framework of these interpretations has been superseded, a great deal of their factual content is still relevant to present purposes.

67. The use of these implements has been inferred from the common occurrence in Yang-shao excavations of perforated stone discs which are most easily interpreted as weights for digging sticks. Ethnological evidence points to the Chinese culture realm as a region where the digging stick was early in use : cf. Fritz L. Kramer, *Distributions of primitive tillage*, Ph.D. dissertation, University of California, Berkeley 1957, p.273 *et seq*.

68. N. I. Vavilov, 'The origin, variation, immunity and breeding of cultivated plants', transl. from the Russian by K. Starr Chester, *Chronica Botanica*, vol.13, nos.1–6 (1949–50). *Andropogon sorghum* was, indeed, the inclusive genus established by Hackel within which *Sorghum* was regarded as a subgenus. Sorghum taxonomy is in a fluid state and for the exact status of the kao-liangs,

which is still debatable, the reader is referred to a recent survey by H. Doggett, 'The development of the cultivated sorghums', in Sir Joseph Hutchinson, *Essays on crop plant evolution.* Cambridge 1965, pp.50–69. What is not in doubt is the African provenance of the cultivated sorghums and their relatively late arrival in China.

69. Michael J. Hagerty, 'Comments on writings concerning Chinese sorghums', *Harvard Journal of Asiatic Studies* (1940), pp.234–63, especially pp.259–60.

70. J. G. Andersson, 'An early Chinese culture' *Bulletin of the Geological Survey of China*, no.5 (Peking, 1923), p.26; Huang-ho Shui-k'u K'ao-ku-tui, Hua-Hsien-tui, 'Shan-hsi [Shensi] Hua-Hsien Liu-tzŭ Chen k'ao-ku fa-chüeh chien-pao', *K'ao-ku*, no.2 (1959), p.73.

71. Li Chi, *Hsi-yin Ts'un shih-ch'ien-ti i-ts'un.* Ching-hua Research Institute, Pei-p'ing and Shang-hai 1927, pp.22–3.

72. Carl Whiting Bishop, 'The Neolithic age in Northern China', *Antiquity*, vol.7 (1933), p.395.

73. Shih Hsing-pang, 'Hsin-shih-ch'i shih-tai ts'un-lo i-chih-ti fa-hsien – Hsi-an-Pan-p'o', *K'ao-ku T'ung-hsün*, no.3 (1955) pp.7–16; K'ao-ku Yen-chiu-so Hsi-an-Pan-p'o Kung-tso-tui, 'Hsi-an-Pan-p'o i-chih ti-erh-tz'ŭ fa-chüeh-ti chu-yao shou-huo', *loc. cit.*, no.2 (1956), pp.23–30; Hsia Nai, 'Our Neolithic ancestors', *Archaeology*, vol.10 (1957), pp.181–7; K'ao-ku-so Pao-chi Fa-chüeh-tui, 'Shan-hsi [Shensi] Pao-chi Hsin-shih-ch'i shih-tai i-chih fa-chüeh chi-yao', *K'ao-ku*, no.5 (1959), pp.222–30 and 241; Huang-ho Shui-k'u K'ao-ku-tui, Hua-Hsien-tui, 'Shan-hsi [Shensi] Hua-Hsien Liu-tzŭ Chen k'ao-ku fa-chüeh chien-pao', *loc. cit.*, no.2, (1959) pp.71–5 and no.11, pp.585–7 and 591; An Chin-huai, 'Cheng-Chou ti-ch'ü-ti ku-tai i-ts'un chieh-shao', *Wen-wu Ts'an-k'ao Tzŭ-liao*, no.8 (1957), pp.16–20; Chao Ch'ing-yün, '1957-nien Cheng-Chou hsi-chiao fa-chüeh chi-yao', *K'ao-ku T'ung-hsün*, no.9 (1958), pp.54–7; Mao Pao-liang, 'Cheng-Chou Hsi-chiao Yang-shao wen-hua i-chih fa-chüeh chien-pao' *K'ao-ku T'ung-hsün*, no.2 (1958), pp. 1–5, An Chih-min, Cheng Nai-wu and Hsieh Tuan-chü, *Miao-ti Kou yü San-li Ch'iao.* Science Press, Pei-p'ing 1959 [Reviewed in *K'ao-ku*, no.1 (1961), pp.22–8 and no.4 (1961), pp.222–6].

74. J. G. Andersson, 'Researches into the prehistory of the Chinese', *Bulletin of the Museum of Far Eastern Antiquities*, vol.15 (1943), pp.1–304.

75. Chang, *Archaeology*, pp.61–2.

76. Chang, *op. cit.*, pp.65–6, and 'Chung-Kuo yüan-ku-shih-tai i-shih sheng-huo-ti jo-kan tzŭ-liao', *Chung-yang Yen-chiu-yüan: Min-ts'u-hsüeh Yen-chiu-so Chi-k'an*, no.9 (1960), pp.254–62.

77. Morton H. Fried, 'On the evolution of social stratification and the state', in Stanley Diamond [ed.], *Culture in history : essays in honor of Paul Radin.* Columbia University Press, New York 1960, pp.713–31.

78. Wu Gin-ding (Wu Chin-ting), 'P'ing-ling fang-ku chi', *Kuo-li Chung-yang Yen-chiu-yüan Li-shih Yü-yen Yen-chiu-so Chi-k'an*, vol.1 (1930), pp.471–86.

79. An Chih-min *et al.*, *Miao-ti Kou yü San-li Ch'iao* (1959).

80. Chang Kuang-chih, 'Chung-Kuo Hsin-shih-ch'i shih-tai wen-hua tuan-tai', *Kuo-li Chung-yang Yen-chiu-yüan Li-shih Yü-yen Yen-chiu-so Chi-k'an*, vol.30 (1959), p.269.

81. Li Chi *et al.*, *Ch'eng-tzŭ Yai*. Academia Sinica, Nan-ching 1934. English translation by Kenneth Starr, Yale University Publication in Anthropology, no.52. Yale University Press, New Haven, 1956; Liang Ssŭ-yung, 'Lung-shan Wen-hua – Chung-Kuo wen-ming-ti shih-ch'ien-ch'i-chih-i' *K'ao-ku Hsüeh-pao*, no.7 (1954), pp.5–14; Liu Yao, 'Lung-shan Wen-hua yü Yang-shao Wen-hua-chih fen-hsi', *Chung-Kuo K'ao-ku Hsüeh-pao*, no.2 (1947), pp.251–82; Yin Ta, *Chung-Kuo Hsin-shih-ch'i Shih-tai*. Peking, 1955, pp.44–66; An Chih-min, 'Shih lun Huang-ho liu-yü Hsin-shih-ch'i shih-tai wen-hua', *K'ao-ku*, no.10 (1959), pp.559–65, An Chih-min, 'I-chiu-wu-liu-nien-ch'iu Ho-nan Shan Hsien fa-chüeh chien-pao', *K'ao-ku T'ung-hsün*, no.4 (1957), p.4, and An Chih-min, 'Chung-Kuo Hsin-shih-ch'i shih-tai k'ao-ku-hsüeh-shang-ti chu-yao ch'eng-chiu', *Wen-wu*, no.10 (1959), pp.20–1; *K'ao-ku*, no.10 (1959), p.531; Mei Fu-ken, 'Hang-Chou Shui-t'ien Fan i-chih fa-chüeh pao-kao', *K'ao-ku Hsüeh-pao*, no.2 (1960), p.95.

82. Li Chien-yung, P'ei Chi and Chia Ngo[O], 'Lo-ning Hsien Lo-ho liang-an ku-i-chih tiao-ch'a chien-pao', *K'ao-ku T'ung-hsün*, no. 2 (1956), pp.52–3; Liu Yao, 'Ho-nan Chün-Hsien Ta-lai Tien shih-ch'ien i-chih' *T'ien-yeh K'ao-ku Pao-kao*, no.1 (1936), p. 75; Liang Ssŭ-yung, 'Hou-kang fa-chüeh hsiao-chi', *An-yang Fa-chüeh Pao-kao*, no.4 (1933), pp. 614–6.

83. Hu Yüeh-ch'ien, 'An-hui Hsin-shih-ch'i shih-tai i-chih-ti tiao-ch'a', *K'ao-ku Hsüeh-pao*, no.1 (1957), p.26; Yang Chien-fang, 'An-hui Tiao-yü T'ai ch'u-t'u hsiao-mai nien-tai shang-chüeh', *K'ao-ku*, no.11 (1963), pp. 630–1.

84. Chang, *Archaeology*, p.92.

85. Chang, *Archaeology*, p.96. Although certain metal implements discovered at Huang-niang-niang T'ai in Kan-su appear to have occurred in a Ch'i-chia (i.e. Lungshanoid) context, it would seem from the report so far published that they were contemporaneous with the Early or Middle Shang [Kuo Te-yung, 'Kan-su Wu-wei Huang-niang-niang T'ai i-chih fa-chüeh pao-kao', *K'ao-ku Hsüeh-pao*, no.2 (1960)].

86. Chang Kuang-chih, 'Chung-Kuo yüan-ku-shih-tai i-shih-sheng-huo-ti jo-kan tzŭ-liao', *Chung-yang Yen-chiu-yüan : Min-ts'u-hsüeh Yen-chiu-so Chi-k'an*, no.9 (1960), pp.264–8.

87. Shih Chang-ju, 'Ku-pu yü kuei-pu t'an-yüan', *Ta-lu Tsa-chih*, vol.8, no.9 (1954), pp.9–13; Chen Hui, T'ang Yün-ming and Sun Te-hai, 'Ho-pei

T'ang-shan Shih Ta-ch'eng-shan i-chih fa-chüeh pao-kao', *K'ao-ku Hsüeh-pao*, no.3 (1959), pp.32–3; Shou T'ien, 'T'ai-yüan Kuang-she Hsin-shih-ch'i shih-tai i-chih-ti fa-hsien yü tsao-yü', *Wen-wu Ts'an-k'ao Tzŭ-liao*, no.1 (1957); Chou Tao, *K'ao-ku*, no.9 (1959); Chao Ch'ing-fang, 'Nan-ching Shih Pei-yin-yang Ying ti-i, erh-tz'ŭ-ti fa-chüeh', *K'ao-ku Hsüeh-pao*, no.1 (1958), p.14.

88. Pei-ching Ta-hsüeh, Ho-pei Sheng Wen-hua-chü, Han-tan K'ao-ku Fa-chüeh-tui, '1957-nien Han-tan fa-chüeh chien-pao'. *K'ao-ku*, no.10 (1959), pp.531–2.

89. Kwang-chih Chang, 'China', in *Courses toward urban life*, p.184.

90. Fried, 'On the evolution of social stratification', pp.721–6.

91. By 'strategic resources' Fried means those things which, given the technological basis and environmental setting of the culture, maintain subsistence. *Vide* Fried, 'The classification of corporate unilineal descent groups', *Journal of the Royal Anthropological Institute*, vol.87 (1957), p.24.

92. Robert J. Braidwood, *The Near East and the foundations for civilization.* Condon Lectures, Oregon State System of Higher Education; Eugene, Oregon 1952, p.41, and 'Levels in prehistory', in Sol Tax, *Evolution of man after Darwin*, vol.2. University of Chicago Press 1960, p.149. In the Middle East the analogue of the Lung-shan stage would be the *'Ubaid-Warqa*; in terms applicable to the world at large *Late Formative* or *Early Florescent.* Cp., for example, Julian H. Steward *et al., Irrigation civilizations : a comparative study.* Pan American Union Social Science Monograph I. Washington, D C 1955; Gordon R. Willey, 'The prehistoric civilizations of nuclear America', *American Anthropologist*, vol.57, no.2, pt.1. Menasha, Wisconsin 1955, pp. 571–93.

93. Robert Redfield and Milton B. Singer, 'The cultural role of cities', *Economic development and cultural change*, vol.3 (1954), p.58. Cf. also Redfield, 'The folk society', *The American Journal of Sociology*, vol.52 (1947), pp.293–308, 'The natural history of the folk society', *Social Forces*, vol.31 (1953), pp.224–8, and *The primitive world and its transformations.* Cornell University Press, Ithaca 1953, Chapter 1.

94. George M. Foster, 'What is folk culture?', *American Anthropologist*, vol.55 (1953), pp.159–73. For comments on this paper see Sidney W. Mintz, 'On Redfield and Foster', *loc. cit.*, vol.56 (1954), pp.87–92.

95. Cf. Redfield, *The little community. The Gottesman Lectures*, vol.5. Uppsala University, 1955, and *Peasant society and culture.* University of Chicago Press 1956.

96. Notably Eric R. Wolf, *Peasants.* Foundations of Modern Anthropology Series, Prentice Hall, Inc., Englewood Cliffs, New Jersey 1966, pp.2–3.

97. Marshall D. Sahlins, 'Political power and economy in primitive society', in Gertrude E. Dole and Robert L. Carneiro [eds.], *Essays in the science of culture. In honor of Leslie A. White.* Thomas Y. Crowell Company, New York 1960, p.408. One aspect of the distinction between folk and urban society was

epitomized by Mencius when he said: 'In courts [that is urbanized society] nobility holds the first place, in villages age holds the first place' (II, ii. 3, 6).

98. Chang, *Archaeology*, p.137.

99. Information in this and subsequent paragraphs relating to the archeology of Shang ceremonial sites (of which the author has no first-hand experience) is drawn from the papers and reports cited in notes 2 and 4, as well as from a fairly wide range of interpretative writings. Full bibliographies of these latter works are readily available in the volumes of Kwang-chih Chang and Cheng Te-k'un mentioned in note 2, so that specific citations will be furnished only when points of unusual significance are not easily traceable there.

100. Chang, *Archaeology*, p.148. Cf. also Cheng-Chou Shih Wen-wu Kung-tso-tsu, 'Cheng-Chou Shih Yin-Shang i-chih ti-ts'eng kuan-hsi chieh-shao', *Wen-wu Ts'an-k'ao Tzŭ-liao*, no.12 (1954), pp.86–95.

101. Ho-nan-Sheng Wen-hua-chü Wen-wu Kung-tso-tui, 'Cheng-Chou Shang-chieh Shang-tai i-chih-ti fa-chüeh', *K'ao-ku*, no.6 (1960), pp.11–12.

102. Chao Ch'üan-ku *et al.*, 'Cheng-Chou Shang-tai i-chih-ti fa-chüeh', *K'ao-ku Hsüeh-pao*, no.1 (1957), pp.56–8; An Chin-huai, 'Cheng-Chou Shih ku-i-chih, mu-tsang-ti chung-yao fa-hsien', *K'ao-ku T'ung-hsün*, no.3 (1955), p.18; Chao Hsia-kuang, 'Cheng-Chou Nan-kuan-wai Shang-tai i-chih fa-chüeh chien-pao' *K'ao-ku T'ung-hsün*, no.2 (1958), pp.6–8; Ch'en Chia-hsiang, 'Cheng-Chou Lo-ta Miao Shang-tai i-chih shih-chüeh chien-pao', *Wen-wu Ts'an-k'ao Tzŭ-liao*, no.10 (1957), pp.48–51; Chao Ch'ing-yün, '1957-nien Cheng-Chou hsi-chiao fa-chüeh chi-yao' *K'ao-ku T'ung-hsün*, no.9 (1958), pp.54–7; Chao Ch'ing-yün and Liu Tung-ya, 'Cheng-Chou Ko-ta-wang Ts'un i-chih fa-chüeh pao-kao', *K'ao-ku Hsüeh-pao*, no.3 (1958), pp.41–62.

103. Cf. note 4 above; also Ho-nan Wen-hua-chü, *Cheng-Chou Erh-li Kang*.

104. Cf. the Lungshanoid settlements described above, and pp.386–99 below.

105. In European English usage, and predominantly in the English-language reports of the Chinese archeologists, *hang-t'u* is translated as 'stamped earth' (cf., for example, Chang, *Archaeology*, pp.55, 137, 143, 342, *et al.*), but in American usage the term is usually rendered as 'tamped earth'. In French archeological writing, and in some English-language journals, it is translated as 'terre pisée'.

106. Cp. note 167 to Chapter Five.

107. In the above translation I have borrowed eclectically from previous authors and am only too obviously indebted especially to Professor Bernhard Karlgren and Dr Arthur Waley. Nevertheless, my rendering of the second stanza may appear idiosyncratic to those accustomed to more orthodox versions, although an appreciation of the onomatopoeic nature of the lines surely underlay Dr Waley's translation:

They tilted in the earth with a rattling,
They pounded it with a dull thud,
They beat the walls with a loud clang,
They pared and chiselled them with a faint *p'ing p'ing* . . .
    [*The Book of Songs*. George Allen and Unwin, Ltd, 1937, p.249].

Professor Karlgren, on the other hand, essayed what I believe to be the impossible task of trying to ascribe a rational meaning to the onomatopoeic graphs: 'In long rows they collected it (sc. the earth for the buildings), in great crowds they measured it out, they pounded it, (the walls) rising high; they scraped and (repeated =) went over them again, (so they became) solid . . .' [*The Book of Odes*. Chinese text, transcription and translation. A reprint of two papers in the *Bulletin of the Museum of Far Eastern Antiquities*, vols.16 and 17, 1944 and 1945 (The Museum of Far Eastern Antiquities, Stockholm 1950), p.190].

For a more prosaic account of the construction of *hang-t'u* walls, this time round the city of ****Ngįən** (*Yin*) in 597 BC, see *Tso Chuan*, Duke **Sįwan (Hsüan), 11th year.

108. According to Chang Kuang-chih, only two or three such hairpins have come to light outside the enceinte [*Archaeology of Ancient China*, p.151].

109. An Chin-huai, *Wen-wu Ts'an-k'ao Tzŭ-liao*, no.8 (1957), p.18; Chao Ch'üan-ku *et al.*, *K'ao-ku Hsüeh-pao*, no.1 (1957), p.58.

110. Chao Ch'üan-ku *et al.*, *K'ao-ku Hsüeh-pao*, no.1 (1957), pp.70-2; Ch'en Chia-hsiang, 'Cheng-Chou Lo-ta Miao Shang-tai i-chih shih-chüeh chien-pao', *Wen-wu Ts'an-k'ao Tzŭ-liao*, no.10 (1957), p.51; Ma Ch'üan, 'Cheng-Chou Shih Ming-kung Lu hsi-ts'e-ti Shang-tai i-ts'un', *Wen-wu Ts'an-k'ao Tzŭ-liao*, no.10 (1956), pp.50-1; An Chin-huai, *Wen-wu Ts'an-k'ao Tzŭ-liao*, no.8 (1957), p.19.

111. Chao Ch'üan-ku *et al.*, *K'ao-ku Hsüeh-pao*, no.1 (1957), p.58.

112. Chao Ch'üan-ku *et al.*, *op. cit.*, p.57; Ma Ch'üan, *Wen-wu Ts'an-k'ao Tzŭ-liao*, no.10 (1956), pp.50-1; Chou Chao-lin and Mou Yung-hang, 'Cheng-Chou fa-hsien-ti Shang-tai chih-t'ao i-chi' *Wen-wu Ts'an-k'ao Tzŭ-liao*, no.9 (1955), pp.64-6.

113. An Chin-huai, *Wen-wu Ts'an-k'ao Tzŭ-liao*, no.8 (1957), pp.16-20; Yin Huan-chang, 'Pa-ko-yüeh-lai-ti Cheng-Chou wen-wu kung-tso kai-k'uang', *Wen-wu Ts'an-k'ao Tzŭ-liao*, no.9 (1955), pp.56-8.

114. Chao Ch'üan-ku *et al.*, *K'ao-ku Hsüeh-pao*, no.1 (1957), p.72.

115. Liao Yung-min, 'Cheng-Chou Shih fa-hsien-ti i-ch'u Shang-tai chü-chu yü chu-tsao-t'ung-ch'i i-chih chien-chieh', *Wen-wu Ts'an-k'ao Tzŭ-liao*, no.6 (1957), pp.73-4.

116. An Chin-huai, 'Shih-lun Cheng-Chou Shang-tai ch'eng-chih – Ao-tu', *Wen-wu*, nos.4-5 (1961), p.78; Li Yang-sung, 'Tui Wo-Kuo niang-chiu ch'i-yüan-ti t'an-t'ao', *K'ao-ku*, no.1 (1962), pp.41-4.

117. Cf. Cheng Te-k'un, *Shang China*, p.19: 'The localities excavated had been so badly disturbed at the beginning of the excavation that the materials unearthed were treated together as remains of the later Shang period.' Also p.43.

118. Cf. note 2 above. Vol.1 of the reports is entitled *The site. Its discovery and excavations (I-chih-ti fa-hsien yü fa-chüeh)* and was published in 1959.

119. Kuo Pao-chün, 'I-chiu-wu-ling-nien-ch'un Yin-hsü fa-chüeh pao-kao', *K'ao-ku Hsüeh-pao*, no.5 (1951), p.2. Cf. also Shih Chang-ju, 'Yin-hsü tsui-chin-chih chung-yao fa-hsien. Fu : Lun Hsiao-T'un ti-ts'eng', *Chung-kuo K'ao-ku Hsüeh-pao*, no.2 (1947), p.76.

120. Li Chi, *Hsüeh-shu Hui-k'an*, no.1 (1944), pp.1–14, and *The beginnings of Chinese civilization.* University of Washington Press, Seattle 1957.

121. Tsou Heng, 'Shih-lun Cheng-Chou hsin-fa-hsien-ti Yin-Shang wen-hua i-chih', *K'ao-ku Hsüeh-pao*, no.3 (1956), pp.77–103.

122. Cheng Te-k'un, *Shang China*, pp.37–8.

123. Chang, *Archaeology*, pp.164–5.

124. Tung Tso-pin, *Kuo-li Chung-yang Yen-chiu Yüan Li-shih Yü-yen Yen-chiu-so Ch'ing-chu Ts'ai Yüan-p'ei Hsien-sheng liu-shih-wu-sui lun-wen chi.* Pei-ching, 1933, pp.323–424; 'Yin-tai li-chih-ti hsin-chiu liang-p'ai', *Ta-lu Tsa-chih*, vol.6, no.3 (1953), pp.1–6; and *Chia-ku-hsüeh Wu-shih-nien.* T'ai-pei, 1955. For dissenting views see Ch'en Meng-chia, *Yin-hsü Pu-tz'ŭ Tsung-shu.* Pei-ching, 1956); Kaizuka Shigeki and Ito Michiharu, *Tōhō Gakuhō*, vol.23. Kyōto, 1953; and, particularly, Noel Barnard's review of Jao Tsung-i's *Yin-tai cheng-pu jen-wu t'ung-k'ao* in *Monumenta Serica*, vol.19 (1960), pp.485–6.

125. Tung Tso-pin, *Ta-lu Tsa-chih*, vol.6, no.3 (1953).

126. This Linnaean-style manipulation of the vast quantities of data available from An-yang is well exemplified, for example, by Shih Chang-ju's classification of underground constructions ['Hsiao-T'un Yin-tai-ti chien-chu i-chi', *Kuo-li Chung-yang Yen-chiu-yüan Li-shih Yü-yen Yen-chiu-so Chi-k'an*, vol.26. T'ai-pei 1955, pp.131–88]. This classification is also reproduced in Cheng Te-k'un, *Shang China*, pp.44–8.

(1) *Hsüeh*
(a) Round pits with steps built against the wall.
(b) Round pits with steps leading down into the middle of the pit.
(c) Oval pits with a single flight of steps against the wall.
(d) Oval pits with two flights of steps against the wall on opposite sides of the pit.
(e) Oval pits with steps leading down into the middle of the pit.
(f) Square pits with steps against one of the walls.

(2) *Chiao*
(a) Pits without foot-holes.

(*b*) Pits with two flights of foot-holes in opposite walls.

(*c*) Pits with two flights of foot-holes in the same wall.

(*d*) Pits with two flights of foot-holes in the same corner.

(*e*) Pits with two flights of foot-holes, one in a wall, the other at a corner.

(*f*) Pits with a flight of steps and a series of foot-holes.

   (3) *Tou*

(*a*) Holes with a flat bottom and no foot-holes.

(*b*) Holes with a convex bottom and no foot-holes.

(*c*) Holes of such a narrow width that no foot-holes were necessary.

(*d*) Holes with two series of foot-holes, one in each of two opposite walls.

(*e*) Holes with two series of foot-holes in the same wall.

(*f*) Gourd-shaped holes with two series of foot-holes.

   (4) *Mu*

(*a*) Rectangular pits with a *kuo* chamber.

(*b*) Rectangular pits with a *yao-k'eng* pit.

(*c*) Rectangular pits with no coffin hole.

(*d*) Rectangular pits with a square bottom.

(*e*) Small rectangular pits about half the size of a normal *mu*.

(*f*) A round pit incorporating *hang-t'u*.

   (5) *K'eng*

(*a*) Chariot pits.

(*b*) Horse pits.

(*c*) Ox pits.

(*d*) Sheep pits.

(*e*) Dog pits.

(*f*) Ox and sheep pits.

(*g*) Sheep and dog pits.

(*h*) Pig pits.

(*i*) Fowl pits.

   (6) *K'an*

(*a*) Elongated caves with irregular sides.

(*b*) Irregularly shaped caves with four sides.

(*c*) Oval irregular caves.

(*d*) Crooked caves.

   (7) *Kou*

(*a*) Broad channels with irregular walls.

(*b*) Channels with post impressions in the walls.

(*c*) Channels without post impressions but incorporating *hang-t'u* constructions.

127. Shih Chang-ju, *Yin-hsü chien-chu i-ts'un*, vol.1, fasc.2 (1959). Cf. also Tung Tso-pin, 'Chung-Kuo wen-tzŭ-ti ch'i-yüan', *Ta-lu Tsa-chih*, vol.5, no.10 T'ai-pei 1952.

128. Ling Ch'un-sheng, 'Pu-tz'ŭ-chung she-chih yen-chiu', *Kuo-li T'ai-wan Ta-hsüeh K'ao-ku Jen-lei Hsüeh-k'an* nos.25–6 (1965), pp.1–15.

129. *Vide* Ling, *loc. cit.*

130. Shih Chang-ju, 'Yin-tai ti-shang-chien-chu fu-yüan-chih i-li', *Kuo-li Chung-yang Yen-chiu-yüan Yüan-k'an*, vol.1 (1954), pp.267–80.

131. Tai-Chen, *K'ao-kung chi t'u*, vol.2 (1746; reprinted Shanghai 1955), p.104.

132. *Vide* Bernhard Karlgren, 'The early history of the *Chou li* and *Tso chuan* texts', *Bulletin of the Museum of Far Eastern Antiquities*, vol.3 (1931), pp.2–8, 35–8, 50–7; K. Nagasawa, *Geschichte der Chinesischen Literatur, und ihrer gedanklichen Grundlage*. Transl. from the Japanese by E. Feifel. Fu-jen University Press, Pei-p'ing 1945, p.122.

133. Tung Tso-pin, 'Chung-Kuo wen-tzŭ-ti ch'i-yüan', *Ta-lu Tsa-chih*, vol.5, no.10. T'ai-pei 1952.

134. Liang Ssŭ-yung and Kao Ch'ü-hsün', *Chung-Kuo K'ao-ku Pao-kao Chi*, vol.3, pt.2. T'ai-pei, 1962; Kao Ch'ü-hsün, 'The royal cemetery of the Yin dynasty at Anyang', *Kuo-li T'ai-wan Ta-hsüeh K'ao-ku Jen-lei Hsüeh-k'an*, no.13. T'ai-pei 1959, pp. 1–9; Li Chi, *Kuo-li Chung-yang Yen-chiu-yüan Li-shih Yü-yen Yen-chiu-so Chi-k'an*, vol.29 (1958), pp.809–16.

135. Paul Pelliot, 'The royal tombs of An-yang', in *Independence, convergence and borrowing in institution, thought and art*. Harvard University Press 1937, pp. 265–72.

136. Cheng Te-k'un, *Shang China*, p.77.

137. Shih Chang-ju 'Ho-nan An-yang Hou-Kang-ti Yin-mu', *Kuo-li Chung-yang Yen-chiu-yüan Li-shih Yü-yen Yen-chiu-so Chi-k'an*, vol.13 (1948), pp.21–48.

138. Kuo Pao-chün, *K'ao-ku Hsüeh-pao*, no.5 (1951), pp.1–61.

139. Tung Tso-pin, 'An-yang Hou-chia Chuang ch'u-t'u-chih chia-ku wen-tzŭ', *T'ien-yeh K'ao-ku Pao-kao*, no.1 (1936), pp.91–166.

140. Tung Tso-pin, *ibid.*; Kwang-chih Chang, *The archaeology of ancient China*, p.166.

141. Ma Te-chih, Chou Yung-chen and Chang Yün-p'eng, 'I-chiu-wu-san-nien An-yang Ta-ssŭ-k'ung Ts'un fa-chüeh pao-kao', *K'ao-ku Hsüeh-pao*, no.9 (1955), pp.25–90.

142. Chao Hsia-kuang, 'An-yang Shih hsi-chiao-ti Yin-tai wen-hua i-chih' *Wen-wu Ts'an-k'ao Tzŭ-liao*, no.12 (1958), p.31; Liu Tung-ya, 'Ho-nan An-yang Hsüeh-chia Chuang Yin-tai i-chih, mu-tsang ho T'ang-mu fa-chüeh chien-pao' *K'ao-ku T'ung-hsün*, no.8 (1958), pp.23–6.

143. Kuo Pao-chün and Lin Shou-chin, 'I-chiu-wu-erh-nien ch'iu-chi Lo-yang tung-chiao fa-chüeh pao-kao', *K'ao-ku Hsüeh-pao*, no.9 (1955), pp.91–116; Kuo Pao-chün *et al.*, 'Lo-yang Chien-pin ku-wen-hua i-chih chi Han-mu', *ibid.*, no.1 (1956), pp.11–28; An Chih-min and Lin Shou-chin, 'I-chiu-wu-

ssŭ-nien ch'iu-chi Lo-yang hsi-chiao fa-chüeh chien-pao', *K'ao-ku T'ung-hsün*, no.5 (1955), p.26; Ho-nan Wen-wu Kung-tso-tui Ti-erh-tui Sun-ch'i T'un Ch'ing-li Hsiao-tsu, 'Lo-yang Chien-hsi Sun-ch'i T'un ku-i-chih', *Wen-wu Ts'an-k'ao Tzŭ-liao*, no.9 (1955), pp. 58–64.

144. Kuo Pao-chün, Hsia Nai *et al.*, *Hui-Hsien Fa-chüeh Pao-kao*. Science Press, Peking, 1956. See also Li Te-pao, 'Ho-nan Wei-ho Chih-hung kung-ch'eng-chung-ti k'ao-ku tiao-ch'a chien-pao', *K'ao-ku T'ung-hsün*, no. 2 (1957), pp.32–5.

145. Chang, *Archaeology*, pp.163–4.

146. Yang Chi-ch'ang, 'Ho-nan Shan-Hsien Ch'i-li P'u Shang-tai i-chih-ti fa-chüeh', *K'ao-ku Hsüeh-pao*, no.1 (1960), pp.25–47.

147. Wang Ming-jui and Chin Shih-hsin, 'Ho-nan Hsin-hsiang Lu-wang Fen Shang-tai i-chih fa-chüeh pao-kao', *K'ao-ku Hsüeh-pao*, no. 1 (1960), pp.51–60.

148. Wen-wu Kung-tso Pao-tao, Ho-nan Sheng 'T'ang-yin Chao-ko Chen fa-hsien Lung-shan ho Shang-tai-teng wen-hua i-chih' *Wen-wu Ts'an-k'ao Tzŭ-liao*, no.5 (1957), p.86.

149. Yu Ch'ing-han, 'Ho-nan Nan-yang Shih Shih-li Miao fa-hsien Shang-tai i-chih, *K'ao-ku*, no.7 (1959), p.370.

150. Yang Tzŭ-fan, 'Chi-nan Ta-hsin Chuang Shang-tai i-chih k'an-ch'a chi-yao', *Wen-wu Ts'an-k'ao Tzŭ-liao*' no.11 (1959), pp.8–9; Li Pu-ch'ing, 'Chi-nan Ta-hsin Chuang i-chih shih-chüeh chien-pao', *K'ao-ku*, no.4 (1959), pp.185–7.

151. An Chih-min, 'Ho-pei Ch'ü-yang tiao-ch'a-chi', *K'ao-ku T'ung-hsün*, no.1 (1955), pp.39–44.

152. See Ho-pei Sheng Wen-hua-chü Fa-chüeh-tsu, 'Hsing-T'ai-shih fa-hsien Shang-tai i-chih', *Wen-wu Ts'an-k'ao Tzŭ-liao*, no.9 (1956), p.70; [T'ang] Yün-ming, Lo P'ing, and [Ch'eng] Ming-yüan, 'Hsing-T'ai Shang-tai i-chih-chung-ti t'ao-yao', *ibid.*, no.12 (1956), pp.53–4; T'ang Yün-ming, 'Hsing-T'ai Nan-ta-kuo Ts'un Shang-tai i-chih t'an-chüeh chien-pao', *ibid.*, no.3 (1957), pp.61–3; T'ang Yün-ming, 'Hsing-T'ai Ts'ao-yen Chuang i-chih fa-chüeh pao-kao', *K'ao-ku Hsüeh-pao*, no.4 (1958), pp.43–50; T'ang Yün-ming, 'K'ao-ku tung-t'ai : Ho-pei Hsing-T'ai Tung-hsien-hsien Ts'un Shang-tai i-chih tiao-ch'a', *K'ao-ku*, no.2 (1959), pp.108–9; T'ang Yün-ming, 'Hsing-T'ai Yin-kuo Ts'un Shang-tai i-chih chi Chan-Kuo mu-tsang shih-chüeh chien-pao', *Wen-wu*, no.4 (1960), pp.42–5 and 69.

153. *Vide* Max Weber, *Wirtschaft und Gesellschaft*, vol.2. Second edition, J. C. B. Mohr Tübingen, pp.679–752.

154. *Shih-Chi*, chüan 3, f.1 recto et verso. Cp. *Shih-Ching*, ***G'iwen-tiôg* (Hsüan-niao : Mao CCCIII):

Heaven commanded the black bird

To descend and give birth to Shang (***Śi̯ang*)

Who dwelt in the vasty land of Yin (**·*Ɉən*).

Although *g'iwen-tiôg* (= dark or black bird) has traditionally been understood as a swallow, Kuo Mo-jo [*Ch'ing-t'ung Shih-tai*. Shanghai 1946, p.11] believed that the phrase denoted a phoenix and symbolized the male sex organ. In *Ch'u-Tz'ŭ* (**Lia-Sôg : Li-Sao* and **T'ien-Mįwən : T'ien-Wen*) it is **Tieg-K'ôk (Ti-K'u) who sends the mysterious bird. For a discussion of the implications of this myth see Chang Kuang-chih, 'Shang-Chou shen-hua-chih fen-lei', *Chung-yang Yen-chiu-yüan : Min-ts'u-hsüeh Yen-chiu-so Chi-k'an*, no.14 (1962), p.67. The **Sįang-Dz'įung (Shang-Sung)*, the section of the *Shih-Ching* from which *G'iwen-tiôg* is taken, is generally considered to preserve the dynastic odes of the state of **Sông (Sung), the territory ruled over by the descendants of the old house of Shang (cf. *Shih-Chi*, chüan 3, f.13 recto), while the culture of **Tṣ'įo (Ch'u), where the *Ch'u-Tz'ŭ* were composed, is also held to have incorporated numerous elements derived from Shang civilization. It is not unlikely, therefore, that both works, Eastern Chou rifacimentos though they be, reflect to some extent authentic Shang values.

155. Kwang-chih Chang, 'Some dualistic phenomena in Shang society', *The Journal of Asian Studies*, vol.24, no.1 (1964), pp.45–61. There is an earlier statement by the same author entitled 'Shang-wang miao-hao hsin-k'ao', in *Chung-yang Yen-chiu-yüan: Min-ts'u-hsüeh Yen-chiu-so Chi-k'an*, no.15 (1963), pp.65–95.

156. E.g. Ting Su, 'Lun Yin-wang-p'i shih-fa', *Chung-yang Yen-chiu-yüan : Min-ts'u-hsüeh Yen-chiu-so Chi-k'an*, no.19 (1965), pp.71–9; Hsü Cho-yün, Kuan-yü "Shang-wang miao-hao hsin-k'ao" i-wen-ti chi-tien i-chien', *loc. cit.*, pp.81–7; Lin Heng-li, 'P'ing Chang Kuang-chih "Shang-wang miao-hao hsin-k'ao"-chung-ti lun-cheng-fa', *loc. cit.*, pp.115–19; Hsü Chin-hsiung, 'Tui Chang Kuang-chih Hsien-sheng-ti "Shang-wang miao-hao hsin-k'ao"-ti chi-tien i-chien', *loc. cit.*, pp.121–37.

157. Chang Kuang-chih, 'Kuan-yü "Shang-wang miao-hao hsin-k'ao" i-wen-ti pu-ch'ung i-chien', *Chung-yang Yen-chiu-yüan : Min-ts'u-hsüeh Yen-chiu-so Chi-k'an*, no.19 (1965), pp.53–70. The **dįog-mįôk system is described in the *Wang-Chih* section of the *Li-Chi* (*Record of Rites*), a Han-time compilation which nevertheless includes material from earlier times, some possibly from the 5th century BC (though even at that time it was no more than an imperfectly understood tradition).

158. Raymond Firth, *We, the Tikopia*. Allen and Unwin, London 1936.

159. Marshall D. Sahlins, *Social stratification in Polynesia*. American Ethnological Society, Seattle 1958.

160. Morton H. Fried, 'The classification of corporate unilineal descent groups', *Journal of the Royal Anthropological Institute*, vol.87 (1957), pp.1–29.

161. Liu Pin-hsiung, 'Yin-Shang wang-shih shih-fen-tsu-chih shih-lun',

Chung-yang Yen-chiu-yüan : Min-ts'u-hsüeh Yen-chiu-so Chi-k'an, no.19 (1965), pp.89–114.

162. The combinations of the ten Heavenly Stems in the five patrilineal descent groups would have been *Chia-i, ping-ting, wu-chi, keng-hsin* and *jen-kuei*, and the two matrilineal moieties *Chia-ping-wu-keng-jen* and *I-ting-chi-hsin-kuei* [*loc. cit.*, pp.106–8].

163. Paul Kirchhoff, 'The principles of clanship in human society', *Davidson Journal of Anthropology*, vol.1 (1955), pp.1–10. Also pp.374–7 below.

164. Kwang-chih Chang, 'Some dualistic phenomena', pp.46 and 52–3.

165. Twelve kings ruled during the An-yang period but the last, **Tieg-sjĕn, is supposed to have perished in the flames of his palace when the capital was captured by the Chou armies.

166. Chang, 'Some dualistic phenomena', p.52.

167. *Li-Chi, Wang-Chih* section. Cf. Ling Ch'un-sheng, 'Chung-Kuo tsu-miao-ti ch'i-yüan', *Chung-yang Yen-chiu-yüan : Min-ts'u-hsüeh Yen-chiu-so Chi-k'an*, no.7 (1959), pp.141–84.

168. Shih Chang-ju, *Yin-hsü chien-chu i-ts'un*.

169. *Li-Chi, Wang-Chih* section. This idealized arrangement of the ancestral shrines within the temple compound is depicted in a plan, based on an exposition by Chu-Hsi, in the great Ch'ien-lung edition of the *Li-Chi*.

170. A full account of the Shang system of government in so far as it can be reconstructed is conveniently accessible in Ch'en Meng-chia's *Yin-hsü Pu-tz'u Tsung-shu*. Pei-ching 1956, pp.249–332 and 503–22. See also Kaizuka Shigeki (ed.), *Kodai Inteikoku*. Misuzu Shobu, Tokyo 1957.

171. Wolfram Eberhard, *A history of China*. Second edition, University of California Press, Berkeley and Los Angeles 1960, p.24.

172. L. Carrington Goodrich, *A short history of the Chinese people*. Harper Torchbook 3015, New York 1963, p.14.

173. William Watson, 'A cycle of Cathay', in Stuart Piggott (ed.), *The dawn of civilization*. McGraw-Hill Book Co., Inc., New York 1961, p.271.

174. Jao Tsung-i, *Yin-tai Chen-pu Jen-wu T'ung-k'ao*, 2 vols. Hong Kong, 1959; Ch'en Meng-chia, *Yin-hsü Pu-tz'ŭ Tsung-shu*. Pei-ching 1956.

175. According to Tung Tso-pin, the Shang capital was located at Hsiao-T'un from 1384–1111 BC, a total of 273 years ['Chung-kuo shang-ku-shih nien-t'ai', *Kuo-li T'ai-wan Ta-hsüeh K'ao-ku Jen-lei Hsüeh-k'an*, no.11 (1958), pp.1–4].

176. Reinhard Bendix, *Max Weber. An intellectual portrait*. Doubleday Anchor Book A281, New York 1962, p.334.

177. *Ibid.* Cf. also Thomas F. Tout, *Chapters in the administrative history of medieval England*, 6 vols. Longmans, London 1920–33.

178. Chang, 'Some dualistic phenomena', p.51.

179. Tung Tso-pin, 'Wu-teng Chüeh tsai Yin-Shang', *Kuo-li Chung-yang Yen-chiu-yüan Li-shih Yü-yen Yen-chiu-so Chi-k'an*, vol.6 (1936), pp.413–30.

180. The oldest form of this graph depicts a mouth and a dagger-axe (i.e. army and command) inside an enclosure. Cf. Karlgren, 929.

181. Its former role as a Shang capital may be epitomized in the Shang and Chou forms of the graph, which depict a high building of some sort (Karlgren 773).

[I] The character for ** *B'âk* (*Po*), the name of a Shang ceremonial center, as it appears on an oracle bone.

182. Li Hsüeh-ch'in, *Yin-tai Ti-li Chien-lun*. Pei-ching 1959.

183. One such benefice apparently carried the title of ** *Śįu-dzįəg tsįəg* (*Shu-szŭ tzŭ*) or Heritable Lordship of Frontier Defense [Bronze inscription 26.50 : *vide* Kuo Mo-jo, 'An-yang yüan-k'eng-much-ung ting-ming k'ao-shih', *K'ao-ku Hsüeh-pao*, no.1 (1960), pp.1–5]. Noel Barnard [review article in *Monumenta Serica*, vol.22. fasc.1 (1963), p.219] has suggested that the form of this title implies that the benefice had become associated with a permanent office connected with the outer regions of Shang dominion, and draws attention [*ibid*] to an office of ** *slįəg-śįu* (*shih-shu*) mentioned on a bronze vessel (insc. 6.5) recently excavated near Ling-yüan in Jehol, a district remote from the metropolitan territory of Shang.

The oracle-bone graph for *śįu* depicts, appropriately enough, a man and a so-called dagger-axe.

184. 'Liturgical' was the term used by Max Weber to denote payments in kind made to a central authority [after the liturgies of the ancient city-states in which certain groups of the population were charged with the provision and maintenance of naval vessels or the furnishing of theatrical performances]. *Vide* Weber, *The Theory of social and economic organization*. Oxford University Press 1947, pp.310–15.

184a. Cf. Ting Shan, *Chia-ku-wen so-chien Shih-tsu chi-ch'i Chih-tu*. Pei-ching 1956.

185. Shih Chang-ju, 'Yin-hsü fa-chüeh tui-yü Chung-kuo ku-tai wen-hua-ti kung-hsien', *Hsüeh-shu Chi-k'an*, vol.2 (1954), pp.8–23. Cf. also Hayashi Minao, *Tōhō Gukuhō*, vol.29. Kyōtō 1959, pp.155–284.

186. Bendix, *Max Weber*, p.365.

187. Max Weber, *Staatssoziologie*. Duncker and Humblot, Berlin 1956, p.103.

187a. If, as Creel contends [cf. note 40], the *Shang-Sung* does indeed preserve some remembrance of Shang government, then the following passage from the *Shih-Ching* [Mao CCCV] affords no support for the theory that that government was in any way feudal:

Heaven charged the many princes
To establish the capital where Yü (**Gįwo) had labored;
They came [to court] in connection with their yearly service,
[Saying] Do not punish or reprove us –
We have not neglected our husbandry.

There is no question of an impersonal contractual relationship here, but rather an implication of personal benefices held at the royal pleasure.

188. *Shih-Chi*, chüan 3, f.3 recto : cf. *Meng-tzŭ*, v, i, 7.

189. Chang Kuang-chih, 'Shang-wang miao-hao hsin-k'ao', pp.85–8 and 'Some dualistic phenomena', pp.53–5.

190. Cf. Bendix, *Max Weber*, pp.367–8.

191. In later times **Mlwan (*Mwan) was a generic name for a congeries of tribal peoples in the southwest. Cf. Fan Ch'o's *Man(*Mwan)-Shu*, written between AD 860 and 865.

192. Based primarily on an analysis by Kwang-chih Chang, *Archaeology*, pp.163–4. Chang's evaluation of the implications of the available archeological evidence is not incompatible with the geography of the Shang culture realm as partially reconstructed by Li Hsüeh-ch'in on the basis of information in the oracle archives : *Yin-tai Ti-li Chien-lun*. The Science Press, Pei-ching, 1959. Reviewed by Hsü I in *K'ao-ku*, no.5 (1959), pp.271–2.

[II] The character for **·įəp (*i*), denoting a ceremonial center, as it appears on Shang oracle bones.

193. In its oracle-bone form the graph for **·įəp depicted an enclosure above a man in the deep-kneel posture, implying presumably an enclosed place where men dwelt. By Chou times it had come to denote a walled city, a fortified burgh, or a seigniorial town, and still later, under the Han, it signified the seat of a subprefecture. No doubt it was used anhistorically in one or other of these senses by Chou and Han authors who wrote about Shang times.

194. Cf. Noel Barnard's review article in *Monumenta Serica*, vol.22 fasc.1 (1963), pp.218–20.

195. Noel Barnard, 'A recently excavated inscribed bronze of Western Chou date', *Monumenta Serica*, vol.17 (1958), pp.33–6.

196. For more detailed discussions of the materials in this and the following sections see Ch'en-Meng-chia, *Yin-hsü Pu-tz'ŭ Tsung-shu*. Pei-ching 1956; and Li Ya-nung, *Yin-tai She-hui Sheng-huo*. Jen-min Press, Shanghai 1955.

197. Exceptions to this generalization which have so far been observed concern certain potters and bronzesmiths working in the neighborhood of the ceremonial enclave at Cheng-Chou : see p.66.

198. Shih Chang-ju, 'Ho-nan An-yang Hou-Kang-ti Yin-mu', *Kuo-li Chung-yang Yen-chiu-yüan Li-shih Yü-yen Yen-chiu-so Chi-k'an*, vol.13 (1948), pp.21–48.

199. The *yao-k'eng* was a smail pit excavated in the floor of the coffin chamber to receive a sacrificial victim, usually a dog.

200. The soil layer in which Shang cultural remains are customarily found, and which is normally drier than other earths in the neighborhood.

201. In the literature relating to the An-yang excavations this platform is referred to as *erh-ts'eng t'ai*.

202. Ma Te-chih *et al.*, 'I-chiu-wu-san-nien An-yang Ta-ssŭ-k'ung Ts'un fa-chüeh pao-kao', *K'ao-ku Hsüeh-pao*, no.9 (1955), pp.25–90; Chao Ch'ing-yün *et al.*, *K'ao-ku T'ung-hsün*, no.10 (1958), pp.51–62.

203. Kao Ch'ü-hsün, 'The royal cemetery of the Yin dynasty at An-yang', *Kuo-li T'ai-wan Ta-hsüeh K'ao-ku Jen-lei Hsüeh-k'an*, no.13 (1959), pp.1–9; Liang Ssŭ-yung and Kao Ch'u-hsün, *Chung-kuo K'ao-ku Pao-kao Chi*, vol.2, pt.3 (1962).

204. Shih Chang-ju, 'Hsiao T'un C-ch'ü-ti mu-tsang ch'ün', *Kuo-li Chung-yang Yen-chiu-yüan Li-shih Yü-yen Yen-chiu-so Chi-k'an*, vol.23 (1952), pp.447–487. It is noteworthy that dog sacrifices in considerable numbers (up to 30 in a single pit and a total of 130 in 8 pits) were associated with the construction of the wall surrounding the ceremonial center at Cheng-Chou [An Chin-huai, 'Cheng-Chou ti-ch'ü-ti ku-tai i-ts'un chieh-shao', *Wen-wu Ts'an-k'ao Tzŭ-liao*, no.8 (1957), p.18].

205. Eberhard, *History of China* (second edition), p.26.

206. Kuo Mo-jo has expounded this point of view in numerous publications over the past forty years, but has perhaps developed his argument most fully in *Nu-li-chih Shih-tai*. Jen-min Press, Pei-ching, 1954. Cf. also Han Hang-soo, 'Die ökonomische Struktur der Gesellschaftsformen in Ostasien', *Archiv für Völkerkunde* (1947), p.166.

207. *Vide*, for example, the discussion of 'Feudalism and gentry society' in Wolfram Eberhard, *Conquerors and rulers. Social forces in Medieval China.* E. J. Brill, Leiden; Second edition 1965, pp.22–47; and Ch'en Meng-chia, *Yin-hsü Pu-tz'ŭ Tsung-shu*. Pei-ching; 1956, p.616.

208. Mao Hsieh-chün and Yen Yen have shown that live slaves suffering from malnutrition were sacrificed during dedication ceremonies for important buildings, that they were buried with their ruler in royal tombs, and that their bodies were used in the manufacture of artifacts ['Dental condition of the Shang dynasty skulls excavated from Anyang and Huü-Xian', *Vertebrata Palasiatica*, vol.3, Pei-ching 1959, pp.79–80].

209. Cf. note 109 above.

210. Cf. note 114 above, and Chou Chao-lin and Mou Yung-hang, 'Cheng-Chou fa-hsien-ti Shang-tai chih-t'ao i-chi', *Wen-wu Ts'an-k'ao Tzŭ-liao*, no.9 (1955), pp.64–6.

211. **Śia*=spread out, set [as a net], etc. Some scholars, presumably reading *śia* as a loan for **g'iəg* (*ch'i*), translate as 'pennant' or 'flag lineage' [e.g. Chang Kuang-chih, *Archaeology*, p.170]. The other two lineages mentioned in this connection, the **Kjər* (*Chi*) and **Ṯjông-g'įwɛr* (*Chung-k'uei*), do not seem to be connected with crafts in any way, but the vocabulary of Archaic Chinese has not survived in all its ramifications and these names may once have carried connotations now lost to us.

212. Chang, *Archaeology*, p.171.

213. Most Chinese archeologists concerned with this topic have included sorghums among the crops grown by Shang farmers, but see note 68 above. For a pioneer study of farm implements and tools in ancient China, based primarily on literary sources, see Hsü Chung-shu, 'Lei-ssŭ k'ao', *Kuo-li Chung-yang Yen-chiu-yüan Li-shih Yü-yen Yen-chiu-so Chi-k'an*, vol.2 (1930), pp.11–59.

214. Hu Hou-hsüan, *Chia-ku-hsüeh Shang-shih Lun-ts'ung*, series II. Ch'eng-tu 1945, p.134.

215. *Ibid.*

216. I know of no evidence that would bear out Hu Hou-hsüan's contention that fertilization was practised, other than by the burning-off of scrub and brush [Hu Hou-hsüan, *Li-shih Yen-chiu*. Pei-ching 1955, p.1].

217. Cf. Hsü Chung-shu, 'Lei-ssŭ k'ao'.

218. Described in An Chih-min, 'Chung-Kuo ku-tai-ti shih-tao', *K'ao-ku Hsüeh-pao*, no.10 (1955), pp.27–52 : also Li Chi, 'Yin-hsü yu-jen shih-ch'i t'u-shuo', *Kuo-li Chung-yang Yen-chiu-yüan Li-shih Yü-yen Yen-chiu-so Chi-k'an*, vol.23 (1952), pp.523–619.

219. The dimensions of this demand are illustrated by inscriptions which contemplate the sacrifice of as many as fifty sheep, or even three hundred cattle, at one time [Lo Chen-yü, *Yin-hsü Shu-ch'i, ch'ien-pien* (1912), III, xxiii, 6 and IV, viii, 4]. Cp. also p.65 above.

220. Cf. Bendix, *Max Weber*, p.364, where the conventionalized hunt is described as 'the natural medium in which the physical and psychological capacities of the human organism came alive and became supple. In this form of "training" the spontaneous drives of man found their outlet, irrespective of any division between "body" and "soul" and regardless of how conventionalized the games often became.'

221. A vast quantity of reportage relating to the industrial technology of Shang times has been compendiously synthesized by Cheng Te-k'un in *Shang China*, Chapters VI–X. For Shang bone technology (not discussed in the text)

see Cheng, *op, cit.*, Chapter VIII, and William Charles White, *Bone culture of ancient China.* University of Toronto Press 1945.

222. Cheng, *loc. cit.*, pp.93–108.

223. *Ibid.*, pp.109–25; Cheng Te-k'un, 'The carving of jade in the Shang dynasty', *Transactions of the Oriental Ceramic Society*, vol.29 (1957), pp.13–30. Li Chi, 'Yen-chiu Chung-Kuo ku-yü wen-t'i-ti hsin-tzǔ-liao', *Kuo-li Chung-yang Yen-chiu-yüan Li-shih Yü-yen Yen-chiu-so Chi-k'an*, vol.13 (1948), pp.179–82.

224. Cp. Cheng Te-k'un, *Shang China*, pp.137–55.

225. T'ang Yün-ming, 'Lung-shan wen-hua yü Yin wen-hua t'ao-ch'i-chien-ti kuan-hsi', *Wen-wu Ts'an-k'ao Tzǔ-liao*, no.6 (1958), pp.67–8.

226. Ma Ch'üan and Mao Pao-liang, 'Cheng-Chou fa-hsien-ti chi-ko-shih-ch'i-ti ku-tai yao-chih', *Wen-wu Ts'an-k'ao Tzǔ-liao*, no.10 (1957), pp. 58–9.

227. Berthold Laufer, *The beginnings of porcelain in China.* Chicago 1917.

228. J.A. Pope, 'An analysis of Shang white pottery', *Far Eastern Ceramic Bulletin*, vol.6 (1949), pp.49–54, and S. Umehara, *Etude sur la poterie blanche dans les ruines de l'ancienne capitale des Yin.* Kyōtō 1932.

229. *Ibid*; Cheng, *Shang China*, p.147.

230. Li Chi, 'Hsiao-T'un t'ao-ch'i chih-liao-chih hua-hsüeh fen-hsi', *Kuo-li T'ai-wan Ta-hsüeh Fu Ku-hsiao-chang Ssǔ-nien Hsien-sheng Chi-nien Lun-wen-chi.* T'ai-pei, 1952, pp.123–38.

231. Cf. W. Hochstadter, 'Pottery and stonewares of Shang, Chou and Han', *Bulletin of the Museum of Far Eastern Antiquities*, vol.24 (1952), pp.81–108; Cheng, *Shang China*, pp. 147–8.

232. Li Chi, *Hsiao-T'un*, vol.3 : *Ch'i-wu*, fasc.1 : *T'ao-ch'i*, pt.1. T'ai-pei 1956.

233. Cheng, *Shang China*, pp.156–76; Mizuno Seiichi, *Chūgokuno chōkoku; sekibutsu, kindobutsu.* Nihon Keizai, Tōkyō 1960.

234. Ch'en Meng-chia, 'Yin-tai t'ung-ch'i', *K'ao-ku Hsüeh-pao*, no.7 (1954), pp.15–59; but for the limitations of analyses derived from unattested or poorly attested bronzes see Noel Barnard's comments in a review article in *Monumenta Serica*, vol.22, fasc.1 (1963), p.230. Cf. also Li Chi, *The beginnings of Chinese civilization.* University of Washington Press, Seattle 1957, p.47. It should be noted, too, that Dr Barnard, in the paper mentioned above, has pointed out that the alloys from which Western bronzes were cast do not appear to have conformed very much more closely to a standard formula than do those of Shang China [*loc. cit.*, pp.229–40].

235. Noel Barnard, *Bronze casting and bronze alloys in ancient China.* Monumenta Serica Monograph XIV. Monumenta Serica, the Catholic University of Nagoya and the Australian National University, Canberra 1961, p.108.

236. Shih Chang-ju, 'Yin-tai-ti chu-t'ung kung-i', *Kuo-li Chung-yang Yen-chiu-yüan Li-shih Yü-yen Yen-chiu-so Chi-k'an*, vol.26 (1955), pp.95–129.

237. Cheng Te-k'un, 'The origin and development of Shang culture', *Asia Major*, series 2, vol.6 (1957), pp.80–98, and *Shang China*, pp.32 and 162–3; Li Chi, *Hsiao T'un, T'ao-ch'i*, pt.1.

238. Like everyone else who writes about Shang bronze foundry, I am indebted in general to Dr Noel Barnard's systematization of the available information (*Bronze casting and bronze alloys in ancient China*), and in this particular instance to his perspicuity in discerning the implications of the type of crucible employed in Shang China. The crucible itself had already been described by Shih Chang-ju and Cheng Te-k'un. Barnard attributes the first notice of the influence of ceramic manufacture on Shang bronze casting to Mrs Wilma Fairbank [*Monumenta Serica*, vol.22, fasc.1, p.235], though Sekino Takeshi had made much the same point in regard to both bronze and iron technology in 1956 [*Chugaku Kōkogaku Kenkyu*. Tōkyō, pp.189–91].

239. See C. Hentze, *Bronzegerät, Kultbauten, Religion im ältesten China der Chang-Zeit*. Antwerpen 1951, and Max Loehr, *Chinese Bronze-Age weapons*. University of Michigan Press, Ann Arbor 1956.

240. Cheng Te-k'un has devised a functional classification of Shang bronzes as follows, which, whatever its other merits, at least illustrates the wealth of forms in the bronzesmith's repertoire, as well as the almost exclusive emphasis on luxury items [*Shang China*, pp.167–8].

(1) *Food vessels*
Li tripod
Ting tripod
Ch'i four-legged vessel
Ting tripod with stove
Hsien tripod
Kuei tripod
Tou bowl
P'ou jar
Kuei bowl
I box
Pi ladle
Tsu table
(2) *Wine vessels*
Ho pot
Chia tripod
Chüeh tripod
Chio tripod
Yu wine-can
Tsun jar

Chih cup
Hu jar
Ku cup
Kung ewer
Bird-and-animal *tsun* cup
Shao spoon
(3) *Water vessels*
Yu water vessel
P'an basin
(4) *Musical instruments*
Nao bell
Ling bell
Ku drum
(5) *Military weapons*
Tsu arrow-head
Pang bow fitting
Mao spear-head
Ko dagger-axe
Ch'u axe
Yüeh axe

Ch'i axe
Tao knife
K'uei armor plate
Chou helmet
   (6) *Tools*
Pen socketed axe
Hsiao knife
K'e-tao incisor
Kou hook
Tsuan drill

   (7) *Miscellaneous*
Ching mirror
Chu chopsticks
Yin seal
Chariot and harness fittings
Pole finial
Mask
Color container
Architectural fittings

241. Kao Ch'ü-hsün, 'Hsiao-ch'en Hsi shih-kuei-ti ts'an-p'ien yü ming-wen', *Kuo-li Chung-yang Yen-chiu-yüan Li-shih Yü-yen Yen-chiu-so Chi-k'an*, vol.28 (1957), pp.593–610; O. Karlbeck, 'An-yang marble sculpture', *Bulletin of the Museum of Far Eastern Antiquities*, vol.7 (1935), pp.61–9; Li Chi, *The beginnings of Chinese civilization*, Fig. 6.

242. Huang Chan-yüeh, 'Chin-nien ch'u-t'u-ti Chan-Kuo Liang-Han t'ieh-ch'i', *K'ao-ku Hsüeh-pao*, no.3 (1957), p.106.

243. Karl Polanyi, 'The economy as instituted process', in Karl Polanyi, Conrad M. Arensberg and Harry W. Pearson, (eds.), *Trade and market in the early empires*. The Free Press of Glencoe, Illinois, and the Falcon's Wing Press 1957, pp.243–70. The quotation is from p.250. In recent years Polanyi's theses have been subjected to severe criticism, notably by Scott Cook ['The obsolete "anti-market" mentality : a critique of the substantive approach to economic anthropology', *American Anthropologist*, vol.68, no.2 (1966), pp.323–45], but for the most part the debate has centered on the epistemological implications of the semantic dichotomy between economics in the substantivist sense of the provision of material goods and in the formal sense of rationalizing calculation. But even if the ideological basis of the substantivist approach to economic problems should ultimately prove untenable, the distinction between symmetrically disposed reciprocal systems and centripetally arranged redistributive organizations still holds as a conceptual framework for analysis of the economic competition which Cook, among others, rightly attributes to so-called primitive societies.

244. *Vide* Tung Tso-pin, *Yin Li P'u*. Li-chuang 1945; and 'Yin-tai-chih li-fa nung-yeh yü ch'i-hsiang', *Hua-hsi Ta-hsüeh Wen-shih Chi-k'an*, vol.5 (1946); Cheng Te-k'un, *Archaeology in China*, vol.2, p.197.

245. Tung Tso-pin, *Yin Li P'u*.

246. Amano Motonosuke, 'Yintai no nogyo to shakai kozo', *Shigaku Kenkyu*, vol.62 (1956), p.11.

247. An Chin-huai, 'Shih-lun Cheng-Chou Shang-tai ch'eng chih – Ao-tu', *Wen-wu*, nos. 4 and 5 (1961), p.77.

248. Li Chi, Preface to Shih Chang-ju's *Yin-hsü chien-chu i-ts'un*, p. iii.

249. Li Chi, *The beginnings of Chinese civilization*, p.53, note 13.

250. Polanyi *et al.*, *Trade and market*, p.250.

251. Cp. Walter C. Neale, 'The market in theory and history' in Polanyi *et al.*, *Trade and market*, p.371.

2

The Diffusion of Urban Life in Ancient China

THE CHOU DYNASTY[1]

According to the traditionally received account of ancient Chinese history the Shang dynasty, corrupted by the exercise of absolute power over several centuries, was overthrown by a coalition of tribes under the leadership of one of its own feudatories which went under the style of Chou (**T̑i̯ôg). According to these same sources the Chou were rude barbarian tribes whose harsh existence on the steppes and hills of the northwest both fitted them to preserve the virtues of ancient times and consequently to deserve the Mandate of Heaven, and endowed them with the martial qualities necessary to wrest supreme power from the effete and decadent Shang dynasty. In the traditional chronology this was achieved in 1122 BC when King **Mi̯wo (Wu), profiting from the absence of the Shang ruler on a military expedition, was able to seize the Shang capital. Much of the success with which the Chou consolidated their victory is attributed to the Duke of Chou, younger brother of King Mi̯wo and *de facto* ruler of the new Chou state during the minority of his nephew Ch'eng (**D̑i̯ĕng). He it was, according to the traditional account, who suppressed a Shang rebellion (or, in the language of bronze inscriptions, effected 'the second conquest of Shang'), pacified the state, and ensured the continuation of the Shang sacrifices by establishing members of the deposed royal lineage in the district of **Sông (Sung) in present-day eastern Ho-nan. In the light of Chinese beliefs in later times this superficially altruistic act can be construed as having been motivated by the desire to avoid retribution at the hands of the powerful Shang ancestors if their sacrifices were discontinued.

This version of the transference of power from Shang to Chou, including as it does the stereotypes of the depraved terminal representative of a dynasty[2] and the able founder of a new line of kings upon whom is conferred the Mandate of Heaven, and who, with the selfless assistance of a virtuous chief minister, establishes a great and glorious new dynasty, has only too obviously been subject to the archetyping process which ultimately produces myth. But in the absence of archeological evidence it has hitherto proved impossible to penetrate to the original events which are now cast in the form of heroic situations.

107

Recently, however, Dr Noel Barnard has used information in the *I Hou Nieh I* inscription (Inscription 121.3 in Barnard's systematization) to demonstrate, first, that the so-called Shang rebellion was in fact more likely to have been but one in a series of Chou attacks on the Shang polity, and second, that the conquest, which the classical texts attribute to the Duke of Chou, was in fact effected by King Ch'eng in person, presumably after he had attained his majority.[3] There can be little doubt that other epigraphic evidence yet to be excavated, when evaluated on the strict principles of interpretation established by Dr Barnard, will introduce further modifications into the traditional history of the Chou conquest.

Both the origin and the ethnic composition of the Chou people are obscure. Their own traditions, as preserved in Chinese classical literature, trace their descent from **G'u-Tsjək (Hou-Chi) or Prince Millet, a legendary ancestor who was also an agricultural deity. According to these same dynastic traditions it was G'u-Tsjək's grandson, Duke **Ljôg (Liu), who welded the Chou tribes into a unitary people, and **Tân-B'jwo (Tan-Fu) who gave them a political identity, at the same time as he brought them from the district of **Pjən (Pin), traditionally identified with present-day Pin-Hsien in Shen-hsi, to settle permanently at the foot of Mount **G'jĕg (Ch'i), customarily equated with the neighborhood of Pao-chi in the Wei valley.[4] Two generations later, under **T'jang (Ch'ang), who subsequently adopted the regnal style of **Mjwən-Gjwang (Wen-Wang), the Chou had come to constitute the most powerful state in the Wei valley, with its cult center at **P'jông (Feng), a site on the southern side of the Wei valley not far from present-day Hsi-an. It was Mjwən-Gjwang's son, **Mjwo-Gjwang (Wu-Wang), who proclaimed the independence of Chou and, from a capital at **G'og (Hao), also in the vicinity of Hsi-an, initiated the conquest of Shang.[5]

Of this archetyped pre-conquest history of Chou, archeology has very little to say, either in confirmation or denial. Although Western Chou artifacts had been discovered in the Wei valley before World War II,[6] it was not until the 'fifties that Su Ping-chi and Wu Ju-tso documented a transition sequence from Lungshanoid (K'ai-jui Chuang II in the terminology of the excavators) to Chou.[7] So far, although a dozen or so Chou sites have been investigated in the vicinity of Hsi-an, it has proved extremely difficult to distinguish pre-conquest from later remains. It is, for example, practically impossible from the published reports to decide whether Chou elements in association with Hsiao-T'un-type finds were indeed contemporary with the Shang or were introduced after the conquest. When the Chou cultural imprint is found together with Shang remains of the Erh-li Kang phase we are on stronger ground – uniquely so for these finds afford the only incontestable archeological evidence for the pre-conquest Chou – but such associations are few and still inadequately analyzed.[8]

In the absence of an established basis of archeologically attested facts, any interpretation of Chou origins must rest on the implications of epigraphic and literary evidence. In the first place the oracle bones leave us in no doubt that the Shang rulers regarded the Chou as constituting one of the benefices in the gift of the Shang king, and were prepared to use troops to enforce their will. Conceivably the Chou may have been one of the **$p\underline{i}wang$ (*fang*) tribes (p. 58 above) whose chieftain had had his authority confirmed and validated by a ceremony of investiture. Of course, this would afford no guarantee that the Chou regarded themselves as dependents of the Shang king and the point may never be settled, for the surviving record of the Chou point of view has passed through the hands of later scholars who have had an intellectual commitment to systematizing the ancient dynasties into a morally acceptable sequence.

According to the received version of Chou history before the conquest, the Chou people had been established in the middle and lower Wei valley for at least four generations before M$\underline{i}$wo-G$\underline{i}$wang asserted his independence of the Shang ruler. Some scholars have seen reason to believe that they had previously occupied territories either in the Ordos or at least north of the Wei river, but, however that may be, the late recensions of their annals – which are the only ones extant – intentionally create the impression of a semi-nomadic people who had adopted a sedentary mode of life at some time prior to their conquest of Shang. Ssŭ-ma Ch'ien, who may have drawn his information from an earlier recension of the annals, attributes this transformation specifically to the culture-hero Tân-B'$\underline{i}$wo who, he says, 'rejecting the customs of the **Ń$\underline{i}$ông (Jung) and **D'iek (Ti),[9] organized the construction of an inner and an outer wall, and of houses and chambers, [so that] the settlement (**·$\underline{i}əp : i$) constituted a distinctive environment (*pieh-chü*).' [10] This is the language of Chou documents in later times, and it is more than doubtful if it was applicable to the period of Tân-B'$\underline{i}$wo. However, Chou mythology was not entirely inconsistent in its picture of the pre-urban way of life, for there are sundry other hints that these tribes had developed the pastoral aspects of their economy in early times, and it may not be wholly fortuitous that the *Chu-shu Chi-nien* records that, after Duke **K$\underline{i}$wɐd-liek (Chi-li) of Chou had subdued the **D$\underline{i}$o-m$\underline{i}$wo (Yü-wu) tribes of the Ń$\underline{i}$ông, King **T'âd-tieng (T'ai-ting) of Shang appointed him to be Chief of Herdsmen (**$m\underline{i}$ôk-s$\underline{i}ər : mu$-*shih*).[11] This is a situation very similar to that envisaged above in which a tribal chieftain was accorded a Shang title and absorbed, first into the Shang polity, and then into the Shang culture group.

Intimations such as these of a difference between the Shang and Chou ways of life have induced speculation by modern scholars as to the possibility of the two peoples representing distinct ethnic groups and even linguistic stocks. In the earlier years of this century, the Chou were regarded simply as the first of a succession of nomadic invaders from the steppelands of Central Asia. In 1942 Wolfram Eberhard concluded from an analysis of such information as was available on the tribal federations which made up the Chou armies that at the time of the conquest the ruling house was ethnically Turkish, while the tribesmen were, generally speaking, of mixed Turkish and Tibetan stock.[12] At just about the same time Owen Lattimore, interpreting the same evidence in the light of ecological rather than linguistic considerations, came to precisely the opposite conclusion, namely that the Chou were of the same ethnic group as the Shang.[13] It is perhaps necessary to explain at this point that, according to Lattimore's hypothesis, the emergence of Chinese civilization out of a relatively uniform Lungshanoid culture was associated with the development of improved farming techniques. Lattimore placed particular emphasis on the adoption of irrigation, for which there is, in fact, no evidence in prehistoric China (cf. p. 68 above), but this is not seriously detrimental to his theory, as practically any other innovation in agricultural technology, whether the introduction of new methods of tillage or new crops, could have brought about the same result, namely more certain harvests, heavier yields per man and perhaps per acre, and ultimately an intensification of population density and a higher degree of social solidarity. Lattimore does not spell out this process in detail, and neither does he analyse the social processes involved, but presumably he is envisaging some sort of transformation such as that reported by Ralph Linton and Abram Kardiner when the Tanala of Madagascar changed from dry to wet padi cultivation.[14] Those communities on the North China plain which experienced these changes developed a consciousness of shared understandings and common aims and values which would ultimately provide the foundations for Chinese civilization. Those groups, on the other hand, who, by reason of circumstance or inclination, failed to accept technical innovation, were gradually forced out of the proto-Chinese community and into still poorer peripheral and interstitial territories, where they had no option but to elaborate the pastoral sectors of their economies. In extreme cases this might lead to fully nomadic ways of life in which farming played only a vestigial role. On this view the age-long conflict between sedentary Chinese and nomadic 'barbarians' was initiated as much by Chinese expansion as by nomadic inroads. It is in the context of this interpretation of Chinese history that Lattimore places both the Shang and the Chou – and, incidentally, the Hsia as well – among the nuclear Sinic communities.

Only the progress of archeological investigation will ultimately decide the ethnic status of the pre-conquest Chou, and even then the evidence will not be easy to interpret. But the whole question is not so purely academic as it may at first appear, for on it depends our interpretation of the origin and nature of the Western Chou polity and, consequently, of the status of the city in the political system of the time (cf. pp. 112–14 below).

The idea that the Chou were nomadic intruders into the Chinese culture realm led on to the notion that their culture at the time of the conquest was inferior to the civilization of Shang, and during the first half of this century this disparity in the cultural attainments of the two groups was held as an article of faith by virtually all Western historians of China. The Chou have been envisaged most frequently as rugged 'defenders of the marches and pioneers of the high-lands',[15] whose continual struggle against both a harsh environment and hostile neighbors had bred in them the martial skills which eventually enabled them to overcome the Shang. The four generations since the time of Tân-B'įwo, during which they had been established in the Wei valley, had been insufficient for their élite to acquire more than a veneer of Shang culture, so that when Mįwo-Gjwang acceded to control of the premier polity in East Asia he brought with him a band of battle-hardened retainers more familiar with the mores and values of the camp than with the niceties of ritual and protocol.[16] The texts provide no real basis for this interpretation – which is hardly surprising since they preserve the version of events authorized by the Chou themselves – and archeology offers little evidence beyond the presence of metal artifacts in the Wei valley in pre-conquest times. On present evidence it is still possible to argue either that the early Chou were only a Neolithic Lungshanoid group somewhat affected by the absorption of selected Shang culture traits, or that they had already developed one of the Lungshanoid regional traditions to the point where it should be classed as a civilization running on a course parallel to that of the Shang. However, this choice may not be open to us for much longer, for Dr Noel Barnard has recently voiced some pertinent observations in this con-nection. He has pointed out that, whereas the Shang restricted their bronze inscriptions – as far as can be ascertained from scientifically attested specimens – to two or three characters recording names or emblems, the Chou, even before they had finally completed the conquest of Shang, were engraving texts of con-siderable length. The *I Hou Nieh I* inscription is, of course, the prime example. On a matter on which I am far from expert I cannot do better than quote Dr Barnard's conclusion to his evaluation of this inscription:

'The facts which face us are simply these – the Shangs made short inscriptions in bronze of little historical value; the Chous, even before the Shang state was entirely vanquished, manufactured bronze texts that are truly historical documents of tremendous interest. It is tempting to suggest that the Chous were possibly possessors of a somewhat more advanced culture than that of the Shangs – the two civilizations, however, exhibiting much the same form of culture; for example, the written scripts were identical in most respects but the contents of the more permanent documents differed. Much of Shang writing was connected with divination – the Chous, however, were apparently more concerned with lay affairs and had practical reasons to record, in a permanent form, matters for the instruction of posterity.'[17]

It is possible that Barnard's investigations have not yet quite reached the point at which they can support unaided the edifice of interpretation which he has erected upon them. In any case his conclusion requires that he disregard a considerable number of Shang bronze inscriptions containing up to a score or so of characters[18] which he considers, probably correctly, to be not properly attested, a phrase which he construes in rigorous fashion to mean 'acquired through scientifically controlled excavation'. Nevertheless, his fundamental arguments are extremely persuasive and based on analysis of a much more austere and punctilious character than has usually been accorded the oracle texts. In some respects Barnard's suggestion – and it is only a suggestion – is not in conflict with the inescapable conclusion of archeology that the post-conquest Chou culture was a lineal descendant of that of the Shang 'and the Conquest involves no major discontinuity as far as the civilizational growth of the Yellow River valley is concerned.'[19] Such a conclusion surely implies that the two cultures were much of a muchness at the time of the conquest.

STATE AND GOVERNMENT

When the Chou rulers finally found themselves in control of the Shang kingdom, together probably with some other eastern districts which had been outside the sphere of Shang dominion, they were faced with the problem of extending their version of patrimonial government to territories beyond the reach of personal authority. In response to this need they apparently instituted a network of garrisons designed to assert their control over virtually the whole of the North China plain. Many, perhaps most of these garrisons, constituted islands of ethnically Chou composition in a sea of Shang and other indigenes, but occasionally former Shang benefice holders were allowed to retain their lands provided they transferred their allegiance to the new rulers. One of the traditional annals records that no less than 1,773 dependent territories were established in this manner by the Chou king.[20] There is no independent confirmation of this figure but the order of magnitude at least implies that most settlements of any size were placed under a Chou chieftain or a Chou adherent. The Chou themselves retained direct control of their homeland in the Wei valley.

A proportion of the Chou vassals were doubtless kinsmen of the royal house, but the system of classificatory kinship nomenclature[21] was extended to include benefice holders who, despite their propagation of fictitious genealogies,[22] are now known to have had no biological connection with the Chou royal clan. In addressing a territorial magnate bearing the same surname as that of the royal house the Chou king used the term 'paternal uncle', whereas a lord with a different surname was addressed as 'maternal uncle'. In this way familial relations were not only integrated into the political framework of the state but also provided a model for the conduct of government. The authority of the Chou court was sustained by a series of ceremonies and rituals in which political duties were conceived on the pattern of family loyalty, and both linked with

112

religion in a manner which accorded divine sanction to the system of government. In these circumstances the Chou king was able to rely on the majority of
his vassals favoring the divinely ordained *status quo*, as against the innovator
who failed to conform to the sacrally validated pattern. Long after the Chou
ruler had ceased to wield significant secular power, he continued to exercise
ritual authority, adjudicating in claims of legitimacy and, by sanctioning innovations when the force of events rendered them inevitable, easing strains in
a developing society. In this respect the Chou capital shared something in
common with Sumerian Nippur, and perhaps to a lesser extent with the Greek
Delphi and Yoruba Ile Ifẹ, all of which were cult centers from which emanated
culturally unifying influences[23] although they themselves were not especially
powerful politically. Particularly this is true of the situation in China after the
middle of the 8th century when the royal Chou had lost most of its power to
influence events outside its own territory.

Traditionally the Chou has been pictured as a largely static era characterized
by a gradual decline of centralized power. In a sense this image can be traced
back to the Chou dynasty itself, for the philosophers of the age had evolved the
myth of a preceding era of unity, peace, and prosperity as offering a model for
an alternative to the conflict and misery of their time. Some four or five centuries later the Han rulers propagated just such an idealized version of the past
as a demonstration of the benefits to be derived from a unified kingdom under
a strong paternalistic monarch, an interpretation which of necessity forced the
expositors of this thesis to treat the barely forgotten strife of the later years of
the Chou dynasty as civil war.[24] This is the version of events which has come
down to the present and which is still current in numerous writings by Chinese,
Japanese and Western scholars. However, from the second decade of the
present century a group of Chinese scholars, among whom the most prominent
has been Ku Chieh-kang, have penetrated behind the veil of Han exegesis and
revealed the so-called Chou dynasty in a very different light, and their interpretation has subsequently been adopted in its essentials by most Western
specialists in this field.[25]

How long the Chou royal family retained effective control over their conquered territories is unknown, but after some three centuries of rule external
forces intervened to diminish whatever degree of power they still exercised. In
771 BC internal disturbances resulted in the loss of the Chou capital of *G'og* to
non-Chinese tribes from the west, from whom it was eventually recovered not
by the Chou king but by the ruler of the former dependency of **Dz'i̯ĕn*
(Ch'in). The seat of government of the Chou domain was transferred to
***Glâk-di̯ang* (*Lo-yang*), which had hitherto functioned as the eastern capital
of the realm. The royal house of Chou never recovered from this reverse, and
by the end of the century had sunk to the level of her former vassals. In fact,
the Chou court maintained its existence only by exploiting its validatory and

consecratory functions, and by allying itself with the most powerful of its neighbors.

The three centuries or so of Chou hegemony prior to 771 BC have been designated by Chinese historians as the period of the Western Chou. From then until the final extinction of the dynasty in 221 BC is an era now known as the Eastern Chou dynasty, which is customarily sub-divided into two periods designated by names drawn from the literature of their time. The earlier of these, the Ch'un-Ch'iu (**T̂'i̯wən-T̂s'i̯ôg) or Spring and Autumn period, denotes the epoch covered by a history of the same title, namely 772–481 BC; the later, also named after a collection of Chou annals, is known as the period of the Contending States (Chan-Kuo; **T̂i̯an-Kwək). Its beginning is variously assigned to 475, 468 or 403, but it has been found convenient in the present study to date the period from 463, the year following the last entry in the *Tso-Chuan*, the most important of several commentaries on the *Ch'un-Ch'iu*. As has been stated previously, precise dates are not a prime requisite in an evolutional study such as this, and in any case the Eastern Chou constitutes a period of continuous political development rather than two developmentally discrete epochs articulating at a major break in time.

That the Chou king was no longer master of the whole Chinese culture realm at the end of the 8th century is evident from one of the earliest glosses in the *Tso-Chuan*, which records the defeat of the royal troops in 707 BC by an army of **D'i̯ĕng (Cheng).[26] At that time there were about 170 states[27] which, far from feuding within the framework of a unified empire as the traditional annals imply, exercised *de facto* sovereignty over their individual territories. Naturally not all these states were of equal importance. In the old culture hearth of North China the leading contenders for power were **Lo (Lu) **D'i̯ĕng (Cheng), **Gi̯wad (Wei), **Sông (Sung), **K'i̯əg (Ch'i), **D'i̯ĕn (Ch'en), **Dz'ôg (Ts'ao), **Ts'âd (Ts'ai), **Dz'i̯ər (Ch'i) and, of course, Royal Chou itself.[28] At the beginning of the Ch'un-Ch'iu period these states were the most powerful of the polities, and had evolved among themselves ritually sanctioned instruments of formal communication within the framework of a political system in which the Chou domain was of supreme ceremonial significance. Second only to Chou in prestige, though less powerful than some of its neighbors, was the state of Lo, whose authority derived partly from its alleged foundation by the Duke of Chou, and partly from the related circumstance that its ceremonial ritual and protocol, its **li̯ər (*li*), approximated very closely to those of the old Chou court.[29] Generally speaking, these central states – the Chung-Kuo – at the beginning of the Ch'un-Ch'iu period also possessed the most advanced technologies and the most highly developed economies.

Further removed from the ceremonial center of ancient China was a zone of peripheral states which had come within the ambience of Chinese culture in relatively recent times and which, during the 8th and even later centuries, still preserved some of the old barbarian culture traits. To the northwest, in present-day Shen-hsi and Shan-hsi, were the states of **Dz'i̯ĕn (Ch'in), **Tsi̯ĕn (Chin), **Ngi̯wo (Yü), **Kwăk (Kuo) and **Li̯ang (Liang), while in the northeast, in the vicinity of modern Pei-ching, was the state of **·Ian (Yen). In the south, extending in a belt along the Yang-tzŭ valley, were **Tṣ'i̯o (Ch'u), **Dzwia (Sui), **Śi̯ĕn (Shen), **Si̯ək (Hsi), **Dzi̯o (Hsü), **D'əng (T'eng), **Kŏg (Chiao), **Ṭi̯ôg (Chou)[30] and **På (Pa), and still further towards the southeast, in present-day Chiang-su and Che-chiang respectively, were the states of **Ngo (Wu) and **Gi̯wăt (Yüeh). Finally, a third and outer zone was inhabited by barbarian tribes known under the general terms of **D'iek (Ti) in the north, **Di̯ər (I) in the east, **Mlwan (Man) in the south, and **Ńi̯ông (Jung) in the west. Some of these latter groups appear to have possessed fairly substantial and permanent settlements. In fact a process of sinicization was continually changing the status not only of these peripheral tribal peoples but also of the states themselves. Tsi̯ĕn, for example, was admitted to the company of the Central States in fairly early times, and subsequently assumed the leadership of these states.

The degree of political consolidation achieved during the era of the Western Chou is uncertain,[31] but from the middle of the 8th century the process can be documented in considerable detail. By this time the city-states, the ·i̯əp, which had originally constituted the domains of the Chou vassal lords, had been transformed into fully fledged territorial states. Within the inner circle of these states expansion was, generally speaking, possible only at the expense of territories already pre-empted by members of the group[32] and, as we have seen, by the end of the 8th century the contemporary political ethos based on the fiction of a unified empire was at variance with the realities of chronic interstate conflict. Henceforward, Chou political evolution manifested itself in a continuous process of absorption of smaller political units by larger ones, and the Chou technical vocabulary for territorial appropriation and state extinction[33] became increasingly prominent in the annals of the time.

Interstate relations came to be conducted more and more in terms of the expediential dictates of a power struggle rather than according to a sacrally sanctioned moral law. Government by customary morality (li̯ər) and by individuals was subordinated to government by law (**pi̯wăp : fa);[34] in Max Weber's terminology traditional had been replaced by rational-legal authority,[35] and the old ethical code was invoked only when it might add a semblance of legality to power politics. Moreover, as conflict tended to promote a concentration of power, so the more potent among the Chou territorial magnates began to arrogate to themselves some of the functions that had previously been royal prerogatives. A major step in this direction was the assumption in 679 B C by the ruler of the state of Dz'i̯ər of the title of **Păg (Pa) or Hegemon, a role not too dissimilar from that of the Shogunate in 19th-century Japan. As president of the assembly of nobles in the imperial capital, and sure of the support of the most powerful of all the states, this Păg was able to impose some degree of directional unity on the foreign policies of the states, to restrain to some extent the antagonisms of competing factions, and to achieve a measure of relative peace over a span of nearly forty years. Between 681 and 644 BC, he convened assemblies of the nobles (**g'wâd : hui) on at least twenty-four occasions,[36] and these face-to-face confrontations doubtless contributed to a general easing of tensions at a difficult period of interstate rivalry. Subsequently the hegemony passed to Dukes of Dz'iĕn, Sông, and Tsiĕn, and significantly, ultimately to a king of Tṣ'io in the Yang-tzŭ valley. The institution of the Hegemon finally lapsed in 591, when a rough parity of power among the states prevented any particular ruler exercising political control over the others.

Although it had provided some support for the later fiction of a unified political entity on the North China plain, the institution of Hegemon had protected rather than strengthened the Chou court, which had, if anything, declined in prestige during the 7th century. The erosion of the aura of charisma that had attended the royal Chou in the earlier years of the dynasty is reflected very clearly in the debasement of the royal style **Giwang (Wang). Originally this had been a prerogative of the Son of Heaven (**T'ien-tsiag : T'ien-tzŭ), who alone could offer to Heaven the supreme sacrifices and thus maintain the parallelism between the macrocosmos and the microcosmos without which no state could prosper. He it was who, in the words of Marcel Granet, was 'à la fois l'auteur de tout péché, l'émissaire de toute expiation, le bénéficiaire de toute grâce, le principe de toute puissance.' In the universe of the early Chou there could be only one filial mediator between heaven and earth, and giwang, as his style, was sacrosanct. The exception was to be found in the Yang-tzŭ valley state of Tṣ'io, in which aboriginal customs formed a much larger element in the élite culture than they did in North China. Here the ruler had styled himself giwang since the beginning of the Eastern Chou, and he retained the title when, during the Ch'un-Ch'iu, Tṣ'io forced acceptance of itself as a major power in the Chinese culture realm. Towards the end of the Ch'un-Ch'iu period the rulers of two other southern states, Ngo and Giwăt, followed the example of the Duke of Tṣ'io. Even though there was no precedent in their own past for the use of this designation, yet they, like Tṣ'io, were of aboriginal, mainly Giwăt and **T'âd (T'ai), culture and it is unlikely that the Chou religion of Heaven had ever made much appeal to their élites.[37] Adoption of the Chou royal style in these cases probably signifies no more than the adaptation of a prestigious honorific to an already existing institution. When the custom began to spread among the inner circle of Chou states, however, it implied a rejection of the divinely sanctioned system of universal order on which the authority of the Chou monarch ultimately rested, and as such marked an important stage

116

in the evolution of Chinese political forms. By the end of the 4th century A D, the rulers of at least five, and perhaps six, of the more powerful states had assumed the style of *giwang*.[38]

During the Ch'un-Ch'iu period, then, the smaller polities at first found themselves acting as buffer-states between more powerful contending neighbors and, after vainly attempting to preserve their identities by means of alliances, were ultimately absorbed into the territories of their aggrandizing neighbors. By the beginning of the 5th century B C there were no more than thirteen states of any importance, of which five lay outside the specifically Chou culture sphere.[39] During the rest of the life of this alleged dynasty the remaining states engaged in a protracted conflict of mutual extermination. Finally the dialectic of power, working itself out in a manner not totally dissimilar from that of the dialectic of ideology in present-day China, resolved itself into two polarized entities, in this case the state of Dz'ĭĕn in the north contending against the state of Tṣ'ĭo in the south. In a series of campaigns between 230 and 221 B C, the former overcame Tṣ'ĭo and its ruler re-established the unity of the Chinese polity, the outcome of more than half a millennium of political evolution. Discarding the discredited style of *Gĭwang*, which had symbolized the old concept of government according to a divinely ordained moral law, the ruler of Dz'ĭĕn assumed the title of ****Tieg* which, because of its attachment during the Contending States period to some of the more recently created culture heroes of mythological antiquity, had acquired overtones of universality something after the manner of the concept of *cakravartin* adopted by the Mauryas. Had Shih Huang-ti, the first Emperor of Dz'ĭĕn, known the term, he would certainly have claimed to be a *digvijayin*, a conqueror of the four quarters of the world.

It was not only in the sphere of interstate relations that conflict concentrated power : an analogous change was effected concomitantly within the individual states, and it is fortunate that this process has recently been analyzed with exemplary rigor and perspicacity by Professor Cho-yün Hsü.[40] The internal administrations of almost all the states were characterized by struggles between nobles and rulers as well as between noble and noble. It was to be expected that, under the familialistic type of government of Western Chou times, close relatives of a ruler would monopolize important political offices. Brothers of rulers, in particular, often played very important roles in state government.[41] One of the earliest political changes discernible during the Ch'un-Ch'iu period was the replacement of these brothers in seats of power by an oligarchical aristocracy,[42] which was in turn often ruined by interfamilial conflicts. By the beginning of the 5th century B C this class of noble ministers had been virtually eliminated, and the great ministerial families had become things of the past (apart, of course, from the few who had managed to acquire supreme rule within their states). By the beginning of the Contending States epoch a new type of political entity had emerged, in which a ruler exercised despotic power over a bureaucracy the selection of whose personnel was not wholly divorced from merit, although neither had ascriptive principles of appointment been entirely abandoned. Generally speaking, in Max Weber's conceptualization of the nature of state government, the bureaucracies of the Contending States should be classed with those in which the ruler's administrative staff are separated from the *means* of administration (whether these be money, building, war material, vehicles, horses or other things), in contrast to the administrative staffs of the Ch'un-Ch'iu period who had predominantly owned their own means of administration.[43] In the latter (Ch'un-Ch'iu) case the ruler had shared his domination with an autonomous aristocracy, whereas by Chan-Kuo times he had assumed direct control while yet delegating executive power to qualified officials, men whom Weber categorized as 'propertyless strata having no social honor of their own.'[44] We shall have more to say of this new class of administrators subsequently.

The question of feudalism. 'Le mot "féodal" est un terme expressif, commode, – et dangereux.'[45] It has been applied to several periods of Chinese history – sometimes to almost all periods prior to 1949 – and particularly to the decentralized rule of the Chou dynasty. Such broad interpretations stem from generalized definitions of feudalism such as that of Dubrowsky,[46] in which virtually the only requirement for a society to be deemed feudal appears to be the existence of a class of landowners who appropriate the unpaid products of the immediate producers. According to this definition not only Chinese society, but most other Asian societies as well, have remained feudal until well into the 20th century. This, in fact, is the way in which the word is customarily employed in the language of the press and in political propaganda,[47] but, defined thus broadly, it can hardly serve any analytical purpose. At the other extreme there are those who restrict the term to the socio-political systems of certain parts of Western Europe at certain times in the Middle Ages.[48] Among these latter are, first, those who use the word as a generic classifier for a particular dominant political and social organization at a particular time and, second, those who confine it to the description of technical arrangements by which a graded system of land rights comes to correspond to an extreme development of the mode of personal dependence, a state of society in which public rights and duties are inextricably interwoven with the tenure of land and in which 'the whole government system – financial, military, judicial – is part of the law of private property.'[49] In the first instance the institutional structure is defined within the framework of a preconceived time span and limited area,[50] in the second instance the time span is adjusted to correspond with the persistence of a particular institutional complex.[51] Both the institutionally and the chronologically restricted definitions have proved attractive to European historians, who have thus been able to pursue their analyses of the system in the light of their own historical experience.[52] The drawback to this method of inquiry is, of course, that it affords no guarantee that the system under discussion is unique, and not merely one manifestation of a structural uniformity recurring in a series of disparate cultures. Nor does it help us to distinguish incidental and specifically European characteristics from structurally recurrent features common to all cultures in which the institution is found. Defined thus narrowly, the term can hardly serve any comparative purpose, let alone throw light on socio-political conditions during the Chou dynasty.

It is necessary, I think, to remember that at best the idea of feudalism is a high-order abstraction, evolved originally in the minds of European historians to describe a category of institutional complex that had become defunct some half millennium before the term was coined.[53] It seems not unreasonable that other scholars should then seek to discover if the structural characteristics inherent in the abstraction recur in other cultures. Whether or not they find them depends on how they define the institutional complex. It cannot be denied that the texts relating to the Western Chou depict a basically agrarian society in which a supreme ruler delegated sovereign powers to members of a hierarchically structured aristocracy. From the same texts other scholars have cited additional features customarily, though by no means exclusively, associated with European feudalism, notably a personalized government exhibiting a comparatively weak separation of political functions, hereditability of office, regularization of the rights of the lord over the peasant, the maintenance of private armies, and a code of honor stressing military obligations.[54] This complex of features certainly constitutes part of the image projected by the classical literature of China, and has been accepted by most scholars in this field as reflecting more or less truthfully the general lineaments of the Western Chou governmental system. Ch'i Ssŭ-ho, for example, acknowledged it as such in his comparison of Chinese and European feudal institutions,[55] at the same time as he assumed that the *Ch'un-Ch'iu* witnessed the dissolution of a unitary kingdom into civil war. From that point of view he was able, without being guilty of any gross inconsistency, to recognize the more important structural features of Chou feudalism as persisting through the Ch'un-Ch'iu era and beginning to disappear only during the period of the Contending States.[56]

The fact that the Ch'un-Ch'iu can now be categorized as a period of expansion, consolidation and centralization of the power of sovereign states, and that the socio-political aspects of the idealized system can be defined with some degree of confidence, does not mean that the information available is anything like adequate – with the analytical tools presently to hand, at any rate – to permit an assured dynamic historical interpretation of the reality behind the Han image of the Chou era. It is still a matter of debate, for instance, how the Western Chou system of government evolved. Wolfram Eberhard,[57] on the one hand, interpreting the evidence in terms of Alexander Rüstow's theory of

119

feudal societies,[58] sees the Western Chou as a classic exemplar of feudalism resulting from suprastratification, in this instance the imposition of a Chou aristocracy on a substratum of Shang agriculturalists. Eberhard's belief in an ethnic difference between Chou and Shang further leads him to the conclusion that Chou feudalism was the outcome not merely of suprastratification, but of an *ethnic* suprastratification. On the other hand, Owen Lattimore, as already mentioned, interprets the same evidence as indicating an internally generated social stratification.[59] Between these two extremes lies a wide variety of intermediate opinions, including those which derive Chou feudalism from the disintegration of a powerful Shang empire,[60] which only serve to accentuate our ignorance of the true relations between Shang and Chou both before and after the conquest. Neither is there a consensus as to the precise stage at which feudalism may be said to have been established. Whereas Eberhard seems to assume that a feudal situation was initiated at the time of the conquest, Derk Bodde believes that such a system could have evolved only after a gradual evolutionary process had run its course. Feudalism, he says on one occasion, 'means something more than the mere existence of vassalship ties between a single group of territorial nobles on the one hand and a single ruling house on the other. In order to constitute a true feudal system, it should include a network of similar ties linking these same territorial nobles with a descending hierarchy of lesser and more localized dignitaries beneath them, until, ideally, virtually the entire population is integrated into a complex pyramid of delegated powers and responsibilities. . . . One or even two centuries may have been required before a fairly crystallized and broadly inclusive system emerged.'[61] Bodde finds some support for this point of view in Maspero's thesis that sub-infeudation was not practised in early Chou times, although it became fairly common later on when lesser fief-holders had become assimilated into the hierarchy of state nobility.[62] This, together with the evident looseness with which aristocratic titles were used in the early Chou, would seem to imply that a process of political evolution had been taking place. However, both Noel Barnard and Cho-yün Hsü claim to have recognized instances of sub-infeudation under the Western Chou.[63]

Definitive statements on matters such as this must await the attention of specialists, as well as more rigorous definition of the technical terms employed. Meanwhile it is apparent, even through the archetyped glosses of later exegetes, that the Western Chou system of government did present points of comparison with feudal Europe, but the degree of structural similarity involved is a matter for future investigation. To the present author it appears that the complex contractual and legal concepts of European feudalism were either absent or but poorly developed under the Western Chou. There was certainly a hierarchical aristocracy whose members received landed estates and titles from the Chou sovereign. Collectively they were known as the **$t\underset{.}{i}o$-$g'u$ (*chu-hou*), and ranked for ceremonial purposes according to the precedence of the particular **$ts\underset{.}{i}ok$

(*chüeh*) or patent granted to them by the Chou monarch.[64] In late and idealized
Chou books of ritual the five degrees of nobility are each ascribed territorial
fiefs (**kwɔk : kuo*) of fixed areal extent,[65] but Richard Walker has shown
that, at conferences convened after the middle of the 7th century B C, the states
ranked according to their power positions.[66] There were, in addition, **b'iu-
dịung (*fu-yung*) or 'attached' territories, whose rulers were denied direct access
to the Chou king but who rendered their services to neighboring lords. What is
of primary interest in the present context is the ceremony of investiture at
which the noble was confirmed in the possession of his lands, and which was
held in the Royal Chou ancestral temple.[67] After a fairly extended acquaintance
with the texts which prescribe the ritual forms for this ceremony (which,
incidentally, are all relatively late in time) it seems to the present author that
the investiture, in the idealized form in which it has been transmitted to us,
signified not so much the assumption of contractually determined obligations
on the part of the lord in return for a fief but rather a sacrally sanctioned induc-
tion into the hallowed community of the Chinese aristocracy. As Marcel
Granet expressed it in his posthumously published work *La Féodalite chinoise*,
'En recevant l'investiture (*fong*) qui lui permettait d'élever sur sa terre un
Autel du Sol à la chinoise, un chef devenait à la fois un Chinois et un Seigneur.'[68]
Certain undertakings were indeed required of the candidates for investiture but
they were, in my opinion, in the nature of adherence to sacred family loyalties
rather than secular contractual arrangements. The terms of investiture, in so
far as we can know them, seem to have partaken of the character of an *exequatur*
rather than of the *commendatio* of medieval Europe – or so I believe.[69] Of
course, when ambivalent texts have to be interpreted not merely through the
refracting lens of an alien culture, but also through the dark glass of the pur-
posed idealization of a later age, such conclusions are bound to incorporate
a high degree of subjectivity, and consensus is not likely to be achieved
easily.

John Hall has argued forcibly that a feudal society cannot be categorized
under a single inclusive concept, and that feudalism as an ideal type need not be
exemplified in its totality by any particular society which is alleged to be feudal.[70]
A feudal society is to be viewed as a mode of social, political, and economic
integration which subsumes a range of essential variables. In defining such a
system it is particularly necessary to pay attention to the limits of variability
of these elements. The essential variables as isolated by Hall in his thought-
provoking paper are : a lord-and-vassal relationship the crux of which 'is not
a specific form of contract but rather the personal nature of the association . . .
and its military origin'; arms-bearing as a class-defining profession; a distribution of goods and services closely integrated with the hierarchy of social
statuses; a landed, or locally self-sufficient, economic base 'with the merchant
community essentially outside the feudal nexus'; a long-term restriction on the

mobility of the bulk of the population; and a direct personal relationship of land manager to cultivator which, as Hall phrases it, 'places the cultivator under feudalism somewhere between slavery on one side and free tenancy on the other.'[71] I agree with the general structure of this model with one reservation. Whereas *a particular* form of contract may not be specific to feudalism, a strongly contractual basis is, in my opinion, essential to the feudal condition : otherwise how can it be distinguished from the patrimonial mode of socio-political integration? A final conclusion on the question of feudalism under the Western Chou and early Ch'un-Ch'iu – or rather on the question of varieties of feudalism in the different political entities of Chou China : Tṣ'jo appears to have been an autonomous state from the earliest times until 223 B C – must await the outcome of a great deal of scholarly investigation of the degree of variability of the essential elements, both in the generalized model of feudalism and in the particular Chinese experience. Until comparative historians have provided a more refined structural definition of the phenomenon of feudalism in general, and not just a description of English or French or Russian or Japanese feudalism, it will be unprofitable to argue determinedly for or against feudalism in Chou China. Nevertheless, I cannot but express my belief that the evidence available for the Western Chou and earlier Ch'un-Ch'iu periods can, in the present unsatisfactory stage of historical analysis, be construed as testimony to a continuation of the patrimonial style of Shang government more readily than as proof of a feudal system of vassalage.[72] In any case, by Ch'un-Ch'iu times the Western Chou empire – if indeed such an entity had ever existed – had been replaced by a congeries of states which, even though they shared certain cultural understandings and acknowledged the supremacy of a common ritual center, enjoyed *de facto* political sovereignty.

SOCIETY

As literacy was a prerogative of the ruling élites, it was inevitable that the literature of the Chou period should reflect almost exclusively the actions, values and attitudes of those groups. But the extant writings of the Chou do not preserve simple statements about these matters : the actions have been archetyped, the values idealized, and the characters heroized. For the Western Chou even this genre of record is exiguous, and it is a matter of great difficulty to ascertain precisely how the various social groups actually functioned, as opposed to how later annalists and exegetes said they functioned. The idealized texts, for example, describe five grades of nobility in a fixed hierarchy of descending rank, but there is no shortage of evidence that in early Chou times the terms denoted types of benefice rather than ranks.[73] Moreover, the very early *I Hou Nieh I* inscription mentions three classes of people, King's men, counts and serfs, without reference to the traditional five noble ranks.[74] The King's men clearly enjoyed the highest status among these three groups and alone are accorded the enumerator **sĕng : sheng* (for **sįĕng : hsing* = family name), while the counts and serfs are merely listed under the general category of husbandmen. What the relation was between these three classes and the traditional rankings we have no means of knowing.

Turning from these negative aspects of the study of Chou society to matters about which it is possible to speak more positively, it can be stated with certainty that in the time of the Western Chou, society was disposed in a pyramidal form, with the king and a virtually closed aristocracy as an apex, supported by a broad base of peasant agriculturalists. In the early post-conquest period the king may well have been the supreme ruler that he always claimed to be, but by the end of the 8th century the royal clan of Chou had lost virtually all political power outside its own domain, and had in fact sunk to the level of its former vassals. Only the superior charisma associated with the king's ritual role as Son of Heaven distinguished the royal family from other minor rulers' courts situated at strategic points on the North China plain. Not that charisma was solely a prerogative of the royal Chou. In later times all the state rulers also believed that they were different from other men. In fact they all traced their descent from ancient culture heroes, adapted genealogies to prove it – a process which in the case of lords of other than imperial descent involved the transformation of not a few unpretentious local deities into emperors and dukes [75] – and undertook an annual schedule of sacrifices to ensure the welfare of their realms.

Associated with the ruler's role as the chosen instrument for communication with the ancestors was an elaborate, but in early times apparently unwritten, code of ceremony and etiquette subsumed under the Chinese term *liər* (*li*). As in the case of the Chou king himself, it was the punctilious attention of the ruler to *liər* which, combined with his personal **tək* (*te*) or *virtus*, ensured the prosperity of the state. Marcel Granet has delineated the role of the ruler in evocative terms which express clearly the close association of religious ritual and legitimate sovereignty. [76]

'Le seigneur est donc, partout, le principe de toute fécondité, de toute fertilité. Il est, dans chaque domaine, un principe universel de fructification, de stabilité, de santé. Les joncs, les chrysanthèmes poussent vigoureusement tant que sont vigoureux la vertu, le *tao-tö*, [77] le *mana* princiers; le plantain a des milliers de graines et le peuple des enfants en foule, tant que ce *tao-tö* ne s'épuise point; tant que le seigneur a assez de *mana* pour vivre vieux, nul, parmi le peuple, ne meurt prématurément. Ni l'eau, ni la chaleur ne manquent en temps voulu, et les chevaux courent vite et les chevaux courent droit, et aucune invasion de sauterelles n'ose pénétrer, et aucun brigand n'ose lever la tête, ou aucun démon faire des siennes dans un pays où le prince conserve, entière, sa Vertu.'

During the Ch'un-Ch'iu period the ruling houses, from the genealogical point of view, fell into three groups, the **Tsjəg (Tzŭ) lineage, which had provided rulers for the old kingdom of Shang but which now ruled only in Sông; the descendants of Chou princes who were considered to have received their fiefs from King Mįwo at the time of the conquest, and who consequently bore the clan name of **Kįəg (Chi); and those who ruled over states which had joined the Chinese community subsequently as a result of a process of sinicization.[78] Both the Shang and Chou rulers claimed descent from gods, but the others traced their origins to ancient emperors, most of whom were eventually systematized into dynasties which today constitute an important part of the mythology of ancient China.

During the Western Chou the rank next below the rulers was filled by ministers of the government, whose relation to their rulers was functionally analogous to that of the Chou king to his dukes (using this latter term in the general sense of *tįo-g'u* (cf. p. 120 above). There were two grades of ministers, the **k'įăng (ch'ing), the higher rank, whose offices were hereditable and who were relatively few in number, and the **t'âd-pįwo (tai-fu), who were more numerous and who functioned as assistants to the k'įăng. There were, in fact, several grades of t'âd-pįwo, some of which seem also to have been hereditable. Together a ruler and his ministers constituted the power group in a state and, at least in the idealized texts of later times, were classificatory kin to one another. On the lower fringes of the power group, in some instances overlapping with it but in others falling far below it, was a class of **dẓ'įag (shih), men who were descendants of rulers or ministers and trained in the six arts of propriety, music, archery, chariot driving, writing, and arithmetic, but who were often, perhaps predominantly, unlanded. Although ranked among the **kįwən-tsįəg (chün-tzŭ)[79] or gentlemen of good birth, such dẓ'įag might be no more than officials in the bureaucracy or in a noble household. Others, who were fortunate enough to possess small estates, might have a few tenants to till their fields or might even work the land themselves. It was the code of behavior that had developed among the dẓ'įag which was formalized and infused with additional moral content by Confucius in the period of the Contending States.

Apart from a few of the dẓ'įag, none of the ruling classes engaged in agricultural or artisan activities, so that virtually the whole structure of society was supported by the labors of the peasantry, who were referred to variously as **mįən (min: = people), or **śįag-ńįĕn (shu-jen : = the masses), or **dẓ'įan (chien : plebeians), or simply as **sįog-ńįĕn (hsiao-jen : = the mean people). In contrast to the aristocracy, these people possessed no family names, and therefore had no need of genealogies; they participated in no ancestral cult and had little understanding of the nature and formalities of lįər. They did not own the land they cultivated but were transferred with it whenever it changed hands. Whether the lord exercised formally recognized rights, inherent in the granting of his benefice, over the lives of the śįag-ńįĕn, or whether the conditions of the time simply afforded no opportunity for the peasant to change his master, is uncertain, though Maspero tends to prefer the latter interpretation.[80] In any case, for all practical purposes the peasant was effectively *adscriptus glebae* and obliged to surrender a portion of his harvest to his overlord, at the same time as he was subject to corvée for construction work and sometimes to conscription into the lord's private army. Indeed, in this largely self-sufficient manorial type of economy there was little to distinguish official state business from the private affairs of a lord. Eberhard is certainly correct in applying the term 'serfs' to these 'men of few rights, few opportunities and few pleasures'.[81]

Included among the *śịag-ńịĕn* were artisans and merchants, both of whom seem to have been attached to manorial-style communities, probably as retainers of noble households. There is no evidence of even partially autonomous associations comparable to the guilds of medieval Europe, though there are some not wholly unambiguous indications that in the Ch'un-Ch'iu period both merchants and craftsmen were sometimes treated as collective entities.[82] Finally, at the very bottom of the social scale was a class of menials and true slaves.[83] The latter were mainly captives and criminals, and could be purchased; the prevailing price was low.[84] There are, too, a few records of slaves being interred in the tomb of their master.[85] Generally speaking, slaves seem not to have been very numerous and, indeed, appear to have occupied a position external to the main structure of Chou society.[86]

The preceding remarks apply primarily to conditions in the earlier centuries of the Chou era, but it will be apparent that, when social and political stratification coincide as closely as they did in ancient China, political transformations of the magnitude of those described above must have been accompanied by equally momentous social changes. These changes have recently been studied in considerable detail by Professor Hsü Cho-yün, and it is his researches which provide the basis for the following remarks.

Already by the middle of the Ch'un-Ch'iu period, say by 600 BC, there were unmistakable signs that the old social order of the Western Chou was crumbling. We have already seen that members of rulers' families had become progressively less powerful during the 7th century, and had sunk in the social scale at the same time as a new class of hereditary ministers had arisen. During the 6th century this ministerial class in turn lost power to a more impersonal bureaucracy, which offered opportunities of advancement to able men who yet lacked the advantages of powerful family influence. Thus the second half of the Ch'un-Ch'iu witnessed the disintegration of the higher social strata of Chinese society, and the upward rise of individuals on the basis of ability. And it was not only the civil bureaucracy which was able to make use of technical skills dissociated from noble birth : the high incidence of warfare during the Chan-Kuo also facilitated the rise of able commoners to positions of military command. At the same time the population base from which they were selected was broadened when infantry were substituted for the ritualized chariot warfare and archery of earlier centuries and a formalized system of military conscription reached deep into the villages.

Concomitant with these political and social changes was another series associated with economic changes to be discussed in a later section. When, towards the end of the Ch'un-Ch'iu, the use of serf labor was replaced by a system of taxes and rents and the old patrimonial relationship of lord and serf gave way to that between landlord and tenant, the way was opened for the emergence of a class of men who owned land but not rank. As these investors increased their holdings and with them their wealth, so, at the other end of the scale there began to appear a class of landless peasants. Thus these opposing, yet complementary, spirals induced an economic stratification, which in time hardened into class distinction and transformed the very basis of society. Meanwhile, the development of commercial activity was effecting a parallel trend within the framework of urban society. By the 5th century there had appeared a class of urban merchants who were using their wealth to acquire political influence. By investing their surplus wealth in land, this group also contributed to the formation of a landless peasantry and furthered the crystallization of class distinctions. These were the types of entrepreneurs who served as models for Ssŭ-ma Ch'ien's generalizations in the chapter of his history entitled *Huo-Chih*.[87] Among them were the members of the **Tŏk (Cho) family, originally from **D'jog (Chao) state,[88] the **K'ung (K'ung) family of **·Iwăn (Yüan),[89] **D'jĕng-D'jĕng (Ch'eng-Cheng), from **Bljəm-g'jung (Lin-ch'iung),[90] **Kwâk-Tsjung (Kuo-Tsung) of G'ân-tân,[91] and the **Pjăng (Ping) family of Dz'ôg (Ts'ao), all of whom made fortunes in the iron-smelting business during the closing decades of the Chan-Kuo period. **·Ia-Twən (I-Tun) achieved equal success in salt production, and was bracketed with Kwâk-Tsjung as a man whose wealth could be compared with that of a ruler of a kingdom.[92] In the district known as Within the Pass, the **D'ien (T'ien), **Ljĕt (Li) and **D'o (Tu) were the dominant merchant families.[93] By the final years of the Chou dynasty the widow **Ts'jĕng (Ch'ing) had amassed such wealth by skilful manipulation of the profits on the sale of cinnabar cakes in Pǎ (Pa) and **Ɖjuk (Shu) that the first emperor of Dz'jĕn entertained her and built the **Njo-g'wɛr-ts'jĕng (Nü-huai-ch'ing) terrace in her honor.[94] A not inconsiderable proportion of the successful entrepreneurs whose achievements are described by Ssŭ-ma Ch'ien were of humble, sometimes picaresque, origins. **Dz'jĕn-Djang (Ch'in-Yang) was a ploughman, **K'juk-Śjôk (Ch'ü-Shu)[94a] was a grave robber, **G'wân-Pjwăt (Huan-Fa) was a gambler, **·Jung Glâk-ɖjĕng (Yung Lo-ch'eng) was a peddler, **·Jung-Păk (Yung-Po) began as a purveyor of fats, the **Tjang (Chang) family as vendors of syrups, the **Tjĕd (Chih) family as knife sharpeners, the **Tŭk (Cho) family as dealers in dried sheep stomachs, and **Tjang-Ljəg

126

(Chang-Li) as a horse doctor. But the prince of all Chan-Kuo businessmen, and exemplar of the new age, was **B'ăk-Kiweg (Po-Kuei), a native of Chou in the time of Marquis **Mįwən (Wen) of Ngįwər. His story, as told by Ssŭ-ma Ch'ien and felicitously translated by Dr Burton Watson,[95] is reproduced below and can stand as symbolic of the entrepreneurial spirit of the times.

'... Po Kuei delighted in watching for opportunities presented by the changes of the times.

> What others throw away, I take;
> What others take, I give away,

he said. "When the year is good and the harvest plentiful, I buy up grain and sell silk and lacquer; when cocoons are on the market, I buy up raw silk and sell grain. When the reverse marker of Jupiter is in the sign *mao*, the harvest will be good, but the following year the crops will do much worse. When it reaches the sign *wu*, there will be drought, but the next year will be fine. When it reaches the sign *yu*, there will be good harvests, followed the next year by a falling off. When it reaches the sign *tzŭ*, there will be a great drought. The next year will be fine and later there will be floods. Thus the cycle revolves again to the sign *mao*."

By observing these laws, he was able to approximately double his stores of grain each year. When he wanted to increase his money supply, he bought cheap grain, and when he wanted to increase his stock, he bought up high-grade grain. He ate and drank the simplest fare, controlled his appetites and desires, economized on clothing, and shared the same hardships as his servants and slaves, and when he saw a good opportunity, he pounced on it like a fierce animal or a bird of prey. "As you see," he said, "I manage my business affairs in the same way that the statesmen I-Yin and Lü-Shang planned their policies, the military experts Sun-Tzŭ and Wu-Tzŭ deployed their troops, and the Legalist philosopher Shang-Yang carried out his laws. Therefore, if a man does not have wisdom enough to change with the times, courage enough to make decisions, benevolence enough to know how to give and take, and strength enough to stand his ground, though he may wish to learn my methods, I will never teach them to him!"

Hence, when the world talks of managing a business it acknowledges Po-Kuei as the ancestor of the art.'

Of this new breed of men in general Ssŭ-ma Ch'ien has this to say:

'None of them enjoyed any titles or fiefs, gifts, or salaries from the government, nor did they play tricks with the law or commit any crimes to acquire their fortunes. They simply guessed what course conditions were going to take and acted accordingly, kept a sharp eye out for the opportunities of the times, and so were able to capture a fat profit. They gained their wealth in the secondary occupations and held on to it by investing in agriculture; they seized hold of it in times of crisis and maintained it in times of stability. There was a special aptness in the way they adapted to the times. . . .'[96]

In short, the Eastern Chou can be characterized as a period when the power élites of a congeries of *de facto* sovereign states were reconstituted, when political influence ceased to be wholly ascriptive and came to be based to a large extent on achievement, and when new political and economic stratifications congealed into social classes. At the same time there was an increase in vertical social mobility, as the upper strata of society lost a good deal of their former kin-based cohesiveness and allowed a proportion of their members to sink in the scale, while the development of bureaucratic institutions, by introducing competition for high positions, facilitated the rise of able individuals on merit alone.

ECONOMY

As compared with that of the Shang period, the economy of Chou China was influenced by significant changes in both environmental and technological considerations. Let us look at the environment first.

Environment. The Chou period witnessed a marked enlargement of the *Lebensraum* of the Chinese, but even more important was the increased diversity of the resource base which accompanied this extension of territory. The original Chou benefices or fiefs (according to whether the government is considered patrimonial or feudal) occupied an area not greatly in excess of that of the old Shang kingdom – or perhaps more accurately of the Shang culture realm as revealed by archeology (cf. Fig. 8). There were, in fact, only two significant additions to those territories, one in the west and one in the east. Chou itself had built up its power in the Wei valley in central Shen-hsi and maintained its capital and the royal domain there until 771 BC, after which the region became the territory of Dz'jĕn. This valley, together with the lower reaches of the Ching, Lo and other tributaries of the Huang, is essentially a sheltered extension of the North China plain protruding into the more rigorous environment of the löss uplands, but in Chinese history it has fulfilled a dual role. By reason of the potential fertility of its lössic soils wherever water could be made available, it has afforded a productive agricultural base for political and military activity,[97] and by reason of its location and physiography it has provided the entrance to the main routeway from the Chinese heartland to Central, and ultimately to Western, Asia. On the eastern marches of the North China plain the Western Chou conquests brought firmly within the Chinese culture realm a fringe of territories that had apparently resisted Shang encroachments until the very end of the dynasty. In this direction the early Chou probably extended their political control to the shores of the Po-Hai and the edges of both the Shantung highlands and the Huai marshes.

128

By the beginning of the Ch'un-Ch'iu period the Chung-Kuo or Central States (as defined on p. 114) still occupied this territory which had constituted the original kingdom of the Chou, but they were now surrounded by a zone of peripheral states which, during the Western Chou, had become acculturated – though sometimes imperfectly – to the Chinese way of life. In the far north, in the embayment of the North China plain which now constitutes the environs of Peking, was the state of ·Ian; to the northwest, in present-day southern Shan-hsi, was Tsįĕn, which subsequently disintegrated into the three smaller states of **D'įog (Chao), **Ngįwər (Wei), and **G'ân (Han)⁹⁸; in the west Dz'įĕn ruled the former Chou homeland in the Wei valley; and in the south the Han and Yang-tzŭ lowlands afforded territorial bases for at least eight states, of which Tṣ'įo and Ngo were both territorially the most extensive and politically the most powerful. Somewhat later Gįwăt, in the present province of Che-chiang, forced itself into the Chinese comity of states. In the north this expansion of the Chinese culture realm effected no great changes, though it did establish the Chinese mode of ecological adaptation on the löss upland of Shan-hsi. In the south, however, Tṣ'įo, Ngo, and Gįwăt constituted a bridge between North China, a climatically rigorous land of limited and uncertain rainfall, and South China, a land of benign climate and abundant moisture; between predominantly level, dust-blown plains and dissected, verdure-clothed hills; between growing seasons of seven or eight months and year-round continuous growth; between wheat and millet on the one hand and rice on the other; in short between precarious livelihood and potentialities for prodigal abundance.⁹⁹ Tṣ'įo extended particularly far south, reaching deep into Hu-nan in the vicinity of the Tung-t'ing lake. When, towards the close of the 3rd century B C, Shih Huang-ti welded the last survivors of the Contending States into a unitary polity, his empire reached from the löss uplands in the west to the Yellow Sea in the east, and from the north of present-day Ho-pei to northern Hu-nan.

The diversity of this environmental base is explicitly evident in two of the oldest Chinese geographical documents extant, and is implicit in numerous other writings from the Chou period. The oldest of these accounts is the **Gįwo-Kung or Tribute of Gįwo [Yü], which now constitutes a chapter in the Shu-Ching. Gįwo was a culture hero, probably of central Chinese origin, who, during the period of the Contending States,¹⁰⁰ was incorporated into the systematized dynasties of ancient times as founder of the Hsia. For this reason, and also because it includes information about the Yang-tzŭ valley, the Gįwo-Kung is itself today usually ascribed to the Chan-Kuo period. This is undoubtedly true of the text, but may be less than the truth so far as the substantive material which it contains is concerned. In the first place the schedule of tribute products is arranged on the basis of natural regions, with no allusion to the political structure of the Contending States. The organizational framework is that of another, and presumably much older, age. In the second place the inventory of natural resources and products is fuller for the three inner provinces, which occupied approximately the territories of the old Chung-yüan, than for the six outer provinces, which may be held to imply that the text was originally compiled in this metropolitan area. In the light of these considerations it would appear not unlikely that the *Gjwo-Kung* is a cumulative text, cast in its present form during the era of the Contending States, but incorporating material from one or more earlier periods. In later times it exercised great influence on the thinking of Chinese scholars, and it may well be that some of the material was already old, perhaps almost sacrosanct, when the present recension was made. Possibly the hallowed name of Gjwo, in view of that culture-hero's achievements and the legends associated with his bronze cauldrons, was likely to become attached to any serious compendium of geographical information, and an original nucleus of matter may have been repeatedly augmented as it was transmitted across the centuries under his name. The Ptolemaic corpus provides an interesting parallel in the Western world. What is of interest in the present context is the evidence of this document for a tribute system which reflected a natural environment of considerable diversity.

The second work which attests the regional diversity of the Chou realm is the chapter entitled **$T\!\!\!/jak$-$pjwang$-$djeg$ (*Chih-fang-shih*) in the *Chou-Li*. This work, in the form in which it now exists, may well be of Han date, and is certainly not earlier than the Chan-Kuo, but its contents are equally certainly cast in an antique mould. The attribution of 'profitable items', that is natural products, accords fairly well with that of the *Gjwo-Kung*, and both works may in fact derive from a common, but ancient, tradition.

Of greater significance than the mere fact of diversity is the implication of scattered fragments of evidence of an incipient regional specialization in handicrafts,[101] but apart from the production of salt on the coast and various forms of mining in the interior, this could hardly have gone farther than the fabrication of exotic luxuries. And, according to the *K'ao-kung Chi*, a primitive lack of craft specialization still prevailed in Gjwăt, ·Ian, and Dz'jĕn, where every man was, respectively, his own blacksmith, armourer, and spear maker.

Technology. Throughout the Chou period the basis of the economy was agriculture, but there is little evidence of technical innovation during the first half of the dynasty. During the Western Chou, cultivation seems to have been effected by men working in pairs and using caschrom-like, wooden implements known as **$ljwar$-$dzjag$ (*lei-szŭ*).[102] At least some of the fields were cultivated on a swidden cycle, and the crops were those of Shang times, although rice became of vastly greater importance as the Yang-tzŭ valley states were absorbed into the Chinese culture realm. Iron hoe blades and sickles began to appear towards the end of the Ch'un-Ch'iu,[103] though it is doubtful if they became at

all common until another century or two had passed, and had certainly not
wholly supplanted bronze and stone tools even at the close of that era. More
significant was the introduction of the ox-drawn plough and more efficient
methods of fertilization in the period of the Contending States. At the same
time there was a great expansion in the practice of hydraulic engineering, both
for irrigation of crops and for transport of commodities, a development which
is partially documented in the latter, and therefore non-mythical, part of the
chapter on 'The Yellow River and its canals' in *Shih-Chi* (chüan 29). Early in
the Contending States an irrigation system based on the **Ṭịang (Chang)
river brought prosperity to the district of **G'â-nəp (Ho-nei) in Ngịwər.[104]
At the end of the 4th century BC a scheme was initiated for the control of the
waters of the Ch'eng-tu plain[105] and the completed system, only slightly
modified, is still functioning today. In the north a vast area of Dz'ịĕn territory
was rendered productive when a giant canal, over 300 *li* in length, was constructed between the Ching and Lo rivers in Shen-hsi.[106] It was claimed that on
the completion of this project the Lands-within-the-Passes were converted into
fertile fields, yields were raised five-fold,[107] and the people of Dz'ịĕn no longer
suffered from lean years.[108] Contemporaneously there was an improvement in
the efficiency of water-lifting devices, notably the introduction of the counter-
balanced bailing bucket (*chieh-kao*), first mentioned in a well-known passage
of the *Chuang-tzŭ*.[109] Yet, despite these innovations, Chan-Kuo farming was
still relatively primitive, with few safeguards against the vagaries of the weather.
Li-K'uei, a jurist and minister at the court of Gịwad in about 400 BC, is alleged
to have reckoned the variation in yields as oscillating between a fifth of, and
four times, the average.[110]

The diffusion of iron technology during the Contending States period has
already been mentioned in connection with the introduction of hoes and
plough-shares. The Chinese had been familiar with techniques of iron casting
since the end of the 6th century[111] – which is not surprising in view of their
splendid tradition of bronze foundry. It is usually accepted that the first literary
reference to the use of iron refers to the 29th year of Duke **D'ịog (Chao), that
is 513 BC, but the earliest tools so far excavated date only from the 5th century
BC. From late in the 4th century iron began to be forged,[112] but this innovation
seems to have had a greater effect on the form of weapons than on that of agricultural implements. It was at just about this time that long iron swords came
into use, first it would seem in the armies of Tṣ'ịo and later in those of Dz'ịĕn.
In the 3rd century long single-edged blades, which occur in some quantity on
archeological sites, may have been instrumental in establishing the supremacy
of the Dz'ịĕn armies.

Meanwhile the old Shang traditions of ceramic manufacture, jade carving,
lacquering, and bronze foundry continued into the early Chou, together with
the working of stone, bone and shell. These last three industries remained in the

Shang tradition, but pottery and jade craftsmanship achieved major advances from the point of view of both technology and aesthetics. Bronze working, too, underwent technological improvement, chiefly in the process of the casting-on of accessories, although there was a decline in general quality during the Contending States. Each of these traditions is worthy of, and indeed is a subject of, study in its own right, and the fact that they are not discussed in the present instance reflects only their lack of direct relevance to the study of urban origins and diffusion.

Land Tenure. A comparison has frequently been made between the economic institutions of the Western Chou and those of the manorial system of Western Europe. Certainly the early Chou economy was based on predominantly self-sufficient agricultural units in the form of fiefs of noble households, within which neither exchange nor labor specialization was very important. A peasant worked both the fields allotted to his family and, probably, part of his lord's demesne land as well. We need only note in passing the long-standing controversy over the precise nature of the **tsi̯ĕng-d'ien* (*ching-t'ien*) or well-field system of land settlement which is described in the *Mencius*[113] and, derivatively, in the *Chou-Li.*[114] In this system, it is alleged, eight peasant families each cultivated its own holding (**si̯ər-d'ien : ssŭ-t'ien*), at the same time as all joined together to cultivate a centrally located demesne tract belonging to the lord (**kung-d'ien : kung-t'ien*).[115] It is extremely unlikely that such a checkerboard pattern of landholdings could have been established as rigorously as Mencius implies over any considerable area, and certainly not even the territory of a single benefice, let alone the whole of the Chou kingdom, could have been carved up in this fashion. Beyond that there is little agreement among scholars as to the implications of the texts. There are those who regard the whole system as an idealization conceived in the minds of later writers purely for didactic purposes,[116] and there are those, K'ang Yu-wei among them,[117] who have accepted it as a practical mode of agricultural colonization devised by sages in some socialist millennium of antiquity. Between these two polar views is ranged a spectrum of opinions which between them take account of almost all possible interpretations. One of the most interesting of these is Wolfram Eberhard's suggestion that the *tsi̯ĕng-d'ien* units arose as semi-military *colonia*-style settlements of Chou tribesmen under the direction of their clan leaders, and amid an initially hostile Shang population.[118] In this case the system would have been a prerogative of the Chou conquerors. Probably a majority of Chou scholars today concede that the notion of *tsi̯ĕng-d'ien* does perpetuate some kind of social and economic land system of Western Chou times in which both agricultural land and its produce were communally shared, with the fief holder pre-empting a ninth part of the harvest. If this were so Ch'i Ssŭ-ho does not exaggerate unwarrantably when he compares the *kung-d'ien* with the demesne land of the European manor and the *sįər-d'ien* with the land held in villeinage.[119] Whether the name *tsįěng-d'ien* implies that the nine units of cultivation did in fact share a common well, or whether the term arose because of a graphic resemblance of the idealized Mencian layout to the character for well, is still a topic of contention which need not, however, delay us at this time.

During the Ch'un-Ch'iu period it is possible, ambivalent though the evidence proves to be, to discern a change in the relationship between lord and cultivator. There are increasingly frequent indications that taxes in kind were being substituted for labor services. The *Tso-Chuan*, for example, ascribes the imposition of the first tax of this kind in the state of Lo to the year 594 BC,[120] and it is implied in the *Lun-Yü* that the rate was customarily a tenth of the harvest,[121] a figure that is almost certainly too low. When the cultivator paid such a tax to a member of the landholding nobility he had become virtually a rent-paying tenant, but with the elimination of the less powerful noble houses and the concentration of political power in the hands of progressively fewer territorial magnates, the peasant not infrequently found himself the tenant of a landowner who occupied the supreme position in the state, of the ruler in fact. It is unknown if the figment of Royal Chou suzerainty subsumed a claim to personal ownership of all the territory of the Chinese culture realm, but it is evident that in practice land was annexed, ceded and exchanged without reference to the wishes of the Chou monarch. As Hsü Cho-yün remarks, what mattered was not the ritually sanctioned claim to territory by a universal ruler, but the control which a member of the power élite could exercise over it,[122] and 'possession' is consequently a more apt term than 'ownership'. In any case, what is certain is that the tenant who paid a tax to a state – or, in other terms, a rent to a ruler – had freed himself from the bonds of serfdom. He was in essentially the same position as those other farmers who, during the Ch'un-Ch'iu and the Chan-Kuo periods, had brought waste land into cultivation or reclaimed fields abandoned during the ever-recurring wars, and not greatly different, so far as tenure was concerned, from those who were awarded grants of land in return for signal services to their ruler. All were virtually private landowners.

But if land was now often in private ownership, it had also become a purchasable commodity and the way was open for its concentration in the hands of the economically powerful. There is abundant evidence that this process was accelerated during the Chan-Kuo period, when a new class of merchant-capitalists turned the profits of trade towards the acquisition of land, the only form of investment, given the insecurity of the times and the relatively primitive character of economic instruments, available to them. But the lands which went to make up the estates of this new class of 'nobles without rank and lords without scepters'[123] were acquired at the expense of a peasantry poorly equipped to weather the storms of economic change. The social and political tracts of the time emphasized two mutually interacting factors as operating especially powerfully to prise land out of peasant hands, namely a combination of heavy taxation and unseasonable labor service bearing on the cultivator on the one hand, and the ready availability of concentrations of capital in the hands of merchants on the other. And to mediate the interaction between these two groups there was evolved the instrument of usury, the oppressive character of which is described graphically enough in the *Kuan-tzŭ*.[124] The final outcome was that, by the end of the Chan-Kuo, in most of the states for which information is available, there had emerged a class of landless laborers owning 'not an inch of soil', as the saying went. The cycle did not everywhere run its course with the same rapidity, but the trend was universal during the later years of the Contending States, always involving an apparently inevitable progression from a familial lord-and-subject bond, through the contractual lien of creditor and debtor, to the impersonal relationship of master and hired hand.

Commerce. In the Spring-and-Autumn period, and presumably in earlier centuries, merchants figured among the retainers of noble households but, in a context of self-sufficient manorial-style socio-economic units, and in view of the concomitant absence of an active market and a developed monetary system, their role in the conduct of exchanges could have been of only relatively small significance. The commodities which passed through their hands were probably restricted to salt, metals and a fairly narrow range of luxury items. On the dissolution of the Chou kingdom into politically autonomous states, a multiplication of toll stations further hampered the development of commerce, though the Ch'un-Ch'iu era did witness the negotiation of some mutual agreements on border tariffs.[125] Not until the latter half of this period is there evidence of the emergence of a powerful merchant class, presumably encouraged at that time by the establishment of centralized governments over larger and larger tracts of territory, the improvement of roads and the construction of waterways, and the incipient delineation of a regional specialization and interdependence in natural products and craft goods consequent upon the extension of Chinese culture into new and varied environments.[126] *Pari passu* with this expansion of commerce bronze money came into general use. Strings of cowries seem to have been used as media of transaction, and therefore fulfilled some of the functions of money, during Shang times, and metals and cloth were both used in the same way in later centuries, when salaries were also paid in grain. In fact commodities were used to make payments throughout the Chou era, but a metallic currency of fixed value was introduced in either the 4th or 3rd century B C,[127] thus fostering more complex modes of exchange and facilitating capital accumulation.

The instruments of exchange employed by Chan-Kuo merchants are not readily apparent from the archetyped texts of classical China, but it can be inferred with confidence that they attained only a low degree of economic sophistication. The volume of trade is attested less by direct references in the texts than by the resources commanded by some parvenu merchants, as evidenced by their ability to acquire large landed estates.

THE ARCHEOLOGICAL RECORD

It cannot be doubted today that the only material which can be regarded as of primary character for the study of urbanism during the Western Chou – possibly for the whole of the Chou period – is properly attested archeological evidence, while the transmitted texts must be considered as of only secondary importance. In these circumstances it is doubly unfortunate that archeological discoveries pertaining to the Western Chou period are exiguous in the extreme, often of doubtful scientific validity, and restricted largely to tombs. We have seen already that evidence relating to the Chou before the conquest is of even smaller quantity and poorer quality, and it will be demonstrated subsequently that material is by no means abundant for the era of the Eastern Chou. Numerous of the Chou settlement sites are occupied by present-day cities, so that archeological investigation is often limited to chance exposures revealed during construction work. Other sites have been ploughed so frequently during the last twenty centuries that the imprint of urban life has been wholly obliterated, while many ancient cities remain as yet unlocated. Although the ruins of nearly a score of Chou cities are known, not one has been subjected to thorough investigation. Indeed, most have been surveyed rather than excavated. And although a proportion can be identified as foundations of ancient times, only rarely can they be ascribed dates accurate to within a century or so.

THE WESTERN CHOU

Although literary sources refer to the founding of cities in pre-conquest times, so far no archeological evidence of urban life at that time has been brought to light. Before World War II Shih Chang-ju carried out a preliminary survey of those districts in which the pre-conquest capitals were traditionally supposed to have been located, but he apparently failed to find any remains of indisputably urban forms.[128] However, both Shih and subsequent investigators[129] have established with certainty that pre-conquest Chou culture developed out of a Lungshanoid regional tradition strongly influenced by secondary diffusion from – and, if the traditional literary texts are to be trusted, political domination by – the Shang metropolitan territory. It should be noted that, although no distinctively urban features have been demonstrated at pre-conquest archeological sites, yet one of the settlements constituted a more or less fully occupied area of some 480,000 square meters.[130]

Several settlement sites of Western Chou date have been excavated, notably those at Chang-chia-p'o[131] near Hsi-an, at Hsi-kuan-wai[132] near Hsing-T'ai, at Tung-Chai in Cheng-Chou,[133] at Wang-wan in Lo-yang,[134] at San-li T'un

135

in Chiang-su,[135] and at Chin-p'en in Hung-an in the middle Yang-tzǔ valley,[136] but the only investigations which have revealed indications of urban form are those of Ch'eng-tzǔ Yai, near Chi-nan in Shan-tung.[137] This was the site in ancient times of the capital of the small state of **D'əm (T'an), allegedly founded by a Shang benefice holder whose descendant featured in Eastern Chou times as a *tsįəg*.[138] An examination of the relevant literary sources led Tung Tso-pin[139] to conclude that this ceremonial center was established in about 1200 BC, and was still in existence as late as 200 BC, even though the Ch'un-Ch'iu recorded its destruction (**mįat : mieh) by Dz'iər in 684 BC.[140] Indeed, the excavators of the city have claimed to see evidence of this event in two mass burials, both devoid of funerary furniture, which were found close under the north wall of the city. Probably the walls were razed at that time but, if so, they appear to have been subsequently restored.

The city had been built on a site long occupied by a Lungshanoid people. The walls, which formed a more or less rectangular enclosure of approximately 450 × 390 meters, were of a composite character. The Chou – or, if Tung Tso-pin is correct in his conclusions, perhaps the Shang – builders had incorporated into their new structures old Lungshanoid walls that were already in an advanced state of dilapidation. Both elements were of *hang-t'u* construction. Near the wall were four pottery kilns manufacturing typical Chou grey ware.

THE CH'UN-CH'IU PERIOD

Lo-yang. In Chou times there were two cities in the neighborhood of present-day Lo-yang. According to transmitted texts **Dįěng-Tįôg (Ch'eng-Chou), built to house the population of the old Shang capital, lay to the east of the modern city, with the Ch'an river to its west and the Lo river on its southern flank, while **Gįwang-Dįěng (Wang-Ch'eng) or the Royal City, also known as **Kap-ńįuk (Chia-ju), was situated to the west of present-day Lo-yang, in an angle between the Chien and Lo rivers (Fig. 10). Both cities were mentioned in literary and bronze epigraphic texts, but the *Ch'un-Ch'iu* leaves us in no doubt that, during most of the 7th and 6th centuries at any rate, Gįwang-Dįěng, the city where King Mįwo (Wu) was believed to have deposited Gįwo (Yü) the Great's nine cauldrons, was considered the more important. This is not surprising in view of the fact that the city, as its name implies, became the capital of the Royal Chou when the court was transferred from G'og in the Wei valley to the east in 771 BC. It retained this status for twelve generations, but in about 509 **Klįǎng-Gįwang (Ching-Wang) chose Dįěng-Tįôg, which had meanwhile attracted to itself the sobriquet of **G'å-to or Lesser Capital, as his metropolis. Towards the end of the Chan-Kuo, however, the honor was restored to Gįwang-Dįěng by **Nan-Gįwang (Nan-Wang), penultimate ruler of the Chou dynasty. Archeological investigation has been focused exclusively

136

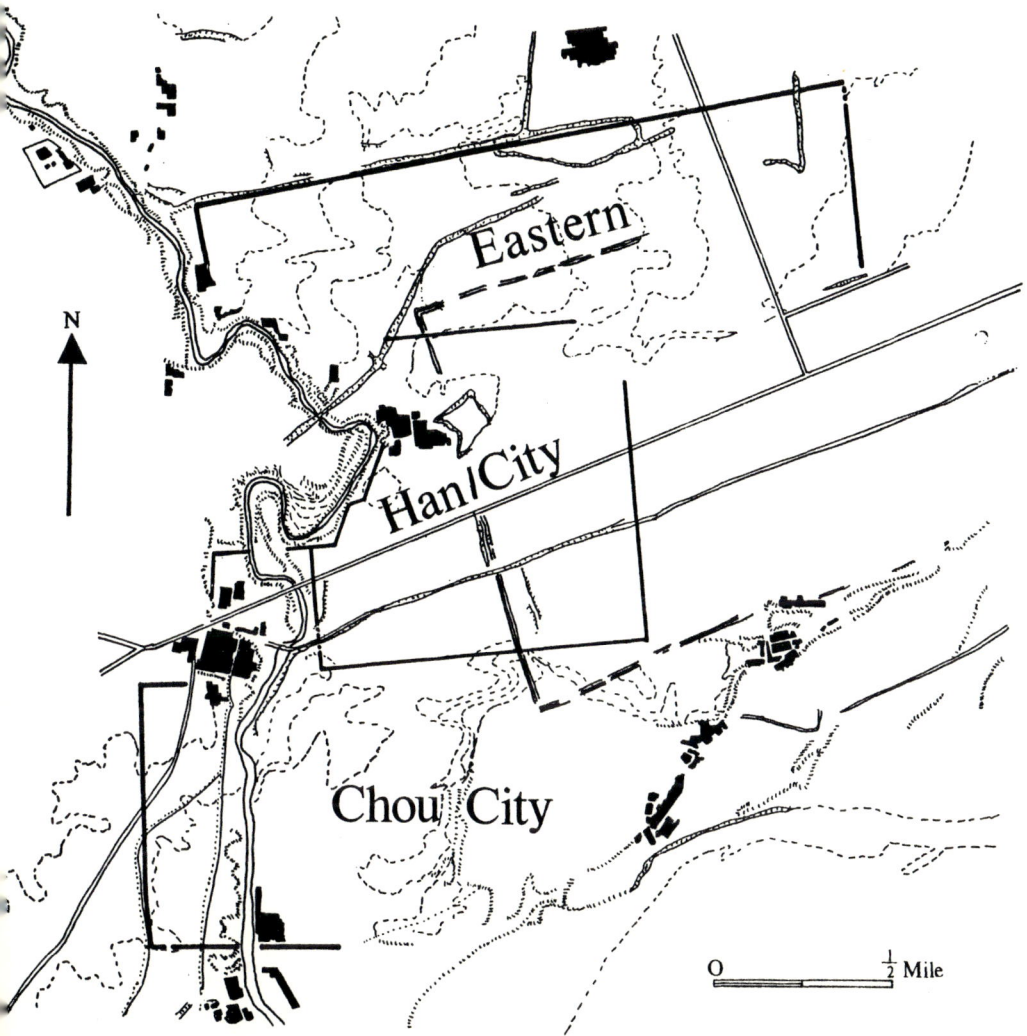

[10] **Gi̯wang-ḍi̯ĕng (Wang-Ch'eng), royal city of the Eastern Chou.
Based on Ch'en Kung-jou, 'Lo-yang Chien-pin Tung-Chou ch'eng-chih fa-
chüeh pao-kao', *K'ao-ku Hsüeh-pao*, no. 2 (1959), fig. 1. This record of excavation can be contrasted with the stylized symbolism that was attributed to
Gi̯wang-ḍi̯ĕng in the Chinese literary canon and which is depicted in fig. 23
on p. 415.

on the Royal City but, even though work began more than a decade ago, to date only preliminary reports have been published.[141]

Sections of walls of *hang-t'u* construction which have been traced imply that the city was in the form of a rough square with sides of about 3,000 meters and an area of no less than 8,000,000 square meters. So far only the northern wall, the northern section of the eastern wall, both northern and southern sections of the western wall, and a part of the southern wall where it forms the southwestern corner, have been traced, but these are sufficient to show that the thickness of the walls varied considerably. At their narrowest in the west they barely exceeded five meters, whereas at their widest in the east they attained a thickness of fifteen meters. More than two and a half millennia after their construction the surviving portions range from one-and-a-half to four meters in height. To date no traces of the street plan or of the gates have been uncovered, but it has been suggested that quantities of pottery tiles bearing *t'ao-t'ieh* and cloud-scroll patterns may point to the central and southern sectors of the city as the former sites of the Chou royal palace and other important buildings. A pottery kiln was excavated in the northwestern sector of the enceinte, together with an adjacent house foundation presumed to be the dwelling of a craftsman, and workshops for the manufacture of bone tools and stone ornaments have been brought to light in the same general area. At various points water channels have been uncovered, but there is so far no way of knowing if they formed part of an integrated drainage system. Analysis of the cultural remains found in different parts of the city indicates that the walls were built before the middle of the Ch'un-Ch'iu period and were already undergoing repairs as early as the Chan-Kuo, and that the site was occupied continuously until late in Former Han times, a conclusion which is fully in accord with the literary evidence. Subsequently a much smaller city was constructed within the crumbling walls of Gįwang-Ḋįĕng and served as the seat of government for Ho-nan county.[142]

Hou-ma Chen. The choice in 1955 of the historic locality in southern Shan-hsi, known in Chou times as the **Sįĕn-D'ien (Hsin-T'ien) or New Fields, for the site of the planned industrial town of Hou-ma Shih led to the mounting of an archeological salvage operation which revealed two partially superimposed cities (Fig. 12, III), dating from the second half of the Ch'un-Ch'iu. These were identified as capitals of Tsįĕn state during the rule of no less than thirteen princes.[143]

The earlier of the two cities appears to have been that which is situated close to the present-day village of Niu. Its stamped earth walls, now only about one meter high, formed a quadrangular enclosure with sides of 1,340, 1,100, 1,740 and 1,400 meters respectively. Despite this irregularity in the lengths of the sides, the fact that the western and southern walls meet in a right angle imparts a general impression of cardinal orientation to the plan of the city. A section of ditch six meters wide and three or four deep on the outer side of the south wall is probably all that remains of a former defensive moat. Somewhat to the north of the geometrical center of the enceinte is a square, cardinally oriented platform of *hang-t'u* construction, which has sides of 52·5 meters and a height of 6·5. Whereas the northern edge is bounded by a vertical face, the southern is constructed in the form of a ramp. Sherds of pots and tiles would seem to indicate that the platform was surmounted by an architectural structure of some sort. Within the enceinte the excavators have revealed a section of road running from north to south and, in its excavated sector at least, wide enough for two or three chariots to advance abreast. Another road apparently ran round the inner face of the wall.

The second, and later, city is known by the name of the neighboring village of P'ing-wang. It was intruded into the northwest corner of the Niu-Ts'un settlement and it is, in fact, only this intrusive sector of its enceinte which has so far been traced. It is also clear that there was a cardinally oriented, triple-terraced platform of *hang-t'u* somewhere towards the center of the enclosure, though its precise geometrical relationship to the overall plan of the city will be determined only when the line of the rest of the walls has been traced. The excavators' reports leave the impression that this platform, with its three stages, was of more complex construction than that at Niu-Ts'un. It was certainly larger, measuring 75 meters at the base of each side and rising to a height of 8·5 meters. Like the platform at Niu-Ts'un, it was provided with a ramp on the southern side but descended vertically to ground level on the north. And, also like the Niu-Ts'un structure, it carried on its upper level a building of imposing dimensions. The excavators of these sites refer to both the platforms as 'palace foundations', though it seems more likely that they were the mounds on which were raised successive ancestral temples of the Tsjĕn ruling family. Certainly they were impressive structures, facing over the city and approached by long ramps.

Remains of dwellings have been discovered both within the city enceinte and grouped in villages to the south and east of the Niu-Ts'un settlement. The dwellings were all semi-subterranean in character, and a high proportion had tiled roofs. Their doorways invariably faced south. Interspersed among them were subterranean and semi-subterranean storage pits, some of unusually large capacity and measuring several meters in both width and depth, together with a number of wells. Not infrequently a storage chamber was linked with a living space to form one habitation complex.

The excavators leave us in no doubt that craft activities were not restricted to the environs of the city but were dispersed through the surrounding country-side. For example, two bronze foundries were located near the southernmost of the villages mentioned in the preceding paragraph, and it is significant that there is good evidence that they engaged in specialized production. Whereas at one site the moulds were designed exclusively for the manufacture of spades, chisels and *pu*-type coinage, at the other emphasis was equally strongly directed towards the manufacture of belt hooks and chariot fittings. In the same neighborhood as these foundries were two workshops, for bone and antler respectively, while a third was found a kilometer and a half to the southeast of Niu-Ts'un. Finally, not far distant from this last site was a craft settlement devoted solely to potting, where kilns and their ancillary apparatus occupied an area of half a square kilometer. Kwang-chih Chang has justly remarked on the similarity of this settlement morphology to that of some Shang urban forms, in which dispersed agricultural and craft villages were integrated into a political, social and economic nexus organized for the support of a ceremonial center. Presumably the groups of animal burials discovered half a kilometer south and three kilometers east of Niu-Ts'un constituted yet another element in this functional unity. The animals – chiefly horses, together with some sheep and a few cattle – had been placed, alive but with their feet tied, upside down in a series of pits arranged regularly in groups of either two or four. One of the pits contained an elephant which had been entombed in the same manner. Bronze and jade ornaments accompanied most of the burials and, although the precise purpose of these entombments is unknown, the excavators are surely right in suggesting that they were associated with important rituals conducted at the Tsjĕn court during Ch'un-Ch'iu times.

A third city has been discovered about ten kilometers to the east of the Sjĕn-D'ien.[144] The remains explored so far consist of a double enclosure oriented a few degrees east of north. The original form of the inner enceinte was probably that of a square with a side of 1,100 meters, but the K'uai river has eroded the southern edge of the city so that now only 600 and 1,000 meters of eastern and western wall respectively remain. The surviving walls now reach a maximum height of only three meters and are usually considerably less, but the foundations show that they were originally about twelve meters wide. The outer enceinte was of similar construction, though only the northern and western walls remain, respectively somewhat more than 3,100 and 2,600 meters in length, up to four meters high and nine thick. Some idea of the extent of this city can be gained from the fact that the distance between the two enceintes on the northern side is 1,400 meters, and about the same on the west. The space between the two eastern walls, though, is only a quarter as far, so that the inner city is not centrally placed in relation to the outer. The situation on the south has been irretrievably obscured by the encroachment of the K'uai river. Traditionally this locality was believed to be the site of the capital of **·Ok (Wo), a small independent territory which was occupied by a marquis of Tsjĕn in the 8th century BC. Subsequently it became the seat of the Tsjĕn rulers until they transferred their capital to the New Fields. The excavators seem inclined to follow literary tradition by equating these remains with ·Ok, but the ruins and associated cultural relics appear to be of rather later date. Certainly the city was occupied right through Chan-Kuo and into Han times, though this is not to deny that there may have been a continuity of occupance from earlier periods.

Chao-k'ang Chen. In 1959 a brief report was published recording the discovery of an ancient rectangular enceinte at Chao-k'ang Chen in Hsiang-fen, Shan-hsi, and in 1963 the meager information in this notice was amplified in a some-what longer article.[145] Apparently the sections of *hang-t'u* wall remaining were sufficient to imply dimensions of five kilometers from north to south and four from east to west. A broad avenue connected opposing gaps, presumably denoting former gates, in the eastern and western walls. A similar opening was observed in the northern wall, but the southern was so poorly preserved that no positive evidence could be adduced for such a gate on that side of the city, although it is to be presumed that such a one did exist. Another section of wall also came to light inside the southeastern corner of the enceinte, but cannot at present be satisfactorily related to the overall plan of the city. Conceivably it could have been part of an inner city such as we have seen existed at ·Ok. The dating of the foundation of this city cannot be precise, but early Eastern Chou potsherds recovered from the *hang-t'u* of the wall imply that it cannot have been established later than the Ch'un-Ch'iu period.

Wu-chi Chen. Two ruined cities have been observed as still existing in districts to the southwest of Wu-an Hsien in southern Ho-pei, territory which formed part of the ancient state of D'jog.[146] The more westerly, at Wu-chi Chen, was investigated in 1956 and reported to be unusually well preserved. It comprised a roughly rectangular enceinte 889 meters from east to west, 768 from north to south, and enclosing some 680,000 square meters of land. The walls varied from eight to thirteen meters in width and are still between three and six meters high. There was a gate in each wall after the manner of the site at Chao-k'ang Chen, but in the present case there were also the remains of paved roads leading into the city. Most attention in the preliminary survey – which has been the only investigation undertaken so far – was directed to a series of pottery kilns producing vessels, tiles and bricks, but semi-subterranean dwellings, burials and wells were also noted in the western sectors of the city. The remains in their totality indicate a period of occupation extending from the Eastern Chou through the Former Han.

No information is yet available about the second city in this neighborhood.

THE CHAN-KUO PERIOD

Altogether thirteen cities of Chan-Kuo date have been investigated at least cursorily.

**G'ân-tân* (*Han-tan*). It has long been recognized in traditional literature that the ruins situated some four kilometers to the southwest of the present city of Han-tan in southern Ho-pei are those of the ancient capital of D'įog state. The city itself was in the form of a cardinally oriented and only slightly irregular square, with two sides each of 1,475 meters, one of 1,456 and one of 1,387 (Fig. 11).[147] The Japanese excavators of the site provided us with one of the very few estimates of the original dimensions of a city wall : they accorded it a reconstructed height of no less than fifteen meters and a reconstructed width at the base of more than twenty meters. They also discovered gaps in the wall which were associated with debris of brick and tile, and consequently interpreted as gates, but their occurrence was irregular. Whereas there was only one in the east and two in both south and west, there were three in the north, which, given the predominantly southerly orientation of Chinese town planning, is a somewhat singular arrangement.

Within the city the north-south axis of the enceinte was delineated by four *hang-t'u* platforms. The most southerly, known locally as Lung T'ai or Dragon Terrace, was the largest : 13·5 meters high, and with sides of 210 × 288 meters at the base. Surprisingly no cultural remains of any significance were discovered on its summit. By contrast, the next platform to the north, 4·5 meters high and with basal dimensions of 49 × 51 meters, apparently supported a two-storey structure, for two parallel rows of stone pillar foundations were found *in situ*, together with flanking rows of bricks. The third platform, three meters high and 60 × 70 meters at the base, yielded tiles, pottery, knife-money and a few bronze and iron implements, but no stone foundations. Finally, the fourth and northernmost platform differed from the others in being circular, with a diameter of 62 meters and a height of 7·5.

This then is the city proper, but this simple plan which has formed the basis for numerous subsequent Chinese cities is, in this instance, complicated by the addition of an eastern annex. This consists of an enclosure about half the size of that of the main city, the eastern wall of which forms the western wall of the annex. The southern and northern walls of the annex are each 875 meters in length, and the eastern and western walls exceed those of the city proper by a few meters only. The annex also contains two square, cardinally oriented platforms arranged along a line parallel to, and to the west of, the north-south axis. There is, too, an as yet unexplained section of wall, more than 520 meters in length, running due north from the northern wall of the city proper, which it joins slightly to the east of the mid-point. Finally, both inside and outside the enceintes there are ten additional *hang-t'u* platforms, all square or rectangular apart from one which is circular, and all bearing bricks and tiles on their summits.

The cultural debris associated with this city points unequivocally to the Chan-Kuo period, which is why it is being discussed at this point, but G'ân-tân

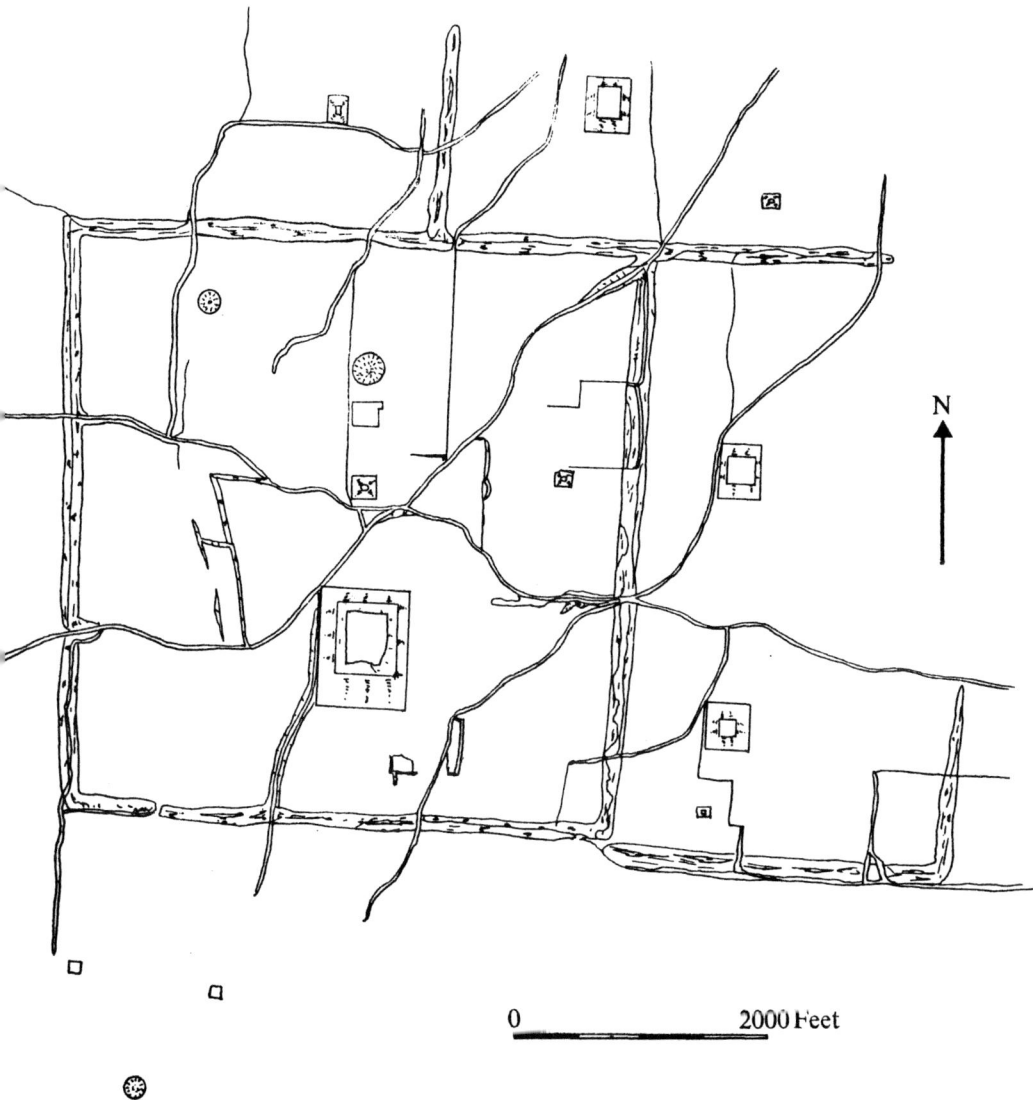

[11] * *G'ân-tân (Han-tan), capital of the state of *D'i̯og (Chao) from
386 to 228 BC. Redrawn from Komai Kazuchika and Sekino Takeshi, 'Han-
tan', *Archaeologia Orientalis*, series B, vol. 7 (1954), fig. 2.

was first mentioned as a city of Tsįĕn in reference to the year 500 BC.[148] However, it was not until 386 BC that it was chosen as the capital of the succession state of D'įog. It continued in that role until D'įog was extinguished (*mįat*) by the armies of Dz'įĕn in 228 BC.

G'ǎ-to (= *the Lesser Capital*). Excavations were carried out on the site of this ancient city of the state of ·Ian, near I-Hsien in Ho-pei, as early as 1930, and were resumed in 1958.[149] As it exists today the enceinte takes the form of an irregular figure with maximum measurements of 8,300 meters from east to west and 3,930 from north to south (Fig. 12, V). However, this curiously shaped enclosure gives all the indications of having been built up through time from a more or less regularly ordered nucleus, perhaps a square or rectangular enceinte, by the addition of sundry extensions and annexes. Indeed, excavations have already revealed that the southeastern sector was at one time separated from the rest of the city by a wall so that it constituted a smaller enclosure of 4,500 × 3,200 meters. Even today the average height of the walls exceeds five meters.

A distinctive feature of this settlement as it exists at present is a scatter of more than fifty *hang-t'u* platforms. They occur both inside and outside the enceinte but are particularly numerous in the northern sectors. Most are believed to have been burial mounds, but several in the northeastern parts of the city may have served as raised foundations for temples, much in the manner that similar structures in G'ân-tân did. The largest of these platforms, which attains a height of more than eight meters and which is known to the local people as Lao-lao T'ai (the Old Dame's Terrace), is actually outside the northern wall. It is square in shape with three terraces carved from its southern face, and it is surmounted by a circular mound, an arrangement which is reminiscent of the two parts of the diviner's board (*shih*), in which a discoidal plate representing the heavens (*t'ien-p'an*) was superimposed on a square earth plate (*ti-p'an*).[150] Architectural remains, pottery, bronze and iron weapons, ornaments, and coins were found on the upper terrace of this structure in some quantity.

It is thought that the inner enclosure was the site of the more important buildings in the city when G'ǎ-to was the capital of ·Ian. It is in the northern part of this area that the excavators found most of the more imposing platforms, together with a row of *hang-t'u* foundations arranged symmetrically in relation to the platforms and perpendicular to the inner northern wall, a pattern of construction which led them to infer that this was the palace precinct. Immediately to the southwest of this enclave are the remains of iron and bronze foundries, and in the southern part of the inner enclosure are relics of what has been interpreted as *sįag-ńįĕn* quarters, perhaps those of artisans or retainers. The city was probably occupied more or less continuously from 697 to 226 BC, but the cultural remains so far revealed relate exclusively to the Chan-Kuo period.

**Mịwo-Dịĕng (*Wu-Ch'eng*). The ruins of this city, which at one time formed part of the state of D'iog, are enclosed within a cardinally oriented enceinte approximately square in shape and with sides of 1·1 kilometers. The walls are twelve meters in thickness at the base, and five openings have been uncovered in each of the northern and western sides. Although the enceinte has been traced on the other two sides, the walls are in such poor condition that it has not been possible to elicit the arrangement of their gates. A ditch some 20–30 meters in length, below the outer edge of the northern wall, would appear to have formed part of a moat. Within the enclosure tiles, potsherds, *pu* coins, spindle whorls and bronze arrowheads indicate a floruit during the period of the Contending States.[151]

Ts'ai-Chuang. This locality, situated to the southwest of Chou-k'ou Tien in Ho-pei, is the site of the remains of another, but much smaller, city of ancient ·Ian. The walls can be traced on three sides, being in places still as much as three meters high, but evidence is lacking for the northern boundary. However, it is believed that the enceinte was originally square with sides of about 300 meters. A protruding section adjacent to the western wall may indicate the existence of a former annex or merely a reinforcement of a city gate.[152]

Lin-tzŭ. The ruins of an ancient city at Lin-tzŭ in northern Shan-tung, which has been identified as the capital of Dz'iər state during the Chan-Kuo period, was investigated by Japanese archeologists in 1940–1 and again by Chinese in 1958.[153] The *hang-t'u* walls formed a roughly rectangular shape, with approximate cardinal orientation and overall dimensions of 3,000 meters from east to west and 4,000 from north to south. The southeastern corner, which disturbs the regularity of the rectangular shape (Fig. 12, VI), may have been an addition to an essentially regular figure. Moreover, a smaller enceinte in the form of a square of about 1,350 meters side has been constructed over the southwestern corner of the main enclosure. Sekino Takeshi, the archeologist who excavated at this site in 1940, suggested that the smaller enclosure was the palace precinct of the prince of Dz'iər. If so, an oval-shaped *hang-t'u* platform, some 65 × 73 meters in size at ground level and situated just to the west of the center of this enclosure, may have been the supremely sacred spot of the Dz'iər territories, the altar to the Dz'iər god of the soil. A wide range of cultural remains have been found at sites scattered through the rest of the city, including tiles, bricks, potsherds, knife-money, bronze arrow heads and, allegedly, cowry shells, a clay mould for the making of bronze mirrors and a clay seal – though these last were obtained by purchase from present-day inhabitants rather than by excavation.

Ch'ü-fu. To the northeast of Ch'ü-fu in central Shan-tung are the ruins of a capital of the old state of Lo.[154] Its walls enclose an irregularly bounded oval measuring some 3·5 kilometers from west to east and about 2·5 from north to south. There is evidence of a single gate in the east, of two in the south and, curiously enough, of three in the north, but no trace has so far been uncovered of any entrances in the western side.

T'eng-Hsien. The ruins of two ancient cities have been discovered in T'eng-Hsien in southern Shan-tung.[155] The first, lying about twenty kilometers to the southeast of the present-day hsien city, are the remains of the capital of the former state of **Sịat (Hsüeh). They are enclosed in a rectangular enceinte of 3·6 × 2·8 kilometers, the walls of which still in places reach up to ten meters in height. There are the remains of one gate on the eastern side, and of two on both north and south, but again no evidence of an entrance on the west.

The second cluster of ruins in the vicinity of T'eng-Hsien are those of the ancient city of **D'əng (T'eng).[156] The general plan of the settlement is reminiscent of that of ·Ok, for it consists of a rectangular inner precinct of 900 × 600 meters, surrounded by an outer enceinte of 1,500 × 1,000 meters. The inner wall averages about three meters in height and its thickness varies from six to nine meters. There are traces of four gates, one on each side of the city.

Ch'ang-Chou. South of Ch'ang-Chou (Wu-chin) in Chiang-su are the ruins of the former capital of the ethnically Gịwăt state of **·Ịam. The layout of this capital is more complex than any discussed previously.[157] At the heart of the settlement is a roughly square enceinte oriented a few degrees east of north and measuring about a kilometer in circumference. It is known today as the Tzŭ-Ch'eng or Prince's City. Surrounding this innermost enclosure is another, also roughly square and of similar orientation, which is known as the Inner Wall. It is about three kilometers in circumference and was formerly bordered on its outer side by a moat. Finally, both these enceintes are set eccentrically within a third some six kilometers in circumference and known, appropriately enough, as the Outer Wall. This third wall was roughly circular rather than square, and was also moated on its outer side. Today both Outer and Inner Walls are razed almost to ground level, but the boundary of the Tzŭ-Ch'eng is even yet a prominent feature in the landscape. Between the Outer and Inner Walls in the western sector of the city is still to be seen a row of three earthen mounds bearing evidence of former buildings on their summits. Cultural remains associated with this settlement consist predominantly of pottery, stone tools, bronze vessels and, in the moat surrounding the Inner Wall, three dugout canoes, representing a mode of transport appropriate to the water-threaded terrain of the Yang-tzŭ delta.

146

Figure 12 (on the two pages following)

Plans of representative Chou cities on a uniform scale.

I. **Mịwo-dị̆ěng (Wu-Ch'eng), a city of **D'ịog (Chao) during the period of the Contending States. Based on Ao Ch'eng-lung, 'Ho-pei Tz'ŭ-Hsien Chiang-wu Ch'eng tiao-ch'a chien-pao,' *K'ao-ku*, no.7 (1959), fig.3.

II. **G'ân-tân (Han-tan), capital of **D'ịog (Chao) from 386 to 228 BC. Redrawn from Komai Kazuchika and Sekino Takeshi, 'Han-tan,' *Archaeologia Orientalis*, series B, vol.7 (1954), fig.2.

III. Remains of a capital of the Prince of **Tsị̆ěn (Chin) in a late phase of the Spring-and-Autumn period. Based on Ch'ang Wen-chai, 'Hou-ma ti-ch'ü ku-ch'eng-chih-ti hsin-fa-hsien' *Wen-wu Ts'an-k'ao Tzŭ-liao*. no.12 (1958), fig.1.

IV. **Gịwang-dị̆ěng (Wang-Ch'eng), royal city of the Eastern Chou. Based on Ch'en Kung-jou, 'Lo-yang Chien-pin Tung-Chou ch'eng-chih fa-chüeh pao-kao,' *K'ao-ku Hsüeh-pao*, no.2 (1959), fig.1.

V. The **G'å (Hsia) capital in the state of **·Ian (Yen). Based on Hsieh Hsi-i, 'Yen Hsia-tu i-chih so-chi,' *Wen-wu Ts'an-k'ao Tzŭ-liao*, no.9 (1957), p.61, and Huang Ching-lüeh, 'Yen Hsia-tu ch'eng-chih tiao-ch'a pao-kao,' *K'ao-ku*, no.1 (1962) fig.1.

VI. An ancient city at Lin-tzŭ which has been identified as a capital of **Dz'iər (Ch'i). Based on Shan-tung Sheng Wen-wu Kuan-li-ch'u, 'Shan-tung Lin-tzŭ Ch'i-ku-ch'eng shih-chüeh chien-pao,' *K'ao-ku*, no.6 (1961), fig.1.

147

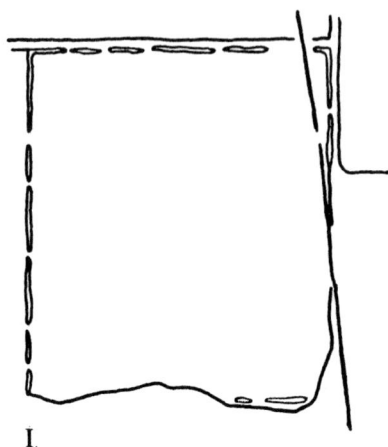

I.

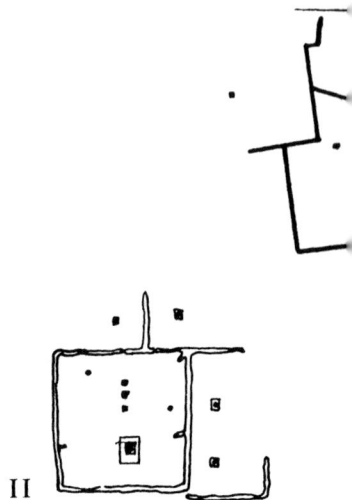

II

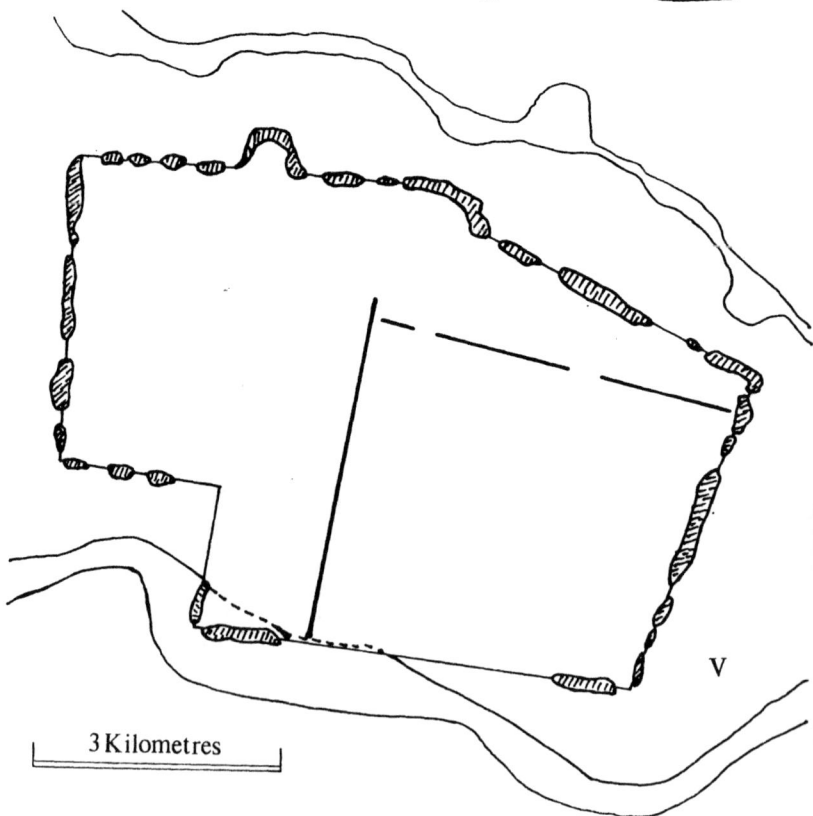

V

3 Kilometres

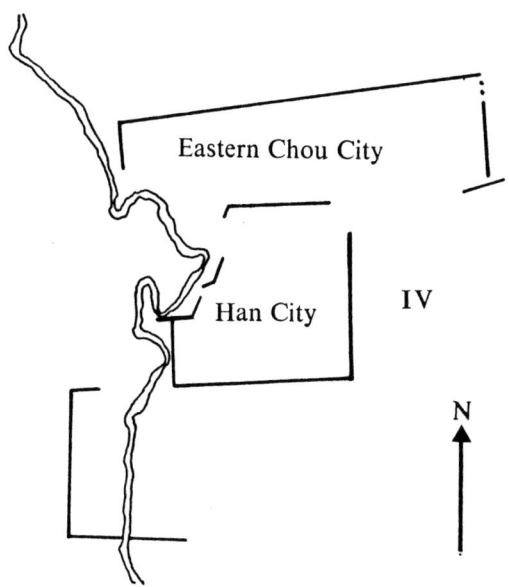

Eastern Chou City

Han City

IV

N

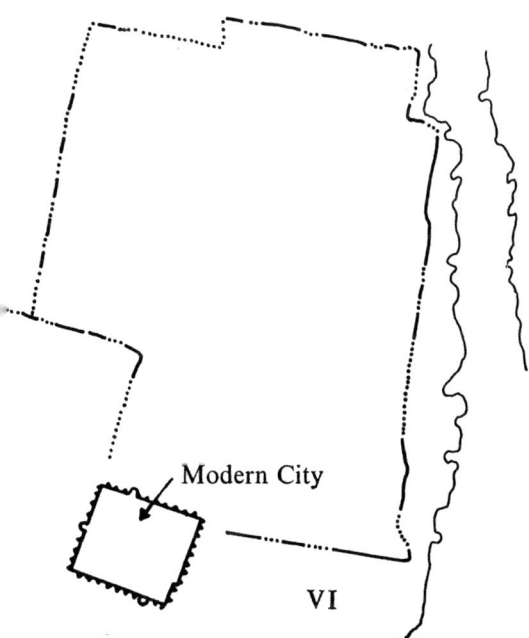

Modern City

VI

149

Hsi-Shan Hsien. The ruins of an ancient city have been discovered about a kilometer and a half northeast of present-day Hsi-Shan in southwestern Honan.[158] It was much smaller than most of the examples we have discussed, being roughly in the form of a rectangle only 800 meters from east to west and 850 from north to south. There can be no doubt that the settlement was constructed with the needs of defence in mind, for both its eastern and western flanks are set atop of sheer precipices, while the northern and southern walls are protected by moats.

Nan-yang Hsien. The present *hsien* city of Nan-yang occupies a part of an earlier and much larger enceinte on the same site. So far no excavation has been undertaken and the site has received only cursory notice.[159] The northeastern corner of the ancient enclosure is more than two kilometers to the northeast of the present city, and its *hang-t'u* walls have been traced for a kilometer and a half in roughly western and southern directions. At their base they were formerly about seven meters thick.

Hua-yin Hsien. At Yüeh-Chen in Hua-yin Hsien in Shen-hsi ruins have been found [160] which are thought to have been those of **·Jəm-tsjĕn (Yin-chin), a fortress city built by the Gjwad rulers close to their frontier with Tsjĕn and constituting an important node in a defensive system of which the great wall of Gjwad was perhaps the most impressive feature. The ancient city was roughly oval in shape, with its longer axis running approximately north-south. Sections of wall survive only in the north and west, the other two sides having been razed to the ground. The walls were 7·4 meters wide at the base, but were reinforced by an additional thickness of 5·6 meters where they adjoined a gate, and the gate itself revealed traces of additional fortification.

There has also been a cursory survey of a walled city of Ho-nan which is thought to have formed part of ancient G'ân, one of the succession states of Tsjĕn. So far no more than a short note on the morphology of the site has appeared in print, and it is impossible to evaluate the significance of the city beyond pointing out that it appears to have some pretensions to cardinal orientation and axiality.[161]

LITERARY SOURCES

The fact that only scientifically acquired archeological evidence can be considered primary for the study of Western, and perhaps later, Chou urbanism does not mean that the transmitted texts are completely worthless, but it is true that their value is different from that accorded them by traditional Chinese scholarship. They are not so much records of events as vehicles for the aspirations and values of subsequent ages. In a word, they have been archetyped, partly through an unconscious process natural to the passage of time and partly

150

through consciously undertaken historiographical editing and exegesis at least from Ch'un-Ch'iu times onwards.

There is a relatively extensive literature relating to the Chou dynasty but none of it is devoted specifically to the character of cities, so that materials for a history of Chou urbanism have to be abstracted from a large corpus of texts dealing with Chou civilization in general. They include works of an annalistic and genealogical character, prescriptions for rituals and ceremonies, folk lore and folk songs, dynastic hymns, philosophical treatises, moral tracts, and divination texts. The vast bulk of this material stems from the Eastern Chou and later, so much so in fact that reliable written records of Western Chou times are scarcely more numerous than are those for the Shang era. Indeed, the same literary sources often serve for both periods. The more important of these, such as the *Shu-Ching, Chu-shu Chi-nien, Shih-Chi* and *Shih-Ching* have already been discussed in connection with Shang urbanism in Chapter One.

As the activities of editors have been so pervasive, it is a matter of great difficulty to distinguish those texts which contain authentic accounts of genuine events from those which have been intentionally amended to afford support for later value systems and moral judgments. So intractable does this problem appear at first sight that some scholars, among whom Lou Kan-jou is fairly representative,[162] have eschewed the use of all texts other than the *Ch'un-Ch'iu, Tso-Chuan* and *Kuo-Yü*. Just after World War II Professor Bernhard Karlgren made an attempt to evaluate the available texts from the standpoint of their historical reliability. From a combined philological and historical point of view he distinguished what he called 'free' pre-Han texts from 'systematizing' or 'reconstructive' pre-Han texts, and both from Earlier and Later Han systematized texts.[163] Free texts are those in which, in his own words, 'accounts of ancient men, happenings and cults are given *en passant*, either as occasional records of events or inserted in speeches of politicians and philosophers, who refer to current traditions in elucidating some moral or political theme.'[164] Such, for example, are the *Shu-Ching, Shih-Ching, Tso-Chuan, Kuo-yü, Chan-kuo Ts'e, Lun-yü, Meng-tzŭ, Mo-tzŭ, Chuang-tzŭ, Li-Sao,* and *T'ien-Wen.* Systematizing texts, on the other hand, 'are the products of scholars who deliberately tried to lay down laws or make a consistent whole of the ancient traditions and ritual ideas. Their goal was to work up and compile a diffuse and heterogeneous material, to create a system.'[165] To this class belong, say, the major part of the *Li-Chi* and the whole of both the *I-Li* and *Chou-Li,* together with numerous later texts. Karlgren, by reason of his long familiarity with the texts and immense sinological erudition, was confident that he could distinguish between them. However, not all sinologists have been so confident. Wolfram Eberhard, in particular, has argued strongly that the distinction between these two classes of texts is not made anything like so easily as Karlgren supposed.[166] As an example of one of Karlgren's free texts which does in fact contain interpolations from Han times we may cite the *Tso-Chuan*, in which were inserted passages designed to validate the legitimacy of the usurper Wang-Mang's newly established dynasty.[167] If this is true of the *Tso-Chuan*, then, as the texts are closely related from the point of view of filiation, the same must also hold for the *Kuo-Yü*. On the other hand, what formerly appeared to be imaginative glosses on the genealogy of the Shang kings in Ssŭ-ma Ch'ien's *Shih-Chi* have since been confirmed by fully attested inscriptions from the oracle archives of that dynasty, a situation which can only be explained by hypothesizing that Ssŭ-ma Ch'ien had access to some treatise now lost, possibly, as Karlgren himself suggests, a genealogical list preserved by the ruling house of Sông.[168]

According to Eberhard, the consistency with which legends and beliefs are presented in the free texts, even in those of the most opposed schools, stems not, as Karlgren believed, from the preservation of their pristine form and freedom from corruption but from the unity of the *Weltanschauung* of the men who transmitted, and only too frequently amended and edited, them. In short, Eberhard denies the validity, and even in many instances the possibility, of assigning a particular text to one of Karlgren's categories, and argues that each section and aspect of a work should be examined on its intrinsic merits, in terms – as he puts it – of its structural matrix.[169] From this standpoint all texts are in a manner of speaking authentic in that all preserve versions of events presented in the context of their respective authors' ideological predilections. Some will have emphasized an aspect of which they approved, others will have suppressed it in the interests of denigration or, possibly, have selected an entirely different episode with which to press their point, but none of this was a prerogative of Han exegetes : Chou authors were no less prone to view the past in terms of their own present. What makes the Han glosses so prominent in our thought is that they frequently provide the form in which the text has been preserved until our own time. But even these glossifiers sometimes had access to texts no longer available to us, and an apparently late (because not confirmed by an extant earlier mention) version of events may sometimes be more reliable than that preserved in an earlier, but no less severely amended, recension. This is not to deny the immensity of the problems associated with the transmission of Chou texts or, in many instances, the opacity of Han glosses, but rather to question the absolute validity of a dichotomy into free and systematized texts in the sense in which Karlgren used those terms.

It would clearly be impracticable at this juncture to attempt a critical evaluation of all the literature relevant to urban evolution in Chou times, for that would encompass virtually all the literature relevant to Chou political, social, and economic development. The following notes are, therefore, restricted to a few of the texts of more than usual importance for present purposes. The most valuable corpus of written evidence for the period of the Eastern Chou is without doubt that incorporated in the *Ch'un-Ch'iu* and its associated commentaries. *Ch'un-Ch'iu*, meaning literally 'Springs and Autumns', was a generic name applied in Middle Chou times to the archival records of at least some of the Chou states,[170] but all have been lost, perhaps destroyed during the proscription of 213 BC, except a condensed and apparently garbled recension of the chronicles of the state of Lo from 722 to 481 BC. This is the *Ch'un-Ch'iu* which we have today, and which owes its preservation in no small measure to the fact that it was supposed to have undergone some unspecified form of editing by Confucius.[171] It has traditionally been held that in the process of redaction the Sage passed moral judgments on the actors, and thus handed on to posterity a grammar of political ethics. The difficulty resides in the fact that he expressed his judgments not by explicit statements but by a discriminatory use of terminology, a device which encouraged the rise of competing schools of exegesis. Confucius did, it is alleged, expound some of his judgments orally to his disciples, and these explanations were supposedly incorporated in explicatory traditions (*chuan*), of which three are still extant. Two of these, the *Kung-yang Chuan* (*The Tradition according to Kung-Yang*) and the *Ku-liang Chuan* (*The Tradition according to Ku-liang*),[172] are concerned principally to expatiate on the principles allegedly informing Confucius's moral judgments, but the third, the *Tso-Chuan* (*The Tradition according to Tso*[173]) confines itself mainly to elaborating the background to events which the Master had chronicled in terse, often elliptical, phrases. Towards the close of the Chou dynasty Tso's chronicle was arbitrarily combined with the annals of Tsi̯ĕn, Tṣ'i̯o, and Gi̯wad, and the whole subsequently distributed as a fragmented commentary on the separate sections of the *Ch'un-Ch'iu*. It is, consequently, quite proper to regard it as an historical compendium sectionalized so as to fit into the framework of a condensed version of the annals of Lo, and it is this combination of documentarily attested historical fact and supplementary oral tradition which constitutes the single most important literary source for the history of the Ch'un-Ch'iu period. In its present form it is said to comprise 170,000 Chinese characters, which would be the equivalent of at least 300,000 words in translation into any European language.

As we now reject the traditional view that the *Tso-Chuan* was solely Confucius's exposition of the esoteric implications of the *Ch'un-Ch'iu*, so we can equally disregard the belief which was espoused by the *avant-garde* historians of the sceptical movement at the beginning of this century that it was deliberately forged by Liu-Hsin (or by one of his associates) for political ends.[174] Analyses by Karlgren, Maspero and Ojima have disposed of any basis for such an argument. As early as 1926 Karlgren concluded that the Tso Tradition exhibited a homogeneous grammar consonant with a 4th-century date.[175] Subsequently, he was able to demonstrate that the text was known to Mao-Heng and Mao-Ch'ang when they wrote their famous commentary on the

Shih-Ching at some time prior to the middle of the 2nd century BC.[176] Meanwhile, Maspero,[177] utilizing some previous investigations by Ojima,[178] had succeeded in establishing that the ritual and ethical tradition contained erroneous references to winter solstices and eclipses which must have been calculated between 352 and 238 BC, while the chronicle sections incorporated exact prophecies of events which actually occurred as late as 327 BC, so that their redaction must have taken place after that date. Analysis of the same prophecies led Liu Ju-lin to conclude that the chronicle sections were compiled between 375 and 340 BC.[179] These scholars are by no means in complete agreement among themselves, but their combined efforts point uncompromisingly towards a date in the 4th century, and probably in the second half of that century, for the compilation of the Tso-Chuan. However, William Hung has also shown that several passages contain ideas which first entered into the amalgam of Chinese thought in later centuries, notably in Han times when Liu-Hsin set his imprint upon the work.[180] There is also reason to believe that sections of commentary were incorporated into the text at different times so that, although the Tso-Chuan demonstrably preserves a great deal of ancient material, it is prudent to adopt a sceptical attitude to the moralizings which occur from time to time. Such passages are easily concocted, and were the favorite media of redactors who wished to use a classical text for propaganda purposes. As early as Sung times, scholars such as Lin-Li questioned the authenticity of numerous of the paragraphs beginning with the phrase 'The superior man says . . .' and Legge passed the warning on to the modern world, together with a list of passages which he considered dubious.[181] And, clearly, passages which successfully predict events whose outcome could not have been known to their authors have been tampered with at some time or other. In the present work I have eschewed such passages as sources of factual information about events in ancient times but, even so, the Tso-Chuan remains a massive repository of material for any scholar concerned with Chou society.

Much the same situation obtains with regard to the voluminous Kuo-Yü (Discourses on the States), for long believed to have been fashioned from the materials on the Chou states other than Lo which were accumulated by Tso-ch'iu Ming during his preparation of the Tso-Chuan. As such it has traditionally been classified as an External Tradition (Wai-Chuan), while the Tso, Kung-yang and Ku-liang have been designated Internal Traditions (Nei-Chuan). Since Sung times, however, doubt has increasingly been cast on the common authorship of the Tso-Chuan and Kuo-Yü. Bernhard Karlgren in recent times, for instance, has, on grammatical and linguistic grounds, attributed these works to different authors working contemporaneously in the same school.[182] William Hung, on the other hand, has concluded that the Kuo-Yü is older than the Tso-Chuan and has attributed it to the very end of the Chan-Kuo period.[183] Hung's thesis is, in fact, a more sophisticated version of an interpretation put forward in 1891 by K'ang Yu-wei, who maintained that the *Tso-Chuan* was excised from a truly massive recension of the *Kuo-Yü* by Liu-Hsin.[184] Whatever view be taken in this matter, it is evident that this text must be used with caution.

Two other works which partake of the same general character as those we have been discussing also require discriminating attention. The *Lü-Shih Ch'un-Ch'iu* (*Master Lü's Springs and Autumns*), in twenty-six chüan, is an apparently eclectic collection of moral and political essays, compiled under the patronage of the Dz'iĕn chancellor Lü Pu-wei.[185] According to a codicil which has found its way into the middle of the book, it was completed in 239 BC. A great deal of the material which goes to make up this work has been traced back by Li Chün-chih and Liu Ju-lin [186] to its origins in the lore of the competing schools of the Chan-Kuo period so that, although subject to redaction in Ch'in times, it does preserve a reasonably faithful record of some aspects of Chan-Kuo thought. It appears virtually certain that a numerological symbolism underlies the form of this work. It is divided into three main sections symbolizing the Chinese trinity of Heaven, Earth and Man. The first of these sections is sub-divided into twelve chapters, each of which begins with a schedule of the rites and functions appropriate to a particular month of the year. The number associated with Heaven is, of course, twelve, but each of these chapters is further sub-divided into five sub-sections, representing the five elements which govern the workings of Heaven. The second main section is composed of eight chapters, each of eight sub-sections, eight being the figure numerologically assigned to the Earth. Man, symbolized by the third main section, is represented by six chapters, each with six sub-sections.

The second of these works is the *Chan-Kuo Ts'e* (*Intrigues of the Contending States*), one of the earliest of a class of writings known to the Chinese since Sui times as *Tsa-Shih* or *Miscellaneous Histories*. The authors of the patently discrete sections of this work are unknown, but the materials seem to have been selected from the records of Chan-Kuo diplomats, strategists and politicians which had been preserved in the Han Imperial Library, and the resulting collectaneum edited either then, or later by the scholar Liu-Hsiang. Since that time the book has undergone extensive alteration, chiefly at the hands of Sung exegetes, who attempted to replace lacunae in the text with imaginative glosses. The *Chan-Kuo Ts'e* in its present form contains numerous anachronisms, duplications and inconsistencies, which reveal only too clearly its composite, and even cumulative, character, but nevertheless the society, institutions and values which it portrays are essentially those of Chan-Kuo times.[187]

The books of ritual which at first sight appear to convey so much information about ancient China, and which have provided the material for numerous expository accounts of Chou institutions, are in fact nearly all later compilations. It was these works to which Karlgren pointed as prime exemplars of his class of systematizing texts (p. 151), and there is no doubt that they are, as he said, 'the products of scholars who deliberately tried to lay down laws or make a consistent whole of the ancient traditions and ritual ideas'. Nevertheless, it can also be shown that some at least of their information is based on fact deriving from even as early as the Western Chou period. The records of investiture ceremonies preserved on bronze ritual vessels, for example, bear out in a general way the prescriptions of the *Li-Chi*, and the arrangement of the tablets in the ancestral temples as detailed in the same work [188] has been partially confirmed by archeological investigation. Of the fifty-five investiture ceremonies described in Western Chou epigraphy and published by Kuo Mo-jo,[189] forty-four took place, as the *Li-Chi* prescribes, in the royal ancestral temple. For nine no locality was mentioned, and only two were definitely performed outside the capital. One of these was carried out at D'jĕng (Cheng), a site which possessed considerable ritual significance in the early years of the dynasty and which was itself to become the Chou capital in 509 B C, while the other took place at **G'ân-ts'jĕg (Han-tz'ŭ) when the king was undertaking a ceremonial progress through the realm.[190] In this particular instance the investiture was still carried out in the presence of the royal court. There is, of course, the possibility that bronze inscriptions similar to those studied by Kuo Mo-jo may have been used by Han systematizers as a model for an idealized ceremony, but, if so, this only serves as a guarantee of the accuracy of their reconstruction of the event. Of a more disruptive character are the warnings of Noel Barnard against epigraphic forgery, possibly on a considerable scale.[191] But on the whole it would seem that the testimony of epigraphy affords no inconsiderable support for the authenticity of certain sections of the ritual books.

A nucleus of what was later to be constituted as the *Chou-Li* (*Chou Ritual*) seems to have been in existence in some form late in the Chou era, because it featured among the works most actively suppressed by Shih Huang-ti in 213 B C. In the middle of the 2nd century B C a copy in archaic script, which had somehow escaped the proscription, was presented to the imperial library, where in about 40 B C it came to the notice of Liu-Hsiang. Unfortunately the last section of this copy was missing, and it was as a replacement for it that Liu-Hsiang substituted the *K'ao-kung Chi* (*Record of Artificers*), a work itself of some antiquity, possibly originally an official document of the state of Dz'iər. During the Han the whole work was known as the *Chou-Kuan* (*Officers of Chou*), a name which was changed during the *Tsjĕn* (Chin) dynasty to *Chou Kuan-li* (*Official ritual of the Chou*). Only in the T'ang did *Chou-Li* become the official title. During the Sung, scholars in general tended to discredit the work as a source for the study of Chou institutions, and Hu An-kuo went so far as to brand it a forgery of Liu-Hsin. However, Chu-Hsi's researches did much to re-establish the authenticity of the *Chou-Li*, which was not again questioned until K'ang Yu-wei mounted his attack on the veracity of the classics at the end of the 19th century. K'ang's allegations were in turn refuted by Ojima, Maspero, and Karlgren (cp. p. 151).[192] But none of this debate has done much to elucidate the crux that faces all researchers into Chou government and society, namely to what extent does the elaborately structured hierarchy described in the *Chou-Li* reflect actual conditions during the Western Chou period? After a recent re-evaluation of the evidence, Dr Sven Broman concluded that the Chou-Li 'depicts a governing system which, in all its essentials, prevailed in middle and late feudal Chou in the various states and has its roots in the system pertaining to late Yin and early Chou.'[193] If this were so, then Western Chou administration was of a rigidity unparalleled in any other known governmental system. My own reading of inscriptional materials and of the available 'unsystematizing' (Karlgren's 'free') texts does not lead me to the same conclusion, and, although Broman has adduced an impressive quantity of evidence, I am not convinced that it really implies such an involuted and inflexible system of government as that which the ritual texts portray. Nevertheless, faced with Broman's closely reasoned arguments, I am no little encouraged to find that Professor Creel shares my opinion.[194] His interpretation seems to accord closely with the general implications of the little that we know or can infer about Western Chou government from other sources. Briefly, he believes that the *Chou-Li* preserves a late Chan-Kuo elaboration of a system of government which did actually exist at one time, but that the relative contributions of Western Chou ritualists and later systematizers is still unsettled.

The *Li-Chi* (*Record of Rituals*) and *I-Li* (*Ceremonies and Rituals*) are less pertinent to present purposes and need not be discussed here. Both are essentially similar in character to the *Chou-Li*, that is they are 2nd-century compilations, systematizations in Karlgren's phrase, of earlier materials, which subsequently underwent further modification.[195]

The *Kuan-tzŭ*, in twenty-four chüan, is another of those ancient works which would be a valuable source for the background of Chou urbanism if its text could be dated with any degree of certainty. Although best known for its discussion of early economic theory, in particular an application of the quantity theory of money, this series of treatises contains a great deal of material relating to the ideologies of Chou China, political and administrative organization, etiquette, logic, natural phenomena, and even a chüan of what should perhaps be described as wisdom literature. Already by the 2nd century BC there was in existence a corpus of materials attributed to Kuan-Chung, chief minister of Duke Huan of Dz'iər during part of the 7th century BC. Late in the 1st century BC these materials were reconstituted by Liu-Hsiang, and it is essentially this recension which we have today.[196]

As early as the 3rd century AD Fu-Hsüan recognized that the then current version of the *Kuan-tzŭ* could not have come from the hand of Kuan-Chung.[197] Since that time there has developed a large exegetical literature dealing with the character, origin and transmission of the work, but only recently has there been any sustained attempt to evaluate the status of the text on a chapter-by-chapter basis. The first scholar to adopt this method of approach was Lo Ken-tse in 1931,[198] but the most successful use of this technique has been achieved by Professor Rickett.[199] In a work published only very recently he has been able to ascribe positive datings to twelve of the chüan, and even to parts of certain chüan. He has shown, for example, that the *Ta-K'uang* (** *D'âd-K'įwang*) chüan is composed of two discrete sections, an historical romance and a fragment of a philosophical treatise. Both were, on internal evidence, written in about the middle of the 3rd century BC, and probably combined by Liu-Hsiang more than two centuries later. The chüan entitled *Nei-Yeh* (** *Nəp-Ngįǎp*), by contrast, may have been written as early as the end of the 4th century BC and certainly not later than the beginning of the third. The *Fa-Fa* (** *Pįwǎp-Pįwǎp*) chüan is another composite chapter, consisting this time of three separate sections which may have been the work of one man or of three men belonging to the same school. All three sections should probably be dated to the end of the 3rd century BC. And each of the other chapters is of a similar nature and must be judged independently. Rickett has also endorsed the widely accepted theory that the nucleus of writings around which the *Kuan-tzŭ* crystallized was produced in the famous Chi-hsia (** *Tsįək-g'å*) Academy, founded by King Hsüan (** *Sįwan*) of Dz'iər in about 302 BC. Probably the collection began to take shape towards the middle of the 3rd century BC, was added to for another couple of centuries or so and finally stabilized by Liu-Hsiang perhaps between 230 and 220 BC.[200]

Numerous other works can be made to contribute fragments of information to the study of Chou urbanism, among them the *I-Ching* (*The Book of Changes*), the Taoist classics *Chuang-tzŭ* (*The Book of Master Chuang*) and *Tao-Te Ching* (*The Canon of the Way and its Power*), the *Hsün-tzŭ* (*The Book of Master Hsün*), the *Han-Fei-tzŭ* (*The Book of Master Han-Fei*), the *Meng-tzŭ* (*The Book of Master Meng*), and the *Lun-Yü* of Confucius (usually rendered into English as *The Analects*), but the exiguous quantity of material that can be extracted from their pages does not justify extended discussion of their authenticity. Suffice it to say that they are all composite and, what renders them the more difficult to handle from our present point of view, cumulative texts. Each of them – indeed, each fragment extracted from them – must be evaluated on its own merits and from the standpoint of the argument to which it is directed. In the present work I have been at pains to use these sources with discretion. This does not imply a simple process of acceptance or rejection, but rather of selection according to circumstance. A chance remark in, say, one of the Confucian classics may have no value in the documentation of an historical happening in the Western Chou period to which it purports to relate, but may yet be an authentic record of a Chan-Kuo belief. More often than not, however, even this kernel of truth will be enveloped in a cocoon of Han and later editing,

158

which must be carefully peeled away before the Chan-Kuo evidence is ready for use. Consequently the analysis of Chou institutions only too often becomes an exercise in the penetration of layers of interpretation and value judgments from later centuries. And, not infrequently, deep in the heart of the cocoon there lies not a record of a Western Chou event, perhaps not even an echo, but only the faint memory of an echo smothered in the resonant sounds of subsequent exegesis. Needless to say, only very rarely can this earliest memory be isolated from the web of values and ideas in which it has been encapsulated. Neither is it always possible to discriminate between the results of the process of archetyping which accompanies the passage of time and the deliberate emendation of texts in the interests of ideology. All of which helps to explain why literary sources relating to Chou urbanism must be used with extreme care.

Even though it has been mentioned in Chapter One it is perhaps necessary, in conclusion, to say a further word or two about the post-Chou *Shih-Chi*, for it is the earliest extant example of systematic Chinese historiography and is the only major source (secondary though it be in the sense defined on p. 135) for Chou history which belongs to that genre. Moreover, it is, among the works with which we are presently concerned, the one that has suffered least at the hands of redactors. Text and subsequent commentaries have been kept rigorously separate and, although at least one chapter is now missing in its entirety and several others appear to be incomplete or even fragmentary, the *Shih-Chi* is the best preserved among the works that we have consulted.

Collection of the material for, and apparently the conception of, a history of the Chinese people were initiated by Ssŭ-ma T'an, Grand-'Historian' at the court of Emperor Wu of Han, shortly after that ruler's accession in 141 BC. But the working out of the design, most of the actual writing, and certainly the general flavor of the history we owe to his son Ssŭ-ma Ch'ien. He it was who labored for more than twenty years to produce a monumental history, in 130 chüan, of the Chinese culture realm from the earliest times down to his own lifetime, say the end of the 2nd century BC, and in so doing forged a new medium for the transmission of political and social experience. Here, of course, we are concerned only with those sections of his work which relate to the Chou dynasty.

The *Shih-Chi* consists of five major sections, respectively *Pen-Chi* (*Basic Annals*), *Nien-Piao* (*Chronological Tables*), a series of Treatises (*Shu*) on rituals, music, astronomy, religious affairs and economics, thirty chapters entitled *Shih-Chia* (*Hereditary Houses*) which deal mainly with the pre-Dz'iĕn states, and finally seventy chapters of *Lieh-Chuan* (*Organized Traditions* or *Biographies*). Of these sections the *Annals* and the *Hereditary Houses* are both cast in the old annalistic mould which had characterized the historiography of Chou times, but Ssŭ-ma Ch'ien extended both the scope of the enquiry and the quantity of information handled. Most of the improvements, however, came with the later chapters relating to the Han dynasty, and for the earlier periods

Ssŭ-ma Ch'ien did little more than string together extracts from ancient works. As already mentioned, he appears to have had access to sources now lost which preserved in secondary form genealogical materials going back as far as the Shang dynasty. The *Tables*, in fact, are largely a systematization of such materials, but the attempt at a synchronization of events related in the old annals was new. The technical treatises are also innovations, as are the biographies. They represent new means of organizing material, around institutions and persons respectively, and mark the beginnings of an analytical study of the past. However, not a little of the biographical section is of an anecdotal or romantic character, which betrays its origins in the ancient tradition of historical romance, of which the first part of the *Ta-K'uang* chüan of the *Kuan-tzŭ* is a good example.[201]

For Karlgren, who apparently believed that no pre-Ch'in texts extant in the Han era had been lost since that time,[202] Ssŭ-ma Ch'ien was often no better than a forger. It is certainly true that the historian selected evidence to suit his purpose and fitted it into a framework in which it would do just that, namely render justice to the virtuous and cast reproach upon the unworthy, but I am aware of no specific instance in which it can be positively asserted that he manufactured the evidence. Where, as in the paragraphs relating to Huang-Ti, he is the earliest author to provide extant material, it may be hypothesized that he had access to texts now lost or that the record had been preserved orally, either among the Little Traditions of China (using that term in the technical sense advocated by Robert Redfield) through the centuries or, perhaps for a much shorter period of about four generations since the proscription of 213 BC, by individual families. Our conclusion is that, although Ssŭ-ma Ch'ien was by no means an objective historian, he was not a counterfeiter.[203]

EPIGRAPHIC EVIDENCE

Inscriptions on bronze vessels are of such importance, both actual and potential, for the history of the Western Chou that it is proper that they should receive brief mention here. However, for most of that period they derive from bronzes of the Royal Chou, and only towards the end of the era do vessels of other than Chou states begin to appear. The inscriptions are also restricted to a narrow sector of the total spectrum of Chou life, chiefly that concerned with ritual and ceremonial. Although this has implications for institutions not specifically of a religious nature, notably those of a political and social character, it is of only indirect relevance to the study of urbanism. During the Ch'un-Ch'iu, bronze inscriptions were still connected preponderantly with state functions, but it is observable that some powerful ministers were also beginning to use them in their private ceremonies. Finally, by Chan-Kuo times inscriptions were appearing on a wider range of vessels as well as on weapons, coins and a variety of other objects. It is one of the minor ironies of

Chinese history that, in the period when the secularization of epigraphy began to introduce a wider range of topics into inscriptions, the significance of those very inscriptions was greatly reduced by the preservation of much longer texts written in other media. Nevertheless, the bronze inscriptions do afford direct, if limited, access to the ideas of the time in a way that archetyped and edited texts do not, and as such provide an important check on the classical literature of the Chou era. They make a particularly valuable contribution to the study of the Western Chou, when other evidence, both literary and archeological, is exiguous.

THE SPREAD OF URBANISM IN CHOU TIMES

THE WESTERN CHOU

It has been shown in Chapter One that urban development in Shang times was, on present archeological evidence, restricted to an arcuate zone of the Chung-Yüan. On the outer edge of this zone was a fringe of territory apparently characterized by incipient urbanism. Literary records of dubious reliability refer to contemporary urban forms in the middle Wei valley, but such have not so far been attested archeologically.

During the early decades of Chou hegemony there is no reason to think that the situation was radically different. Presumably the spatial pattern of urbanism at that time comprised two main elements : Shang cities persisting into the later age, and the new foundations of the Chou conquerors. There is no way of knowing how many of the Shang cities survived into the new era, and speculation on this point will depend largely on the view taken of the Shang polity. If political complexity, despite the demonstrable cultural unity of the Shang people, had not advanced beyond the level of the city-state, for instance, then there is probably less likelihood of the pattern of Shang urbanism having persisted for long under Chou domination; for, when city and state are one, reorganization of the political framework tends to eliminate the *raison d'être* of a proportion of the urban foci. Cities with developed specialist functions outside the sphere of politics and administration are those which stand the best chance of survival. On the other hand if, as the transmitted texts would lead us to believe, there was indeed a Shang territorial state controlling a sizable tract of North China, within which cities enjoyed a degree of administrative (though not political) autonomy, then the old urban pattern would be more likely to have persisted under the new dynasty. The assumption of power by the Chou conquerors need not have precipitated a major dislocation of the urban network. But all this is supposition and serves little purpose beyond directing attention to a matter requiring further investigation. There were, in any case, ritual and cosmological aspects of urban life which have to be taken into account in this connection, and which are discussed in Chapter Five.

L   161

It is more profitable to turn to a discussion of the pattern of urban distribution during the Western Chou dynasty. After the conquest, the Chou king established his benefice holders in fiefs scattered strategically throughout the old Shang culture realm and, apparently, even farther afield, particularly in the east, on lands that had never been brought wholly within the Shang dominion and certainly not under Shang political control. Whereas some of these fief seats were entirely new foundations in the shape of garrison establishments created *de novo* by Chou aristocrats in both Shang and tribal territories, others may have been old Shang settlements adapted to new purposes. In any case they constituted a network of garrison posts, which were at the same time cult centers for members of the nobility. The number of such settlements is, as already mentioned, reported very differently in different texts, the figures ranging from 1,773 to considerably fewer than a hundred (p. 112 above and Note 20). No more than twenty-six of these seats are mentioned by name in any text, and that of a much later date. It is, in fact, the *Tso-Chuan*, under the 24th year of Duke **Xįǝg (Hsi : 635 B C), which enumerates the benefices established after the conquest.

'The King was incensed [at happenings which need not concern us here] and wished to invade D'jěng with the help of the D'iek. **Pįŭg-Ɗjǝn (Fu-Ch'en) remonstrated with him, saying "Forbear to do this. Your servant has heard that in high antiquity the populace was kept in tranquillity by virtue. In later times it was customary to show favor to relatives. Formerly the Duke of Ţįôg, grieved by a lack of accord with the two younger brothers [of King Mįwo], beneficed his relatives as fences and screens [to protect] Ţįôg. The [princes of] **Kwân (Kuan), **Ts'âd (Ts'ai), **Ɗjěng (Ch'eng), **Xwâk (Huo), **Lo (Lu), **Gįwad (Wei), **Mog (Mao), **T'nâm (T'an), **Kôg (Kao), **·Įung (Yung), **Dz'ôg (Ts'ao), **D'ǝng (T'eng), **Pįět (Pi), **Ngįwǎn (Yüan), **P'įông (Feng), and **Dzįwěn (Hsün) were descendants of [King] Mįwǝn in the d̂įog (chao) generation.[204] Those of **Gįwo (Yü), **Tsįěn (Chin), **·Įǝng (Ying), and **G'ân (Han) were descendants of [King] Mįwo in the *mįôk* (*mu*) generation. Those of **B'įwǎm (Fan), **Tsįang (Chiang), **G'ieng (Hsing), **Môg (Mao), **Dz'âg (Tsu) and **Kįwǝr (Kuei) were descendants of the Duke of Ţįôg (Chou).'

These benefices were identified by Ch'i Ssŭ-ho in a paper in 1946,[205] and subsequently plotted on a map by Chang Sen-dou, who took them as 'roughly representing the walled cities at that time'.[206] There are, I think, five, and possibly six, reasons why it is unlikely that this map presents an accurate – or even an impressionistic – picture of urban development in North China in about 1100 B C. First, the passage in which the schedule of benefices occurs is incorporated in a work compiled probably between seven and eight hundred years after the event, and fashioned into its present form some three centuries after that. Thus, at least a millennium elapsed between the alleged apportionment of the

162

benefices and the final redaction of the record, during which time the epic of the Chou accession to power had been archetyped, sanctioned by the invention of the theory of the mandate of Heaven, and integrated into a scheme of genealogies designed to validate the power exercised by the principal ducal houses of North China and the Yang-tzŭ valley. That this particular paragraph is not to be relied upon is confirmed by the implications of the *I Hou Nieh I* inscription with regard to the role of the Duke of T̂i̯ôg, which have been discussed in an earlier section of the present work (p. 108).

In the second place the notice in question is one of the moralizing passages which, we have already seen, are likely to be later interpolations. It purports to recount the remonstrance of a perspicacious and virtuous minister to a ruler about to embark on a course of action of dubious morality, and the schedule of names has all the hallmarks of a literary device rather than the similitude of an actual debate. I think there is every chance that the coupling of the reference to the Duke of T̂i̯ôg and the early days of the dynasty with the tale of Fu-Ch'en represents the fusion of a literary with an oral tradition in a manner that is only too characteristic of the *Tso-Chuan*.

Third, the genealogies on which this apportionment of benefices is based are more than dubious, but – and this is the fourth point – even were they reliable, it would appear that the schedule is incomplete, for additional territories are listed in a passage in the *Shih-Chi* (chüan 4), where **Tsi̯og (Chiao) was allegedly granted by King Mi̯wo to a descendant of Shen-Nung (**D̂'i̯ĕn-Nông), **T̂i̯ok (Chu) to a descendant of Huang-Ti (**G'wâng-Tieg), **G'i̯ĕg (Chi) to a descendant of Yao (**Ngi̯og), **D'i̯ĕn (Ch'en) to a descendant of Shun (**Śi̯wən), and **K'i̯əg (Ch'i) to a descendant of Yü (Gi̯wo [the Great]). In a second part of the same passage Mi̯wo is recorded as bestowing other benefices on ministers (mostly relatives) who had rendered distinguished service or sage counsel in the Chou cause. Some of the later territories are those which appear in the passage translated above, but one, **·Ian (Yen), is an additional name. I do not mean by this to imply that the map would be rendered accurate simply by combining these two lists of benefices. Clearly both are part of the lore of ancient Chinese genealogy, which embodies kernels of garbled fact [207] enmeshed in a tissue of imaginative glosses, and which can be accepted at its face value only at the scholar's peril. Were a third list still extant, no doubt it would afford yet a third variation on the theme.

Fifth, Ch'i Ssŭ-ho's identifications of the names in the passage from the *Tso-Chuan* are based not on research in the tangled thickets of toponymy in early Chou times but on the glosses of a long line of scholars, who in turn have relied predominantly on local tradition and, failing that, on standards of toponymic analysis which are presently unacceptable. Of course, there is no real doubt as to the position of the territory of Lo (although its boundaries cannot be delimited with anything approaching precision), or of Gi̯wad or even Ts'âd, but the locations of others of these benefices are by no means so certain. Karlgren expressed the very strongest doubts as to the traditional identifications of place names proposed by Chinese commentators.[208] Perhaps he was, as Eberhard contends,[209] a little too pessimistic, but the difficulties of relating names, which are not infrequently *hapax legomenon*, to localities in early Chou times are often insuperable. Certainly not all Ch'i Ssǔ-ho's identifications can be accepted.

About the sixth reason I am prepared to be less dogmatic. But a cursory check through the literary texts – by no means reliable sources, as I have been at pains to emphasize – leads me to conclude that, although they mention only twenty-six aristocratic seats by name, they imply a rather higher number. Furthermore, a total of twenty-six holdings, together with the domain of the Royal Chou, scattered through some 350,000 square miles of North and Central China, would imply benefices of a massive size compared with the inferred territories of the pre-conquest Shang city-states. This last is not a strong argument, but its deficiencies do not weaken my main contention that the notice in the *Tso-Chuan* is an inadequate basis for a map of early Chou urbanism.

Under the circumstances I can see no alternative but to abandon the attempt to map the distribution of urban centers at the beginning of the Western Chou dynasty. The most that can be said is that urban foundations either persisted or were established throughout the nuclear area of Shang culture, that is throughout the Chung-Yüan, and, within a relatively short space of time, were disseminated eastwards into the hitherto tribal territories of present-day Shantung, which came to constitute the state of Dz'iər. There seems also to have been a significant early development of urban forms in the valleys of the Wei river and its tributaries, which were the old Chou domain, but to what extent this had been initiated in pre-conquest times is still uncertain.

So exiguous is the archeological evidence, and so ambivalent and intractable are the literary sources available even for later periods of the Western Chou, that it is debatable whether it is worth trying to map the information that can be gleaned from them. However, Fig. 13, for what it is worth, is just such an attempt. On it are depicted all the Western Chou urban forms to which I have found reference in pre-Han texts, together with those which I have culled from Ssǔ-ma Ch'ien's *Shih-Chi* (completed at the beginning of the 1st century BC) and from the *Chu-shu Chi-nien*. The basis of the distribution derives from the *Shih-Chi*, but I am not unaware that in the relevant sections of that work Ssǔ-ma Ch'ien was reproducing older archetyped material. When abstracting references to urban forms from the *Shu-Ching* I have used only the orthodox

---

[13] Recorded urban settlement during the period of the Western Chou. For the limitations of this distribution see pp. 164–8 of the text. Note: the river systems shown on this map are no more than skeletal approximations based on very inadequate evidence.

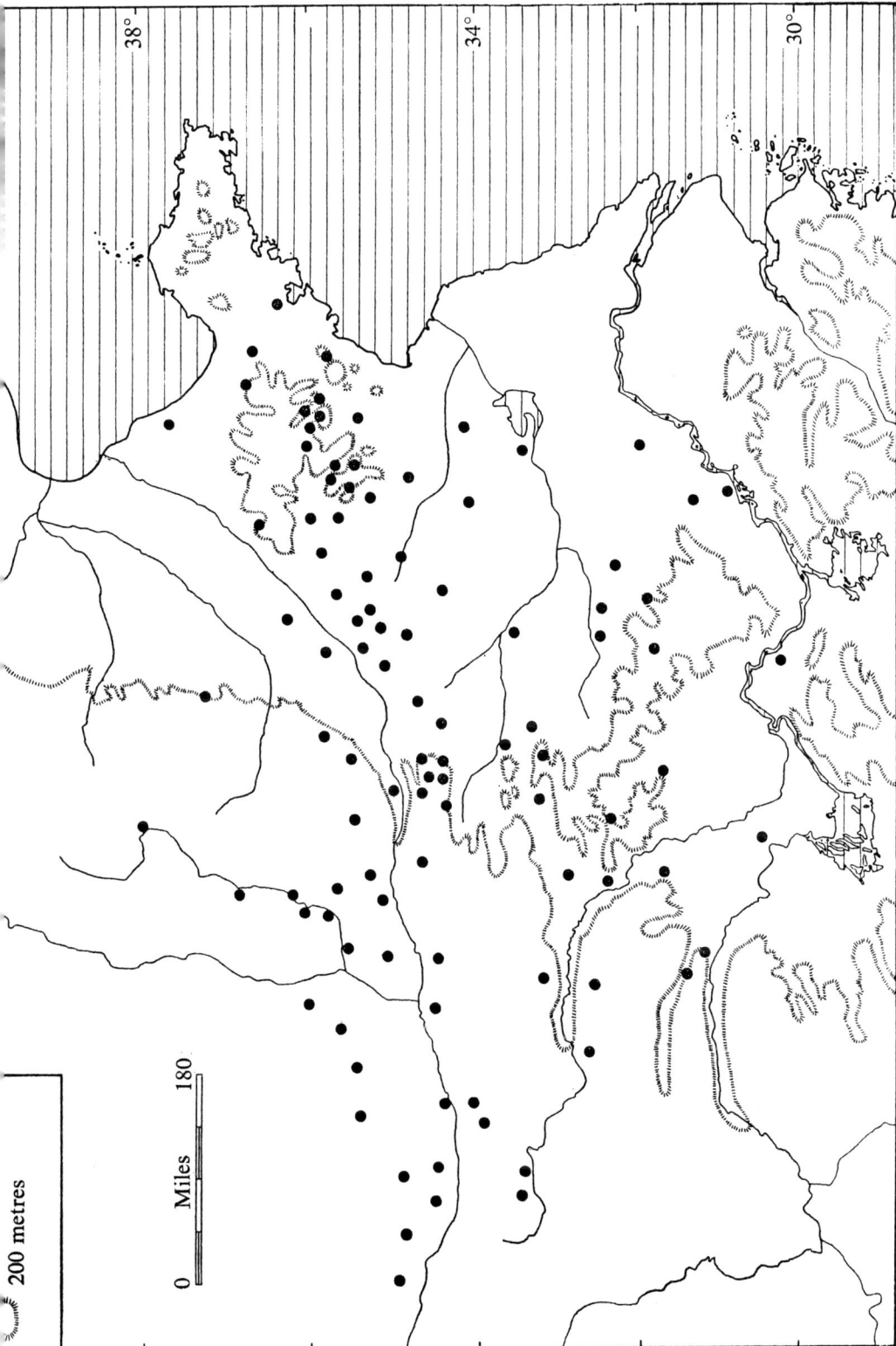

Miles

0   180

38°

34°

30°

ku-wen text (cf. p. 13). With regard to the *Chu-shu Chi-nien*, I have drawn only upon those references occurring in Wang Kuo-wei's reconstitution of the early text.[210] I am by no means convinced that the so-called modern text is valueless for present purposes[211] but, compared with that of the *Shih-Chi*, the contribution of the *Chu-shu Chi-nien* is relatively minor in any case, while the quantity of additional materials to be extracted from the 'modern' text (as opposed to those provided by the reconstructed version) does not justify the long excursus that would be necessary to evaluate their reliability. Scraps of information quarried from other Chou sources have been used with the caution advocated in previous pages.

In the matter of place-name identification I have perforce had to settle for a wide range of probability. I have followed to their sources, with Karlgren's strictures in mind, the correspondences suggested in Chavanne's magnificent *apparatus criticus* to his translation of the Chou chapters of the *Shih-Chi*,[212] and have rejected them wherever they appeared to be based on unduly suspect traditions. However, very few of the traditions are firmly based, so that the exercise became one of selecting the least unreliable from among predominantly equivocal traditions. This was not quite such a profitless undertaking as might at first appear, for the aim was not to attain absolute accuracy so much as to arrive at a regional location for a name. Of course, a handful of toponyms, chiefly ducal capitals, can be identified with a high degree of certainty and occasionally located with considerable accuracy (it should be noted in passing that identification and location are not the same thing), but a high proportion can be assigned only an approximate locality. Perhaps, for example, a settlement is recorded as having been in the vicinity of, close to, or not far from, the capital. Or it may have been described as midway between two known points. Or, only too frequently, it may be implied only that it was situated in a particular part of a state. All such identifications are, I think, worth plotting. States in the inner group (cf. p. 114 above), which are those with which Western Chou records are mainly concerned, were not large and, on the scale at which Fig. 13 is reproduced, a symbol plotted on the eastern border of, say, Kwân would be only an eighth of an inch from one plotted on the western border. Although Lo was apparently wider latitudinally, its northern and southern frontiers were no farther apart than were those of Kwân. When it is recorded, for example, that the army of Sông invaded **Dz'ôg in 489 BC and established five ·jəp on the frontier,[213] it is not introducing any significant error to locate five urban symbols along the relatively short border zone between those two states. It must be remembered though that, whereas the capital of a state can often be fixed with a fair measure of confidence, only very rarely can the frontiers be located with any degree of accuracy. Yet, even so, in this case the error of the placement on Fig. 13 can hardly exceed one-quarter of an inch. There is inevitably a large element of subjectiveness in the selection of toponyms on this principle, and I can only say in justification of this enterprise that I have, generally speaking, plotted only those names which seemed to be both identified and located by traditions that stood a reasonable chance of being genuine. In one or two instances I have plotted a settlement which could be located but not identified.

Subjectiveness was not restricted to the plotting of place names : it also lay at the basis of the decision as to what constituted an urban settlement. **Kwək (*kuo*), a word which was sometimes used metonymically to denote the fortified cult center of a noble as well as his territory, and **to (*tu*), capitals of states and benefices, were accepted as urban forms, and the justification for this will be presented in the next chapter, but **·iəp (*i*) is more difficult to evaluate. It, too, could, and often did, denote a ceremonial center, usually surrounded by a *hang-t'u* wall, but difficulties arise when we try to estimate to what extent it exercised urban functions as those are defined in Chapter Four. The texts are seldom explicit on this point. Sometimes the word ·iəp, for example, seems to carry no implication beyond that of 'place', or 'locality' or 'district', or 'settlement'. Whereas in the *Lun-Yü* (V, 27), Confucius is alleged to have alluded to 'a ·iəp of ten households', the *Appended Judgment* (*Hsi-Tz'ŭ*) to the **Dzjung (*Sung*) hexagram in the *I-Ching* apparently implies that 300 households constituted a representative size of ·iəp.[214] I have had to make my judgments in the general context of the source concerned, in the light of the events being described and, not least important, with due consideration of the nature of the narrative. After acquiring some familiarity with the texts I have come to sense that highly archetyped passages, particularly those fragments of folklore incorporated in a literary tradition, tend to upgrade settlements in the urban hierarchy. ·Iəp in such contexts was certainly intended to denote a city but, contrariwise, because virtually all settlements in such contexts had been archetyped as cities, was regarded with suspicion when I came to plot the map. Once again I can only say that I included in the distribution solely those settlements which seemed to be something more than villages with their inhabitants working the surrounding fields. To be classified as urban (in the sense defined in Chapter Four) a settlement had to appear to be an instrument for the organization of the surrounding territories, not merely the locus of a labor force. That the method of categorization is unsatisfactory I do not deny, but the attempt may be justified by the purpose for which the map was constructed. It was, in fact, designed simply to provide a visual impression of the broad pattern of urban development under the Western Chou. Hopefully, it will be the first in a series of distributions tracing the evolution of the spatial pattern of urban development in China from the earliest times to the present. The nature of the sources dictated that the pattern be cumulative throughout the era of the Western Chou, but the fact that cities were destroyed or moved to new sites during the three centuries of that dynasty means that it does not depict conditions at the end of that period. It is a record of those settlements mentioned in classical texts which are believed to have manifested urban characteristics at any time during the dynasty, together with the sole archeologically attested and indisputably urban capital of the state of D'əm (p. 136 above). The qualifications to this statement should be noted. The classical texts are concerned predominantly with the central states, so that there may have been more urban foundations in the larger outer states (where incidentally it was more hazardous locating a toponym whose position was specified only in general terms) than appear on the map. This is, I think, particularly true of Tṣ'ịo, which may have developed urban foci at a relatively early date but whose cities are at any time only sparsely represented in the records. It will be recalled that Duke **Snịang (Hsiang) of Lo in 541 incurred the opprobrium of his ministers and subjects when he had a palace built for himself in the style of those of Tṣ'ịo.[215] Presumably this act by the ruler of one of the technologically most advanced of the central states reflects the existence of a developed urban architectural style in contemporary Tṣ'ịo. There is, of course, no reason to think that the record of urban centers is complete for the central states, but neither is there any reason to suppose that it does not afford a more or less representative sample of Chou cities in those states.

Despite its inadequacies, Fig. 13 does show that the three centuries of the Western Chou had witnessed a significant areal extension of urban society. Even allowing for the inchoate state of the archeological investigation of Shang remains and the consequent deficiencies of Fig. 13, there can be no doubt but that urban settlements had both become more numerous in the central states and had extended far beyond the borders of the Shang culture realm. The highest incidence of cities appears from the map to have occurred in the old states of Lo, Sông, Gịwad, D'ịĕng and the Chou domain, though there was already a fairly dense scatter in Tsịĕn, Dz'ịĕn and southern Dz'ịər; but, as mentioned above, this distribution may reflect the character of the sources rather than the pattern of urbanism in Chou China. There seems a strong likelihood, however, that the center of gravity of urban development was shifting from the Shang hearth in northern Ho-nan eastwards towards a point in Lo or Gịwad. To the south distinctively urban settlements were to be found in the Han valley and along the middle Yang-tzŭ, where they signified the introduction of new modes of social organization into hitherto tribal territories.

---

[14] Recorded urban settlement during the Ch'un-Ch'iu period. For the limitations of this map see pp. 170–2 of the text. Note especially that the pattern of distribution is cumulative over some two and a half centuries, so that more than one capital may occur within the territory of any particular state. The river systems shown on this map are no better than skeletal approximations based on very inadequate evidence.

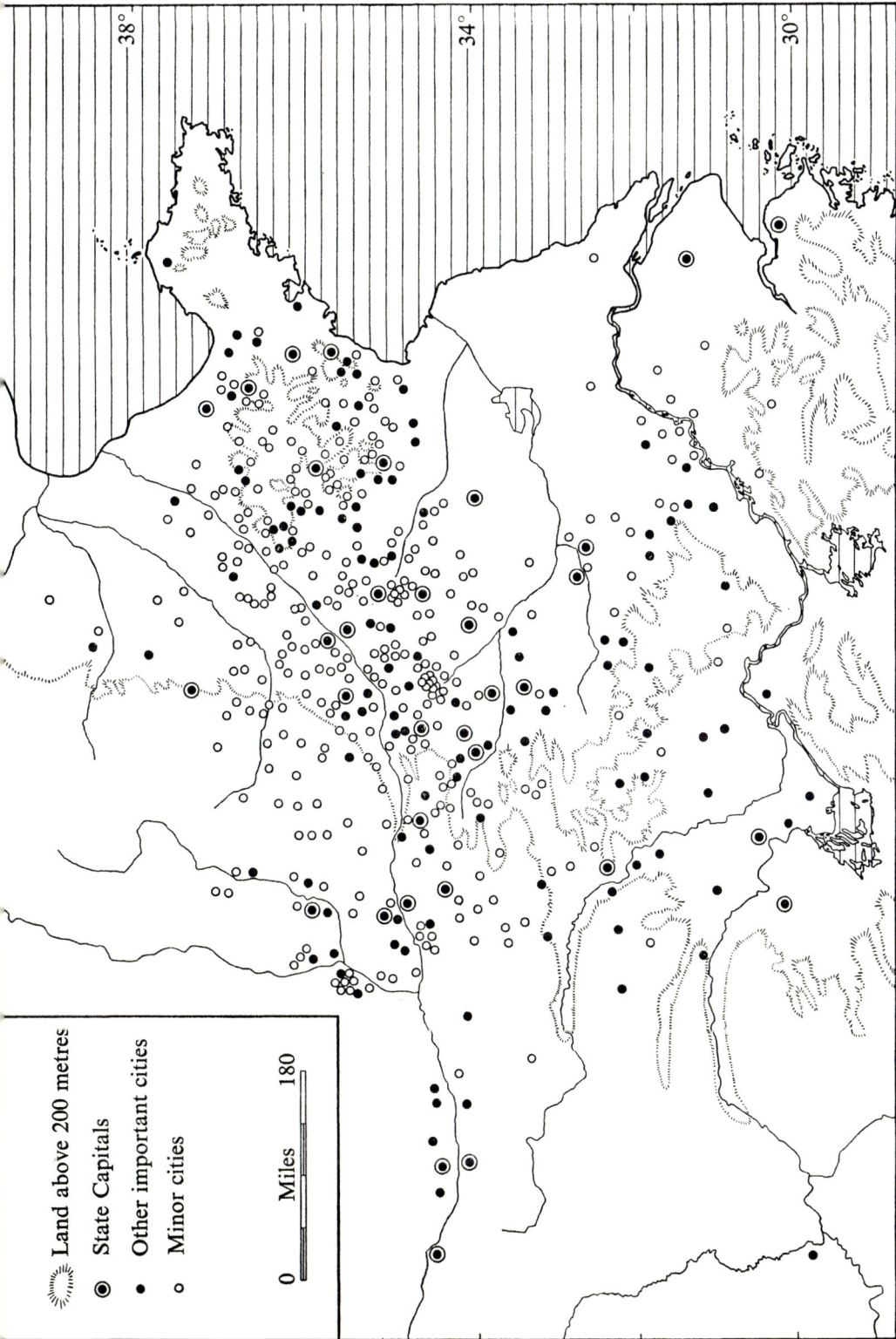

Land above 200 metres

State Capitals ◎

Other important cities ●

Minor cities ○

Miles

0   180

38°

34°

30°

THE EASTERN CHOU

Fig. 14 is based essentially on the *Tso-Chuan*, augmented by a variety of other sources discussed on pp. 150–160 and by a sprinkling of archeologically attested sites, some of which are in any case mentioned in the relevant texts. It depicts, therefore, those settlements mentioned in classical sources and archeological reports which are believed to have exercised urban functions (again as defined in Chapter Four) during the Spring and Autumn period. Originally I had toyed with the idea of analyzing this pattern of urban distribution in terms of the twelve twenty-year periods used by the late Professor George Kennedy in his seminal paper on the process of historical development depicted in the *Ch'un-Ch'iu*[216] and subsequently by Richard Walker in his study of Chou political systems,[217] but the doubtful degree of reliability of the evidence available rendered such an undertaking impracticable. Not the least intractable of the problems which sabotaged my attempt were the continual, and often abrupt, fluctuations in the frontiers of the states. This was important because many of the urban centers could be located only in relation to frontiers, or even more frequently, with respect to one particular tract of territory within the state. In some instances the broad outlines of such fluctuations can be determined with confidence, and Richard Walker has done this for the state of Dz'iər.[218] By connecting the outermost localities assigned to Dz'iər by the *Ch'un-Ch'iu* and *Tso-Chuan*, he was able to depict on a map sequent changes in the extent of the core territory of the state. I myself performed the same exercise for Lo and Tsjĕn but in all instances, including that of Dz'iər, there remained a strong likelihood that the actual boundaries of the states had extended well beyond the core area delimited on the map. Indeed, the texts seldom mentioned frontier zones in precise terms unless they were the sites of captured cities or battlefields.

Dz'iər affords an instructive example of this problem. Until about 660 B C the state was restricted to a tract of territory, with maximum dimensions of from 300 to 350 miles by from 60 to 70, situated principally among the western hills of Shan-tung. By 600 B C, mainly under the hegemon Duke **G'wân (Huan) and his advisor **Kwân-D'jông (Kuan-Chung), the frontiers had been pushed northwestwards across the **Dz'iər (Ch'i) or eastern distributary of the **G'wâng (Huang) river, and eastwards across the Wei-Hsien valley into the eastern uplands of the Shan-tung peninsula. Already the Dz'iər government had 'imposed terms' (g'ông) on **Tjang (Chang) and 'removed' (ts'jan) **Djang (Yang), as well as persuading a noble of the principality of **Kjəg (Chi) voluntarily to agree to the incorporation of his territory, **G'iweg (Hsi), in the Dz'iər polity. During the ensuing half century or so the small states of **Ləg (Lai) and **D'âng (T'ang) were 'destroyed' (mjat) and **Kăd-kən (Chieh-ken) 'annexed' (ts'ju), thereby extending the boundaries of Dz'iər significantly southwards. Finally, by 480 B C the state had come to include some of the valleys and plains of the Tung-wen river system on the southern flanks of the western highlands. This five-fold increase in the area of the state, during which altogether fourteen neighboring territories were absorbed into Dz'iər, can be documented in broad terms, but only seldom can a border be determined with precision. It is more than probable, for example, that by the close of the Ch'un-Ch'iu period the Dz'iər writ ran throughout most of the seaward tracts of the G'wâng delta and eastward to the tip of the Shan-tung peninsula, but, as no written references to these territories survive, they can be included in the Dz'iər kingdom only by inference.[219] It follows that to plot the cities of this one state during twenty-year periods would, on the imprecise evidence available, be extremely difficult, not to say hazardous, but to plot the urban development of all the Chinese states on the same principle would be an impossibility.

For these reasons, Fig. 14 represents the cumulative pattern of urban distribution for the whole of the Ch'un-Ch'iu period. From even a cursory glance at the map it is evident that the extent of territory supporting urbanized societies had not changed greatly since the time of the Western Chou. The rise of ·Ian in the embayment of present-day Pei-ching, and the emergence of Ngo and Gįwăt in the Yang-tzŭ delta and modern Che-chiang, had introduced urban forms somewhat farther north and among the very definitely non-Chinese peoples of the southeast, but elsewhere the spatial frontiers of urban society at the end of the Ch'un-Ch'iu were essentially those of the Western Chou. Apparently, during the intervening two and a half centuries, the social and economic changes adumbrated above had induced an intensification of urbanism both within the old core of central states and in some of the outer polities such as Tṣ'įo. To what extent the apparent increase in density of urban foundations reflects the greater detail of the *Ch'un-Ch'iu* and related texts, as compared with the rather meager sources for the Western Chou period, is uncertain. Certainly nothing like 367 cities (the difference in the number of symbols on Figs. 13 and 14) are recorded as having been founded during those two and a half centuries. In fact, by collating information from the *Tso-Chuan* and the *Kung-yang Chuan*, Oshima Riichi was able to find mention of the foundation of only seventy-eight cities during this period,[220] usually expressed in some such phrase as, 'In the summer [of 713] **Lâng (Lang) was walled', 'In the winter [of 695] **Xįang (Hsiang) was walled', or on one occasion, 'The Marquis [of Tsįĕn in 660] walled **K'įuk-·ok (Ch'ü-wo) for his son'.[221] If the distribution of Fig. 14 approximates to, or understates, the actual distribution of cities during the Ch'un-Ch'iu, then either the vast proportion of instances of city founding are indeed unrecorded or the number of Western Chou cities is underrepresented on Fig. 13. My own feeling is that both factors are operative. I have emphasized already that Fig. 13 depicts only those Western Chou cities which happened to play a more or less decisive role in the history of a handful of states; and, as for the Ch'un-Ch'iu distribution, on perusing the texts one does in fact get the impression that, generally speaking, only cities established by the state governments were considered worthy of mention. This would not be altogether unexpected in view of the fact that the basic annalistic materials around which the framework of the *Tso-Chuan* and *Ch'un-Ch'iu* was constructed were originally court archives. In any case the *Tso-Chuan* deals primarily with the conflict between the northern states of Dz'iǝr and Tsjěn on the one hand and the southern state of Tṣ'įo on the other, so it should come as no surprise that the former two kingdoms accounted for one-sixth of the cities mentioned and Tṣ'įo for nearly a quarter.

Sen-dou Chang, drawing his materials from Ch'en P'an's revision of Ku Tung-kao's *Ch'un-Ch'iu Ta-shih Piao*,[222] has published a map showing ninety-seven walled cities of the Ch'un-Ch'iu period.[223] It is not clear why Chang used this secondary source, published between 1957 and 1959, in preference to the original texts, but in any case there can be no dispute about the fact that his map depicts only a fraction of the number of cities in existence in Ch'un-Ch'iu times. If, as Oshima claims, there are references to the actual founding of seventy-eight cities during that era (and these, it is to be remembered, are only the *recorded* foundings), then Chang's figure would imply that there were less than a score of urban settlements in the whole of the Chinese culture realm at the end of the Western Chou. Such was certainly not the case.

All the limitations and inadequacies discussed in relation to the distribution of Western Chou cities apply with equal cogency to Fig. 14. Subjectivism, illation, relativism, even compromise, all played their part in the construction of the map, and will doubtless render it liable to modification in the future as more sophisticated techniques become available for the analysis of ancient Chinese society.

The reader who has persisted this far may well expect to find at this point a map depicting the distribution of cities during the era of the Contending States. The reason such a map is not included is that the sources for the spatial study of Chan-Kuo urbanism are less satisfactory from the point of view of both quantity and quality than are those relating to the Ch'un-Ch'iu period, and the only map that can be compiled from them simulates a less detailed version of Fig. 14. In other respects, though, the Chan-Kuo sources are more informative. In fact, they reveal the advent of important changes in the nature of the city at that time, which will be touched upon in subsequent sections of this work.

It may be of interest before closing this section to interpolate a few comments on the results of an inquiry into the city-building activities of the Chou Chinese published by Dr Li Chi as long ago as 1928.[224] This author based his study on materials in the *Ch'in-ting Ku-chin T'u-shu Chi-ch'eng*, an encyclopedia prepared – as the title says – by imperial order, under the general editorship of Ch'en Meng-lei. It was completed in 1726.[225] Section VI of this work contains the dates at which walled cities were established in the various provinces of China, the information having been extracted from the great tradition of local gazetteers that form such an important strand in the web of Chinese historical and geographical writing.[226] The provincial scholars who produced these local histories and topographies through the centuries without significant exception drew their information on ancient times from the archetyped and edited classical texts discussed above. It follows, therefore, that they, followed by the scholars who labored on the *Ch'in-ting Ku-chin T'u-shu Chi-ch'eng*, and ultimately by Li Chi, made use of a great deal of information which we have found it necessary to reject. Consequently it is not surprising that Li Chi's estimates of the number of cities in Chou China are higher than the number of symbols on Figs. 13 and 14. For the period prior to 722 BC, the beginning of the Ch'un-Ch'iu, he had discovered references to the building of 163 cities, and for the period from 722 to 207 BC, that is for the remainder of the Chou dynasty, he had counted no less than 585. In addition 233 of uncertain age were mentioned for the first time during the latter period. These figures are to be compared with the 91 for the Western Chou on Fig. 13, and 466 plotted on Fig. 14, which relates to the Ch'un-Ch'iu (722–481 BC). While maintaining that Li Chi's estimates are based on unacceptable evidence, we must admit that our own figures are too low, because there is absolutely no reason to suppose that anything like all the cities in Chou China were mentioned in the sources that we judge reliable – or in any other sources for that matter. This is, in fact, merely an oblique way of drawing attention to the ironic situation in which Li Chi's estimates may be nearer the truth than our own, but for reasons that are unacceptable to us. Both are, in any case, too low. In the matter of relative, as opposed to absolute, incidence of building activity, by contrast, we are in substantial agreement with Li Chi. He finds that prior to 722 BC, urban life was restricted to the five provinces of Kan-su, Ho-nan, Shen-hsi, Chih-li and Shan-hsi (he uses the old Manchu provincial names appropriate to the source of his materials), from which it extended during the Eastern Chou into Shan-tung, Hu-pei, and Chiang-su. We have drawn the limits of urban development somewhat more narrowly during both periods, chiefly as a result of having adopted more stringent criteria of source evaluation. It is more than doubtful, for example, if Kan-su, Chih-li, and Chiang-su should figure as prominently in the history of Shang and Chou urbanism as Li Chi contended.[227] But he was certainly correct in postulating a shift in the focus of building activity from the Chung-yüan, hearth of the Shang culture, out into the eastern parts of the plain and the foothills of Shan-tung.

THE NATURE OF CHOU URBANISM

THE FUNCTION OF THE CHOU CITY

The mosaic of settlements spread over the North China plain early in the

Western Chou comprised old Shang foundations dating from before the conquest, tribal villages which had existed outside the framework of an organized polity until the advent of Chou overlords, and, perhaps most important of all, the garrison establishments of the new dynasty. Each of these settlement forms was integrated into the political structure of the Chou kingdom, and each sooner or later, despite its distinctive origins, assumed a role in the emergence of a hierarchy of cities, each unit of which at each level of the system combined ceremonial, military, and agricultural functions. At the apex of the hierarchy was the imperial capital at G'og in the Wei valley, the style center whence diffused the intellectual, religious, social, and aesthetic values of Western Chou culture. At various levels in the hierarchy the seats of benefice holders reproduced a proportion of these functions and, finally, in interstitial and peripheral locations were to be found the lowest levels of urban development, the seats of ministers, members of ruling families, and even of tribal chieftains in process of assimilation to the Chinese way of life. The level at which an urban center articulated with the political and administrative structures of the state was reflected, at least in the phraseology of later texts, in the term used to describe it: **t̯iông-to (chung-tu) for the capital of the Son of Heaven, **to (tu) for the seat of a powerful aristocrat, and **·i̯əp (i) for that of a lesser landholder or the chief of a b'i̯u-d̯iung (fu-yung). In some of these later texts the several ranks within the hierarchy were rationalized as representing an evolutionary sequence. In the Shih-Chi, for example, we read that, 'On the first occasion when Shun (Śi̯wən, one of the legendary model emperors) migrated he built a ·i̯əp; on the second occasion he founded a to; and on the third occasion he established a **kwək (kuo : = city-state), to which he attracted nobles from the four directions.' Similar statements occur in the Lü-Shih Ch'un-Ch'iu, the Kuan-tzŭ and the Chuang-tzŭ, but we shall see in Chapter Three that the actual process of urban genesis was probably somewhat different from that postulated by systematizing Chinese editors.

That some hierarchical distinction was also recognized by the compiler of the Tso-Chuan is evident in a gloss on a passage in the Ch'un-Ch'iu dealing with the enclosing of a settlement at **Mi̯ər (Mei). 'Mi̯ər', he wrote, 'was not a to. All ·i̯əp having ancestral temples providing a lodging for their former rulers were designated to, those without such a temple were termed ·i̯əp. A ·i̯əp is said to be enclosed (**t̯iôk : chu), a to is said to be fortified (**d̯i̯ĕng : ch'eng).'228 It is implicit in the second sentence of the passage just quoted that ·i̯əp denoted all urban foci other than state or benefice capitals. In the wider context of Chou literature it seems in fact to have included settlements that were hardly more than hamlets. We have, for example, already mentioned the reference in the Lun-Yü (V, 27) to a ·i̯əp of only ten households. It is important, therefore, that each reference to a ·i̯əp be evaluated in the light of its context and not assumed uncritically to have been urban in character.

One of the two essential features of the Western Chou city, at whichever level of the hierarchy it occurred, was the altar to the god of the soil (*she* : **$d\underset{.}{i}\hat{a}$*), which, like the *apadana* of Xerxes (p. 439 below), was always kept open 'to receive the hoar frost, dew, wind, and rain, and to allow free access by the influences of Heaven and Earth' (*Li-Chi*). The roofing-over of this altar signified the extinction both of the ruler's line and of the state and the city. The state might subsequently be reconstituted and the city rebuilt or resuscitated, but for the time being both were extinguished. As the Son of Heaven received his mandate from Heaven, so the noble received his territory, his city, and his people from the Chou king, and piled his altar to the god of the soil around a clod of earth from the great national altar in G'og – or later in the Gịwang-Ḓịĕng at Lo-yang. The other essential feature of the city at this time was the temple of the ancestors (**$m\underset{.}{i}og$* : *miao*), wherein rested the tablets of the agnatic ancestors and their wives in *dịog-mịôk* order. No state could hope to survive without the favor and intercession of its former rulers who, in turn, traced their lineage back to sage emperors or culture heroes of antiquity. When the ancestral sacrifices were discontinued, then also both ruler and state had become extinct. It was this temple of the ancestors which served as the focus for all important state functions, whether religious, political, diplomatic or military. A third feature which – as there was no overlord without a city and, with very few and temporary exceptions, no city without an overlord[229] – was an inevitable (though not essential) concomitant of all urban development, was the ruler's palace. And moving between these ternions of cityhood was the ruler, the animating force of state, city, and temple, whose *d'ôg-tək*[230] caused nature and men to be what they were, who, in Granet's phrase, 'dispensed to men and things their destiny'.[231] As the *Li-Chi* has it : 'When [the former Emperors] presented their offerings to Shang-ti in the outskirts [of the capital], wind and rain were duly regulated, and cold and warmth came each in its appointed season, so that the Sage [Emperor] had only to stand with his face to the south for order to prevail throughout the world.'

The agricultural and military functions of Western Chou cities were closely related. Discussion of the Chou settlement of the North China plain has customarily focused on a nexus of ideas involving the relations between the martial Chou conquerors, 'the hundred lineages', established in fortified settlements, and the food-producing Shang and tribal peoples, 'the black-haired folk'; and the argument has then usually hinged on the nature of the instruments devised by the Chou leaders to ensure the peace of the countryside, and ultimately their own food supply. The most elaborate of the available expositions, and also that which is most hypothetical, was put forward by Wolfram Eberhard a few years ago.[232] This author points out that the Chou were probably often unable, by reason of disaffection or perhaps inability to produce a surplus, to rely on the local populace for their rations, and consequently were obliged to devise alternative arrangements. In the event Eberhard believes, following hints provided in the earlier work of Hsü Chung-shu, that the Chou benefice holders organized their followers in semi-military cadres, each of eight families. These groups, who must have found themselves in much the same situation as the early British settlers among the forest Indians of North America, are held to have gone out from the fortress at the beginning of spring, cultivated parcels of land on a swidden cycle, and returned to the protection of the fortress at the onset of winter. This, according to Eberhard, was probably the origin of the well-field system discussed on p. 132 above. The clearings of the eight families in each cadre, together with an alleged ninth section the produce of which went for the maintenance of the non-cultivating élites in the fortress community, were subsequently idealized by systematizing editors into the regularly shaped and spaced, communally worked, land-settlement scheme which, torn from its contextual setting in Mencius and the *Chou-Li*, has been taken by some more recent but no less systematizing authors as a prototype of 'natural socialism' or 'primitive communism' achieved in the innocence of the world. Contrasting strongly with these agro-military settlements were the villages of the indigenous folk, paying tribute to their new masters but, in the earlier days of the Western Chou, still self-contained and tribally organized. Only with the passage of time were the Chou *colonia* and the Shang or tribal populace fused into the unity of the Chou city. Perhaps this came about through the socially consolidatory medium of markets established under the fortress walls; possibly – as Eberhard suggests – it came about through intermarriage; and most probably through the initiation of a symbiotic process of mutual interdependence, as when the Chou needed to augment their labor force for construction work in the fortress, or when the indigenous folk sought to obtain the implements, tools and ornaments produced in city workshops. In other words the native and tribal territories are to be envisaged as being drawn into the ambit of the fortress through a combined process of political absorption and cultural diffusion. When the tribute of the indigenes was no longer distinguished from the tithe (or rather the ninth part of the harvest, if we accept the well-field as a working system) of the Chou bondsman, then the process was virtually complete. Not all scholars accept Professor Eberhard's interpretation in its entirety, particularly so far as it concerns the well-field system, but that something after this fashion took place in North China during the early years of the Western Chou is beyond dispute.

It is clear that these early Chou cities were primarily administrative and military foundations. Such industrial activities as they generated were restricted to crafts producing prestige items in bronze, jade, lacquer, pottery, and bone for the Chou nobility, while village workshops continued to manufacture the stone and bone implements used by the peasantry in farm and field. It has already been pointed out on p. 134 that in this almost wholly self-contained, manorial-style economy commerce played only an insignificant role. With the political, social and economic transformations of the Ch'un-Ch'iu period, however, the city often became a locus for the enterprises of the new merchant class. The representative Eastern Chou capital never lost its ceremonial functions, but not a few cities developed their commercial activities to a high level. In the ritualized schema of the *K'ao-kung Chi* the market was located behind, that is to the north of, the royal palace.[233] Ssŭ-ma Ch'ien had no doubts about the contribution of trade to the prosperity of certain Chou cities. He reported, for example, that during the Ch'un-Ch'iu period **·Ɉung (Yung), the capital of Dz'ɪĕn, had derived no inconsiderable benefit from its situation in the middle Wei valley, at a point where commodities from **Lɟung (Lung), a district lying astride the approaches to the desert road to Central Asia, converged on those moving northeastwards from **Ɖɪuk (Shu), the region of present-day Ssŭ-ch'uan[234]. Later, under Dukes **Xɪăn (Hsien) and Xŏg (Hsiao) [384–338 BC], the capital had been relocated farther downstream at **Gliok (Li), where its merchants were able, while still retaining command of western and southern trade, to engage in commercial transactions with the succession states of Tsɪĕn to the east.[235] In the Ho-tung, **Dɪang (Yang) and **B'ɪĕng-dɪang (P'ing-yang) exploited their nodal position with relation to the **Dz'ɪĕn (Ch'in) and **D'iok (Ti) barbarians of the west and the **Ɵɪung (Chung) and **D'əg (Tai) of the north.[236] G'ân-tân, the capital of D'ɪog, had profited from its ability to tap the trade of ·Ian (Yen) and **Tŭk (Cho) from the north at the same time as it had attracted to itself the commodities of Gɪwad and D'ɪĕng.[237] Merchants in the Chou capital itself traded with Dz'ɪər and Lo in the east and with **Lɪang (Liang) and Tş'ɪo to the south.[238] ·Ian, too, enjoyed an especially advantageous commercial location, situated as it was in the angle between the **·O-g'wân (Wu-huan) and **Pɪwo-dɪo (Fu-yü) tribes on the north and the **·Ɉwăd-g'lâk (Wei-ho), **D'ɪog-sɪan (Ch'ao-hsien), and **Ɵɪĕn-p'ɪwăn (Chen-p'an) peoples of the east, at the same time as it had unobstructed lines of communication to the metropolitan heart of China to the south.[239] All this and more was apparent to Ssŭ-ma Ch'ien when he came to compose his *Huo-Chih*,[240] and in modern times Miyazaki Ichisada has collated a great deal of information from sources such as the *Tso-Chuan, Kuo-Yü* and *Chan-Kuo Ts'e* showing that during Ch'un-Ch'iu and Chan-Kuo times trade and commerce played no insignificant role in numerous Chinese cities.[241] This was an age when, as Ssŭ-ma Ch'ien tells us, the 'secondary occupations', that is trade, and to a lesser extent handicrafts, were the best source of wealth for a poor man. Anyone in the ·ɪəp or *to* of late Chan-Kuo or early Han China, he says, who managed to sell 1,000 brewings of liquor, 1,000 jars of pickles and sauces, 1,000 jars of syrup, 1,000 carcases of cattle, sheep or swine, 1,000 *chung*[242] of grain, 1,000 cart- or boat-loads of firewood and kindling stubble, 1,000 logs of timber, 10,000 bamboo poles, 100 horse carriages, 1,000 two-wheeled ox carts, 1,000 lacquered wooden vessels, brass utensils weighing 1,000 *chün*,[243] 1,000 *tan*[244] of plain wooden or iron vessels, gardenia and madder dyes, 200 horses, 500 cattle, 2,000 sheep or swine, 100 slaves of either sex, 1,000 *chin*[245] of tendons, horns, or cinnabar, 1,000 *chün* of silk cloth, raw silk, or other fine fabrics, 1,000 rolls of embroidered or patterned silk, 1,000 *shih* of vegetable-fiber fabrics or raw or tanned hides, 1,000 *tou*[246] of lacquer, 1,000 jars of leaven or salted bean relish, 1,000 *chin* of globefish or mullet, 1,000 *shih* of dried fish, 1,000 *chün* of salted fish, 3,000 *shih* of jujubes or chestnuts, 1,000 fox or sable pelts, 1,000 *shih* of lamb or sheep skins, 1,000 felt rugs, or 1,000 *chung* of fruits or vegetables, anyone who could do any of these things 'might live as well as the proprietor of an estate of 1,000 chariots'.[247]

With the passage of time the market quarter became a venue not only for commercial but also for social exchange, a place where the businessman, the stallholder, the teamster, the housewife, the casual passer-by, the idler, and the countryman in town for a few hours could pass the time of day. It combined, in fact, the economic and social functions of the *agora* of the Greek *polis* and the *forum* of the Roman city, and there remained only a tenuous distinction between these facets of its activities. (In China, however, there was – as far as is known – no Aristotle to advocate the separation of these functions on the Thessalian pattern : *Politics*, VII, ii, 2).

In the immediately preceding paragraphs we have traced the evolution of the representative Chou city from its inception as a fortified ceremonial enclave established in an essentially colonial context to its mature development in Chan-Kuo times as a focus of centralized facilities serving a spatially integrated hinterland. Throughout the near millennium of this period there were grafted on to the ceremonial and agro-military roles of the city certain industrial and tertiary economic activities, a process which recalls Max Weber's view of the medieval European city as resulting from the fusion of fortress and market. However, whatever applicability such an interpretation may have to European urbanism, it would be an inadequate conceptualization of the Chinese experience. In the first place, despite the relative space which we have accorded commercial activities, these were but poorly developed by any absolute standard, and the vast majority of city dwellers, not only in Chou times but even in Han and later periods, were cultivators who, in summer at any rate, went out daily through the city gates to work in their fields. In this mass of agrarian labor which constituted the urban population, the craftsmen and merchants generated only a small leavening influence and, more important for urban theory, never constituted an autonomous group able to undertake the collective exercise of power. The cities of Chou China from first to last afforded no locus of countervailing power directed against central authority, but were themselves instruments for the exercise of that power, governed, if not by the ruler of a polity, then by one of his officials. In the second place Weber's concept of European urban origins found no place for the role of the ceremonial center, the axis of the kingdom, where alone the ruler could seek counsel and intercession from the ancestors who had served the state in the past and who now watched over its future, where alone he could preside over the universal harmony that, under a virtuous monarch, manifested itself in the spontaneous co-operation of animate and inanimate nature, and where alone, at the pivot of the universe, he could ensure the continuance of the cosmic process.

The origin of the hsien city. One legacy which the Chou bequeathed to later dynasties was the governmental instrument of the *hsien* (**g'ian*), which subsequently became the basic administrative unit of the empire. Until modern times the capital of the *hsien* has constituted the lowest level of the urban hierarchy through which the central government has exercised its authority directly. As such it has generated a low-order degree of centrality, probably approximately comparable to that assigned to the *Kreisstadt* in Christaller's hierarchy.[248]

It has long been recognized that the creation of the *hsien* was a response to the need for a degree of impersonality and categorization in the developing bureaucracies of the states of Chou China, but the first attempt to localize and date this process had to await the publication in 1938 of Professor Bodde's study of the life and work of Li-Ssǔ (**Ljǝg-Sjěg*).[249] Bodde saw the origin of the *hsien* in two situations : when land was conquered from tribal peoples along the margins of the Chinese culture realm, and when territory was annexed from another state. In either case the ruler of the polity, being under no obligation to delegate sovereign rights or apportion benefices within the newly acquired territory, tended to retain it under his direct control. Government was then carried out by non-hereditary, state-appointed officials. If, as is often asserted, the graph for *hsien* was originally composed of a pictograph of a severed human head, together with the post and cord with which to display it in a public place, the whole character signifying 'to suspend' or 'attach', then the postulated mode of origin of the term as a designation for recently annexed territory may receive some support from etymology.[250] Bodde believed that administrative units on this pattern were first established in Dz'ĕn, where four such are mentioned in extant records as being instituted in a restricted territory in 688 BC.[251] The fact that this erosion of the political privilege of the **djĕg* (*shih*) kin group in favor of bureaucratic control was ascribed to Dz'ĕn, a state which even at the end of the Ch'un-Ch'iu was considered by the literati of the central states as being at least semi-barbarian,[252] was held to give added plausibility to Bodde's interpretation. Certainly it was in that state in 350 BC that the *hsien* was made the basis of a new and more highly centralized system of government.[253] Concurrently the institution had been diffusing among the other states, so that by Chan-Kuo times *hsien* were to be found in each of the seven great states, D'i̯og, Ngi̯wər, G'ân, Dz'i̯ĕn, Tṣ'i̯o, ·Ian, and Dz'i̯ər. This has also been the point of view adopted by most subsequent scholars, including Sen-dou Chang in his exposition of the urban geography of the *hsien* city.[254]

More recently, however, this thesis has been considerably revised by Professor H. G. Creel.[255] In the first place Creel questions whether the *Shih-Chi* reference to *hsien* in Dz'i̯ĕn in 688 and 687 BC was in fact concerned with administrative districts. The phrase ****g'ian-i̯əg* (*hsien-chih*) could – indeed probably does – mean simply that the territories in question were annexed, without any corollary implications as to the manner in which they were integrated into the Dz'i̯ĕn polity. In the whole of the extant corpus of Chou literature there is only one other reference, and that almost certainly a late interpolation, which mentions *hsien* in connection with Dz'i̯ĕn during the Ch'un-Ch'iu.[256] Creel has also pointed out that what little evidence is available would indicate that in Dz'i̯ĕn governmental institutions tended to lag behind those in some other states, notably Tṣ'i̯o. Dz'i̯ĕn, he says, was a borrower rather than an innovator, and, a factor of some importance so far as diffusion of its institutions was concerned, was held in low esteem by its neighbors.[257] He is certainly correct when he denies the existence of conclusive evidence for the existence of *hsien* administrative units in Dz'i̯ĕn in the 7th century, and probably so when he casts doubt on the innovatory proclivities of the Dz'i̯ĕn government.[258]

Hsien are reliably reported during Ch'un-Ch'iu times in only two other states, Tsi̯ĕn and Tṣ'i̯o.[259] So far as Tsi̯ĕn is concerned, the earliest mention relates to the year 627 BC,[260] and Creel has argued that by 543 the whole state was apportioned in *hsien* under administrative officials.[261] It appears also that *hsien* soon became hereditable,[262] which allowed powerful *di̯ĕg*, kin-based corporate groups as Creel defined them, to treat their *hsien* as normal benefices, and thus to retain a great deal of their political privilege at the expense of the development of centralized government. During the 6th and 5th centuries, in fact, Tsi̯ĕn administration exhibited increasingly powerful centrifugal tendencies, which culminated in its disintegration into three separate states in 453. In other words *hsien* administration seems neither to have been particularly congenial to the Tsi̯ĕn political ethos, nor to have persisted in the bureaucratic form in which it was originally conceived. It consequently seems unlikely that it originated in that state.

The only other state in which the *hsien* functioned as an administrative institution during the Ch'un-Ch'iu was Tṣ'i̯o, and it is here that Creel looks for its beginnings.[263] In a detailed excursus he shows that during the Ch'un-Ch'iu and Chan-Kuo periods central authority was much more strongly developed in Tṣ'i̯o than in the northern states, that tenure of office depended to a greater extent on merit, and that hereditary office was almost non-existent. It is possible that a factor contributing powerfully to this situation was the different kinship system obtaining in Tṣ'i̯o, possibly even to the exclusion of the *di̯ĕg* until that institution was adopted into the Tṣ'i̯o cultural inventory during the Ch'un-Ch'iu.[264]

Creel has elicited the further fact that, not only is the *hsien* likely to have existed earlier in Tṣ'i̯o than in any of the northern states, but also that evidence of a system of *hsien* government existed earlier there than elsewhere. The early existence of *hsien* in Tṣ'i̯o is to be inferred from a somewhat cryptic passage in the *Tso-Chuan*. In a statement made in 478 BC[265] a Tṣ'i̯o official recalls that King **Mi̯wən (Wen), who reigned from 689 to 675, converted the states of **Śi̯ĕn (Shen) and **Si̯ək (Hsi) into *hsien*, presumably after the attack which both the *Tso-Chuan* and the *Shih-Chi*[266] record as having been mounted in 688. A subsequent reference to a Tṣ'i̯o *hsien* officer in 664, and the presence of a Śi̯ĕn army under Tṣ'i̯o command in 635, afford some support for Creel's interpretation of the evidence,[267] but even more significant is a report in the *Tso-Chuan*[268] of two districts which were put under **i̯uĕn (*yin*) administration by King **Mi̯wo (Wu) of Tṣ'i̯o, who reigned from 740 to 690 BC. *I̯uĕn* was a title of *hsien* administrators regularly used in Tṣ'i̯o in later years, so it is not unlikely that the institution of the *hsien* existed in that state even as early as the beginning of the 7th century BC. In any case, whether or not this inference proves acceptable, Creel has been able to demonstrate beyond doubt that, well before the beginning of the 6th century, Tṣ'i̯o had an established system of government in which the *hsien* was an important unit.[269]

We have already seen that, whereas in Tṣ'i̯o the *hsien* had been established as an instrument for centralized control, in Tsi̯ĕn it functioned in that way only for a short time, before being subverted in the interests of powerful kin associations. This would seem to presuppose that the *hsien* had not been devised in Tsi̯ĕn, but merely represented an abortive attempt to adopt a political instrument which, in the event, proved not readily assimilable to the structure of Tsi̯ĕn society and politics. Creel is probably correct in his conjecture that the institution of the *di̯ĕg* was significant in this connection. This point of view inevitably raises the question as to how Tsi̯ĕn came to undertake the experiment of *hsien* government, and Creel has also provided a considerable quantity of circumstantial evidence bearing on this problem. In 635, for example, a son of the Tsi̯ĕn ruler returned from an exile spent partly in Tṣ'i̯o to become Duke **Mi̯wən (Wen).[270] According to the *Tso-Chuan*, he had become well acquainted with the role of career officials in the Tṣ'i̯o government. During the reigns of Duke **Mi̯wən and his successors the government of Tsi̯ĕn underwent extensive remodelling, and welcomed into the administration a number of able officials from Tṣ'i̯o.[271] In the *Tso-Chuan*, under the 26th year of Duke **Sni̯ang (Hsiang), there occurs the following passage:

"The high ministers of Tsi̯ĕn," said **Śi̯ĕng-tsi̯əg (Sheng-tzŭ), "are not the equal of those of Tʂʻi̯o ... and like the wood of the medlar and the catalpa, like skins and leather, [administrative talent] is exported from Tʂʻi̯o. Although Tʂʻi̯o possesses the raw material, it is Tsi̯ĕn which puts it to use." It is surely not stretching the bounds of probability to attribute some of the Tʂʻi̯o-style features which appeared in Tsi̯ĕn administration during the 7th and 6th centuries to this influx of talent from the great Yang-tzŭ valley state, and among these features there is good reason to include the institution of the *hsien*, and with it the *hsien* city, which was to play such an important role in later Chinese imperial administration.

MORPHOLOGY OF THE CHOU CITY

For our account of the functioning of Chou cities we have had to depend almost wholly on materials of a secondary character, namely the transmitted texts. When we turn our attention to the morphology of these cities we shall find that the literary sources are still important but that, for the period of the Eastern Chou at least, they are supplemented by a body of archeological evidence which is of considerable value from two points of view. Not only is it a primary source in its own right, but it can also be used as a check on conclusions derived from textual information. Even with this additional increment of primary information, however, it is still not easy to formulate generalizations which hold for the whole of the Chou territories at any one time, and it is not to be expected that urban forms would have undergone no change during the nine centuries or so of Chou hegemony. There are barely a score of known urban sites spread, unequally, through the whole of that period, and there is no reason to doubt that states as far apart as ·Ian and Gi̯wăt, Dzʻi̯ĕn and Dzʻi̯ər developed distinctive regional traditions of urbanism which have so far escaped the eye of the archeologist. Moreover, the remains relate to settlements at different levels in the urban hierarchy. Some were capitals of major states, others of minor polities, and the rest were apparently provincial towns. It follows that such structural uniformities as can be elicited are of a most general order, and the presumed variety of cultural expression has to be almost entirely ignored. There is reason to think that this may be especially deleterious to our concept of the Tʂʻi̯o city, which shared in the architectural traditions of the Yang-tzŭ valley rather than in those of the North China plain. Yet, although the archeological material is exiguous in relation to the territorial and chronological extent of Chou China, its confirmation of certain categories of literary evidence gives it a value out of all proportion to its bulk.

Through the whole Chou period cities were walled, and the importance of this wall is reflected in the fact, which has been frequently remarked, that the same character was used to denote both city and wall. According to the ***Ngi̯wăt-Li̯ĕng* (*Yüeh-Ling*) of the *Li-Chi*, the ritually sanctioned season for the *construction* of city walls was the second month of autumn, which was incidentally a relatively slack season in the farming year. The *repair* of walls and gates was winter work. All the walls investigated so far have proved to be of *hang-t'u* construction though, as was to be expected, their dimensions varied widely not only between different cities but between different sections of wall within the same city. In the Royal City in the neighborhood of present-day Lo-yang, for example, some sections of the western wall are only five meters in width, while certain lengths of the eastern wall are as much as fifteen meters wide. The inner walls of ·*Ok*, with a width of twelve meters, and the outer with a width of nine, fall between the two extremes encountered in the walls of the Royal City. At one of the ruined cities near Wu-an the thickness of the wall varied between eight and thirteen meters. The most massive of the walls recorded in the archeological literature are those of G'ân-tân, which exceeded twenty meters at the base. The Japanese archeologists who investigated this site have also provided the only estimate that I have come across of the original height of a city wall. Their figure for the reconstructed height was fifteen meters, which must have made the city an impressive feature in the flat landscape of southern Ho-pei. On the evidence available I have not been able to discern any correlation between the areal extent of a city and the size of its walls. In at least two instances, the Tsjĕn capital at Niu-Ts'un and the ·Jam capital near Ch'ang-Chou, the walls were flanked on their outer sides by moats, and literary references indicate that this was a common occurrence.[272]

The areas enclosed within the walls also varied enormously : from the square enceinte of 300 meter sides of the ancient ·Ian city at Ts'ai-Chuang, to the very large site of G'å-to with maximum dimensions of 8,300 × 3,930 meters. Among other areally extensive enclaves were those at Lin-tzŭ (3,000 × 4,000 meters), Chao-k'ang Chen (5,000 × 4,000 meters), Lo-yang (3,000 × 3,000 meters), T'eng-Hsien (3,600 × 2,800 meters), Hou-ma Chen (probably approximately 3,000 meters square, though erosion has destroyed the possibility of accurate measurement), and Ch'ü-fu (3,500 × 2,500 meters). Apart from the city at Chao-k'ang, whose status has not been determined, these were the state capitals of, in order, Dz'iər, Royal Chou, Sjat, ·Ok, and Lo. The dimensions of the other capital cities which have been investigated so far are that of Tsjĕn at Niu-Ts'un, the sides of whose quadrangular enceinte varied between 1,340 and 1,740 meters; of D'jog near Han-tan, with a maximum extent of 1,387 × 1,475 meters; and of the small state of D'əng in modern T'eng-Hsien, whose outer rampart measured some 1,000 meters by 1,500. The outer circular enceinte of the old state of ·Jam is best measured in terms of its circumference, which was about 600 meters in length. There is no reason to think that the areal extent of cities was larger at the end of the Chou period than at its beginning. And neither is there any reason to assume that a correlation of size with rank in the urban hierarchy which is adduced in the *Tso-Chuan* was anything more than a late systematization. The passage in question runs, 'The walls of any state capital (*to*) which exceed a hundred **d'*i̯ər* (chih) [in circumference] constitute a danger to the state. According to the institutions (**t̯i̯ad*, chih) of the former kings, the walls of a city of the first order must not exceed one-third the length of that of the capital, that of a second-order city one-fifth, and that of a third-order city one-ninth.'273 That this archetyped notion of the urban hierarchy was indeed a piece of literary furniture brought out to grace a certain type of occasion is rendered the more likely by the inclusion of another passage, expressing very similar sentiments, in a patently moralizing context.

'The King [of *Tṣ'i̯o*] asked **Śi̯ĕn Mi̯wo-gi̯wo (Shen Wu-yü) what was likely to happen if a state contained great cities [in addition to the capital. Śi̯ĕn] replied that in [the state of] **D'i̯ĕng [the existence of] **Kli̯ăng (Ching) and **Gliok (Li) was the real cause of the death of **Mwân păk (Man-pe); [the existence of] **Siôg (Hsiao) and **B'âk (Po) in Sông led to the murder of **Tsi̯əg-Di̯ôg (Tzŭ-Yu); in Dz'i̯ər [the existence of] **G'i̯o-k'i̯ŭg (Ch'ü-ch'iu) was directly responsible for the slaying of **Mi̯wo-Ti̯ĕg (Wu-Chih); in Gi̯wad [the existence of] **B'wo (P'u) and **Ts'iôk (Ch'i) brought about the expulsion of Duke **Xi̯ăn (Hsien). In the light of these examples it must be concluded that [such cities] are injurious to the state. Large branches are sure to break, a large tail cannot be wagged.'274

It would be premature to deny that, at the ceremonies by which benefice capitals were established in the early centuries of the Chou, the formal layouts may not have been conceived according to some descending order of size based on the rulers' positions in the social and political hierarchies (though I know of no independent evidence to support such a contention), but it is inconceivable that such a graded ranking of urban size should have persisted as the pressures of developing tertiary economic activities (modest in scale though these were) began to interact with the ever-present strains of political conflict. In any case, beyond confirming the truism that the more important cities of ancient China had larger enceintes, such archeological evidence as we have affords no confirmation of any such rigorously ordered hierarchy of size.

The shape of Chou urban enclaves is sufficiently significant to merit separate discussion in Chapter Five. Suffice it to note here that there was a strong tendency to regularity in the layout, a regularity which was expressed predominantly in the form of a square, or at least of a rectangle. On several of the occasions on which city plans at first appear to be fortuitously irregular, closer inspection leads to the inference that they were in fact built up by the accretion of individually regular units. Such appears to have happened, for example, in the evolution of the G'å-to. That such a process of accretion did indeed operate from time to time to modify the layouts of Chou cities is attested by the remark in the *Tso-Chuan* that 'in summer [of 667 BC] **Dẓ'i̯əg-Gwia (Shih-Wei), Grand Minister of Works (**D'âd-si̯əg-k'ung : Ta-szŭ-k'ung), walled [presumably implying in this context that he enlarged the walls of] **Kǫng (Chiang) in order to secure a greater depth for the palace.'[275] The archeological reports also reveal a tendency to both cardinal orientation and cardinal axiality of city enceintes. This latter feature is perhaps suggested by the central location of the presumably ceremonial platform in the Tsjĕn capital at Niu, is implied by the arrangement of the gates leading into the enclosure at Chao-k'ang, and is partly traced out in paved roads at the D'jog city near Wu-an. In G'ân-tân it is explicit in the arrangement of the *hang-t'u* platforms along north-south axes. The number and arrangement of city gates were also important elements of city morphology, but are best discussed in connection with the topic of symbolism included in Chapter Five.

A prominent feature of urban design throughout the whole Chou period was the raising of important buildings on platforms of *hang-t'u* construction. At Niu-Ts'un such a platform was located at the geometrical center of the city enceinte; at P'ing-wang one appears to have been similarly located; at G'ân-tân two series were arranged along meridional axes, and an additional ten were scattered both within and without the city; at Lin-tzŭ one was located in a small enclave in the southwest of the main enclosure; at the site of ·Jam three very large examples, situated between the so-called Inner and Outer Walls, were aligned parallel to the western sector of the former; and more than fifty were dispersed in and around the enceinte of the G'å-to. In this latter case a proportion of these small tumuli are believed to have been burial mounds, but elsewhere the platforms have usually been construed as the foundations of palaces and temples, and the localities in which they occur consequently interpreted as palace precincts and ceremonial centers. In plan these platforms were predominantly square and circular, though the one at Lin-tzŭ was oval, and those at ·Jam (Yen) of irregular shape. Of the sixteen platforms at G'ân-tân, fourteen were square and only two circular. Just outside the northern wall of the G'å-to a large square platform, the Lao-lao T'ai, provided a base from which rose a circular mound. This platform was also diversified by three terraces cut in its southern face, a feature which had occurred earlier in the P'ing-wang platform. At both P'ing-wang and Niu-Ts'un the southern edges of the platforms were constructed in the form of ramps. It is tempting to ponder on the different purposes reflected in the varying forms of these *hang-t'u* mounds, but so far archeology has provided no basis for such speculation beyond the presence of architectural remains on the summits of numerous of them.

At several of the earlier urban sites archeologists have reported the existence of workshops not only within the walled enclaves but also dispersed through the surrounding countryside on the old Shang pattern. This dispersed morphology was especially prominent in the Royal City of Chou and in the Tsjĕn capitals in the vicinity of Hou-ma Chen, and, as in Shang times, presumably implies a redistributive mode of economic integration. During the Eastern Chou, however, this dispersed morphology seems to have undergone a major transformation when outer walls were constructed to enclose previously extramural settlements and workshops. Miyazaki Ichisada was apparently the first to notice indications of this process in Chou literary sources,[276] and during the past twenty years his observations have been confirmed by archeological investigation. This scholar seems to have regarded the original enceinte as having at one time provided a site for virtually all urban activities, and to have assumed the role of administrative and ceremonial enclave only after the building of the outer wall. We take a slightly different view, and visualize the inner enclosure as having from the beginning constituted the ceremonial focus, the outer wall being added subsequently to afford protection to the populace and handicrafts that had been attracted to the neighborhood of the cult center. That such a spatial expression of the dichotomy between the two main sectors of society, the *kįwən-tsįəg* and the *dįå-ńįĕn*, the sacrally ordained élite and the mass of the populace, did exist in Chou times is attested by fragmentary references in ancient literature which divide the representative city into two sectors. One, termed alternatively the **to* (*tu*) or **kwâk* (*kuo*), contained the sacred structures without which a state could not come into, or remain in, being, together with the palace of the ruler, and accommodation, usually in early times in the form of semi-subterranean dwellings, for retainers, servitors and some craftsmen. The other sector, known as the **pįəg* (*pi*), housed the rest of the community and provided sites for most of the handicraft workshops serving it. Occasionally the names attached to some of the discrete quarters of these cities have been recorded in Chou literature, chiefly in the *Tso-Chuan*. One quarter of the capital of D'įĕng, for example, was known straightforwardly as the Central District (**Tįông-Pįwən : Chung-Fen),[277] and another within the capital of Sông went by the name of the Southern Neighborhood (**Nəm-Lįəg : Nan-Li).[278] In the suburbs the dwellings were partly of *hang-t'u* and partly of thatch, and in the dry and dusty winter months fire was an ever-threatening hazard. As early as 563 BC precautionary measures were

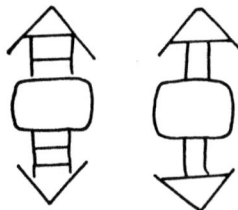

[15] The character denoting the outer wall of an early Chinese city as it appears (right) on Shang oracle bones and (left) on an early Chou bronze [Karlgren, 774b and c].

initiated in the capital of Sông after the city had been devastated by fire. Although the conflagration was denoted in the *Tso-Chuan* by the graph for a calamity sent by Heaven (**tsəg : tsai),[279] the government nevertheless made every effort to prevent the divine will manifesting itself in the same form on a subsequent occasion. **Nglŏk-Xịəg (Yüeh-Hsi), the equivalent of a Minister of Works, appointed an official to supervise preventative measures in those parts of the city which the flames had not reached. Small houses were to be removed altogether and large ones to be rough-cast. Baskets and barrows were to be placed at strategic spots, well-ropes, buckets and water-jars were to be provided, and supplies of earth and mud held in readiness. A fire-watch was to be maintained within the city, and reserve forces were to be summoned from the countryside. Particular attention was to be paid to the safety of the state records in their several repositories, and to the precincts of the palace. This is the only instance of preventative action to have been recorded in such detail, but we may be certain that the problem was one common to all cities of the time.

The fundamental role of the inner wall enclosing the administrative and ceremonial focus of the territory, the axis about which revolved the microcosm of the state, is reflected in the etymology of the word **dịĕng (ch'eng), which came to denote both 'city' and '[the] wall', whereas **kwâk (kuo), the outer wall, acquired overtones associated with fortification and subsequently developed the secondary meaning of 'suburb'.[280] That the two enceintes were not always constructed simultaneously is attested by an account of the founding of **Tṣ'ịo-k'ịŭg (Ch'u-ch'iu), the new Gịwad capital, after the previous city had been razed by the D'iek barbarians. The neighboring states sent contingents to assist in the raising of the inner wall surrounding the ceremonial center in the spring of 657,[281] but the suburbs (**p'ịug : fu) were not walled until the spring of 647, when a D'iek attack appeared to be imminent.[282] The royal capital of Dịĕng-Tịôg (cf. p. 136 above) affords another example. The suburb of **D'iek-dz'ịwan (Ti-ch'üan), site of the royal tombs outside the eastern wall, had certainly come into existence by 517 BC,[283] but was not brought within the wall until 508.[284] In Lo the suburbs of the city of **Dịĕng, which appears to have been mentioned first in 705,[285] were not walled until 557 in the face of an attack by the forces of the Marquis of Dz'iər.[286] And, as a final example, we may point to a brief notice in the *Tso-Chuan* which records the walling of the already existing suburbs of **Dz'ŏg (Ch'ao) and **Kịwɛd-ńịan (Chi-jan) in Tṣ'ịo.[287]

The *Kuo-Yü* expressed the spatial and functional dichotomy of the city rather differently in opposing an administrative enclave (**kwân-pịu : kuan-fu) to a market place (**dịəg-tsịĕng), and realistically also included within the urban sphere the fields that lay beyond its walls (**d'ien-dịǎ). It would seem that Mencius had a similar pattern of land use in mind when he wrote that, if the King were to establish a government of perfect virtue, then 'the officials of the kingdom would all be anxious to establish themselves at Your Majesty's court, the farmers would all be anxious to cultivate Your Majesty's lands, and the merchants would all be anxious to store their goods in Your Majesty's market-places.'[288]

Although it is clear that these changes in urban form took place during the Chou dynasty, because of the relative paucity of archeological evidence and the difficulty of dating the information contained in cumulative and systematizing texts, it is not yet possible to define the stages by which they came about. In any case, there is no reason to suppose that the transformation proceeded contemporaneously in all states. Certainly the old dispersed pattern of urban integration appears to have persisted in the settlements of the New Fields well into the second half of the Ch'un-Ch'iu period, whereas the newer compact urban forms, with their double enceintes, seem to have become common during Chan-Kuo times, with the rise of cities such as the Dz'iər capital at Lin-tzŭ and the D'əng, ·Iam, and ·Ok[289] capitals. Precisely which point of view one adopts in this matter will depend very largely on how one interprets the urban annexes that feature in the plans of some of these cities, notably that of G'ân-tân. Wolfram Eberhard has proposed to group such cities into a class which he calls appropriately 'double cities', each sector of which he regards as inhabited by ethnically distinct populations.[290] In his view most of the Chou *colonia* established after the conquest would have taken this form. It is true that the *I Chou-shu*, which probably preserves material from the beginning of the 3rd century BC, attributes just such a formal dichotomy to **Glâk-·jəp (Lo-i, later known as Djĕng-Tjôg: cf. p. 136 above),[291] and similar divisions are mentioned in connection with the old Chou capitals of P'jông and G'og, but only archeological investigation will ultimately decide if the ancient texts are to be relied upon in this respect. Even if they are, it still remains an open question as to whether the ethnic division of the early Chou *colonia* was the precursor of the class division apparent in later times. All that can be said at present is that such an ethnically based duality does not appear to us to have been a prerequisite for the development of the double enclaves of Chan-Kuo times.

In the idealized city of the Western Chou the ruler's palace was raised exactly in the center of the enceinte, and itself constituted a city within a city. At its very center the hall of audience fronted southwards on to the axial avenue which ran between the altar to the god of the soil and the temple of the ancestors. At the next lower level in the social hierarchy the dwellings of the more powerful families, each grouped round its own great hall, reproduced on a smaller scale the residence of the ruler. As in all classical, which is synonymous with archetyped, literatures, the cities of the Western Chou are represented as splendid creations of Chinese architectural genius. That they were something less, indeed – although they contained the seeds which would later flower into the glories of Ch'ang-an and Pei-ching – often mean and cluttered settlements, has been stated so persuasively by Marcel Granet that I can do no better than quote his description of these ancient cities.[292]

'It appears however that in every country the princely residences were usually humble dwellings, quickly built and rapidly demolished. In 502, for example, a highly placed personage had a house of beaten earth made for his son, at the side of his own palace.[a] There was no hesitation in throwing down entire houses to make way for a funeral.[b] An old ritual rule (which is explained by the constitution of the family) required that sons should not have the same abode as their father : fathers and sons resided (in alternate generations) on the right or left of a building which was supposed to have been the house of the founder of their line. The same disposition held good for the chapels of the ancestral Temple which were consecrated to the most recent ancestors. All these ephemeral dwellings, enclosed within low little walls and separated by narrow alleys, were crowded around a sort of fortress. In time of revolts and vendettas (for example at Chin [*Tsjĕn*] in 549 BC) attackers are seen to leap over the low walls. When they have hoisted themselves upon the gate of the palace, they can rain arrows into the prince's chamber : but a fortified tower serves as an entrenchment for the defenders. At Ch'i [*Dz'iər*], in 538 BC, under a prince famous for his ostentation, the chief minister resides in a low quarter containing the market. He inhabits "a low and narrow house, exposed to the dust". The prince is alone in possessing "a piece of ground which is well lighted, high and dry". Built upon an eminence and flanked by towers, the seigniorial residence looks like a fortified village dominating the low-lying outskirts of a market.[c]'

[Granet's footnotes refer to Séraphin Couvreur's French translation of the *Ch'un-Ch'iu* and *Tso-Chuan* in 3 volumes (Mission Press, Hochienfu, 1914) : (*a*) vol. 3, p. 547; (*b*) vol. 3, p. 291; (*c*) vol. 2, p. 293, and vol. 3, pp. 59, 60, 736.]

SIZE OF THE CHOU CITY

The level of intensity of archeological excavation of Chou urban sites does not permit us to use the dimensions of the enceintes described in the preceding section to estimate the populations of these cities in the manner in which, say, Henri Frankfort was able to calculate early urban densities for Lower Meso-potamia.[293] Of the density of dwellings within either or both enceintes we have practically no idea. The problem is especially intractable in the case of the dis-persed settlement form associated with the Shang and earlier centuries of the Chou. To judge from analogous developmental stages of urban evolution in other parts of East Asia and Nuclear America, by no means all the space within the city walls was under structures of any kind, let alone residential buildings (cf. also p. 436 below). In default of a sound archeological basis for calculation, we can only fall back on the few population estimates which occur in Chou literature. The *Chan-Kuo Ts'e* (chüan 8), for example, credits the Dz'iər capital at Lin-tzŭ with 210,000 inhabitants. In view of what we have said about such texts in a previous section, it is doubtful if this figure can be relied upon. When the Gi̯wad capital was re-established at **Tṣ'i̯o-k'i̯ŭg (Ch'u-ch'iu) after its sack at the hands of the D'iek barbarians in 659 B C, it was reputed to have had a mere 5,000 inhabitants,[294] including the people of two smaller settlements, **Ki̯ung (Kung) and **D'əng (T'eng), who had been brought into it. Presumably the population of the earlier capital had been somewhat larger. That many, perhaps most, Ch'un-Ch'iu urban settlements were much less populous than this is implicit in numerous passages in the literature of the time. It was proposed, for example, to invest a single Gi̯wad minister with as many as sixty ·i̯əp,[295] which surely implies that each was a relatively small settlement; and we have already drawn attention to the implication in an appendix to the *I-Ching* that some three hundred households constituted a reasonable population for a representative ·i̯əp (p. 167). It must be remembered, of course, that, whatever its pretentions, this particular appendix was composed, at the earliest, towards the end of the Chou period, and its assumptions are those of the era of the Contending States or later.

Notes and References

1. I have made no attempt to furnish primary documentation for this introductory section, but these notes do provide a skeleton bibliography of secondary and exegetical writings which should help a student of urbanism to acquire an appreciation of the background against which Chou cities evolved.

2. For pertinent comments on this stereotype see Arthur F. Wright, 'Sui Yang-ti: personality and stereotype', in Wright [ed.], *The Confucian persuasion*. Stanford University Press, Stanford, California 1960. Reprinted in Wright [ed.], *Confucianism and Chinese civilization*. Atheneum Paperback no.64, 1964.

3. Noel Barnard, 'A recently excavated inscribed bronze of Western Chou date', *Monumenta Serica*, vol.17 (1958), pp.12–46, and review article in vol.22, fasc.1 of the same journal (1963), pp.223–4. In any case, the canonical view of the role of the Duke of Chou was probably only an elaboration of events by genealogists of the ducal house of **Lo (Lu), who claimed him as their ancestor. Confucians would naturally be well disposed towards the progenitor of the royal house whose early rulers were revered by their master. On the other hand, the Duke of Chou is mentioned only twice in the *Shih-Ching*, and not at all in the *Shang-Sung* section.

4. There are indications that **Tân-B'įwo (Tan-Fu) may have been a culture-hero who at one time rivalled the Chou progenitor **G'u-Tsjək (Hou-Chi). It is possible, for example, that one of the **D'âd-Ngâ (*Ta-Ya*) Odes [Mao 237] associates him with the gourd seeds from which, in certain East Asian mythologies, germinated the human race [cf. Arthur Waley, *The Book of Songs*. George Allen and Unwin Ltd, London 1937, pp.246–7], whereas G'u-Tsjək was traditionally associated with domesticated plants : 'he understood the ways of the earth [so that] appropriate grains were planted and the harvest gathered in' [*Shih-Chi*, chüan 4, f.1 verso]. The fact that Tân-B'įwo was eventually assigned to a later period than G'u-Tsjək is no guarantee of the chronological priority of the latter's myth : indeed, such is the nature of early Chinese historiography, it may well be held to imply an earlier date for the Tân-B'įwo legend.

5. This is the pre-conquest history of the Chou people as it is recorded in *Shih-Chi* : in other ancient sources the detail varies but the general tenor of the account remains substantially the same.

6. Shih Chang-ju, 'Kuan-chung k'ao-ku tiao-ch'a pao-kao', *Kuo-li Chung-yang Yen-chiu-yüan Li-shih Yü-yen Yen-chiu-so Chi-k'an*, vol.27 (1956),

pp.205–323; Su Ping-chi, *Tou-chi T'ai Kou-tung-ch'ü Mu-tsang.* National Academy of Pei-p'ing 1948.

7. Su Ping-chi and Wu Ju-tso, 'Hsi-an fu-chin ku-wen-hua i-ts'un-ti lei-hsing ho fen-pu', *K'ao-ku T'ung-hsün,* no.2 (1956), pp.32–8.

8. For discussions of these materials, and particularly the *T'ien-wang Kuei,* an inscribed bronze vessel which may date from the pre-conquest period of Chou history, see Sun Tso-yün, 'Shuo "T'ien-wang Kuei" wei Wu-wang mieh Shang i-ch'ien t'ung-ch'i' *Wen-wu Ts'an-k'ao Tzŭ-liao,* no.1 (1958), pp.29–31, and "Tsai lun 'T'ien-wang Kuei' erh-san-shih," *Wen-wu,* no.5 (1960), pp.50–52; Ch'ien Po-ch'üan, '"Shuo T'ien-wang Kuei wei Wu-wang mieh Shang i-ch'ien t'ung-ch'i" i-wen-ti chi-tien shang-ch'üeh', *Wen-wu Ts'an-k'ao Tzŭ-liao,* no.12 (1958), pp.56–7; Yin Ti-fei, 'Shih-lun "T'ien-feng Kuei"-ti nien-tai', *Wen-wu,* no.5 (1960), pp.53–4.

9. Generic names for the tribes of the western and northern frontiers respectively. In the *Kuo-Yü* [*chüan* 1, f.2 verso], a ministerial descendant of the Duke of Chou (ᵗi̯ôg) found it more expedient to claim that during the Hsia dynasty the ancestors of the Chou kings 'had hidden themselves among the **Ni̯ông (Jung) and **D'iek (Ti)', while yet retaining their Chinese culture.

10. *Shih-Chi,* chüan 4, f.3 recto.

11. *Chu-shu Chi-nien,* Shang dynasty, *sub* Wen-ting (**Mi̯wən-tieng).

12. Wolfram Eberhard, *Kultur und Siedlung der Randvölker Chinas.* Supplement to *T'oung Pao,* vol.36, E.J.Brill, Leiden 1942; *A history of China.* University of California Press, Berkeley and Los Angeles, second edition, 1960, p.29; and *Conquerors and rulers. Social forces in medieval China.* E.J.Brill, Leiden, second edition, 1965, p.28. Cf. also Gustav Haloun, 'Beiträge zur Siedlungsgeschichte chinesischer Clans', *Hirth-Festschrift der Asia Major.* Leipzig 1922; 'Contributions to the history of clan settlement', *Asia Major,* vol.1. Leipzig, 1924; and 'Die Rekonstruktion der chinesischen Urgeschichte durch die Chinesen', *Japanisch-deutsche Zeitschrift für Wissenschaft und Technik,* vol.3, pt.7 (1925).

13. Owen Lattimore, *Inner Asian frontiers of China.* American Geographical Society, New York 1940, parts II and III. Reprint by the Beacon Press, Boston 1962. Cf. also Lattimore, *Studies in frontier history.* Oxford University Press 1962, p.547 [This paper is a reprint of a review article which first appeared in *Past and Present,* vol.12 (1957)].

14. Ralph Linton and Abram Kardiner, 'The change from dry to wet rice cultivation in Tanala-Betsileo', in *The individual and his society.* Columbia University Press, New York 1939. Reprinted in *Readings in social psychology.* New York 1952, pp.222–31. After the Tanala had adopted the techniques of wet padi cultivation from their Betsileo neighbors Linton was able to document the following concomitant changes in the structure of their society: the gradual emergence of a group of landowners; the disruption of the joint family, endo-

gamy and self-sufficiency; the establishment of permanent settlements; modifications in the patterns of warfare; the attachment of an economic value to slaves and an associated formulation of ransom procedures; and the institutionalization of kingship. Linton further pointed out that the situation to be expected when this transformation – which had been initiated by a change in methods of production – should be consolidated and institutionalized was already apparent in Betsileo society, which he characterized as 'a feudal system of a kind' (*ibid.*, p.227).

15. René Grousset, *The rise and splendour of the Chinese empire*. University of California Press, Berkeley and Los Angeles 1958, p.22. This work is a translation by Anthony Watson-Gandy and Terence Gordon of *Histoire de la Chine*. Fayard, Paris 1942.

16. Herrlee Glessner Creel's evaluation is entirely representative of this school of thought : '. . . we know that the Chou were relatively rude barbarians who overran their more cultivated Shang neighbors and consolidated a large portion of North China under a rule that was necessarily rather harsh. . . . The chiefs of the Chou tribe had neither the experience nor the facilities (communications and a monetary system) necessary for highly centralized government...' [*Confucius: the man and the myth*. John Day Company, New York 1949, p.157: p.146 of the reprinted edition under the title *Confucius and the Chinese way*. Harper Torchbook no.63, New York 1960].

17. Noel Barnard, 'A recently excavated inscribed bronze of Western Chou date', *Monumenta Serica*, vol.17 (1958), pp.35–6, and 'A recently excavated inscribed bronze of the reign of King Mu of Chou', *Monumenta Serica*, vol.19 (1960), p.75, note 8.

18. Barnard regards inscriptions of this kind included in Lo Chen-yü's well known compendia as either spurious or of non-Shang origin (*loc. cit.* p.36, note 21).

19. Kwang-chih Chang, *The archaeology of ancient China*. Yale University Press, New Haven 1963, p.180.

20. Another tradition, neither more nor less reliable than the one quoted, alleges that the Chou ruler destroyed some fifty or so [city-]states and founded seventy, while the *Hsün-tzŭ* (4, i and 8, xii) mentions a figure of seventy-one, of which fifty-three were granted to royal kinsmen. The *I Chou-Shu*, possibly compiled in the 3rd or 4th century BC, states that the Chou armies conquered ninety-nine [city-]states and imposed their authority on 652 others [Chu Yu-tseng's edition, Han-k'ou, 1911, chüan 4, f.7 recto], while the late-Chou *Lü-Shih Ch'un-Ch'iu* mentions figures of 400 and 800 for the two categories respectively.

21. This term is used in the sense advocated by Lewis Henry Morgan, 'The systems of consanguinity and affinity,' *Smithsonian Institution contributions to knowledge*, vol.17 (1877). Cf. also A. R. Radcliffe-Brown, *Structure and function*

in primitive society. The Free Press edition, New York 1965, p.64 : 'A nomenclature is classificatory when it uses terms which apply to lineal relatives, such as "father", to refer also to collateral relatives.'

22. Genealogical tables of rulers and their chief ministers are to be found in the Sung scholar Ch'eng Kung-shuo's *Ch'un-Ch'iu Fen-chi* (in the *Ssŭ-k'u Ch'üan-shu*), Book I, chüan 1–18 : cf. also Sun Yao, *Ch'un-Ch'iu Shih-tai-chih Shih-tsu*. China Book Co., Shanghai 1931. On the spurious nature of, for example, the genealogies of the rulers of **·*Ian* (*Yen*) and **Ngo* (*Wu*) see Ch'i Ssŭ-ho, 'Yen-Wu fei Chou feng-kuo shuo', *Yen-ching Hsüeh-pao*, no.28 (1940), pp.175–96. Cf. also Lou Kan-jou, *Histoire sociale de l'époque Tcheou.* Paris 1935, p.42.

23. The comparison with Nippur is apt in another respect, for there is good evidence that *Kengir*, the only term known to have been used for Sumer as a political unit, originally denoted Nippur itself, and consequently affords a parallel with the term Chou (**tįôg) : *vide* Thorkild Jacobsen, *Journal of the American Oriental Society*, vol.59 (1939), p.487, note 11, and 'Early political developments in Mesopotamia', *Zeitschrift für Assyriologie*, vol.52 (1957), pp.91–140.

24. *Vide* Ku Chieh-kang (ed.), *Ku-shih Pien*, vols.1 and 2, *passim*, and Tjan Tjoe Som [Tseng Chu-sen], *Po-hu T'ung*, vol.1. Brill, Leiden 1949.

25. The first full-scale study of the political structure of pre-Ch'in China in this new idiom was that by Richard Louis Walker, *The multi-state system of ancient China*. The Shoe String Press, Hamden, Connecticut 1953, which presented essentially the interpretation adopted in the present work. Earlier authors who had moved in the same direction but somewhat more hesitantly included Ch'en Shih-ts'ai, *A fragment on the equality of states.* A doctoral dissertation submitted to Harvard College, 1945; and 'The equality of states in ancient China', *American Journal of International Law*, vol.35 (1941), pp.641–650. Hung Chün-p'ei [*Ch'un-Ch'iu Kuo-chi Kung-fa*. China Book Company, Shanghai 1937, Chapter I, pp.1–9] summarizes a variety of previous works in this vein. The first Western author to apply the analytical techniques of modern political science to the multi-state system of the Ch'un-Ch'iu was Roswell Britton, 'Chinese Interstate Intercourse before 700 BC', *American Journal of International Law*, vol.29 (1935).

26. *Tso-Chuan*, Duke **·Įən (Yin), 3rd year and Duke **G'wân (Huan), 5th year.

27. This figure has been computed by modern scholars on the basis of information in the *Ch'un-Ch'iu*, its commentaries, and other relevant texts relating to the early years of the Eastern Chou. Cf. Li Tung-fang, *Ch'un-Ch'iu Chan-Kuo P'ien. Chung-Kuo Li-shih T'ung-lun* series. Commercial Press, Ch'ung-ch'ing 1944, p.65. Ku Tung-kao, in his meticulous chronological systematization of events recorded in the Ch'un-Ch'iu, *Ch'un-Ch'iu Ta-shih*

Piao (preface dated 1748), table 5, pp.1a–15a [in *Huang-Ch'ing Ching-chieh Hsü-p'ien*, ts'e 17–34], lists 209 states which are mentioned in the *Ch'un-Ch'iu* and *Tso-Chuan*, but a proportion of these were drawn into the Chinese culture-realm during, rather than before, the period and consequently were not counted by Li Tung-fang. Cf. also Ch'eng Te-hsü, 'International law in early China (1122–249 BC)', *Chinese Social and Political Science Review*, vol.11 (1927), p.42.

28. The most detailed map of the boundaries of the Ch'un-Ch'iu states is probably that at the end of vol.1 of Otto Franke's *Geschichte des chinesischen Reiches*. Walter de Gruyter, Berlin 1930.

29. In this connection we are reminded that when a **Tsjĕn envoy investigated the **Lo archives in 540 BC, he is reported to have exclaimed, 'The institutes (**liər) of Tjôg (Chou) are all in Lo. Now, indeed, I recognize the virtue of the Duke of Tjôg and understand how [the Duke of] Tjôg attained royal status.'

30. Not to be confused with the Royal Tjôg (Chou), which is denoted by a different character.

31. But see Hou Wai-lu, *Chung-Kuo Ku-tai She-hui-shih*. Shanghai 1948.

32. The exception was the state of Dz'iər, which was able to extend its territory at the expense of non-Chinese peoples on the Shan-tung peninsula, a process which has been analyzed and mapped by Walker, *The multi-state system*, pp.29–30. Eberhard has argued that the peripheral states were also better placed, being farther from the focus of power, to develop their own effective systems of local administration [*Conquerors and rulers*, pp.29–30].

33. E.g. **mjat (*mieh*)=extinguish, exterminate, destroy; **ts'ju (*ch'ü*)= take, seize; **g'ŏng / ?g'lông (*hsiang*)=bring to terms, submit; **ts'jan (*ch'ien*)=remove, be removed.

34. Fung Yu-lan, *A history of Chinese philosophy*. Transl. from the Chinese by Derk Bodde, second edition, Princeton University Press 1952, p.312.

35. Max Weber, *The theory of social and economic organization*. Transl. from the German by A. M. Henderson and Talcott Parsons, The Free Press of Glencoe, Illinois 1947, pp.136–8, 329 *et seq.* and 341 *et seq.*

36. A schedule of these g'wâd (*hui*) has been prepared by Li Tung-fang, *Ch'un-Ch'iu Chan-Kuo P'ien*, Chapter I, note 49.

37. Marcel Granet, *La féodalité chinoise*. Instituttet for Sammenlignende Kulturforskning. H. Aschehoug, Oslo 1952, p.66.

38. These were Tş'jo, Dz'iər, Dz'jĕn, **G'ân (Han, a succession state which emerged on the dissolution of Tsjĕn at the end of the 5th century) and ·Ian. **D'jog (Chao), another succession state, followed suit at about this time but the precise year is uncertain.

39. Ssŭ-ma Ch'ien (*Shih-Chi*, chüan 14 and 15) refers to twelve states but enumerates thirteen. This apparent anomaly is usually explained either by

assuming that Ngo was still counted as barbarian, un-Chinese, or that the term 'Twelve Rulers' had become a synecdochic synonym for the whole Chinese culture-realm before Ngo was admitted to the group, and was retained subsequently.

40. Cho-yün Hsü [Hsü Cho-yün], *Ancient China in transition. An analysis of social mobility, 722–222 B C*. Stanford University Press 1965, Chapter 4.

41. Cf. the genealogy of the *Lo* ducal house on p.79 of Hsü's work, and the commentary which accompanies it on pp.78–9.

42. Cf. Table 2, p.30 in Hsü's *Ancient China*.

43. Cf. Max Weber, 'Politik als Beruf', *Gesammelte Politische Schriften*. München 1921, pp.396–450. According to Gerth and Mills this paper was originally presented as a speech at München University in 1918, and published by Duncker and Humblot in the following year. There is an English translation in H. H. Gerth and C. Wright Mills, *From Max Weber*. Galaxy Book no.13, Oxford University Press, New York 1958, pp.77–128. This change in the nature of Chou administration has already been noted by Professor Cho-yün Hsü, *Ancient China*, p.92.

It must be emphasized that direct evidence of Western Chou government is extremely meager, so that there is an unavoidable tendency to regard changes such as those discussed in the present instance as having been initiated in the Ch'an-Ch'iu period. However, it is worthy of note that Professor H. G. Creel has recently drawn attention to the existence under the Western Chou of officials who might reasonably be called proto-bureaucrats (although it is difficult to say to what extent they functioned in the domains of vassals as well as in those of the king). 'It appears quite possible,' he writes, 'that there was [early in the Western Chou] . . . a more effective and centralized administration than critical scholars have usually been willing to suppose'. ['The beginnings of bureaucracy in China : the origin of the *Hsien*', *The Journal of Asian Studies*, vol.23, no.2 (1964), p.169, note 75].

44. Gerth and Mills, *From Max Weber*, p.82.

45. Granet, *La féodalité chinoise*, p.20.

46. S. Dubrowsky, 'Über das Wesen des Feudalismus', *Agrar-Probleme*. Moscow and Munich 1929, p.214. The relevant passage has been translated into English by Wolfram Eberhard in *Conquerors and rulers*, p.24, which also contains a discussion of several theories of feudalism as applied to China.

47. In contemporary Chinese historiography 'feudalism' is the only permitted epithet for some three millennia of the Chinese past, a truth revealed, if not discovered, by Chairman Mao himself in the famous phrase 'feudal from Chou and Ch'in' : Mao Tse-tung, *Chung-Kuo Ke-ming ho Chung-Kuo Kung-ch'an-tang*. Hong Kong 1949.

48. This attitude is typified by the remark of Joseph Calmette [*La société féodale*, Third edition, Paris 1925, p.1 : 'En réalité, la féodalité est proprement

196

occidentale et mediévale'], and is very close to that of Bryce Lyon, *The Middle Ages*, p.13.

49. F. W. Maitland, *The constitutional history of England.* Cambridge University Press 1908, pp.22–3.

50. This is the class of definition which John W. Hall has termed 'particularistic' ['Feudalism in Japan – a reassessment', *Comparative Studies in Society and History*, vol.5, no.1 (1962), p.21].

51. This is Hall's 'linear or developmental conception of feudalism', *loc. cit.*, p.23.

52. Attempts to define feudalism in ethnocentric terms have certainly not been confined to Western Europe. S. B. Veselovsky, for example, spent a lifetime in study of the political and manorial aspects of feudalism in northeastern Russia from the 14th to the 16th century, and, although methodologically he relied on Seebohm, Maitland and Fustel de Coulanges, his conclusions, so far as they were published, related only to one part of Russia. Cf. *Feodal'noe zemlev-ladenie v Severo-Vostochnoĭ Rusi.* On the other hand, S. Yushkov [*Voprosy Istorii*, vol.7 (1946)] adduced interesting parallels between societies as diverse as those of Kievan Russia prior to the 11th century, the Mongol realm prior to Činggis Khan, and the Anglo-Saxon kingdoms before the 9th century AD.

53. It appears that the term 'feudalism' was first coined by the Comte de Boulainvilliers and given wider currency by Montesquieu. Cf. Marc Bloch, *Feudal Society*, transl. from the French by L. A. Manyon. Chicago University Press 1961, pp.xvii–xviii. Learning of this abstraction, Chinese historians rendered it by a term which subsumed a rich store of associations from classical times, namely *feng-chien chih-tu*. According to the Chin philologist Chang-I, both *feng* and *chien* meant 'to establish', and either could be used alone to

[III] The character for ***pi̯ung* (*feng*), signifying 'a mound' or 'to raise a mound', as it appears in a Chou bronze inscription.

denote enfeoffment [*Vide* Chang-I, *Kuang-Ya*, with commentary by Wang Nien-sun (1879), chüan 4, f.22 verso]. Moreover, *feng* (***pi̯ung*) had in early Chou times signified a mound, the raising of a mound, and to earth up a plant. In fact, in Chou bronze inscriptions the character depicts a hand beside a plant rooted in soil, and presumably implies the act of piling earth around a plant. According to books of ritual composed in much later times, the Western Chou ceremony of investiture involved the implanting, in the capital of the new benefice, of a clod of earth from the altar of the national God of the Soil. The new altar mound (*feng*) was then raised around the clod, whence the use of the term (*feng*) to signify enfeoffment. This was the word, with its aura of mellow, half-hallowed classical associations, which Chinese historians used to translate the European concept of feudalism, but many of them, often less familiar with the specialist studies of medieval European history than with Japanese translations of works of Marxian socialism, perceived the lineaments of feudalism as permeating all Chinese history prior to the 20th century, with the exception, of course, of a pre-feudal period lost in the mists of prehistory. For others feudalism developed out of a slave society, and the exigent problem then was to devise a periodization appropriate to these two societies. Cf., for example, Lü Chen-yü, *Chung-Kuo Cheng-chih Ssŭ-hsiang-shih*. Shanghai 1937; and *Chung-Kuo She-hui Shih-kang*, 2 vols. Shanghai 1947; Chien Po-tsan, *Chung-Kuo Shih-kang*, 2 vols. Shanghai 1946. The more sophisticated approach to the study of Chinese feudalism by Ch'i Ssŭ-ho is mentioned below.

54. These are the additional features cited by Derk Bodde in a paper in which he evaluated previous studies of the Chinese experience in the light of the findings of an interdisciplinary conference on comparative feudalism, held at Princeton University in 1950. *Vide* Bodde in Rushton Coulborn (ed.), *Feudalism in History*. Princeton University Press 1956, p.90. Granet [*La féodalité chinoise*, pp.24–8], who considered that the institutional parallels between ancient Chinese and medieval European society were sufficiently close for the former justly to be termed 'feudal', cited as the distinctive characteristic of both societies the dichotomy between a noble warrior class living according to an elaborate code of honor and performing military service in return for enfeoffment on the one hand, and a peasantry who lacked the code, possessed no rights to the land they worked, and served in war only as conscripted levies on the other.

55. Ch'i Ssŭ-ho, 'A comparison between Chinese and European feudal institutions', *Yenching Journal of Social Studies*, vol.4 (1948), pp.1–13, 'Feng-chien-chih-tu yü Ju-chia ssŭ-hsiang', *Yen-ching Hsüeh-pao*, no.22 (1937), pp.175–223, and 'Chan-Kuo chih-tu k'ao', *Yen-ching Hsüeh-pao*, no.24 (1938), pp.159–219.

56. Ch'i Ssŭ-ho, 'A comparison', p.2.

57. Eberhard, *Conquerors and rulers*, pp.27–8, and *Collected papers, vol.1 : Settlement and Social Change in Asia*. Hong Kong University Press, Hong Kong and Oxford University Press, London 1967, p.25.

58. Alexander Rüstow, *Ortsbestimmung der Gegenwart*, vol.1. Zürich, 1949.

59. Lattimore, *Inner Asian frontiers of China*, Chapters IX and XI.

60. An antecedent empire in process of disintegration is one of the dynamic criteria of feudalism proposed in Coulborn, *Feudalism in history, passim* and, especially, A. L. Kroeber's preface, p.viii : 'Coulborn sees feudalism as a socio-political aid in the revival of civilization when this, following the death of creativity in intellectual endeavor, begins to dry rot . . . its political and

economic fabric disintegrates . . . Feudalism may or may not develop; if it does . . . it is as a rude but healthy reconstructive device from the low point of disintegration and decline and as an instrument of the reconstructing civilisation.' For Owen Lattimore feudalism 'is a complex of economic, social, military, and administrative methods of organisation . . . [which] . . . emerges in periods when, in the relationship between these aspects of society, military striking power has quite wide geographical range, but transport is so cumbrous and expensive that the exchange of food and goods of daily consumption cannot be organized within a common market as wide as the periphery to which military operations can reach' [*Studies in frontier history*, pp.543–4]. Lattimore, together with Joseph Levenson [review of Coulborn's *Feudalism in history* in *Far Eastern Quarterly*, vol.15, no.4 (1956), pp.569–72] and Etienne Balazs [*Far Eastern Quarterly*, vol.16, no.2 (1957), pp.329–32], are among the few China specialists who have considered feudalism as a developmental (and, according to Lattimore and Balazs, a devolutional) stage.

61. Bodde in Coulborn's *Feudalism in history*, pp.53–4.

62. Henri Maspero, 'Le régime féodal et la propriété foncière dans la Chine antique', *Mélanges posthumes sur les religions et l'histoire de la Chine* vol.3. Paris 1950, pp.133, 143–4. Cf. also the same author's 'Les régimes fonciers en Chine, des origines aux temps modernes', *ibid.*, pp.147–92, and 'Les termes désignant la propriété foncière en Chine', *ibid.*, pp.193–208.

63. Barnard [*Monumenta Serica*, vol.17 (1958), p. 32, note 18] writes: '. . . subinfeudation, too, was characteristic and numerous examples may be observed in unattested sources – both bronze texts and traditional literature [I think that Barnard must be using the term in a somewhat different sense from Maspero, at least in so far as literary sources are concerned – Author]. The fully attested Inscription 23.9 excavated at Chün-Hsien in 1936 (see *T'ien-yeh K'ao-ku Pao-kao*, 1936 for details and rubbing) reliably indicates the practice.' Cho-yün Hsü [*Ancient China in Transition*, p.5, note ǂ] draws his example from a bronze inscription published by Kuo Mo-jo in *Liang-Chou Chin-wen-tz'ŭ Ta-hsi K'ao-shih*. Bunkyodo, Tokyo 1935, p.85.

64. The ****tsi̯ok** (*chüeh*) were of five degrees of nobility, all of which are also mentioned in Shang inscriptions [*vide* Hu Hou-hsüan, 'Yin-tai feng-chien-chih-tu k'ao' in *Chia-ku-hsüeh Shang-shih Lun-ts'ung*, first series, vol.1. Ch'eng-tu 1944, pp.32 *et seq.*] : ****kung** (*kung*), ****g'u** (*hou*), ****păk** (*po*), ****tsi̯əg** (*tzŭ*), and ****nəm** (*nan*). The ceremonies and precedences associated with each of these ranks are recounted with great elaboration in *Chou-Li* : cf. p. 156–7.

Hu has gone further and attempted the difficult task of assigning etymologies to these titles, e.g. *kung* originally signified 'patriarch', the ancestral head of a family; *g'u*, depicting an arrow striking a target, was a military title; *păk* denoted 'senior' or 'elder'; *tsi̯əg* meant 'a son', of the king presumably;

and *nəm* meant 'male', possibly with the implication of a warrior age-grade. Cf. Bodde in Coulborn, *Feudalism in China*, pp.55–6.

65. Cf. *int. al.*, *Chou-Li*, and Ma Tuan-lin, *Wen-hsien T'ung-k'ao*, pp.2059 *et seq.*

66. Walker, *The multi-state system of ancient China*, p.26. By Ch'un-Ch'iu times all the rulers of the Chou states were accorded the posthumous rank of duke, irrespective of their ranks in life.

67. The Ch'ing scholar Chu Yu-fu composed no less than seven treatises on Chou investiture ceremonies, but it is only too evident in retrospect that – as was inevitable given the time at which he was writing – he was concerned more to expound the formulations of the classical texts than to penetrate to the reality underlying these relatively late systematizations (cf. pp.150–160 below). For a detailed description of the ceremony of investiture (first mentioned under the term **siek-miǎng* [hsi-ming] in the *I-Ching*, but in other texts referring to the Chou – though not necessarily given their final form during that dynasty – as **sięg-miǎng* [tz'ŭ-ming]), based on contemporary, though not always scientifically attested, bronze inscriptions and idealized literary texts of later times, see Ch'i Ssŭ-ho, 'Chou-tai hsi-ming-li k'ao', *Yen-ching Hsüeh-pao*, no.32 (1947), pp.197–226; also Eduard Chavannes, *Le T'ai Chan : essai de monographie d'un culte chinois*. Bibliothèque d'Etudes : Annales du Musée Guimet, Paris 1910, Appendix entitled 'Le Dieu du Sol dans la Chine antique'; and Marcel Granet, *La féodalité chinoise*, pp.112–13.

68. Granet, *loc. cit.*, p.112. *Fong* = a French transcription of MSC *feng* < **pįung*, a word which is etymologically connected with the idea of the piling up of earth round a plant. Cf. note 53 above.

69. I am not the first to gain this impression from the ritual texts. Marcel Granet has already written, 'Il [the candidate for investiture] ne recevait pas un domaine contre une promesse de fidélité, il ne remettait point des droits éminents sur son domaine contre une garantie de protection, il ne s'inféodait pas au Fils du Ciel. Il déclarait entrer, lui et sa terre, dans la discipline et la civilisation chinoises' [*La féodalité chinoise*, pp.112–13].

The ceremony of investiture of a high official of the Western Chou is related in considerable detail on both the Large K'o and the Mao-kung tripods. The inscription on the former reads as follows:

The king was at the ancestral capital of Chou. At dawn the king arrived at the Mu temple and took his seat. Shan-fu K'o, accompanied by Tung[?] Chi, entered the gate and stood in the middle of the court, facing north. The king commanded Yin-shih to invest Shan-fu K'o, and said, "K'o, formerly I had ordered you to promulgate Our decrees; now I shall [. . .] invest you with a title. I grant you [. . .] land at Yeh and at Pei. I grant you farm households cultivating the land at Yung to serve as your subjects and subordinates. I grant you land at K'ang, at Yen, and at Fu-yüan. I grant

you servitors, drums, bells [. . .]. Be diligent by day and by night, and do not disregard Our order. K'o bowed and made obeisance, and humbly praised the virtues of the king [. . .].
[Ch'i Ssŭ-ho, *Yen-ching Hsüeh-pao* (1947)].
There is an English version in E-tu Zen Sun and John de Francis, *Chinese Social History*. American Council of Learned Societies, Washington, D C 1956, p.45. It is difficult to discern anything exclusively feudal about the investiture ceremony described above.

70. Hall, 'Japanese feudalism', pp.26-7.

71. *loc. cit.*, pp.31-2.

72. Several scholars define feudalism in such broad terms that it subsumes the concept of patrimonialism. Among them is H. G. Creel, for example, who, in a most perspicacious paper, has offered a minimal definition as '. . . a system of government in which a ruler personally delegates limited sovereignty over portions of his domain to vassals' ['The beginnings of bureaucracy in China : the origin of the *Hsien*', *The Journal of Asian Studies*, vol.23, no.2 (1964), p. 163]. For Creel's purpose at the time, namely to contrast feudalism and bureaucracy, this definition may have been entirely adequate, but I personally find it constitutes feudalism as too broad a category for it to prove a useful tool for analyzing the pre- or non-bureaucratic governments and societies of China. It does not, for instance, help to differentiate the Shang from the Ch'un-Ch'iu mode of government, or that of Dz'iər from that of Tş'io. Creel does indeed illuminate our idea of the nature of Tş'io government, but he does not use this particular tool to help him do it. In fact, unless 'vassal' be understood in a highly restricted technical sense (and it is apparent from Creel's subsequent discussion of his definition [p.164, note 50] that he did not use it in this way), the definition does not distinguish between feudalism and patrimonialism.

73. Cf. note 64 above.

74. Barnard, *Monumenta Serica*, vol.17 (1958), pp.14 and 35.

75. Students of Chinese mythology commonly denote this process by the term 'euhemerization', even though this word customarily signifies the creation of myth by the archetyping of human actions and situations. Cf. Derk Bodde, 'Myths of ancient China' in Samuel Noah Kramer (ed.), *Mythologies of the ancient world*. Anchor Book 229, Doubleday & Co., Inc. New York 1961, pp.372-6.

76. Granet, *La féodalité chinoise*, pp.122-3.

77. *Tao-tö* is a French transcription of the M S C phrase which is rendered in the Wade-Giles system as *tao-te* < ***d'ôg-tək*. This is a term difficult, perhaps impossible, to define in English. Marcel Granet has an interesting discussion of it in his *Chinese civilization*. Meridian Books No.14, New York 1958 : transl. of *La civilisation chinoise*, second edition, Albin Michel, Paris 1948 : *Evolution de l' Humanité* series no.25; pp.250-1, in which he defines it as

'an animating force of universal essence . . . the characteristic of a Chief whose way (tao) is opened by Heaven and who is invested with it (*ming*) with a specific genius (*tô*) while it bestows upon him the destiny (*ming*) suitable for an overlord' (p.250). This is very close to the quality which Max Weber denoted by 'charisma' : ' "Charisma" soll eine als ausseralltäglich (ursprünglich, sowohl bei Propheten wie bei therapeutischen wie bei Rechts-Weisen wie bei Jagd-führern wir bei Kriegshelden : als magisch bedingt) geltende Qualität einer Persönlichkeit heissen, um derentwillen sie als mit übernatürlichen oder übermenschlichen oder mindestens spezifisch ausseralltäglichen, nicht jedem andern zugänglichen Kräften oder Eigenschaften oder als gottgesendet oder als vorbildlich und deshalb als "Führer" gewertet wird. Wie die betreffende Qualität von irgendeinem ethischen, ästhetischen oder sonstigen Standpunkt aus "objektiv" richtig zu bewerten sein würde, ist natürlich dabei begrifflich völlig gleichgültig : darauf allein, wie sie tatsächlich von den charismatisch Beherrschten, den "Anhängern", bewertet wird, kommt es an' [*Wirtschaft und Gesellschaft*, vol.3 of the collaborative work *Grundriss der Sozialökonomik*, pt.2, second edition, J.C.B.Mohr, Tübingen 1925, pp.133–4]. Elsewhere on the page cited above Granet defines the terms separately : *d'ôg* as 'indicating pure efficacy, concentrated, so to speak, and quite indeterminate', and *tək* as 'the same efficacy in the act of spending itself and becoming particularized'. In these two terms there is something of the complementary opposition of the concepts of power (the production of intended effects : *tək*) and authority (the expected and legitimate possession of power : *d'ôg*). In a sense *d'ôg* is a poten-tial, *tək* a kinetic, quality. In later centuries, of course, different philosophical schools attached different, and in some cases more restricted, meanings to these terms.

78. *Vide* Haloun, *Asia Major*, vol.1 (1924), especially pp.76 *et seq.* and 84 *et seq.*

79. The term *kịwən-tsịəg* (*chün-tzŭ*) is composed of two graphs signifying 'lord' and 'son' respectively, and may originally have denoted sons of rulers, possibly undergoing a subsequent extension of meaning to include all classi-ficatory kin of the ruling houses, by which time it had become a virtual synonym for 'nobility'. This is the basic sense in which the word was used in the *Shih-Ching*, although it had by then already acquired the extended connotation of 'husband'. However, during the later Ch'un-Ch'iu and Chan-Kuo periods the implications of this term were so modified that it came to denote a person of high moral stature, a member of a moral rather than a social élite. Cf. Cho-yün Hsü, *Ancient China in transition*, pp.158–74.

80. Maspero, 'Le régime féodal', p.126.

81. Eberhard, *Conquerors and rulers*, pp.22–3. The quotation is from Hsü, *Ancient China in transition*, p.11.

82. References in Hsü, *Ancient China*, p.11.

83. The general term for slaves in ancient times was **liei* (*li*). Male slaves were also known as **ḍi̯ĕn* (*ch'en*) and females as **ts'i̯ap* (*ch'ieh*).

84. Cho-yün Hsü cites an occasion [*Ch'un-Ch'iu Tso-Chuan Cheng-i*, 12/9 (Hsi 5)] when a slave was ordered to taste some meat suspected of containing poison after a dog had died from eating it, which may indicate that a slave was valued rather below a dog. A bronze inscription probably from the 9th century records that five male slaves were purchased for 100 pieces of metal (**li̯uĕt : lieh*), but the value of these units is unknown. *Vide* Kuo Mo-jo, *Liang-Chou Chin-wen-tz'ŭ Ta-hsi K'ao-shih*. Bunkyodo, Tokyo 1935, p.97.

85. In 679 BC, 66 slaves were interred with Duke Mi̯wo (Wu), and just over half a century later no less than 177 accompanied Duke **Mi̯ôk (Mu) to the grave [Cited in Lou Kan-jou, *Histoire sociale de l'époque Tcheou*, p.112].

86. On slavery in ancient China see E.G.Pulleyblank, 'The origins and nature of chattel slavery in China', *Journal of the Economic and Social History of the Orient*, vol.1, pt.2 (1958), pp.185–220.

87. Chüan 129. *Huo-Chih* (=Augmentation of wealth) is an allusion to Confucius's remark, in an almost certainly corrupt passage of the *Lun-Yü*, to the effect that **Si̯ĕg (Tz'ŭ) was discontented with his lot and was setting out to enrich himself [XI, viii].

88. *Shih-Chi*, chüan 129, f.16 verso.

89. *loc. cit.*, f.17 recto.

90. *loc. cit.*, f.16 verso.

91. *loc. cit.*, f.6 recto.

92. *loc. cit.*, ff.5 verso – 6 recto. The So-yin and Cheng-i commentaries provide much fuller accounts of both **·Ia-Twən (I-Tun) and Kwâk-Tsi̯ung (Kuo-Tsung) than does the *Shih-Chi* itself (*ibid*).

93. *loc. cit.*, f.18 verso.

94. *loc. cit.*, f.6 verso.

94a. Several recensions read **D'ien-Śi̯ôk (T'ien-Shu).

95. *loc. cit.*, ff.5 recto et verso; Burton Watson, *Records of the Grand Historian of China*, vol.2. Columbia University Press, New York and London 1961, pp.482–3.

96. *Shih-Chi*, chüan 129, f.19 recto; Watson, *Records*, pp.498–9.

97. Cf. *Ch'ien-Han Shu*, chüan 28B, ff.6 verso – 7 recto : 'Although the territory of Dz'i̯ĕn comprised [only] one-third of the empire, and although the number of its inhabitants did not exceed three-tenths, yet, if its wealth were to be estimated, it would be found to amount to six-tenths.'

98. The dismemberment of Tsi̯ĕn began in 453 BC, and was formally recognized exactly fifty years later.

99. The contrasting environments of the Huang plains and the Yang-tzŭ valley are very much apparent in the literature of Ch'un-Ch'iu and Chan-Kuo times. In the *Kuo-Yü* [chüan 20, f.20 recto], for example, we read of an

official of Ngo in the Yang-tzŭ delta advising his king not to undertake a military expedition against the northern states : 'Landsmen must live on land and men of the waters near water. If we attack and conquer the Chinese states we still shall not be able to live in their territories nor ride in their chariots. If, on the other hand, we attack and conquer the [southern, non-Chinese state of] Gįwăt, we shall be able to occupy its territories and travel in its boats.' The same theme occurs again in a deposition by a Tş'įo envoy protesting against an invasion by Dz'iər in 655 BC [4th year of Duke Xįəg (Hsi)] : 'Your Grace's territory is by the northern sea, mine by the southern. [So far apart are they that] our very horses and cattle cannot interbreed.'

100. Ku Chieh-kang, 'Yü Ch'ien Hsüan-t'ung Hsien-sheng lun ku-shih-shu', *Ku-Shih Pien*, vol.1 (1926), pp.106–34, 165–86, and 207–10.

101. E.g., swords and other iron weapons from G'ân, Ngo and Gįwăt, sabers from D'įĕng, axes from Sông, blades from Lo, daggers from D'įog, and purple cloth from Dz'iər. Cf. extended remarks on this topic by Hsü, *Ancient China in transition*, pp.120–2.

102. Henri Maspero, 'Contribution à l'étude de la société chinoise à la fin des Chang et au début des Tcheou', *Bulletin de l'Ecole française d'Extrême-Orient*, vol.46, pt.2 (1952–4), pp.349–56. Hsü Chung-shu ['Lei-ssŭ k'ao', *Kuo-li Chung-yang Yen-chiu-yüan Li-shih Yü-yen Yen-chiu-so Chi-k'an*, vol.2, pt.1] has found little support for his contention that the *lei* and *ssŭ* were separate and distinct implements.

103. Hua Chüeh-ming, Yang Ken and Liu En-chu, 'Chan-Kuo Liang-Han t'ieh-ch'i-ti chin-hsiang-hsüeh k'ao-ch'a ch'u-pu pao-kao,' *K'ao-ku Hsüeh-pao*, no.1 (1960), pp.82–3.

104. *Shih-Chi*, chüan 29, f.3 recto.

105. *Shih-Chi*, chüan 29, f.2 verso.

106. *Shih-Chi*, chüan 29, f.3 recto et verso.

107. An estimate arrived at by comparing Ssŭ-ma Ch'ien's reported yield with the average quoted in *Kuan-tzŭ*.

108. *Shih-Chi*, chüan 29, f.3 verso.

109. *Chuang-tzŭ*, chüan 12. Cf. also Liu-Hsiang, *Shuo-Yüan* (*c*.20 BC), chüan 20. There is a study of Chan-Kuo irrigation works by Weng Wen-hao, 'Ku-tai kuan-kai kung-ch'eng fa-chan-shih-chih i-chieh', in *Kuo-li Chung-yang Yen-chiu Yüan Li-shih Yü-yen Yen-chiu-so Ch'ing-chu Ts'ai Yüan-p'ei Hsien-sheng Liu-shih-wu-sui Lun-wen Chi*, vol.2. Academia Sinica, Pei-p'ing, 1935, pp.709–12.

110. Wang Hsien-ch'ien, *Han-Shu Pu-chu*. Ch'ang-sha, 1900, chüan 24A, pp.7–8.

111. Joseph Needham, *The development of iron and steel technology in China*. Second Biennial Dickinson Memorial Lecture, Newcomen Society. London 1958.

112. Sekino Takeshi, *Chugaku Kōkogaku Kenkyu*. University of Tokyo Institute for Oriental Culture 1956, pp.187–8.

113. *Meng-tzŭ*, III A, iii, 19.

114. *Chou-Li*, ts'e 6, chüan 12, f.18 verso (*Ssŭ-pu Ts'ung-k'an* ed., Shanghai 1942).

115. The system as set out in *Chou-Li* is somewhat more complicated than that described in the *Mencius*. According to the former the boundaries between fields and between *tsiĕng* were marked by **ku* (*kou*=drains) and **χiwĕt* (*hsü*=ditches) of sizes varying according to their place in the hierarchy of territorial units. On the outer edges of this *ku-χiwĕt* system the channels must have been very broad and deep indeed. Some scholars have regarded the *tsiĕng-d'ien* and the *ku-χiwĕt* as separate systems [e.g. Chu-Hsi, 'Li-i : Chou-li,' *Chu-tzŭ ch'üan-shu*, ed. Li Kuang-ti (1714), ts'e 15, chüan 37, f.12 verso; Tazaki Masayuki, *Shina kōdai keizai shisō oyobi seido*. Tokyo 1925, pp.495–511], but most have treated them as different versions of one underlying reality.

116. E.g., Hu Shih, 'Ching-t'ien pien', *Hu Shih Wen-ts'un*. Shanghai, 1927. This essay had originally been published in 1920. In 1935 Kao Yün-hui remarked that *tsiĕng-d'ien* had no existence in reality : it was simply a category of social thought, an idealization in the mind ['Chou-tai t'u-ti-chih-tu yü ching-t'ien', *Shih-huo*, vol.1, no.7 (1935), p.12].

117. *Vide* Laurence G. Thompson (transl.), *Ta T'ung Shu : the One-World Philosophy of K'ang Yu-wei*. London 1958, pp.137 and 211. From time to time during Chinese history there had been attempts to use *tsiĕng-d'ien* as a basis for agrarian colonization and social reform [e.g. by Wang-Mang in AD 9, by Wang An-shih in Sung times, and under the Manchu in 1724, when a form of *tsiĕng-d'ien* was established in two counties of Chih-li], but none ever proved successful. For the deployment of *tsiĕng-d'ien* as an instrument of social reform in modern times see Joseph R. Levenson, 'Ill wind in the well-field : the erosion of the Confucian ground of controversy', in *Confucian China and its Modern Fate*, vol.3, *The problem of historical significance*. University of California Press, Berkeley and Los Angeles 1965, pp.16–43. There are general discussions of *tsiĕng-d'ien* in Hsü Chung-shu, 'Ching-t'ien chih-tu t'an-yüan', *Chung-Kuo Wen-hua Yen-chiu Hui-k'an*, vol.4 (1944), pp.121–56; Kuo Mo-jo, *Shih P'i-p'an Shu*. Ch'ung-ch'ing, 1945, pp.1–62; Li Chien-nung, 'Ch'e chu kung', *Ch'ing-hua Ta-hsüeh She-hui K'o-hsüeh Chi-k'an*, vol.9 (1948), pp.25–44, and *Chung-Kuo Ching-chi Shih-kao*, vol.1 (ND), pp.122–38; Lien-sheng Yang, 'Notes on Dr Swann's *Food and Money in Ancient China*', in Yang, *Studies in Chinese Institutional History*. Harvard University Press 1963, pp.85–118.

118. Eberhard, *Conquerors and rulers*, pp.35–6.

119. Ch'i Ssŭ-ho, 'Meng-tzŭ ching-t'ien shuo pien', *Yen-ching Hsüeh-pao*,

no.35 (1948), pp.101–27, especially 124–6. Cf. also Ch'ao-ting Chi, *Key economic areas in Chinese history as revealed in the development of public works for water-control*. George Allen and Unwin Ltd, London 1936, p.58.

120. *Tso-Chuan*, Duke **Sįwan (Hsüan), 15th year.

121. *Lun-Yü*, XII, 9. The precise nature of this tax has elicited a good deal of comment from modern scholars, particularly with regard to its apparent regional and chronological variations. Kato Shigeshi thought he was able to discern both spatial and developmental differences involving labor service, tax on annual yield, and tax at a fixed rate [*Studies in Chinese economic history*, vol.1. Toyo Bunko, Tokyo 1952, pp.555–86]. Cho-yün Hsü, on the other hand, considered 'that this tax was more a developmental phenomenon than a regional difference, since labor service involves both direct control by the landlord over the peasant and annual shifting of fields. The latter practice is necessary for any type of technologically undeveloped agriculture, such as that of the early Ch'un-Ch'iu, whereas a land tax is possible only when the peasants can use their land permanently. The purpose of tax reformation is not merely to increase the burden on the tiller'. [*Ancient China in transition*, p.108]. Miyazaki Ichisada has suggested that the introduction of a so-called tax could more profitably be regarded simply as an extension of the tribute system, hitherto restricted to the nobility, to the peasantry [*Shirin*, vol.18, nos.2 and 3 (1933), pp.1–18]. In any case, whatever the nature of this tax, the outcome of its introduction was as described in the text. Cf. also Maspero, 'Le régime féodal', pp.124 and 138, and Amano Motonosuke, *Toho Gakuho*, vol.30 (1959), pp.141–4.

122. Hsü, *Ancient China in transition*, p.110.

123. *loc. cit.*, p.178.

124. *Kuan-tzǔ*, XV, 11–12 (*Ssŭ-pu Ts'ung-k'an* edition, annotated by Fang Hsüan-ling). One of the best-known instances of unseasonable labor service was the corvée imposed at harvest time by **G'wâng Kwǝk-b'įwo (Huang Kuo-fu), **T'âd-Tsǝg (T'ai-Tsai) under Duke **B'įĕng (P'ing) of Sông, for the purpose of building a terraced platform [*Tso-Chuan*, Duke **Snįang (Hsiang), 18th year].

125. E.g. *Ch'un-Ch'iu*, Duke **D'įĕng (Cheng), 12th year.

126. For the role of merchants and the development of trade see Ku Chi-kuang, 'Chan-Kuo Ch'in-Han-chien chung-nung-ch'ing-shang-chih li-lun yü shih-chi' *Chung-Kuo She-hui Ching-chi-shih Chi-k'an*, vol.7, no.1 (1944), pp.1–22.

127. Yang Lien-sheng, *Money and credit in China*. Harvard University Press 1952, pp.1–2. There is an interesting passage in the *Kuo-Yü* which reports discussions on the possibility of issuing 'heavy coins' in Chou in 524 BC. However, the passage is probably a later interpolation : it is evaluated by Yang, *loc. cit.*, p.33.

128. Shih Chang-ju, 'Chou-tu i-chi yü Ts'ai-t'ao i-ts'un', *Ta-lu Tsa-chih*, supplement no.1 (1952), pp.357–85.

129. Notes 6 and 7 above.

130. Chang Hsüeh-cheng, 'Wei-ho shang-yu T'ien-shui, Kan-ku liang-hsien k'ao-ku tiao-ch'a chien-pao', *K'ao-ku T'ung-hsün*, no.5 (1958), pp.1–5; Jen Pu-yün, 'Kan-su Ch'in-an Hsien Hsin-shih-ch'i shih-tai chü-chu i-chih', *loc. cit.*, pp.6–11; Kuo Te-yung, 'Kan-su Wei-ho shang-yu Wei-yüan, Lung-hsi, Wu-shan san-hsien k'ao-ku tiao-ch'a', *K'ao-ku T'ung-hsün*, no.7 (1958), pp.6–16.

131. Shan-hsi [Shensi] Sheng Wen-wu Kuan-li Wei-yüan-hui, 'Ch'ang-an Chang-chia-p'o Ts'un Hsi-Chou i-chih-ti chung-yao fa-hsien', *Wen-wu Ts'an-k'ao Tzŭ-liao*, no.3 (1956), p.58; Wang Po-hung, Chung shao-lin and Chang Ch'ang-shou, '1955–57-nien Shan-hsi [Shensi] Ch'ang-an Feng-hsi fa-chüeh chien-pao', *K'ao-ku*, no.10 (1959), pp.516–30.

132. T'ang Yün-ming, 'Hsing-T'ai Hsi-kuan-wai i-chih shih-chüeh', *Wen-wu*, no.7 (1960), pp.69–70.

133. Chao Ch'ing-yün, '1957-nien Cheng-Chou hsi-chiao fa-chüeh chi-yao : 4 : Tung-Chai Shang-tai yü Chou-tai wen-hua i-chih-ti fa-chüeh, '*K'ao-ku T'ung-hsün*, no.9 (1958), p.56.

134. Li Yang-sung and Yen Wen-ming, 'Lo-yang Wang-wan i-chih fa-chüeh chien-pao', *K'ao-ku*, no.4 (1961), pp.175–78.

135. Yin Huan-chang *et al.*, 'Chiang-su Hsin-i Hsien San-li Tun ku-wen-hua i-chih', *K'ao-ku*, no.7 (1960), pp.20–2.

136. Wang Ching, 'Hu-pei Hung-an Chin-p'en i-chih-ti t'an-chüeh', *K'ao-ku*, no.4 (1960), pp.38–40.

137. Li Chi *et al.*, *Ch'eng-tzŭ Yai : Tung Tso-pin, 'Ch'eng-tzŭ Yai yü Lung-shan Chen'.* Academia Sinica, Nan-ching 1934, pp.96–8.

138. Cf. Tsang Li-ho *et al.*, *Chung-Kuo Ku-chin Ti-ming Ta-tz'ŭ-tien.* Shanghai 1933, p.1355.

139. Tung Tso-pin, 'T'an "T'an"', ' *Kuo-li Chung-yang Yen-chiu-yüan Li-shih Yü-yen Yen-chiu-so Chi-k'an*, vol.4, pt.2 (1933), pp.159–74. As early as the middle of the 18th century Ku Tung-kao (1679–1759) had included D'əm (T'an), by implication, among those territories which he believed to have been enfeoffed in pre-Chou times [*Ch'un-Ch'iu Ta-shih Piao* (Wan-chüan-lou edition, Wu-hsi, 1748)]. Ku also relied on Sung authors of somewhat dubious reliability in an attempt to show that the clan name of the ruling house of D'əm could be traced back to Shang times, but we now know that such genealogies were manufactured in much later times by rulers of small (and, indeed, often of large) states as instruments of political validation [*Vide* Liang Lü-sheng (1748–93), *Tso-t'ung Pu-shih* in Wang Hsien-ch'ien, *Huang-Ch'ing Ching-chieh Hsü-pien.* Canton 1888; Lo-Pi, *Lu-Shih.* Tun-hua T'ang edition 1611]. There are, indeed, works which state explicitly that D'əm was a Shang foundation.

Yü-Ch'in, for example, arguing against the statement of an otherwise unknown source, the *San-Ch'i Chi*, to the effect that P'ing-ling was the capital of **Tieg- ·įɛt (Ti-i) of Shang, insists that, 'as P'ing-ling was not then in existence, then the site of the capital must have been at Ch'eng-tzŭ Yai'. Needless to say, arguments such as this are based on illusory premises as to the nature of their source materials.

The earliest extant reference to the state of D'əm is to be found in the **Gįwad-Pįŭm (*Wei-Feng*) section of the *Mao Shih*, and the preface to that recension of the *Odes* attributed the ode *Ta-Tung* to a high official of D'əm living at the end of the Western Chou period. A Duke of D'əm also appeared in the genealogical section **Gįwad Ṣįad-kå (*Wei Shih-chia*) of the *Shih-Chi*, under the 5th year of Duke Chuang of Wei (753 BC), and another is mentioned in a later work, the *Feng-su t'ung-i* of Ying-Shao, who lived from AD 140–206. Ssŭ-pu Ts'ung-k'an edition, Shanghai 1929.

140. Duke **Tṣįang (Chuang), 10th year. The Han scholar Tu-Lin elaborated this statement with the further information that *D'əm* 'was southwest of P'ing-ling Hsien in Chi-nan' [Quoted in Tsang, *Chung-kuo Ku-chin Ti-ming Ta-tz'ŭ-tien*, p.1355], and Yü-Ch'in (1284–1333) noted that 'Eastern P'ing-ling is 75 *li* east of Chi-nan. As for the state of *D'əm* mentioned in the Ch'un-Ch'iu, Duke Huan [of *Dz'iər*] destroyed it. The old city was in the southwest, opposite Lung-shan Chen' [*Ch'i-Ch'eng* AD 1781]. Li Tao-yüan [*Shui-Ching Chu* : Northern Wei, late 5th or early 6th century AD] adds : 'The Kuan-lu river rises in the Ma-erh mountains. To the north it flows on the west side of Po-t'ing Ch'eng and continues northwestwards, where it joins the Wu-yüan river at P'ing-ling Ch'eng. This river [the Wu-yüan] issues from low-lying marshland to the south of the city of T'an [D'əm], where it is always known as the Wu-yüan Spring. [Thence] it flows northwards and passes to the east of the city of T'an, which is commonly held to be an ancient foundation. Once more this river flows northwards and passes to the west of the old city of Eastern P'ing-ling . . . farther north it passes to the east of Chü-ho Ch'eng . . . [and eventually] unites with the Kuan-lu river to form the Chü-ho river'. A reconstruction of the course of these rivers in ancient times and the locations of the cities mentioned above is presented in Fig.IV.

141. Ch'en Kung-jou, 'Lo-yang Chien-pin Tung-Chou ch'eng-chih fa-chüeh pao-kao', *K'ao-ku Hsüeh-pao*, no.2 (1959), pp.15–34.

142. Kuo Pao-chün, 'Lo-yang ku-ch'eng k'an-ch'a chien-pao', *K'ao-ku T'ung-hsün*, no.1 (1955), pp.9–21. Pan-Ku, the author of *Ch'ien-Han Shu*, the celebrated commentator Cheng-Hsüan, and Li Tao-yüan, author of *Shui-*

[IV] A reconstruction of the relationship between ancient settlements and the drainage pattern in the neighborhood of Ch'eng-tzŭ Yai. Redrawn from Li Chi *et al.*, *Ch'eng-tzŭ Yai* (Nan-ching, 1934), fig.10, p.103.

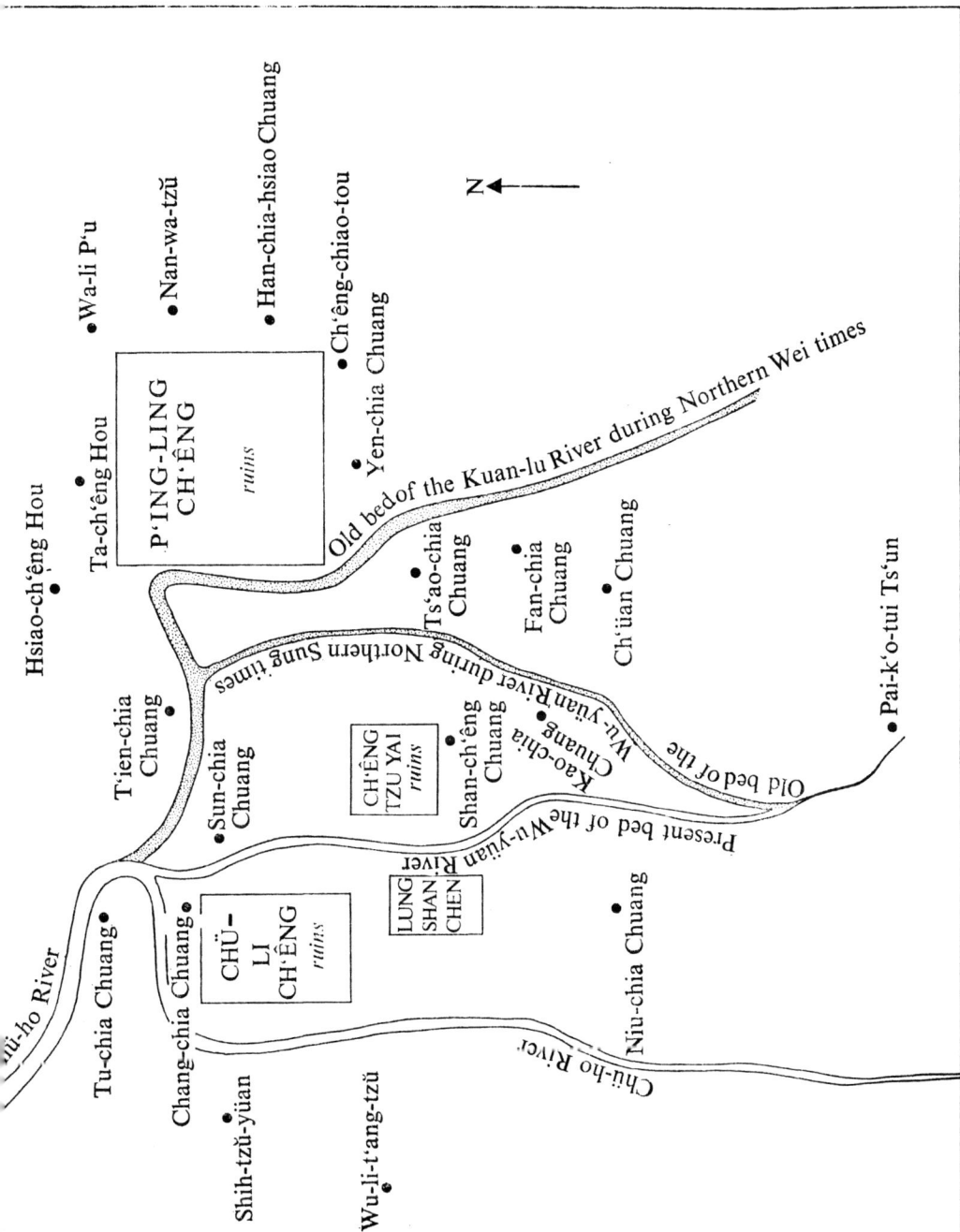

Ching Chu, each in his day confirmed the association of Ho-nan *hsien*-city of the Later Han with the ruins of the old Royal City of Chou, and there can be no doubt that the modern excavators have identified the former correctly.

143. Chang Shou-chung, '1959-nien Hou-ma "Niu-Ts'un ku-ch'eng"-nan Tung-Chou i-chih fa-chüeh chien-pao', *Wen-wu*, nos.8–9 (1960), pp.11–14; Yang Fu-tou, 'Hou-ma-hsi hsin-fa-hsien i-tso ku-ch'eng i-chih', *Wen-wu Ts'an-k'ao Tzŭ-liao*, no.10 (1957), pp.55–6; Ch'ang Wen-chai, 'Hou-ma ti-ch'ü ku-ch'eng-chih-ti hsin-fa-hsien', *loc. cit.*, no.12 (1958), pp.32–3; Ch'ang Wen-chai, Chang Shou-chung and Yang Fu-tou, 'Hou-ma Pei-hsi Chuang Tung-Chou i-chih-ti ch'ing-li', *Wen-wu*, no.6 (1959), pp.42–4; and several continuing anonymous notes in subsequent issues of *Wen-wu*.

144. Shan-hsi Sheng Wen-wu Kuan-li Wei-yüan-hui, 'Shan-hsi Sheng Wen-kuan-hui Hou-ma Kung-tso-chan kung-tso-ti tsung-shou-huo', *K'ao-ku*, no.5 (1959), pp.222–8.

145. Yang Fu-tou, 'K'ao-ku Tung-t'ai : Shan-hsi Hsiang-fen Hsien fa-hsien-ti liang-ch'u i-chih : 2 : Chao-k'ang-Chen-ti Tung-Chou ku-ch'eng-chih', *K'ao-ku*, no.2 (1959), p.107; Ch'ang Wen-chai, 'Shan-hsi Hsiang-fen Chao-k'ang fu-chin ku-ch'eng-chih tiao-ch'a', *K'ao-ku*, no.10 (1963), pp.544–6.

146. Meng Hao, Ch'en Hui, and Liu Lai-ch'eng, 'Ho-pei Wu-an Wu-chi ku-ch'eng fa-chüeh-chi', *K'ao-ku T'ung-hsün*, no.4 (1957), pp.43–7; Meng Hao, 'Ho-pei Wu-an Hsien Wu-chi ku-ch'eng-chung-ti yao-chih', *K'ao-ku*, no.7 (1959), pp.338–42; Ch'en Hui, 'Ho-pei Wu-an Hsien Wu-chi ku-ch'eng-ti Chou, Han mu-tsang fa-chüeh chien-pao', *K'ao-ku*, no.7 (1959), pp.343–5.

147. Komai Kazuchika and Sekino Takeshi, 'Han-tan', *Archaeologia Orientalis*, series B, vol.7 (1954); Sekino Takeshi, *Chugaku Kōkogaku Kenkyu* (Tokyo, 1956), pp.295–302; Pei-ching Ta-hsüeh and Ho-pei Sheng Wen-hua-chü Han-tan K'ao-ku Fa-chüeh-tui, '1957-nien Han-tan fa-chüeh chien-pao', *K'ao-ku*, no.10 (1959), pp.531–6.

148. *Tso-Chuan*, 10th year of Duke **D'ieng (Ting-Kung).

149. Fu Chen-lun, 'Yen-Hsia-tu fa-chüeh pao-kao', *Kuo-Hsüeh Chi-k'an*, vol.3. Peking University 1932, pp.175–82, and 'Yen-Hsia-tu fa-chüeh-p'in-ti ch'u-pu cheng-li yü yen-chiu', *K'ao-ku T'ung-hsün*, no.4 (1955), pp.18–26; Hsieh Hsi-i, 'Yen-Hsia-tu i-chih so-chi', *Wen-wu Ts'an-k'ao Tzŭ-liao*, no.9 (1957), pp.61–3; Huang Ching-lüeh, 'Yen-Hsia-tu-ch'eng-chih tiao-ch'a pao-kao', *K'ao-ku*, no.1 (1962), pp.10–19 and 54. This 'Lesser Capital' should not be confused with the city with the same sobriquet in the vicinity of Lo-yang (cp. p.136).

150. Diagrammatic reconstructions by Wang Chen-to, 'Ssŭ-nan chih-nan-chen yü lo-ching p'an, I', *Chung-Kuo K'ao-ku Hsüeh-pao*, vol.3 (1948) [Reproduced by Joseph Needham, *Science and civilization in China*, vol.4, pt.1. Cambridge 1962, p.263], and Harada Yoshito and Tazawa Kingo, *Rakurō Gokan-en Ō Ku no Fumbo*. Tokyo 1930 [Reproduced by W.C. Rufus, 'Astro-

nomy in Korea', *Journal of the Korean Branch of the Royal Asiatic Society*, vol. 26, pt.1 (1936) and by Needham, *loc. cit.*, vol.3 (1959), plate LXXX].

151. Ao Ch'eng-lung, 'Ho-pei Tz'ŭ-Hsien Chiang-wu Ch'eng tiao-ch'a chien-pao', *K'ao-ku*, no.7 (1959), pp.354–7.

152. Wang Han-yen, 'Pei-ching Shih : Chou-k'ou Tien Ch'ü Ts'ai-Chuang ku-ch'eng i-chih', *Wen-wu*, no.5 (1959), p.73.

153. Sekino Takeshi, *Chugaku Kōkogaku Kenkyu*. Tokyo 1956, pp.241–94; Shan-tung Sheng Wen-wu Kuan-li-ch'u, 'Shan-tung Lin-tzŭ Ch'i-ku-ch'eng shih-chüeh chien-pao', *K'ao-ku*, no.6 (1961), pp.289–97.

154. Sekino, *Chugaku Kōkogaku Kenkyu*, pp.303–25.

155. Sekino, *Chugaku Kōkogaku Kenkyu*, pp.313–23; Chuang Tung-ming, 'T'eng-Hsien Lin-Ch'eng ch'a-te ku-i-chih i-ch'u', and 'T'eng-Hsien Ku-Hsüeh-Ch'eng fa-hsien Chan-Kuo-shih-tai yeh-t'ieh i-chih', *Wen-wu Ts'an-k'ao Tzŭ-liao*, no.5 (1957), p.82.

156. Sekino, *Chugaku Kōkogaku Kenkyu*, pp.305–12.

157. Ni Chen-kuei, 'Yen-Ch'eng ch'u-t'u-ti t'ung-ch'i', *Wen-wu*, no.4 (1959), pp.3–5; Wei Chü-hsien, *Chung-Kuo K'ao-ku-hsüeh-shih*. Commercial Press, Shanghai 1937, p.255; Tseng Chao-yü and Yin Huan-chang, 'Shih-lun "Hu-shu wen-hua", ' *K'ao-ku Hsüeh-pao*, no.4 (1959), p.54; Hsieh Chun-chu, 'Yen-Ch'eng fa-hsien Chan-Kuo-shih-ch'i-ti tu-mu-ch'uan', *Wen-wu*, no.11 (1958), p.80.

158. Han Wei-chou and Wang Ju-lin, 'Ho-nan Hsi-hsia Hsien chi Nan-yang Shih liang-ku-ch'eng tiao-ch'a-chi', *K'ao-ku T'ung-hsün*, no.2 (1956), pp.47–8.

159. *loc. cit.*, pp.49–50.

160. Li Yü-ch'un, 'Shen-hsi [Shensi] Hua-yin Yüeh-Chen Chan-Kuo ku-ch'eng k'an-ch'a-chi', *K'ao-ku*, no.11 (1959), pp.604–5.

161. Chung-Kuo K'e-hsüeh Yüan K'ao-ku Yen-chiu-so Lo-yang Fa-chüeh-tui, '1959-nien Yü-hsi liu-hsien tiao-ch'a chien-pao', *K'ao-ku*, no.1 (1961), p.32.

162. Lou Kan-jou, *Histoire sociale de l'époque Tcheou*. Paris 1935, p.25.

163. Bernhard Karlgren, 'Legends and cults in ancient China', *Bulletin of the Museum of Far Eastern Antiquities*, no.18 (1946), pp.199–366.

164. *loc. cit.*, p.201. On p.351 Karlgren refers to these texts as 'free, narrative texts'.

165. *ibid.*

166. Wolfram Eberhard, Review article in *Artibus Asiae*, vol.9, pt.4 (1946), pp.355–64.

167. *loc. cit.*, p.357.

168. It is true, though, that there are discrepancies between the list of Shang kings provided by Ssŭ-ma Ch'ien and that attested by oracle inscriptions. For example, Ssŭ-ma has confused the sequence by placing **Pôg-tieng (Pao-ting) before, instead of after, **Pôg-iet (Pao-i) and **Pôg-pi̯ǎng (Pao-ping),

has omitted **Tsi̯ĕt and his two sons who are mentioned in both the *Songs of Ch'u* (*T'ien-Wen*) and oracle inscriptions, and, possibly on good grounds, has included a King **T̂i̯ən (Chen), who has not so far been identified in the oracle archives.

169. Eberhard, *Artibus Asiae*, vol.9, p.362. Eberhard also criticizes Karlgren's methodology from the point of view of the sociologist and folklorist : *vide loc. cit.*, p.360.

170. Mo-Ti mentions *Ch'un-Ch'iu* of Chou (T̂i̯ôg) itself, Sông, Dz'i̯ər and ·Ian, but the precise date of Chapter 31 of the *Mo-tzŭ*, in which this reference occurs, is uncertain. Probably it was composed shortly after 400 BC. *Ch'un-Ch'iu* was, of course, an abbreviation of 'spring, summer, autumn and winter', signifying 'years'.

171. This tradition was first voiced, in extant literature, by Mencius some three or four generations after the death of Confucius : 'When the world fell into decay and principles were unimportant . . . Confucius was afraid and put together [*tso*] the *Springs and Autumns*. This work comprises matters proper to the Son of Heaven, wherefore Confucius remarked, 'It is the *Springs and Autumns* by which men will know me, and it is the *Springs and Autumns* by which they will condemn me'' ' [*Meng-tzŭ*, III, ii, IX, 8]. There is, however, no certainty that Mencius was referring to the same text as the one which is extant today.

172. The merits of these rival Traditions were debated in the presence of the Emperor Wu (141–87 BC) by Tung Chung-shu (supporting the *Kung-yang Chuan*) and Chiang-Sheng (espousing the *Ku-liang Chuang*) respectively. For general comments on these Traditions see Wu K'ang, *Les trois théories politiques du Tch'ouen Ts'ieou interprétées par Tong Tchong-chou d'après les principes de l'école de Kong-yang*. Leroux, Paris, 1932, *passim*, but especially pp.172–81.

173. The Tso in question has traditionally been identified as Tso-ch'iu Ming (or perhaps Tso Ch'iu-ming : the precise form is uncertain), who was supposed to have been a disciple of Confucius, but modern scholarship has shown that the *Tso-Chuan* in its present form is a composite work : see below.

174. This notion was first proposed by K'ang Yu-wei, *Hsin-hsüeh Wei-ching k'ao* (Block print edition 1891; Wang-yün Lou lithographic edition, 1891; book and typeset ordered to be destroyed in 1894; presented to the throne in 1898; book and typeset destroyed in 1898 and 1900; Wan-mu ts'ao-t'ang ts'ung shu edition in vermilion, 1917; several subsequent editions, among them the Wen-hua Hsüeh-she edition, Pei-p'ing 1931, in which the reference is to ts'e3A, pp.29–35).

175. Bernhard Karlgren, 'On the authenticity and nature of the Tso chuan', *Göteborgs Högskolas Årsskrift*, vol.32, no.3 (1926), pp.1–65.

176. Bernhard Karlgren, 'The early history of the Chou li and Tso chuan

texts', *Bulletin of the Museum of Far Eastern Antiquities*, vol.3 (1931), pp.1–59.

177. Henri Maspero, 'La composition et la date du Tso tchouan', *Mélanges Chinois et Bouddhiques, Institut Belge des Hautes Etudes Chinoises*, vol.1. Bruxelles 1931-2, pp.137–215; *La Chine antique*. Boccard, Paris 1927 : vol.4 of E. Cavaignac [ed.] *Histoire du Monde*, pp.592–5, and review of Karlgren's 'On the authenticity and nature of the Tso chuan', *Journal Asiatique*, vol.212 (1928), pp.159–65.

178. Ojima, *Shinagaku*, vol.3 (1923), pp.50–61, 127–39 and 452–68.

179. Chang Hsin-cheng, *Wei-Shu T'ung-k'ao*, vol.1. Commercial Press, Ch'ang-sha 1939, pp.408–9.

180. Hung Yeh (William Hung) *et al.*, *Ch'un-Ch'iu Ching-chuan Yin-te*, vol.1. Harvard-Yenching Institute Sinological Index Series, Supplement no.11. Pei-p'ing 1937, pp.1-106. Hung's further conclusion that the *Tso-Chuan* was assembled by Chang-Ch'ang early in Former Han times has not received general assent. Cf. also Ch'i Ssŭ-ho, 'Professor Hung on the Ch'un-ch'iu', *The Yenching Journal of Social Studies*, vol.1, no.1 (1938), pp.50–71. Studies bearing on the nature of the *Tso-Chuan* which have not been mentioned in previous notes include that by Wolfram Eberhard, R. Müller and R. Henseling, 'Beiträge zur Astronomie der Han-Zeit : II', *Sitzungsberichte der preussischen Akademie der Wissenschaften*, philosophisch-historische Klasse, vol.23 (1933), and a magnificent contribution by George A. Kennedy, 'Interpretation of the Ch'un-ch'iu', *Journal of the American Oriental Society*, vol.62, no.1 (1942), pp.40–8.

181. James Legge (transl.), *The Chinese Classics :* vol.5, *The Ch'un Ts'ew* with *The Tso Chuen*. Lane Crawford, Hong Kong and Trübner, London 1872 : photolitho reissue, Hong Kong University Press, 1960, pp.34–5.

182. Karlgren, 'On the authenticity and nature of the Tso Chuan', pp.58–9 and 64–5.

183. Hung, *Ch'un-Ch'iu Ching-chuan Yin-te*, p.lxxxv.

184. K'ang Yu-wei, *Hsin-hsüeh Wei-ching K'ao*, ts'e 4, pp.6–7.

185. Cf. *Lü-Shih Ch'un-Ch'iu*, annotated by Kao-Yu. Ssŭ-pu Ts'ung-k'an edition; Liang Ch'i-ch'ao, *Chu-tzŭ K'ao-shih*. Chung-hua, Shanghai 1936; T'ai-pei reprint 1957, p.104. As this work is not a chronicle of court events, the phrase *Ch'un-Ch'iu* in the title must be used in a metaphorical sense to denote a work of moral and political principle such as the *Ch'un-Ch'iu*, attributed to Confucius at the end of the 3rd century, was conceived to be. Cf. Burton Watson, *Ssŭ-ma Ch'ien, Grand Historian of China*. Columbia University Press 1958, p.103.

186. Li Chün-chih, 'Lü-Shih Ch'un-Ch'iu-chung ku-shu chi-i', *Ku-shih Pien*, vol.6 (1938), pp.321–40; Liu Ju-lin, 'Lü-Shih-Ch'un-Ch'iu-chih Fen-hsi', *loc. cit.*, pp.340–58.

187. *Vide* Ch'i Ssŭ-ho, 'Chan-Kuo Ts'e chu-tso shih-tai k'ao', *Yen-ching Hsüeh-pao*, vol.34 (1948), pp.257–78.

188. *Li-Chi*, Wang-Chih section.

189. Kuo Mo-jo, *Liang-Chou Chin-wen-tz'ŭ Ta-hsi K'ao-shih*. Tokyo. 1935, p.202.

190. Ch'i Ssŭ-ho, 'Chou-tai hsi-ming-li k'ao', p.202.

191. Cf. pp.111–12 above.

192. See particularly Karlgren, 'The early history of the Chou li and Tso chuan texts', pp.2–8, 35–8, 50–7.

193. Sven Broman, 'Studies on the Chou Li', *Bulletin of the Museum of Far Eastern Antiquities*, vol.33 (1961), p.73.

194. Creel, 'The beginnings of bureaucracy in China', p.169, note 75.

195. The history of these texts is summarized succinctly by Charles S. Gardner, *Chinese traditional historiography*. Harvard University Press 1938, pp.56–7, note 69.

196. On the pedigree of this text see Piet van der Loon, 'On the transmission of the *Kuan-tzu*', *T'oung Pao*, vol.41 (1952), pp.357–93. Cf. also Gustav Haloun, 'Legalist fragments: Part I: Kuan-tsï 55 and related texts', *Asia Major*, new series, vol.2, pt.1 (1951), pp.85–120, and 'Das Ti-tsï-tşï, Frühkonfuzianische Fragmente II', *Asia Major*, vol.9 (1933), pp.467–502.

197. Fu-Hsüan (AD 217–278), quoted by Liu-Shu (1032–1078) in the *T'ung-chien Wai-chi*. Subsequently K'ung Ying-ta (574–648), Tu-Yu (735–812), Su-Ch'e (1039–1112), Yeh-Shih (1150–1223), Chu-Hsi (1130–1200) and Huang-Chen (fl. *c.*1270) were all of the same opinion.

198. Lo Ken-tse, *Kuan-tzŭ t'an-yüan* (Chung-hua Shu-chü 1931).

199. W. Allyn Rickett, *Kuan-tzu. A repository of early Chinese thought*, vol.1. Hong Kong University Press 1965.

200. *loc. cit.*, pp.12–13. Rickett's whole book is a confirmation of Karlgren's ['On the authenticity of ancient Chinese texts', pp.173–6] and van der Loon's ['On the transmission of the Kuan-tzu'] rejection of Maspero's [*La Chine antique*, pp.485–6, and review of Gustav Haloun's *Seit wann kannten Chinesen die Tocharer oder Indo-germanen überhaupt?* in *Journal Asiatique*, vol.210 (1927), pp.144–52] thesis that Liu-Hsiang's edition of the *Kuan-tzŭ* was lost and replaced by a modern forgery perpetrated during the 4th and 5th centuries AD.

201. The best introduction to Ssŭ-ma Ch'ien and his work in a Western language is Burton Watson's *Ssŭ-ma Ch'ien, Grand Historian of China*. Columbia University Press 1958. Chapter IV deals specifically with the form of the *Shih-Chi*.

202. Karlgren, 'Legends and cults in ancient China', p.231.

203. For works offering critical analyses of the *Shih-Chi* see Chapter One notes 37, 38, and 39.

204. For the significance of *dįog* and *mįôk* generations see pp.53 and 55.

205. Chi'i Ssŭ-ho, 'Hsi-Chou ti-li-k'ao', *Yen-ching Hsüeh-pao*, no.30 (1946), pp.96–7.

206. Sen-dou Chang, 'The historical trend of Chinese urbanization', *Annals of the Association of American Geographers*, vol.53, no.2 (1963), p.113.

207. The testimony of the *I Hou Nieh I* inscription must now cast doubt on such apparently established events as the beneficing by the Duke of Chou (tįôg) of his son with the territory of Lo (cf. p.108 above).

208. Karlgren, 'Legends and cults', p.302.

209. Eberhard, *Artibus Asiae*, vol.9 (1946), p.360.

210. Wang Kuo-wei, 'Ku-pen Chu-shu Chi-nien chi-chiao', *Hai-ning Wang Chung-ch'io Kung I-shu* (Ch'ang-sha, 1940), with refinements in Fan Hsiang-yung, *Ku-pen Chu-shu Chi-nien Chi-chiao Ting-pu*. Shanghai 1957.

211. This was also the opinion of Henri Maspero, 'La chronologie des rois de Ts'i au IVᵉ siecle avant notre ère', *T'oung Pao*, vol.25 (1927–8), pp.367–86.

212. Edouard Chavannes, *Les mémoires historiques de Se-Ma Ts'ien*, 5 vols. Leroux, Paris 1895.

213. *Tso-Chuan*, Duke **·ər (Ai), 7th year.

214. It is generally agreed that, apart from certain spurious chapters, (of which v is not one), the *Lun-Yü* (which is usually rendered into English as *The Analects*) is an authentic treasury of maxims assembled by students of the Confucian school a generation or so after the Master's death [Cf. Ts'ui Shu, 'Chu-Ssŭ k'ao-hsin yü-lu', in Ku Chieh-kang (ed.), *Ts'ui Tung-pi I-shu*, vol.3 (Shanghai 1936), chüan 2, p.17, and 'Lun-Yü yü-shuo', *loc. cit.*, vol.5, pp.24–35; also Herrlee Glessner Creel, *Confucius and the Chinese Way*. Harper Torchbook, New York 1960, pp.291–4.

The *I-Ching* seems to be an amalgam of peasant superstitions and sophisticated divinatory texts [*Vide* Arthur Waley, 'The Book of Changes', *Bulletin of the Museum of Far Eastern Antiquities*, vol.5 (1933), pp.121–42, and Li Ching-ch'ih, 'Chou-I shih-tz'ŭ hsü-k'ao', *Ling-nan Hsüeh-pao*, vol.8, no.1 (1947), pp.1–66 and 169–73]. Li Ching-ch'ih (*ibid.*) believes that some of the omen texts in this compendium might go back to the 7th or 8th century BC, but that the *T'uan* and *Hsi-Tz'ŭ* did not receive their present form until very late in the Chou dynasty. Other commentaries which now form part of the *I-Ching* were appended in Ch'in and Han times. There is an extremely lucid introduction to this book in Joseph Needham, *Science and civilisation in China*, vol.2 : *History of Scientific Thought*. Cambridge 1956, pp.304 *et seq.*

215. *Tso-Chuan*, Duke **Snjang (Hsiang), 31st year.

216. Kennedy, 'Interpretation of the Ch'un-Ch'iu'.

217. Walker, *The multi-state system of ancient China*, *passim*, but especially p.14.

218. *loc. cit.*, p.30.

219. The sequence of extensions of the Dz'iər borders are conveniently listed in Ku Tung-kao's *Ch'un-Ch'iu Ta-shih Piao*, table 4, ff.7 recto–8 recto.

220. Oshima Riichi, 'Chugaku kodai no shiro ni tsuite', *Tohogakuho*, vol.30 (1959), pp.39–66.

221. These notices occur respectively in *Tso-Chuan*, Duke **·Iən (Yin), 9th year, Duke **G'wân (Huan), 16th year, and Duke **Mįwɛn (Min), 1st year.

222. Ch'en P'an, 'Ch'un-Ch'iu Ta-shih-piao, Lieh-kuo chüeh-hsing chi ts'un-mieh-piao chuan-i [A]', *Kuo-li Chung-yang Yen-chiu-yüan Li-shih Yü-yen Yen-chiu-so Chi-k'an*, vol.26 (1955), pp.59–93; 'Ch'un-Ch'iu Ta-shih-piao, Lieh-kuo chüeh-hsing chi ts'un-mieh-piao chuan-i [B]', *loc. cit.*, vol.27 (1956), pp.325–64, together with 'Chuan-i chung-p'ien pa' (with comments by Lao Kan), pp.365–70; 'Ch'un-Chi'iu Ta-shih-piao, Lieh-kuo chüeh-hsing chi ts'un-mieh-piao chuan-i [C, pt.1]', *loc. cit.*, vol.28 (1956), pp.393–440 and [C, pt.2), *loc. cit.*, vol.29 (1957), pp.513–44.

223. Chang, 'The historical trend of Chinese urbanism', p.114.

224. Chi Li [Li Chi], *The formation of the Chinese people. An anthropological inquiry*. Harvard University Press 1928.

225. This monumental work comprises 10,000 chüan (The Table of Contents alone occupying 40), which, according to Giles's calculation, contain 144 million characters, or from three to four times as much matter as the Eleventh Edition of the *Encyclopaedia Britannica* : Lionel Giles, *An alphabetical index to the Chinese encyclopaedia* (*Ch'in Ting Ku Chin T'u Shu Chi Ch'eng*). British Museum, London 1911, pp.8–9.

226. These gazetteers are termed in general *fang-chih*. If they are concerned with a province they are known as *t'ung-chih*, and variously as *fu-chih, chou-chih* and *hsien-chih* if they deal with smaller units in the administrative hierarchy. There is a brief evaluation of the character of these works in Joseph Needham, *Science and civilisation in China* : vol.3, *Mathematics and the sciences of the heavens and the earth*. Cambridge, at the University Press 1959, pp.517–20. For an excellent introduction in Chinese see Wang Pao-hsin, *T'ung-chih T'iao-i*. Chi Sheng Book Co., Kowloon, 1958. *Vide* also Cheng-siang Chen (Ch'en Cheng-hsiang), *Chung-Kuo Fang-chih-ti Ti-li-hsüeh Chia-chih*. An inaugural address in the Chinese University of Hong Kong (1965).

227. Chi Li (Li Chi], *The formation of the Chinese people*, pp.94 and 100–1.

228. *Ch'un-Ch'iu* and *Tso-Chuan*, 28th year of Duke **Tşįang (Chuang). Although this gloss has all the hallmarks of later systematization, it does show that the compiler of that particular paragraph in the *Tso-Chuan* was able to recognize the basic distinction between these two types of urban settlement in the sources at his disposal, in the same way as we can discern it from the sources available to us.

229. A representative exposition of this belief – one among many – occurs

in the *Tso-Chuan*, Duke **Tṣịang (Chuang), 28th year. Two officers of the Tsịěn court are addressing the Duke : '**K'ịuk-·ok (Ch'ü-wo) is [the precinct of] Your Grace's ancestral temple, **B'wo (P'u) and **Ńịər-k'ịwət (Erh-ch'ü) mark your frontiers. They cannot be without overlords. If your ancestral city be without its overlord, the populace will not stand in awe; if the border mounds are not watched over the Ńịông will be induced to encroach . . .'

230. Cf. p.123 and note 77.

231. Granet, *Chinese civilisation*, p.250.

232. Eberhard, *Conquerors and rulers*, pp.33–40.

233. *Chou-Li*, chüan 12, f.14 recto (1886 edition).

234. *Shih-Chi*, chüan 129, f.7 recto. Ssŭ-ma Ch'ien does, indeed, imply that Duke **Mịwən (Wen) had deliberately located his capital on this site in order to take advantage of the opportunities for trade which it offered. This, I think, is rationalization after the event.

235. *ibid.*

236. *Shih-Chi*, chüan 129, f.8 recto. The text also includes the name **D'ịĕn (Ch'en) as one of the places engaging in this trade, but it appears to be an anomalous interpolation. However, the combination **Dịang (with radical 75 instead of the 163 of the previous folio) B'ịĕng Dịang D'ịĕn recurs on the succeeding folio, from which it appears that a copyist or commentator had at some time read the names as Dịang-b'ịĕng (Yang-p'ing) and Dịang-d'ịĕn (Yang-ch'en).

237. *loc. cit.*, f.8 verso.

238. *loc. cit.*, f.9 recto.

239. *ibid.*

240. Cf. note 87 above.

241. Miyazaki Ichisada, Eastern Studies Fifteenth Anniversary Volume, *Toho Gakkai* (1962). There is also useful information in the same author's paper on what he calls the age of the city-states in China in *Shirin*, vol.33, no.1, (1950), pp.144–63, and 'Les villes en Chine à l'époque des Han', *T'oung Pao*, vol.48, pts.4–5 (1960), pp.376–92.

242. An ancient measure equivalent to 4 *tou*, *q.v.* in note 246 below.

243. A weight of 300 *chin*, *q.v.* in note 245 below.

244. Both a liquid and a dry measure; a weight of 100 *chün*, *q.v.* in note 243.

245. 16 *liang* (oz.) on the Chinese scale. Often translated as 'catty' and stipulated in modern times as 21⅓ oz. avoirdupois (604·53 grammes).

246. A dry measure. Often translated as 'peck' and standardized in modern times as containing 316 cubic inches.

247. Watson, *Records of the Grand Historian*, vol.2, p.495 [transl. from *Shih-Chi*, chüan 129, f.16 recto].

248. Walter Christaller, *Die zentralen Orte in Süddeutschland : Eine*

ökonomisch-geographische Untersuchung über die Gesetzmässigkeit der Verbreitung und Entwicklung der Siedlungen mit städtischen Funktionen. Gustav Fischer Verlag, Jena 1933).

249. Derk Bodde, *China's first unifier. A study of the Ch'in dynasty as seen in the life of Li Ssŭ* (280?–208 BC). E.J.Brill, Leiden 1938. See especially pp.135–9 and Appendix, pp.238–43.

250. Ting Fu-pao, *Shuo-wen Chieh-tzŭ Ku-lin* (1928), pp.3970a–1b. Cf. also Kuo Mo-jo, *Liang-Chou Chin-wen-tz'ŭ Ta-hsi K'ao-shih*, p.203a; Chang Yin-lin, 'Chou-tai-ti feng-chien she-hui', *Ch'ing-hua Hsüeh-pao*, vol.10, no.4 (1935), p.826; and Ku Chieh-kang, 'Ch'un-Ch'iu-shih-tai-ti hsien', *Yü-Kung*, vol.7, nos.6–7 (1937), p.179.

251. Something similar had indeed been hinted at by Chinese scholars somewhat earlier (though Bodde's was the first formal and adequately documented statement): Chao-I, 'Kai-yü ts'ung-k'ao', *Ou-pei Ch'üan-chi* (1877), chüan 16, ff.8 verso–10 recto; Yao-Nai, *Hsi-pao Hsüan Wen-chi* (Ssŭ-pu Pei-yao edition), chüan 2, f.1 recto. Cf. also Ch'i Ssŭ-ho, 'Chan-Kuo chih-tu k'ao', p.214, note 369.

252. In 361 BC Dz'i̯ĕn was not represented at the conferences of rulers, who regarded its government as not greatly superior to that of the Di̯ər and D'iek tribal peoples: *Shih-Chi*, chüan 5, f.17 verso. Even as late as 266 a noble of the state of Ngi̯wər warned his king that, 'Dz'i̯ĕn has the customs of the Ñi̯ông and the D'iek. Its heart is that of the tiger or the wolf. It is avaricious, perverse, desirous of [nothing but] profit, and lacks sincerity. It knows nothing of customary public morality (*li̯ər*), proper relationships (**ngia*) or virtuous conduct (**tək-g'ăng*) ...' [*loc. cit.*, chüan 44, ff.12 verso–13 recto]. Cf. also *Chan-Kuo Ts'e*, Wei section, chüan 26, f.4 recto. Hsün-tzŭ said much the same thing when he observed that the people of Dz'i̯ĕn failed in large measure to practise proper family relationships because they did not observe *li̯ər* and *ngia* [chüan 23].

253. *Shih-Chi*, chüan 5, ff.16–17.

254. Sen-dou Chang (Chang Sheng-tao), 'Some aspects of the urban geography of the Chinese hsien capital', *Annals of the Association of American Geographers*, vol.51, no.1 (1961), p.25. Cf. also W.Allyn Rickett, *Kuan-tzu. A repository of early Chinese thought*, vol.1. Hong Kong University Press, 1965, p.65, note 138.

255. H.G.Creel, 'The beginnings of bureaucracy in China: the origin of the *Hsien*', *Journal of Asian Studies*, vol.23, no.2 (1964), pp.155–83.

256. The passage in question occurs in a conversation between a Tsi̯ĕn pretender and a Dz'i̯ĕn envoy, as reported in the *Kuo-Yü* under the year 651 BC [Ssŭ-pu Pei-yao edition, chüan 8, f.10 verso], but the *Kuo-Yü* is not free from fanciful literary embellishment, and Professor Bodde is doubtless correct in stigmatizing this paragraph as an interpolation [*China's first unifier*, p.243].

257. Creel, 'The beginnings of bureaucracy', p.172. Cf. also note 252 above.

258. *loc. cit.*, pp.172–3.

259. Creel has shown that references to *hsien* in other states during the Ch'un-Ch'iu are either of highly questionable authenticity or afford no confirmation that they connote an administrative institution [*loc. cit.*, p.173, note 97]. Kuo Mo-jo has published an inscription on a bronze vessel ascribed to the reign of Duke **Lieng (Ling) of *Dz'iər* (581–554 BC), which records a grant of 300 *hsien* to a retainer [*Liang-Chou Chin-wen-tz'ŭ Ta-hsi K'ao-shih*, pp.202b–205b] in that state, but both Bodde [*China's first unifier*, p.241] and Creel ['The beginnings of bureaucracy', p.172, note 88] have rejected this inscription as evidence of institutionalized *hsien* administration. The former questioned the authenticity of the inscription on the grounds that the number of *hsien* was impossibly large : according to the *Tso-Chuan* there were only 49 in the whole of the state of Tsjĕn (We may recall here Dr Noel Barnard's warnings against epigraphic forgeries, cf. p.111 above). Creel passed no judgment on the authenticity of the inscription but maintained that *hsien* in this context referred 'only to small "suburban" areas associated with towns'. It is not surprising to find *hsien* attributed to very early times by late systematizing texts, but such testimony is of no more value in a study of Ch'un-Ch'iu times than is Shakespeare's *Coriolanus* for the study of the costume of ancient Rome. The *Huai-nan-tzŭ*, for example, which was put together in the middle of the 2nd century BC, even went so far as to ascribe a *hsien* administration to the kingdom of **G'iat (Chieh), traditionally dated as 1818–1766 BC, [Ssŭ-pu Pei-yao edition, chüan 13, f.9 verso].

260. *Tso-Chuan*, 33rd year of Duke **Xjəg (Hsi).

261. 'The beginnings of bureaucracy', p.173. Creel relies partly on the testimony of the *Tso-Chuan*, 30th year of Duke **Snjang (Hsiang), where the chancellor questions an old man as to his **g'ian d'âd-pjwo (*hsien tai-fu*), thus implying that such an official must have existed, no matter which district the old man hailed from. However, Ku Chieh-kang ['Ch'un-Ch'iu-shih-tai-ti hsien', pp.190–3] had categorized this passage as a forgery of Liu-Hsin and, though not necessarily espousing all Ku's argument, Creel also draws in support of this view on a later passage from the *Tso-Chuan*, 5th year of Duke **Tjog (Chao). This states that in 537 (i.e. only six years after the date of the disputed reference) Tsjĕn had 49 *hsien* able to furnish 4,900 war chariots, an immense force which is possibly the largest attributed to any state in the Ch'un-Ch'iu, and one which must imply that virtually the whole of Tsjĕn territory was apportioned in *hsien* : only eight years later, in 529 [13th year of Duke Tjog], the whole state was apparently able to assemble only a round figure of 4,000 chariots.

262. The evidence for the hereditability of *hsien* in Tsjĕn is complex, obscure and, of course, fragmented so that discussion of apparent individual instances

is hardly, if ever, conclusive, and Creel bases his conclusion on the cumulative impression left by his detailed studies of the Tsįĕn *hsien* in the *Tso-Chuan*. He discusses a selection of the relevant references in 'The beginnings of bureaucracy,' p.173, note 96.

263. Creel himself ['The beginnings of bureaucracy', p.174, note 98] pays tribute to the perspicacity of Hung Liang-Chi (1746–1809), who attributed the creation of *hsien* to Tş'įo, but without citing his evidence or discussing the problems that inevitably accompany such an interpretation ['Ch'un-Ch'iu-shih i ta-i wei hsien shih-yü Ch'u lun', *Keng-sheng-chai Wen Chia-chi* (1802), chüan 2, ff.1–2].

264. Creel, 'The beginnings of bureaucracy', pp.174–9.

265. *Tso-Chuan*, Duke **·ər (Ai), 17th year.

266. *loc. cit.*, Duke **Tşįang (Chuang), 6th year; *Shih-Chi*, chüan 40, f.4.

267. Creel, 'The beginnings of bureaucracy', p.178, note 15.

268. *Tso-Chuan*, Duke Tşįang, 18th year.

269. Creel, 'The beginnings of bureaucracy', p.181, note 124.

270. *Tso-Chuan*, Duke **Xįəg (Hsi), years 23 and 28; *Shih-Chi*, chüan 39, ff.43–5.

271. Cf. also *Tso-Chuan*, Duke **Sįwan (Hsüan), 17th year; Duke **Ḓįĕng (Ch'eng), years 2, 7, 8 and 16; *Kuo-Yü*, chüan 17, ff.3 verso–5 verso.

272. Cf., *int. al.*, *Li-Chi*, *Li-Yün* section : 'It is the purpose [of great men] to make the walls of their cities and suburbs strong, and their ditches and moats secure.'

273. *Tso-Chuan*, Duke **·Įən (Yin), 1st year. It is immaterial, in view of our imprecise knowledge of early Chou measurements, whether 100 *d'įər* be translated as 3,000 cubits [James Legge, *The Chinese Classics*, vol.5 : *The Ch'un Ts'ew with the Tso Chuen*. Hong Kong University Press reprint 1960, p.5] or 4,600 meters [Cho-yün Hsü, *Ancient China in Transition*, p.134]. It would be unrealistic to attempt to match information in a text of this nature with data from present-day archeological investigation. In our opinion the passage in the *Tso-Chuan* is nothing more than a systematization of the simple observation that the more prestigious cities of ancient China tended to have the longer perimeters. Neither, in our opinion and for the same reason, should any significance be attached to the fact that such areal dimensions as archeological research has so far made available are not conspicuously accordant with those of Mencius's representative city, one with a *ḏįĕng* of 3 *li* and a *kwâk* of 7 *li* (Bk. II, pt.2, Chapter i).

274. *Tso-Chuan*, Duke **Ḓįog (Ch'ao), 11th year.

275. *Tso-Chuan*, Duke **Tşįang (Chuang), 26th year.

276. Miyazaki Ichisada, *Rekishi To Chiri*, vol.32 (1933).

277. *Tso-Chuan*, Duke **Snįang (Hsiang), 9th year.

278. *Tso-Chuan*, Duke **Ḓįog (Ch'ao), 21st year.

279. *Tso-Chuan*, Duke **Snįang(Hsiang), 9th year. In the *Kung-yang Chuan* the character for 'fire' (**χwâr : huo) is used instead of that for 'calamity'.

280. Shang and early Chou graphs for *kwâk* (*kuo*) depict a wall with gate towers [Karlgren no.774b,c,d. Cf. Fig.15].

281. *Tso-Chuan*, Duke **Xįəg (Hsi), 2nd year.

282. *Tso-Chuan*, Duke **Xįəg, 12th year.

283. *Ch'un-Ch'iu* and *Tso-Chuan*, Duke **Dįog(Ch'ao), 23rd year. According to the traditional commentators, D'iek-dz'įwan was so named after the D'iek spring and pool on the east of Dįěng-tįôg – a good example of folk etymology if ever there was one.

284. *Tso-Chuan*, Duke D'ieng (Ting), 1st year.

285. *Ch'un-Ch'iu* and *Tso-Chuan*, Duke, **G'wân (Huan), 6th year.

286. *Ch'un-Ch'iu* and *Tso-Chuan*, Duke **Snįang (Hsiang), 15th year.

287. *Tso-Chuan*, Duke **Dįog (Ch'ao), 25th year.

288. *Meng-tzŭ*, Bk.I, pt.1, Chapter VII. Mencius draws the same distinctions again in Bk.II, pt.1, Chapter V.

289. Although literary traditions equate this site with that of the capital of independent ·Ok prior to its absorption by Tsįěn in the 8th century BC, the remains which have been brought to light so far appear to date from the Chan-Kuo (cf. pp.140–1).

290. Wolfram Eberhard, 'Data on the structure of the Chinese city in the pre-industrial period', *Economic Development and cultural change*, vol.3 (1957), pp.258–9.

291. The *I Chou-shu* is the earliest of the *Pieh-Shih* or 'Separate Histories'. It was alleged to have been found, together with the *Chu-shu Chi-nien* (cf. notes 36 and 37 to Chapter One) in an ancient **Ngįwər tomb during the 3rd century AD. If any of its contents are genuine they will date from the end of the 4th and beginning of the 3rd century BC, so that they will almost certainly already have undergone a great deal of systematization before that time, and ideas about urban morphology will be just as likely to relate to the later as the earlier centuries of the Chou. The author of the work is unknown.

292. Marcel Granet, *Chinese civilization*. Transl. from the French by Kathleen E.Innes and Mabel R.Brailsford. Meridian Books Inc., New York, 1958, p.242.

293. Henri Frankfort, *Kingship and the gods*. University of Chicago Press 1947, p.396, note 23.

294. *Tso-Chuan*, Duke **Mįwɛn (Min), 2nd year.

295. *Tso-Chuan*, Duke **Snįang (Hsiang), 27th year.

Glossary of Transcriptions
of Foreign Names, Terms and
Bibliographical References

Glossary of Transcriptions of Foreign Names, Terms and Bibliographical References

Compiled by Mrs T'ung Huang Yih

**·â (o)　阿

**·Â-bʻi̯wang (O-fang)　阿房

**·ăg (ya)　亞

An-hui　安徽

An-nam chí-lược (Việt.)　安南志略

An-nam Chung-tu Hu-fu　安南中都護府

An-nam La-thánh (Việt.)　安南羅城

An-yang　安陽

Âu-lạc (Việt.)　甌雒

Bắc (Việt.)　北

**Bli̯əm-gʻi̯ung (Lin-chʻiung)　臨邛

**Bli̯əm-si̯ĕn (Lin-hsin)　廩辛

**Bʻâk (Po)　亳

**Bʻăk-Kiweg (Po-Kuei)　白圭

**B'jĕng (P'ing)　平

**B'jĕng-djang (P'ing-yang)　平陽

**b'jəng-b'jəng (p'ing-p'ing)　馮馮

**b'ju-djung (fu-yung)　附庸

*B'ju-nậm (Fu-nan)　扶南

**b'jŭg (fu)　婦

**B'jŭg-χôg (Fu-hao)　婦好

**b'jŭk (fu)　簹

**B'jwăm (Fan)　凡

*B'jwɒn Ṣi-mjwɒn (Fan Shih-man)　范師蔓

**B'jwăn (Fan)　繁　樊

**b'jwang (fang)　房

**B'wân-kăng (P'an-keng)　盤庚

*b'wâng (p'ang)　傍

**B'wo (P'u)　蒲

Chan-Kuo (**Ṭjan-Kwək)　戰國

Chan-Kuo Ts'e　戰國策

Chang-chia-p'o　張家坡

Chang-Ch'ang　張敞

Chang-Hua, *Po-wu Chih*　張華　博物志

Chang-I, *Kuang-Ya*　張揖　廣雅

Chang Shou-chieh, *Shih-Chi Cheng-i*　張守節　史記正義

GLOSSARY

Chang-te Fu 彰德府

Chao Chiu-feng, *Ti-li Wu-chüeh* 趙九峯 地理五訣

Chao-k'ang Chen 趙康鎮

Chao-Yeh, *Wu Yüeh Ch'un-ch'iu* 趙曄 吳越春秋

Cheng-Chou 鄭州

Cheng-Hsüan 鄭玄

Cheng-i 正義

Chi 己

Chi-hsia (**Tsjək-g'å) 稷下

Chi-nan 濟南

chia 甲 嘼

chia-chieh 假借

chia-ku hsüeh 甲骨學

Chiang-Sheng 江生

Chiang-su 江蘇

chiao 窖

chieh-kao 桔槹

chien 建

Chien-ho 澗河

chih 觶

Chih-li 直棣

chih-shih 指事

chin 斤

Chin-p'en　金盆

chin-wen　今文

ching　鏡

Ching-Ts'un　荆村

chio　角

Chiu-tsung　九嵕

Chou (**T̂i̯ôg)　周

chou　冑

chou-chih　州志

Chou-k'ou Tien　周口店

Chou-Kuan　周官

Chou-Kung (**T̂i̯ôg-Kung)　周公

Chou-Li　周禮

chu　箸

Chü-ho [Ch'eng]　巨合[城]

Chu-Hsi, *T'ung-chien Kang-mu*　朱熹 通鑑綱目

Chu-shu Chi-nien　竹書紀年

Chu-tzŭ Ch'üan-shu　朱子全書

Chu Yu-fu　朱右甫

Chu Yu-tseng　朱右曾

chuan　傳

chuan-chu　轉注

Chuan-Hsü (**T̂i̯wan-Si̯u)　顓頊

GLOSSARY

Chuang-Chou, *Chuang-tzŭ* 莊周 莊子

chün 鈞

Chün-Hsien 濬縣

chung 鍾

Chung-Kuo K'e-hsüeh Yüan 中國科學院

Chung-yüan 中原

Ch'ang-an (*Ḍ'i̯ang-·ân) 長安

Ch'ang-Chou 常州

Ch'ao-ko 朝歌

Ch'en Meng-lei 陳夢雷

Ch'eng Kung-shuo, *Ch'un-Ch'iu fen-chi* 程公說 春秋分紀

Ch'eng-tzŭ Yai 城子崖

ch'i 氣 鍼

Ch'i-Ch'eng 齊乘

Ch'i-chia 齊家

Ch'i-li P'u 七里舖

Ch'ien-lung 乾隆

Ch'in-ting ku-chin t'u-shu chi-ch'eng 欽定古今圖書集成

Ch'ing-yüan 清苑

ch'ü 钁

Ch'ü-fu 曲阜

Ch'u-Tz'ŭ (**Tṣ'i̯o-Dzi̯əg) 楚辭

Ch'ü-yang 曲陽

GLOSSARY

Ch'un-Ch'iu (**ȶ'ịwən-Ts'ịôg)　春秋

Ch'un-Ch'iu Tso-Chuan Cheng-i　春秋左傳正義

Daigoku-den (Jap.)　大極殿

**dịả-ńịĕn (yeh-jen)　野人

**Dịang (Yang)　陽　楊

**Dịang-b'ịĕng (Yang-p'ing)　楊[陽]平

**Dịang-d'ịĕn (Yang-ch'en)　楊[陽]陳

**Dịĕng (Ying)　郢

**Dịər (I)　夷

**Dịo ·ịĕt-ńịĕn (Yü i-jen)　余一人

**Dịo-mịwo (Yü-wu)　余無

**Dịung-Ḍịĕng (Jung-Ch'eng)　容城

**Dzịo (Hsü)　徐

**Dzịung (Sung)　訟

**Dzịwĕn (Hsün)　郇

**Dzwia (Sui)　隨

**D'âd- ·ịəp (Ta-i)　大邑

***D'âd-Ngả (Ta-Ya)*　大雅

**d'âd-pịwo (tai-fu)　大夫

**D'âd-sịəg-d'o (Ta-ssŭ-t'u)　大司徒

**D'âd-sịəg-k'ung (Ta-ssŭ-k'ung)　大司空

***D'âd-Tung (Ta-Tung)*　大東

GLOSSARY

**D'əg (Tai) 代

**D'əm (T'an) 譚

**D'əng (T'eng) 鄧 滕

**D'i̯an (Ch'an) 瀍

**D'i̯ang-ḍi̯ok (Ch'ang-shao) 長勺

**D'iek (Ti) 狄

**D'iek-dz'i̯wan (Ti-ch'üan) 狄泉

**D'ien (T'ien) 田

**d'ien (t'ien) 田

**D'i̯ĕn (Ch'en) 陳

**d'ien-di̯å (t'ien-yeh) 田野

**D'ien-Śi̯ôk (T'ien-Shu) 田叔

**D'i̯ĕng (Cheng) 鄭

**D'i̯ĕng-D'i̯ĕng (Ch'eng-Cheng) 程鄭

**D'ieng-Kung (Ting-Kung) 定公

**_D'ieng-t̂i̯əg pi̯wang-ti̯ông (Ting-chih fang-chung)_ 定之方中

**d'i̯ər (chih) 雉

**D'i̯og (Chao) 趙

**D'i̯og-si̯an (Ch'ao-hsien) 朝鮮

**D'iok (Ti) 翟

**D'i̯ông-tieng (Chung-ting) 仲丁

**D'o (Tu) 杜

**d'o (t'u) 荼

**D'ôg (T'ao) 陶

*D'uo-γuâ-lâ-puâ-tiei (Tu-ho-lo-po-ti) 杜和羅鉢底

**Dz'ậg (Tsu) 胙

*Dẓ'i-Siep (Shih-Hsieh. Việt : Sī-Nhiêp) 士燮

**dz'ịan (chien) 賤

**dz'ịang (chiang) 匠

**Dz'ịĕn (Ch'in) 秦

**Dz'ịĕn-Dịang (Ch'in-Yang) 秦陽

**dẓ'ịəg (shih) 士

**Dẓ'ịəg-Gwia (Shih-Wei) 士蔿

**Dz'iər (Ch'i) 齊

**Dz'ŏg (Ch'ao) 巢

**Dz'ôg (Ts'ao) 曹

Đại-la (Việt.) 大羅

**ḍịă (she) 社

**ḍịang (shang) 上

**Ḍịang-Tieg (Shang-Ti) 上帝

**ḍịĕg (shih) 氏

**ḍịĕn (ch'en) 臣

**ḍịĕng (ch'eng) 成 城 (Ch'eng) 郕

**Ḍịĕng-Gịwang (Ch'eng-Wang) 成王

**Ḍịĕng-Kung (Ch'eng-Kung) 成公

**Ḍịĕng-Tịôg (Ch'eng-Chou) 成周

$\hat{d}_i \ni g$ (shih) 市

$\hat{d}_i \ni g$-tsi̯ěng (shih-ching) 市井

$\hat{D}_i og$[-Kung] (Ch'ao[-Kung]) 昭[公]

$\hat{D}_i og$-kôg (*Shao-kao*) 召誥

$\hat{d}_i og$-mi̯ôk (chao-mu) 昭穆

$\hat{D}_i uk$ (Shu) 蜀

$\hat{d}$'i̯ǎg (she) 射

$\hat{D}$'i̯ěn-Nông (Shen-Nung) 神農

Erh-li Kang 二里崗

Erh-shih Huang-ti 二世皇帝

erh-ts'eng t'ai 二層台

·ər-Kung (Ai-Kung) 哀公

Fa-Fa (**pi̯wǎp-pi̯wǎp**) 法法

fan-ch'ieh 反切

Fan-Ch'o, *Man* [*Mwan]-Shu* 樊綽 蠻書

fang-chih 方志

Fang Hsüan-ling 房玄齡

Fen 汾

feng : Fr. fong (**pi̯ung) 封

Feng-chia An 馮家岸

feng-chien chih-tu 封建制度

Feng-huang T'ai　鳳凰台

feng-shui　風水

fu-chih　府志

Fu-Hsi (**B'ĭuk-χia)　伏羲

Fu-Hsüan　傅玄

Fu-Sheng　伏生

Fu-yüan　陣原

Giao-châu kí (Việt.)　交州記

**gi̯ək-gi̯ək (i-i)　翼翼

**Gi̯wad (Wei)　衛

***Gi̯wad-Pi̯ŭm (Wei-Feng)*　衛風

***Gi̯wad Śi̯ad-kǎ (Wei Shih-chia)*　衛世家

**gi̯wang (wang)　王

**Gi̯wang-Ḍi̯ĕng (Wang-Ch'eng)　王城

**gi̯wang-ńi̯ĕn (wang-jen)　王人

***Gi̯wang-T̂i̯ad (Wang-Chih)*　王制

**Gi̯wăt (Yüeh)　越

**Gi̯wĕng-śi̯ĕt (Ying-shih)　營室

***Gi̯wo-Kung (Yü-Kung)*　禹貢

**Glâk (Lo)　洛

**Glâk-di̯ang (Lo-yang)　洛陽

**Glâk-·i̯əp (Lo-i)　洛邑

GLOSSARY

Glâk-kôg (Lo-kao) 洛誥

Gliok (Li) 櫟

G'â (Ho) 河

G'å-Mįwo (Hsia-Wu) 下武

G'â-nəp (Ho-nei) 河內

G'â-tân-kap (Ho-tan-chia) 河亶甲

G'å-to (Hsia-tu) 下都

G'ân (Han) 韓 邗

G'ân-tân (Han-tan) 邯鄲

G'ân-ts'įĕg (Han-tzǔ) 寒浞

G'ɛm-djang (Hsien-yang) 咸陽

G'ia (Ch'i) 錡

g'ian d'âd-pįwo (hsien tai-fu) 縣大夫

g'ian tįəg (hsien chih) 縣之

G'įat (Chieh) 桀

G'įĕg (Chi) 薊

G'įĕg (Ch'i) 岐

G'ieng (Hsing) 邢

g'iəg (ch'i) 旗

g'įək (chi) 極

G'įo-k'įŭg (Ch'ü-ch'iu) 渠丘

G'iweg (Hsi) 鄶

g'iwen-tiôg (hsüan-niao) 玄鳥

Hsin-Hsiang　新鄉

Hsing-li Ching-i　性理精義

hsing-sheng　形聲

hsing-shih　形勢

Hsing-T'ai　邢台

Hsing-Tsai　行在

hsiu　宿

Hsü Chih-mo, *Ti-li Cho-yü-fu*　徐之鎮 地理琢玉斧

hsüeh　穴

Hsüeh-chia Chuang　薛家莊

hsün　塤/壎

Hsün-tzŭ　荀子

hu　壺

Hu An-kuo　胡安國

Hua-yin Hsien　華陰縣

Huai-nan-tzŭ　淮南子

Huan Ho　洹河

Huang-Chen　黃震

Huang Ho　黃河

Huang-niang-niang T'ai　皇娘娘台

Hui-Hsien　輝縣

hui-i　會意

Hui-Shih　惠施

GLOSSARY

Hung-an 紅安

Huo-Chih 貨殖

**Xi̯ǎn-Kung (Hsien-Kung) 獻公

**Xi̯ang (Hsiang) 向

**Xi̯əg-Kung (Hsi-Kung) 僖公

**Xi̯o (Hsü) 許

**Xi̯og (Aθ) 罵

**Xiwĕt (hsü) 泄

**Xmwəng-χmwəng (hung-hung) 薨薨

**Xŏg-Kung (Hsiao-Kung) 孝公

**Xwâk (Huo) 霍

**Xwâr (huo) 火

i 彝

I-chang shu Huang-Men 譯長屬黃門

I-Ching 易經

I-Ching, *Ta-T'ang Hsi-yü Ch'iu-fa K'ao-seng Chuan* 義淨 大唐西域求法高僧傳

I Chou-shu, Tso-Lo 逸周書 作雒

I Hou Nieh I 圉厌矢彝

I-Hsien 易縣

I-Li 儀禮

i-mao 乙卯

i-wei　乙未

**·Ia-Twən (I-Tun)　猗頓

Ichisada Miyazaki (Jap.)　宮崎市定

**ı̯uĕn (yin)　尹

**·I̯am (Yen)　奄

**·I̯an (Yen)　燕

*·ı̯ĕn (yin)　印

**·Iɛr-ı̯uĕn (I-yin)　伊尹

**·ı̯ɛt (i)　乙

**·I̯əm-tsı̯ĕn (Yin-chin)　陰晉

**·I̯ən-Kung (Yin-Kung)　隱公

** ·I̯ən-Mı̯wo (Yin-Wu)　殷武

**·I̯əng (Ying)　應

**·ı̯əp (i)　邑

**·I̯ung (Yung)　雍

**·I̯ung Glåk-đı̯ĕng (Yung Lo-ch'eng)　雍樂成

**·I̯ung-Păk (Yung-Po)　雍伯

**·I̯wăd-g'lâk (Wei-ho)　犧貉

**·I̯wăn (Yüan)　宛

Jao Lu　饒魯

jen　壬

Jen-min Kung-yüan　人民公園

Jih-chao　日照

**Kăd-kən (Chieh-ken) 介根

**Kan (Chien) 澗

Kan-su 甘肅

Kao-liang 高梁

Kao-Yu 高誘

**Kăp-ńi̯uk (Chia-ju) 郟鄏

**Kăn-D'iek (Chien-Ti) 簡狄

*Kân-t'â-lji (Kan-t'o-li) 干陁利

**Kăng-tieng (Keng-ting) 庚丁

*Kau-tśi (Chiao-chih) 交趾

keng 庚

keng-hsü 庚戌

**kɛn (chin) 堇

Khâm-định Việt-sử thông-giám Cương-mục (Việt.) 欽定越史通鑑網目

**Ki̯ĕng (Ching) 荆

**Ki̯əg (Chi) 姬

**Ki̯ər (Chi) 饑

**Ki̯ung (Kuŋ) 共

**Ki̯wɛd-Liek (Chi-Li) 季歷

**Ki̯wɛd-Ńi̯an (Chi-Jan) 季然

**Ki̯wɛd-tsi̯əg (Chi-tzŭ) 季子

**Ki̯wɛr (Kuei) 癸

**ki̯wən-tsi̯əg (chün-tzŭ) 君子

2 K

GLOSSARY

****Kįwər-pįwang (Kuei-fang) 鬼方

****klâk-klâk (ko-ko) 閣閣

****Klįǎng (Ching) 京

****Klįǎng-Gįwang (Ching-Wang) 景王

ko 戈

Ko-ta-wang 旭奋王　屹�王

****Kŏg (Chiao) 絞

****Kôg (Kao) 郜

****Kôg-pįwang (Kao-fang) 告方

****Kộng (Chiang) 絳

****kộng/klộng (chiang) 降

kou 鈎

****ku (kou) 溝

ku 觚　鼓

Ku-liang Chuan 穀梁傳

Ku-shih Shih-chiu-shou 古詩十九首

Ku Tung-kao, *Ch'un-Ch'iu Ta-shih Piao* (Wan-chüan-lou)
顧棟高　春秋大事表 (萬卷樓)

ku-wen 古文

kuan 罐

Kuan-Lo, *Kuan-shih Ti-li Chih-meng* 管輅　管氏地理指蒙

Kuan-lu 關盧

Kuan-tzŭ 管子

kuei 簋 圭 簋

kung 觥

**kung (kung) 工 公

**Kŭng (Chiang) 江

Kung-chai Ti-hsing 宮宅地形

**kung-d'ien (kung-t'ien) 公田

Kung-yang Chuan 公羊傳

Kung-yang Kao 公羊高

Kung-yang Shou 公羊壽

kuo 槨

Kuo-li Chung-yang Yen-chiu-yüan Li-shih Yü-yen Yen-chiu-so
國立中央研究院歷史語言研究所

Kuo-Yü 國語

**kwad (kuai) 夬

**Kwăk (Kuo) 虢

**kwâk (kuo) 郭

**Kwâk-Tsi̯ung (Kuo-Tsung) 郭縱

**Kwân (Kuan) 管

**Kwân-D'i̯ông (Kuan-Chung) 管仲

**Kwân-pi̯u (Kuan-fu) 官府

**kwək (kuo) 國

**Kwən-lwən (K'un-lun) 崑崙

Kyōtō (Jap.) 京都

K'ai-feng　開封

K'ai-jui Chuang　開瑞莊

k'an　坎

k'an-kuo　坩鍋

k'an-yü chia　堪輿家

K'an-yü Chin-kuei　堪輿金匱

K'ang (**K'âng)　康

K'ang-hsi Tzŭ-tien　康熙字典

***K'âng-kôg (K'ang-kao)*　康誥

***K'âng-śjôk (K'ang-shu)*　康叔

K'ao-kung Chi　考工記

**K'ât (Ko)　葛

K'e-tao　刻刀

k'eng　坑

**K'ịang (Ch'iang)　羌

**k'ịǎng (ch'ing)　卿

**K'ịəg (Ch'i)　杞

**K'ịu-sịwok (Ch'ü-su)　區粟

**K'ịuk-·ok (Ch'ü-wo)　曲沃

**K'ịuk-Śjôk (Ch'ü-Shu)　曲叔

K'o (**K'ək)　克

k'uei　夔

**K'ung (K'ung)　孔

K'ung An-kuo　孔安國

K'ung Ying-ta　孔穎達

Lạc (Việt.)　雒

**Lâng (Lang)　郎

Lao-Lao T'ai　老姥台

**Ləg (Lai)　萊

li　甹 里

Li Chi　李濟

Li-Chi　禮記

Li Kuang-ti　李光地

Li-K'uei　李悝

Li-Ssŭ (**Ljəg-Sjĕg)　李斯

Li Tao-yüan, *Shui-Ching Chu*　酈道元　水經注

Li Tê-xuyên, *Việt điện u linh tập* (Việt.)　李濟川　越甸幽靈集

**Lia-Sôg (*Li-Sao*)　離騷

liang　兩

**Ljang (Liang)　梁

Liang-ch'eng Chen　兩城鎮

Liang Lü-sheng. *Tso-t'ung Pu-shih* (Wang Hsien-ch'ien, *Huang-Ch'ing Ching-chich Hsü-pien*)

　梁履繩　左通補釋〔王先謙　皇清經解續編〕

Liang-Shu　梁書

Liao-ning　遼寧

Lieh-Chuan 列傳

**liei (li) 隸

lien 鎌

**Lieng-Kung (Ling-Kung) 靈公

**Lįĕt (Li) 栗

**lįəg (li) 吏

*Lįəm-·įəp (Lin-i) 林邑

**Liər (Li) 黎

**liər (li) 禮

**Lįər-kįwɛr (Lü-kuei) 履癸

Lin-Li 林栗

Lin-shan Chai 林山砦

Lin-tzŭ 臨淄

ling 鈴

Ling-yüan 凌源

**Lįôg (Liu) 劉

Liu-Chi, *K'an-yü Man-hsing* 劉基 堪輿漫興

Liu-Hsiang, *Shuo-Yüan* 劉向 説苑

Liu-Hsin 劉歆

Liu-Hsü, *Chiu T'ang-Shu* 劉昫 舊唐書

Liu-Shu, *T'ung-chien Wai-chi* 劉恕 通鑑外紀

**lįuĕt (lieh) 寽

**Lįung (Lung) 隴

**Lịung-pịwang (Lung-fang) 龍方

**lịwər-dzịəg (lei-ssǔ) 耒耜

*Ljwiẹ-lịu (Việt. Luy-lâu) 羸陬

**Lo (Lu) 魯

Lo-ho 洛河

Lo-Pi, *Lu-Shih* 羅泌 路史

Lo-ta Miao 洛達廟

Lu-wang Fen 潞王墳

lui 罍

Lun-Yü 論語

Lũng-khê (Việt.) 隴溪

Lung-shan Chen 龍山鎮

Lung-T'ai 龍臺

Lü Pu-wei 呂不韋

Lü-shih Ch'un-Ch'iu 呂氏春秋

**mǎ (ma) 馬

Ma-erh 馬耳

Ma Tuan-lin, *Wen-hsien T'ung-k'ao* 馬端臨 文獻通考

mao 矛

Mao-Ch'ang 毛萇

Mao-Heng 毛亨

Mao-Kung 毛公

Mao Shih 毛詩

Meng-tzǔ 孟子

**Mịan (Mien) 縣

Miao-ti Kou 廟底溝

**mịat (mieh) 滅

Mien-chʻih 澠池

**mịən (min) 民

***Mịən-log (Min-lao)* 民勞

**Mịər (Mei) 郿

ming (**mịǎng) 命

Ming-kung Lu 銘功路

Ming-Tʻang 明堂

**mịog (miao) 廟

**Mịôk (Mu) 穆

**mịôk (mu) 牧

**mịôk-ṣịər (mu-shih) 牧師

**Mịwěn̈-tịôk (Min-chu) 敏竹

**Mịwɛn-Kung (Min-Kung) 閔公

**Mịwən[-Gịwang] (Wen[-Wang]) 文[王]

***Mịwən-Gịwang gịǔg ṣịěng (Wen-Wang yu sheng)* 文王有聲

**Mịwo-Ḍịěng (Wu-Chʻeng) 武城

**Mịwo[-Gịwang] (Wu[-Wang]) 武[王]¹

**Mịwo-·ịɛt (Wu-i) 武乙

**Mi̯wo-Ti̯ĕg (Wu-Chih) 無知

**Mi̯wo-tieng (Wu-ting) 武丁

**Mlwan (*Mwan, Man) 蠻

Mo-Ti, *Mo-tzŭ* 墨翟 墨子

**Mog (Mao) 毛

**Môg (Mao) 茅

mou-shen 戊申

mu 墓

*Muâ-χiei-śi̯ǝu-lâ (Mo-hsi-shou-lo) 摩醯首羅

*Muâ-tậm (Mo-tan) 摩耽

**Mwân-păk (Man-pe) 曼伯

*Nâ-ka-si̯än (Na-chia-hsien) 那伽仙

*Nậm-Tśi̯äu (Nan-Chao) 南詔

Nan-ching 南京

**Nan-Gi̯wang (Nan-Wang) 報王

Nan-kuan-wai 南關外

Nan-Shih 南史

Nan-yang 南陽

nao 饒

Nara (Jap.) 奈良

Nei-Chuan 內傳

Nei-yeh (**Nǝp-ngi̯ǎp) 內業

**nəm (nan) 男

**Nəm-Li̯əg (Nan-Li) 南里

**ngia (i) 義

**Ngi̯ən (Yin) 沂

**ngi̯o-sli̯əg (yü-shih) 御史

**Ngi̯wǎn (Yüan) 原

**ngi̯wǎn-ḍi̯ěn (yüan-ch'en) 元臣

**Ngi̯wǎt-Li̯ěng (Yüeh-Ling) 月令

**Ngi̯wər (Wei) 魏

**Ngi̯wər-Pi̯ŭm (Wei-Feng) 魏風

**Ngi̯wo (Yü) 虞

**Nglǒk-χi̯əg (Yüeh-Hsi) 樂喜

**Ngo (Wu) 吳

**Ngo-ki̯əp (Wu-chi) 午汲

**Ngog (Ao) 隞

**ngwâd (wai) 外

ni shui 逆水

**Ńi̯ak (Jo) 若

**ńi̯ěn (jen) 人

Nien-Piao 年表

**Ńi̯ěn-pi̯wang (Jen-fang) 人方

**ńi̯əng-ńi̯əng (jeng-jeng) 陾陾

**Ńi̯ər-k'i̯wət (Erh-ch'ü) 二屈

GLOSSARY

**Ni̯o-gʻwɛr-tsʻi̯ĕng (Nü-huai-chʻing) 女懷清

**Ńi̯ông (Jung) 戎 (Sung) 娀

Niu-Chai 牛砦

Niu-Hsiṅg 紐星

Niu-Tsʻun 牛村

Nü-kua (**Ni̯o-Kwa) 女媧

**Ńi̯ĕt-nəm : *Ńźi̯ĕt-nậm (Jih-nan) 日南

**ńźi̯uĕn (jun) 閏

**·O-gʻwân (Wu-huan) 烏桓

**·Ok (Wo) 沃

**·Ok-kwək (Wo-kuo) 沃國

Ou-yang Hsiu, Sung-Chʻi, *Hsin Tʻang-Shu* 歐陽修 宋祁 新唐書

**På (Pa) 巴

**Păg (Pa) 霸

Pai-chia Chuang 白家莊

**păk (po) 伯

Pan-Ku, *Chʻien-Han Shu* 班固 前漢書

Pan-pʻo Tsʻun 半坡村

Pan-Shan 半山

pang 榜

Pao-chi 寶雞

Pei 淖

Pei-Ch'en 北辰

Pei-ching 北京

Pei-Shih 北史

pen 錛

Pen-Chi 本紀

**Pək-[χịang]-g'o, *Pək-[χịang]-γuo (Pei-[hsiang]-hu) 北[嚮]户

Phạm Công-trứ, *Đại-Việt sử-ki toàn-thư, ngoại kỉ toàn-thư* (Việt.)
范公菁 大越史記全書 外紀全書

pi 璧 匕

Pi-sha Kang 碧沙岡

**Pjăng (Ping) 邴

pieh-chü 别居

Pieh-Shih 别史

**pjĕk-địĕn (p'i-ch'en) 辟臣

**Pjĕt (Pi) 畢

**pjəg (pi) 鄙

**Pjən (Pin) 豳

Pin-Hsien 邠縣

ping 丙

ping-wu 丙午

**pjôk-d'ôg (fu-tao) 複道

**Pjŭg-Địən (Fu-Ch'en) 富辰

**pi̯wang (fang) 方

**pi̯wăp (fa) 法

**Pi̯wo-di̯o (Fu-yü) 夫餘

  Po-Hsien 亳縣

  Po-t'ing Ch'eng 博亭城

**Pôg-·i̯ɛt (Pao-i) 報乙

**Pôg-pi̯ăng (Pao-ping) 報丙

**Pôg-tieng (Pao-ting) 報丁

  pu 布

**puk (pu) 卜

**Pŭng (Pang) 邦

  p'an 盤

  P'an-ku (**B'wân-ko) 盤古

  p'ang 旁

  P'ei-Yin 裴駰

  p'en 盆

  P'ing-ling [Hsien/Ch'eng] 平陵[縣/城]

  P'ing-wang 平王

**P'i̯ông (Feng) 豐 酆

**p'i̯ug (fu) 郙

**P'i̯wăn-ngi̯u (P'an-yü) 番禺

**p'i̯wo (fu) 撫

  p'ou 瓴

GLOSSARY

**Sâk-pịwang (*Shuo-fang*) 朔方

San-Ch'i Chi 三齊記

San-fu Huang T'u 三輔黃圖

San-li T'un 三里墩

**Sĕng (*sheng*) 生

Shan-fu K'o (**Ɖịam-pịwo K'ǝk*) 善夫克

Shan-hsi 山西

Shan-Hsien 陝縣

Shan-tung 山東

Shang (**Śịang*) 商

Shang-chieh 上街

Shang-Chou 商州

Shang-lo 商洛

shao 勺

Shen-hsi 陝西

Shen Huai-yüan, *Nan-Yüeh Chi* 沈懷遠 南越記

Shih 室

shih 栻

Shih-Chi : see Ssŭ-ma T'an

Shih-Chia 世家

Shih-Ching 詩經

Shih-li Miao 十里廟

Shih-li P'u 十里舖

Shu 書

Shu-Ching 書經

Shun (**Śi̯wən) 舜

Shuo-wen Chieh-tzŭ 說文解字

**Si̯ang (Hsiang) 相

**Si̯at (Hsieh) 契

**Si̯at (Hsüeh) 薛

**Si̯ĕg (Tzʻŭ) 賜

***Si̯ĕg-kân* (*Ssŭ-kan*) 斯干

**Si̯ĕg-mi̯ăng (Tzʻŭ-ming) 賜命

**Siek-mi̯ăng (Hsi-ming) 錫命

**Si̯ĕn-dʻien (Hsin-tʻien) 新田

**si̯ĕng (hsing) 姓

**Si̯əd-tʻo (Ssŭ-tʻu) 四土

**Si̯ək (Hsi) 息

**si̯ər-dʻien (ssŭ-tʻien) 私田

**si̯og (hsiao) 小

**Siôg (Hsiao) 蕭

**si̯og-d̂i̯ĕn (hsiao-chʻen) 小臣

**Si̯og-·i̯ɛt (Hsiao-i) 小乙

**si̯og-ńi̯ĕn (hsiao-jen) 小人

**Si̯og-si̯ĕn (Hsiao-hsin) 小辛

**Si̯wan-Kung (Hsüan-Kung) 宣公

**slịəg (shih) 史

**slịəg-śịu (shih-shu) 史戍

**Snịang-Kung (Hsiang-Kung) 襄公

So-yin 索引

**Sông (Sung) 宋

Ssŭ-ma Cheng 司馬貞

Ssŭ-ma T'an, Ssŭ-ma Ch'ien, *Shih-Chi* 司馬談 司馬遷 史記

Su-Ch'e 蘇轍

Su-Shih 蘇軾

Sui 隋

Sui-Shu 隋書

Sung-Shih 宋史

**Śia (Shih) 施

**śịag-ńịěn (shu-jen) 庶人

**Śịang-Dzʻịung (Shang-Sung) 商頌

**Śịap (She) 葉

**Śịěn (Shen) 申

**Śịěn Mịwo-gịwo (Shen Wu-yü) 申無宇

**Śịěng-tsịəg (Sheng-tzŭ) 聲子

**śịu-dzịəg tsịəg (shu-ssŭ tzŭ) 戍嗣子

**tâ-ḓịěn (to-ch'en) 多臣

Ta-hsin Chuang 大辛莊

**Tâ-ˌi̯ĕn (To-yin) 多印

Ta-Kʻuang (**Dʻâd-Kʻi̯wang) 大匡

Ta-ssŭ-kʻung Tsʻun 大司空村

Ta-tu 大都

Tai-Chen, *Kʻao-kung Chi Tʻu* 戴震 考工記圖

**Tân (Tan) 旦

tan 擔

**Tân-Bʻi̯wo (Tan-Fu) 亶父

tao 刀

tao-te (Fr. tao-tö; **dʻôg-tək) 道德

Tao-te Ching 道德經

**tək (te; Fr. tö) 德

**tək-gʻăng (te-hsing) 德行

**təng-ńi̯ĕn (teng-jen) 登人

**təng-təng (teng-teng) 登登

**təng-ˌi̯ông ńi̯ĕn (teng-chung jen) 登衆人

ti-pʻan 地盤

ti-chung 地中

**Ti̯ang (Chang) 張

**Ti̯ang-Li̯əg (Chang-Li) 張里

**Tieg/tieg (Ti/ti) 帝

**Tieg-ˌi̯ɛt (Ti-i) 帝乙

**Tieg-Kʻôk (Ti-Kʻu) 帝嚳

**Tieg-sįĕn (Ti-hsin) 帝辛

**tieng (ting) 丁

**tįĕng-ńįĕn (chen-jen) 貞人

**Tiər (Ti) 氏

ting 鼎

**tįôk (chu) 築

**tįông (chung) 中

**Tįông-Pįwən (Chung-Fen) 中分

**Tįông-Śįang (Chung-Shang) 中商

**tįông-to (chung-tu) 中都

**tįung-t'o (chung-t'u) 冢土

**to (tu) 都 堵

**Tŏk (Cho) 卓

tou 籩 豆 斗

Tsa-Shih 雜史

Tsai-Chi 載記

**Tsâk mįog gįək-gįək (Tso miao i-i) 作廟翼翼

**tsâk-ts'ĕk (tso-ts'e) 作冊

tseng 甑

**tsəg (tsai) 災

**Tsįang (Chiang) 蔣

**Tsįang-Kung (Chuang-Kung) 莊公

**Tsįĕn (Chin) 晉

*Tśi̯ĕn-lâp (Chen-la) 真臘

**Tsi̯ĕng (Ching) 井

**tsi̯ĕng-dʻien (ching-tʻien) 井田

**Tsi̯əg/tsi̯əg (Tzŭ/tzŭ) 子

**Tsi̯əg-Di̯ôg (Tzŭ-Yu) 子游

**Tsi̯og (Chiao) 焦

**Tsi̯ok (Chʻüeh) 雀

**tsi̯ok (chüeh) 爵

tso 作

Tso-chʻiu Ming : Tso Chʻiu-ming 左丘明

Tso-Chuan 左傳

**Tso-·i̯ɛt (Tsu-i) 祖乙

**Tso-kăng (Tsu-keng) 祖庚

**Tso-kap (Tsu-chia) 祖甲

tsu 鏃 俎

tsuan 鑽

tsun 尊

tsung 琮

Tu-Lin 杜林

Tu-Yu 杜佑

*Tuən-suən (Tun-sun) 頓遜

**Tŭk (Cho) 濁 涿

Tung-Chai 董砦

GLOSSARY

Tung-Chi 矗季

Tung Chung-shu, *Ch'un-Ch'iu Fan-lu* 董仲舒 春秋繁露

Tzǔ-ching Shan 紫荊山

Tzǔ-Ch'eng 子城

Tzǔ-ch'ih T'ung-chien 資治通鑑

tzǔ-hsü 自序

**T'âd (T'ai) 泰

**T'âd-Ḋịad (*T'ai-Shih*) 泰誓

**T'âd-·ịɛt (T'ai-i) 大乙

**T'âd-tieng (T'ai-ting) 太丁

**T'âd-Tsəg (T'ai-Tsai) 大宰

T'ai-chi 太極

*T'âi-g'ịək Kịung (T'ai-chi Kung) 太極宮

T'ai-p'ing Huan-yü Chi 太平寰宇記

T'ai-p'ing Yü-lan 太平御覽

T'ai-shih Kung Shu 太史公書

**t'âk-t'âk (t'o-t'ǫ) 橐橐

t'an 壇

T'an-kung 檀弓

**T'âng (T'ang) 湯

T'ang Hui-yao 唐會要

**T'âng Ṱịĕng (*T'ang Cheng*) 湯征

T'ang-yin Hsien 湯陰縣

t'ao-t'ieh 饕餮

T'eng-Hsien 滕縣

T'ien-chin 天津

**T'ien-g'jək (T'ien-chi) 天極

T'ien-li-chih tsun 天理之尊

**T'ien-Mįwən (T'ien-Wen) 天問

t'ien-p'an 天盤

T'ien-Shu 天樞

**T'ien-tsjəg (T'ien-tzǔ) 天子

T'ien-wang Kuei 天亡毁

**T'nâm (T'an) 聃

**T'o (T'u) 土

**T'o-pįwang (T'u-fang) 土方

t'uan 彖

t'un-t'ien 屯田

t'ung-chih 通志

**t̑įad (chih) 制

**T̑įang (Chang) 漳 鄣

**T̑įĕd (Chih) 郅

**T̑įĕn-p'įwǎn (Chen-p'an) 真番

**t̑įĕng (cheng) 正

**T̑įək-pįwang-dįĕg (Chih-fang-shih) 職方氏

**T̑įən (Chen) 振

**t̂i̯o-gʻu (chu-hou) 諸侯

**T̂i̯ôg (Chou) 州

**T̂i̯ok (Chu) 祝

**T̂i̯ông-gʻi̯wɐr (Chung-kʻuei) 終葵

**T̂i̯ông-kʻi̯ŭg (Chung-chʻiu) 中丘

**t̂i̯ông-ńi̯ĕn (chung-jen) 冢人

**T̂i̯ung (Chung) 種

**T̂ʻi̯ang (Chʻang) 昌

**Tsʻâd (Tsʻai) 蔡

Tsʻai-Chuang 蔡莊

Tsʻao-yen Chuang 曹演莊

**tsʻĕk (tsʻe) 冊

**Tsʻi̯am (Chʻien) 岍

**tsʻi̯an (chʻien) 遷

**tsʻi̯ap (chʻieh) 妾

**Tsʻi̯ĕng (Chʻing) 清

**_Tsʻieng-tsʻieng li̯əng-d̮i̯ang păk (Chʻing-chʻing ling-shang pai)_
青青陵上柏

**Tṣʻi̯o (Chʻu) 楚

**Tṣʻi̯o-kʻi̯ŭg (Chʻu-chʻiu) 楚丘

**Tsʻi̯ôk (Chʻi) 戚

**tsʻi̯u (chʻü) 取

Tsʻui Shu 崔述

GLOSSARY

Wai-Chuan 外傳

Wang An-shih 王安石

Wang I-yung 王懿榮

Wang-Mang 王莽

Wang Nien-sun 王念孫

Wang-Wan 王灣

Wang-Wei, *Huang-Ti Chai Ching* 王微 黃帝宅經

Wei 渭

Wei-Wang [Li] T'ai, *Kua-ti Chih* 魏王[李]泰 括地志

Wen-ting (**Mįwən-tieng) 文丁

wu 戊 午

Wu-an Hsien 武安縣

Wu-kuan Ts'un 武官村

Wu-yüan 武原

ya-men 衙門

yang 陽

Yang-shao [Ts'un] 仰韶[村]

Yang-tzŭ 揚子

Yang Yün-sung, *Ch'ing-nang Ao-chih* 楊筠松 青囊奧旨

Yao (**Ngiog) 堯

Yao Chan-ch'i, *Yin-yang Erh-chai Ch'üan-shu* 姚瞻旂 陰陽二宅全書

yao-k'eng 腰坑

Yeh (**Dįå) 垫

Yen (**·Įăn) 匽

Yen Shih-ku 顏師古

Yin (**·Įən) 殷

yin 陰

Yin-hsü 殷墟

Yin-kuo Ts'un 尹郭村

Yin Pen-chi 殷本紀

Yin-shih (**Įuěn-ḑįĕg) 尹氏

Ying-che 縈澤

Ying-Shao, *Feng-su T'ung-i* 應劭 風俗通義

yu 卣 酉

Yung 畂

Yung-lo Ta-tien 永樂大典

Yü (**Gįwo) 禹

Yü-Ch'in 于欽

yüeh 鉞

GLOSSARY

BIBLIOGRAPHICAL REFERENCES
Journals

Chung-Kuo K'ao-ku Hsüeh-pao
中國考古學報

Chung-Kuo She-hui Ching-chi-shih Chi-k'an
中國社會經濟史集刊

Chung-Kuo Wen-hua Yen-chiu Hui-k'an
中國文化研究彙刊

Chung-yang Yen-chiu-yüan : Min-ts'u-hsüeh Yen-chiu-so Chi-k'an
中央研究院民族學研究所集刊

Ch'i-hsiang Hsüeh-pao
氣象學報

Ch'ing-hua Hsüeh-pao
清華學報

Ch'ing-hua Ta-hsüeh She-hui K'o-hsüeh Chi-k'an
清華大學社會科學季刊

Hsüeh-shu Chi-k'an
學術季刊

Hsüeh-shu Hui-k'an
學術彙刊

Hua-hsi Hsieh-ho Ta-hsüeh Chung-Kuo Wen-hua Yen-chiu-so Chi-k'an
華西協合大學中國文化研究所集刊

Hua-hsi Ta-hsüeh Wen-shih Chi-k'an
華西大學文史集刊

K'an-tao Yüeh-k'an
康導月刊

K'ao-ku
考古

GLOSSARY

K'ao-ku Hsüeh-pao

考古學報

K'ao-ku T'ung-hsün

考古通訊

Kuo-li Chung-yang Yen-chiu-yüan Li-shih Yü-yen Yen-chiu-so Chi-k'an

國立中央研究院歷史語言研究所集刊

Kuo-li Chung-yang Yen-chiu-yüan Yüan-k'an

國立中央研究院院刊

Kuo-li Pei-ching Ta hsüeh Kuo-hsüeh Chi-k'an

國立北京大學國學季刊

Kuo-li T'ai-wan Ta-hsüeh K'ao-ku Jen-lei Hsüeh-k'an

國立臺灣大學考古人類學刊

Kuo-li T'ai-wan Ta-hsüeh Wen-shih-che Hsüeh-pao

國立臺灣大學文史哲學報

Ling-nan Hsüeh-pao

嶺南學報

Shih-huo [Pan-yüeh-k'an]

食貨[半月刊]

Ta-lu Tsa-chih

大陸雜誌

T'ien-yeh K'ao-ku Pao-kao

田野考古報告

Tung-fang Tsa-chih

東方雜誌

Wen-hsüeh Nien-pao

文學年報

Wen-wu

文物

Wen-wu Ts'an-k'ao Tzŭ-liao

文物參考資料

GLOSSARY

Yen-ching Hsüeh-pao

燕京學報

Yü-kung [Pan-yüeh-k'an]

禹貢[半月刊]

Authors, Books and Papers

An Chih-min, 'Cheng-Chou Shih Jen-min Kung-yüan fu-chin-ti Yin-tai i-ts'un'.

安志敏　鄭州市人民公園附近的殷代遺存

An Chih-min, 'Chung-Kuo Hsin-shih-ch'i shih-tai k'ao-ku-hsüeh-shang-ti chu-yao ch'eng-chiu'.

安志敏　中国新石器时代考古学上的主要成就

An Chih-min, 'Chung-Kuo ku-tai-ti shih-tao'.

安志敏　中國古代的石刀

An Chih-min, 'Ho-pei Ch'ü-yang tiao-ch'a-chi'.

安志敏　河北曲陽調查記

An Chih-min, 'I-chiu-wu-erh-nien ch'iu-chi Cheng-Chou Erh-li Kang fa-chüeh-chi'.

安志敏　一九五二年秋季鄭州二里岡發掘記

An Chih-min, 'I-chiu-wu-liu-nien-ch'iu Ho-nan Shan-Hsien fa-chüeh chien-pao'.

安志敏　一九五六年秋河南陝縣發掘簡報

An Chih-min, 'Kuan-yü An-yang Hou-kang hsün-tsang yüan-k'eng-ti shuo-ming'.

安志敏　關於安陽後岡殉葬园坑的説明

An Chih-min, 'Shih-lun Huang-ho-liu-yü Hsin-shih-ch'i shih-tai wen-hua'.

安志敏　試論黃河流域新石器时代文化

An Chih-min, Cheng Nai-wu, Hsieh Tuan-chü, *Miao-ti Kou yü San-li Ch'iao*.

安志敏　郑乃武　謝端琚　廟底溝與三里橋

GLOSSARY

An Chih-min, Chiang Ping-hsin, Ch'en Chih-ta, '1958–1959-nien Yin-hsü fa-chüeh chien-pao'.

安志敏 江東信 陈志达 1958–1959 年殷墟发掘簡報

An Chih-min, Lin Shou-chin, 'I-chiu-wu-ssŭ-nien ch'iu-chi Lo-yang hsi-chiao fa-chüeh chien-pao'.

安志敏 林壽晋 一九五四年秋季洛陽西郊發掘簡報

An Chin-huai, 'Cheng-Chou Shih ku-i-chih, mu-tsang-ti chung-yao fa-hsien'

安金槐 鄭州市古遺址、墓葬的重要發現

An Chin-huai, 'Cheng-Chou ti-ch'ü-ti ku-tai i-ts'un chieh-shao'.

安金槐 郑州地区的古代遺存介绍

An Chin-huai, 'Shih-lun Cheng-Chou Shang-tai ch'eng-chih – Ao-tu'.

安金槐 試論郑州商代城址—隞都

An Chin-huai, 'T'ang-yin Ch'ao-ko Chen fa-hsien Lung-shan ho Shang-tai-teng wen-hua i-chih'.

安金槐 湯陰朝歌鎮發現龙山和商代等文化遺址

Ao Ch'eng-lung, 'Ho-pei Tz'ŭ-Hsien Chiang-wu Ch'eng tiao-ch'a chien-pao'.

教承隆 河北磁縣講武城調查簡報

Chang Chien-chung, 'Cheng-Chou Shih Pai-chia Chuang Shang-tai mu-tsang fa-chüeh chien-pao'.

張建中 鄭州市白家莊商代墓葬發掘簡報

Chang Hsin-cheng, *Wei-shu T'ung-k'ao*.

張心澂 僞書通考

Chang Hsüeh-cheng, 'Wei-ho shang-yu T'ien-shui, K'an-ku liang-hsien k'ao-ku tiao-ch'a chien-pao'.

張學正 渭河上游天水、甘谷兩縣考古調查簡報

Chang Kuang-chih, 'Chung-Kuo Hsin-shih-ch'i shih-tai wen-hua tuan-tai'.

張光直 中國新石器時代文化斷代

Chang Kuang-chih, 'Chung-Kuo yüan-ku-shih-tai i-shih-sheng-huo-ti jo-kan tzŭ-liao'.

張光直 中國遠古時代儀式生活的若干資料

Chang Kuang-chih, 'Kuan-yü "Shang-wang miao-hao hsin-k'ao" i-wen-ti pu-ch'ung i-chien'.

張光直　關於"商王廟號新考"一文的補充意見

Chang Kuang-chih, 'Shang-Chou shen-hua-chih fen-lei'.

張光直　商周神話之分類

Chang Kuang-chih, 'Shang-wang miao-hao hsin-k'ao'.

張光直　商王廟號新考

Chang Shou-chung, '1959-nien Hou-ma "Niu-ts'un ku-ch'eng"-nan Tung-Chou i-chih fa-chüeh chien-pao'.

張守中　1959年候馬"牛村古城"南东周遺址发掘簡报

Chang Tung-sun, 'Ssŭ-hsiang yen-lun yü wen-hua'.

張東蓀　思想言論與文化

Chang Yin-lin, 'Chou-tai-ti feng-chien she-hui'.

張蔭麟　周代的封建社會

Chao Ch'ing-fang, 'Nan-ching Shih Pei-yin-yang Ying ti-i, erh-tz'ŭ-ti fa-chüeh'.

趙青芳　南京市北陰陽營第一、二次的發掘

Chao Ch'ing-yün, '1957-nien Cheng-Chou hsi-chiao fa-chüeh chi-yao : 4 : Tung-Chai Shang-tai yü Chou-tai wen-hua i-chih-ti fa-chüeh'.

赵青云　1957年郑州西郊发掘記要 四 董砦商代与周代文化遺址的发掘

Chao Ch'ing-yün, Chao Shih-kang, Liu Hsiao-ch'un, Chang Ching-an, '1958-nien-ch'un Ho-nan An-yang Shih Ta-ssŭ-k'ung Ts'un Yin-tai mu-tsang fa-chüeh chien-pao'.

赵青云　赵世網　刘笑春　張靜安　1958年春河南安阳市大司空村殷代墓葬发掘簡报

Chao Ch'ing-yün, Liu Tung-ya, 'Cheng-Chou Ko-ta-wang Ts'un i-chih fa-chüeh pao-kao'.

趙青雲　劉東亞　鄭州旭甶王村遺址發掘報告

Chao Ch'üan-ku, Han Wei-chou, P'ei Ming-hsiang, An Chin-huai, 'Cheng-Chou Shang-tai i-chih-ti fa-chüeh.'

趙全古　韓維周　裴明相　安金槐鄭州商代遺址的發掘

GLOSSARY

Chao Hsia-kuang, 'An-yang Shih hsi-chiao-ti Yin-tai wen-hua i-chih'.

趙霞光　安阳市西郊的殷代文化遺址

Chao Hsia-kuang, 'Cheng-Chou Nan-kuan-wai Shang-tai i-chih fa-chüeh chien-pao'.

趙霞光　鄭州南關外商代遺址發掘簡報

Chao I, 'Kai-yü ts'ung-k'ao,' *Ou-pei Ch'üan-chi.*

趙　翼　陔餘叢考　甌北全集

Cheng-Chou Shih Wen-wu Kung-tso-tsu, 'Cheng-Chou Shih Yin-Shang i-chih ti-ts'eng kuan-hsi chieh-shao'.

鄭州市文物工作組　鄭州市殷商遺址地層關係介紹

Chien Po-tsan, *Chung-Kuo Shih-kang.*

翦伯贊　中國史綱

Chou Chao-lin, Mou Yung-hang, 'Cheng-Chou fa-hsien-ti Shang-tai chih-t'ao i-chi'.

周兆麟　牟永杭　鄭州發現的商代製陶遺跡

Chou Hung-hsiang, *Shang-Yin Ti-wang Pen-chi.*

周鴻翔　商殷帝王本紀

Chou Tao, 'K'ao-ku Tung-t'ai : Ho-nan Hsin-hsiang Lung-shan wen-hua i-chih tiao-ch'a'.

周　到　考古動態：河南新乡龙山文化遺址調查

Chu K'o-chen, 'Erh-shih-pa hsiu ch'i-yüan-chih ti-tien yü shih-chien.'

竺可楨　二十八宿起源之地點與時間

Chuang Tung-ming, 'T'eng-Hsien Ku-Hsüeh-Ch'eng fa-hsien Chan-Kuo-shih-tai yeh-t'ieh i-chih'.

庄冬明　滕县古薛城發現战国时代冶铁遺址

Chuang Tung-ming, 'T'eng-Hsien Lin-Ch'eng ch'a-te ku-i-chih i-ch'u'.

庄冬明　滕县临城查得古遺址一处

Chung-Kuo K'e-hsüeh Yüan K'ao-ku Yen-chiu-so Lo-yang Fa-chüeh-tui, '1959-nien Yü-hsi liu-hsien tiao-ch'a chien-pao'.

中国科学院考古研究所洛陽發掘隊　1959年豫西六县調查簡报

GLOSSARY

Ch'ang Wen-chai, 'Hou-ma ti-ch'ü ku-ch'eng-chih-ti hsin-fa-hsien'.

暢文斎　侯馬地区古城址的新发现

Ch'ang Wen-chai, 'Shan-hsi Hsiang-fen Chao-k'ang fu-chin ku-ch'eng-chih tiao-ch'a'.

暢文斎　山西襄汾赵康附近古城址調查

Ch'ang Wen-chai, Chang Shou-chung, Yang Fu-tou, 'Hou-ma Pei-hsi Chuang Tung-Chou i-chih-ti ch'ing-li'.

暢文斎　张守中　楊富斗　侯馬北西庄东周遺址的清理

Ch'en Cheng-hsiang, *Chung-kuo Fang-chih-ti Ti-li-hsüeh Chia-chih.*

陳正祥　中國方志的地理學價值

Ch'en Chia-hsiang, 'Cheng-Chou Lo-ta Miao Shang-tai i-chih shih-chüeh chien-pao'.

陳嘉祥　郑州洛达庙商代遺址試掘簡报

Ch'en Hui, 'Ho-pei Wu-an Hsien Wu-chi ku-ch'eng-ti Chou, Han mu-tsang fa-chüeh chien-pao'.

陳　惠　河北武安县午汲古城的周、漢墓葬发掘簡报

Ch'en Hui, T'ang Yün-ming, Sun Te-hai, 'Ho-pei T'ang-shan Shih Ta-ch'eng-shan i-chih fa-chüeh pao-kao'.

陳　惠　唐雲明　孫德海　河北唐山市大城山遺址發掘報告

Ch'en Kung-jou, 'Lo-yang Chien-pin Tung-Chou ch'eng-chih fa-chüeh pao-kao'.

陳公柔　洛陽澗濱東周城址發掘報告

Ch'en Meng-chia, 'Shang-tai-ti shen-hua yü wu-shu'.

陳夢家　商代的神話與巫術

Ch'en Meng-chia, *Yin-hsü Pu-tz'ŭ Tsung-shu.*

陳夢家　殷墟卜辭綜述

Ch'en Meng-chia, 'Yin-tai t'ung-ch'i'.

陳夢家　殷代銅器

Ch'en P'an, 'Ch'un-Ch'iu Ta-shih-piao, Lieh-kuo chüeh-hsing chi ts'un-mieh-piao chuan-i'.

陳　槃　春秋大事表列國爵姓及存滅表譔異

GLOSSARY

Ch'en Yin-k'o, *Sui-T'ang Chih-tu Yüan-yüan Lüeh-lun-kao.*

陳寅恪　隋唐制度淵源略論稿

Ch'eng Kuang-yü, Hsü Sheng-mo, *Chung-Kuo Li-shih Ti-t'u-chi.*

程光裕　徐聖謨　中國歷史地圖集

Ch'i Ssŭ-ho, 'Chan-Kuo chih-tu k'ao'.

齊思和　戰國制度考

Ch'i Ssŭ-ho, 'Chan-Kuo Ts'e chu-tso shih-tai k'ao'.

齊思和　戰國策著作時代考

Ch'i Ssŭ-ho, 'Chou-tai hsi-ming-li k'ao'.

齊思和　周代錫命禮考

Ch'i Ssŭ-ho, 'Feng-chien-chih-tu yü Ju-chia ssŭ-hsiang'.

齊思和　封建制度與儒家思想

Ch'i Ssŭ-ho, 'Hsi-Chou ti-li-k'ao'.

齊思和　西周地理考

Ch'i Ssŭ-ho, 'Meng-tzŭ ching-t'ien shuo pien'.

齊思和　孟子井田説辨

Ch'i Ssŭ-ho, 'Yen Wu fei Chou feng-kuo shuo'.

齊思和　燕吳非周封國説

Ch'ien Po-ch'üan, ' "Shuo T'ien-wang Kuei wei Wu-Wang mieh Shang i-ch'ien t'ung-ch'i" i-wen-ti chi-tien shang-ch'üeh'.

錢柏泉　"説天亡毀为武王灭商以前銅器"一文的幾點商榷

Ch'üan Han-sheng, 'Nan-Sung Hang-Chou-ti hsiao-fei yü wai-ti shang-p'in-chih shu-ju'.

全漢昇　南宋杭州的消費與外地商品之輸入

Ch'üan Han-sheng, 'Nan-Sung Hang-Chou-ti wai-lai shih-liao yü shih-fa'.

全漢昇　南宋杭州的外來食料與食法

Fan Hsiang-yung, *Ku-pen Chu-shu Chi-nien Chi-chiao Ting-pu.*

范祥雍　古本竹書紀年輯校訂補

Fu Chen-lun, 'Yen-Hsia-tu fa-chüeh pao-kao'.

傅振倫　燕下都發掘報告

GLOSSARY

Fu Chen-lun, 'Yen-Hsia-tu fa-chüeh-p'in-ti ch'u-pu cheng-li yü yen-chiu'.

傅振倫　燕下都發掘品的初步整理与研究

Fu Ssǔ-nien, 'Shih-Ching Chiang-i-kao', *Fu Meng-chen Hsien-sheng Chi*.

傅斯年　詩經講義稿　傅孟真先生集

Han Wei-chou, Wang Ju-lin, 'Ho-nan Hsi-hsia Hsien chi Nan-yang Shih liang-ku-ch'eng tiao-ch'a-chi'.

韓維周　王儒林　河南西峽縣及南陽市兩古城調查記

Hang Te-chou, Lo Chung-ju, T'ien Hsing-nung, 'T'ang Ch'ang-an Ch'eng ti-chi ch'u-pu t'an-ts'e'.

杭德州　雒忠如　田醒農　唐長安城地基初步探測

Ho-nan Sheng Wen-hua-chü, *Cheng-Chou Erh-li Kang*.

河南省文化局　鄭州二里岡

Ho-nan Sheng Wen-hua-chü Wen-wu Kung-tso-tui, 'Cheng-Chou Shang-chieh Shang-tai i-chih-ti fa-chüeh'.

河南省文化局文物工作队　鄭州上街商代遺址的發掘

Ho-nan Wen-wu Kung-tso-tui Ti-erh-tui Sun-ch'i T'un Ch'ing-li Hsiao-tsu, 'Lo-yang Chien-hsi Sun-ch'i T'un ku-i-chih'.

河南文物工作隊第二隊孫旗屯清理小組　洛陽澗西孫旗屯古遺址

Ho-pei Sheng Wen-hua-chü Fa-chüeh-tsu, 'Hsing-T'ai Shih fa-hsien Shang-tai i-chih'.

河北省文化局發掘組　邢台市發現商代遺址

Hou Wai-lu, *Chung-Kuo Ku-tai She-hui-shih*.

侯外廬　中國古代社會史

Hsieh Ch'un-chu, 'Yen-Ch'eng fa-hsien Chan-Kuo-shih-ch'i-ti tu-mu-ch'uan'.

謝春祝　奄城发現战国時期的独木船

Hsieh Hsi-i, 'Yen-Hsia-tu i-chih so-chi'.

謝錫益　燕下都遺址瑣記

Hsieh Wei-chieh, *Chin-T'ang Hsien Chih*.

謝惟傑　金堂縣志

Hsü Chin-hsiung, 'Tui Chang Kuang-chih Hsien-sheng-ti "Shang-wang miao-hao hsin-k'ao"-ti chi-tien i-chien'.

許進雄　對張光直先生的"商王廟號新考"的幾點意見

GLOSSARY

Hsü Cho-yün, 'Kuan-yü "Shang-wang miao-hao hsin-k'ao" i-wen-ti chi-tien i-chien'.

許倬雲　關於"商王廟號新考"一文的幾點意見

Hsü Chung-shu, 'Ching-t'ien chih-tu t'an-yüan'.

徐中舒　井田制度探原

Hsü Chung-shu, 'Lei-ssŭ k'ao'.

徐中舒　耒耜考

Hsü I, ' "Yin-tai Ti-li Chien-lun" p'ing-chieh'.

許　藝"殷代地理簡論"評介

Hu Chih-hsin, 'Chuang-tzŭ k'ao-cheng'.

胡芝薪　莊子攷證

Hu Hou-hsüan, *Chia-ku-hsüeh Shang-shih Lun-ts'ung*.

胡厚宣　甲骨學商史論叢

Hu Hou-hsüan, *Li-shih Yen-chiu*.

胡厚宣　歷史研究

Hu Hou-hsüan, *Wu-shih-nien Chia-ku-hsüeh Lun-chu-mu*.

胡厚宣　五十年甲骨學論著目

Hu Hou-hsüan, *Yin-hsü Fa-chüeh*.

胡厚宣　殷墟發掘

Hu Hou-hsüan, 'Yin-tai feng-chien-chih-tu k'ao', *Chia-ku-hsüeh Shang-shih Lun-ts'ung*.

胡厚宣　殷代封建制度考　甲骨學商史論叢

Hu Shih, 'Ching-t'ien pien', *Hu-Shih Wen-ts'un*.

胡　適　井田辨　胡適文存

Hu Yüeh-ch'ien, 'An-hui Hsin-shih-ch'i shih-tai i-chih-ti tiao-ch'a'.

胡悅謙　安徽新石器時代遺址的調查

Hua Chüeh-ming, Yang Ken, Liu En-chu, 'Chan-Kuo Liang-Han t'ieh-ch'i-ti chin-hsiang-hsüeh k'ao-ch'a ch'u-pu pao-kao'.

華覺民 楊 根劉恩珠　戰國兩漢鐵器的金相學考查初步報告

Huang Chan-yüeh, 'Chin-nien ch'u-t'u-ti Chan-Kuo Liang-Han t'ieh-ch'i'.

黃展岳　近年出土的戰國兩漢鐵器

GLOSSARY

Huang Ching-lüeh, 'Yen-Hsia-tu ch'eng-chih tiao-ch'a pao-kao'.

黃景略　燕下都城址調查報告

Huang-ho Shui-k'u K'ao-ku-tui Hua-Hsien-tui, 'Shan-hsi [Shensi] Hua-Hsien Liu-tzŭ Chen k'ao-ku fa-chüeh chien-pao'.

黃河水庫考古隊華縣隊　陝西华县柳子镇考古发掘简报

Huang-ho Shui-k'u K'ao-ku-tui Hua-Hsien-tui, 'Shan-hsi [Shensi] Hua-Hsien Liu-tzŭ Chen ti-erh-tz'ŭ fa-chüeh-ti chu-yao shou-huo'.

黃河水庫考古队華縣队　陝西華縣柳子鎮第二次發掘的主要收獲

Hui Tung, *Ming-T'ang Ta-tao Lu*.

惠　棟　明堂大道錄

Hung Chün-p'ei, *Ch'un-Ch'iu Kuo-chi Kung-fa*.

洪鈞培　春秋國際公法

Hung Liang-chi, 'Ch'un-Ch'iu-shih i ta-i wei hsien shih-yü Ch'u lun', *Keng-sheng-chai Wen Chia-chi*.

洪亮吉　春秋時以大邑爲縣始于楚論　更生齋文甲集

Hung Yeh, Nieh Ch'ung-ch'i, Lee Shu-ch'un, Ma Hsi-yung, *Ch'un-Ch'iu Ching-chuan Yin-te*.

洪　業　聶崇岐　李書春　馬錫用　春秋經傳引得

Jao Tsung-i, *Yin-tai Chen-pu Jen-wu T'ung-k'ao*.

饒宗頤　殷代貞卜人物通考

Jen Pu-yün, 'Kan-su Ch'in-an Hsien Hsin-shih-ch'i shih-tai chü-chu i-chih'.

任步雲　甘肅秦安縣新石器時代居住遺址

Kao Ch'ü-hsün, 'Hsiao-ch'en Hsi shih-kuei-ti ts'an-p'ien yü ming-wen'.

高去尋　小臣艅石殷的殘片與銘文

Kao Yün-hui, 'Chou-tai t'u-ti-chih-tu yü ching-t'ien'.

高耘暉　周代土地制度與井田

Ku Chi-kuang, 'Chan-Kuo Ch'in-Han-chien chung-nung-ch'ing-shang-chih li-lun yü shih-chi'.

谷霽光　戰國秦漢間重農輕商之理論與實際

Ku Chieh-kang, 'Ch'un-Ch'iu-shih-tai-ti hsien'.

顧頡剛　春秋時代的縣

Ku Chieh-kang, *Han-tai Hsüeh-shu Shih-lüeh.*

顧頡剛　漢代學術史略

Ku Chieh-kang, 'Yü Ch'ien Hsüan-t'ung Hsien-sheng lun ku-shih-shu', *Ku-Shih Pien.*

顧頡剛　與錢玄同先生論古史書　古史辨

Ku Chieh-kang, Lo Ken-tse, *Ku-Shih Pien.*

顧頡剛　羅根澤　古史辨

Ku Yen-wu, *Li-tai Ti-wang Chai-ching-chi : Han Ch'ang-an Ku-ch'eng.*

顧炎武　歷代帝王宅京記　漢長安故城

Kuo Mo-jo, 'An-yang yüan-k'eng-mu-chung ting-ming k'ao-shih'.

郭沫若　安陽圓坑墓中鼎銘考釋

Kuo Mo-jo, *Ch'ing-t'ung Shih-tai.*

郭沫若　青銅時代

Kuo Mo-jo, *Chung-Kuo Ku-tai She-hui Yen-chiu.*

郭沫若　中國古代社會研究

Kuo Mo-jo, *Liang-Chou Chin-wen-tz'ŭ Ta-hsi K'ao-shih.*

郭沫若　兩周金文辭大系攷釋

Kuo Mo-jo, *Nu-li-chih Shih-tai.*

郭沫若　奴隸制時代

Kuo Mo-jo, *Pu-tz'ŭ T'ung-tsuan.*

郭沫若　卜辭通纂

Kuo Mo-jo, *Shih P'i-p'an Shu.*

郭沫若　十批判書

Kuo Pao-chün, 'I-chiu-wu-ling-nien-ch'un Yin-hsü fa-chüeh pao-kao'.

郭寶鈞　一九五〇年春殷墟發掘報告

Kuo Pao-chün, 'Lo-yang Chien-pin ku-wen-hua i-chih chi Han-mu'.

郭寶鈞　洛陽澗濱古文化遺址及漢墓

Kuo Pao-chün, 'Lo-yang ku-ch'eng k'an-ch'a chien-pao'.

郭寶鈞　洛陽古城勘察簡報

Kuo Pao-chün, Hsia Nai, *Hui-Hsien Fa-chüeh Pao-kao.*

郭寶鈞　夏　鼐　輝縣發掘報告

GLOSSARY

Kuo Pao-chün, Lín Shou-chin, 'I-chiu-wu-erh-nien ch'iu-chi Lo-yang tung-chiao fa-chüeh pao-kao'.

郭寶鈞　林壽晉　一九五二年秋季洛陽东郊發掘報告

Kuo Te-yung, 'Kan-su Wei-ho shang-yu Wei-yüan, Lung-hsi, Wu-shan san-hsien k'ao-ku tiao-ch'a'.

郭德勇　甘肅渭河上游渭源、隴西、武山、三县考古調查

Kuo Te-yung, 'Kan-su Wu-wei Huang-niang-niang T'ai i-chih fa-chüeh pao-kao'.

郭德勇　甘肅武威皇娘娘台遺址發掘報告

K'ang Yu-wei, *Hsin-hsüeh Wei-ching K'ao.*

康有爲　新學僞經考

K'ao-ku-so Pao-chi Fa-chüeh-tui, 'Shan-hsi [Shensi] Pao-chi Hsin-shih-ch'i shih-tai i-chih fa-chüeh chi-yao'.

考古所宝雞發掘隊　陝西宝雞新石器时代遺址發掘記要

K'ao-ku Yen-chiu-so Hsi-an Pan-p'o Kung-tso-tui, 'Hsi-an Pan-p'o i-chih ti-erh-tz'ŭ fa-chüeh-ti chu-yao shou-huo'.

考古研究所西安、半坡工作隊　西安半坡遺址第二次發掘的主要收穫

Lao Kan, 'Ch'un-Ch'iu Ta-shih-piao, Lieh-kuo chüeh-hsing chi ts'un-mieh-piao Chuan-i chung-p'ien Pa'.

勞　榦　春秋大事表 列國爵姓及存滅表 譔異中篇跋

Li Chi, *An-yang Fa-chüeh Pao-kao.*

李　濟　安陽發掘報告

Li Chi, *Ch'eng-tzŭ Yai.*

李　濟　城子崖

Li Chi, *Hsi-yin Ts'un shih-ch'ien-ti i-ts'un.*

李　濟　西陰村史前的遺存

Li Chi, 'Hsiao-T'un t'ao-ch'i chih-liao-chih hua-hsüeh fen-hsi', *Kuo-li T'ai-wan Ta-hsüeh Fu Ku-hsiao-chang Ssŭ-nien Hsien-sheng Chi-nien Lun-wen-chi.*

李　濟　小屯陶器質料之化學分析　國立臺灣大學
傅故校長斯年先生紀念論文集

Li Chi, *Hsiao-T'un : Yin-hsü Ch'i-wu : T'ao-ch'i.*

李　濟　小屯　殷虛器物　陶器

Li Chi, 'Lun "Tao-sen-shih Hsiao-jen" an-chien chi yüan-shih tzŭ-liao-chih chien-ting yü ch'u-li'.

李　濟　論「道森氏、曉人」案件及原始資料之鑒定與處理

Li Chi, 'Yen-chiu Chung-Kuo ku-jü wen-t'i-ti hsin-tzŭ-liao'.

李　濟　研究中國古玉問題的新資料

Li Chi, 'Yin-hsü yu-jen shih-ch'i t'u-shuo'.

李　濟　殷墟有刄石器圖説

Li-Chi, 'Yu chi-hsing yen-pien so-k'an-chien-ti Hsiao-T'un i-chih yü Hou-chia Chuang mu-tsang-chih shih-tai kuan-hsi'.

李　濟　由笄形演變所看見的小屯遺址與侯家莊墓葬之時代關係

Li Chien-nung, 'Ch'e chu kung'.

李劍農　徹助貢

Li Chien-nung, *Chung-Kuo Ching-chi Shih-kao.*

李劍農　中國經濟史稿

Li Chien-yung, P'ei Ch'i, Chia Ngo [O], 'Lo-ning Hsien Lo-ho liang-an ku-i-chih tiao-ch'a chien-pao'.

李健永　裴　琪賈　峩　洛寧縣洛河兩岸古遺址調查簡報

Li Ching-ch'ih 'Chou-I shih-tz'ŭ hsü-k'ao'.

李鏡池　周易筮辭續考

Li Chün-chih, 'Lü-Shih-Ch'un-Ch'iu-chung ku-shu chi-i', *Ku-Shih Pien.*

李峻之　呂氏春秋中古書輯佚　古史辨

Li Hsüeh-ch'in, *Yin-tai Ti-li Chien-lun.*

李學勤　殷代地理簡論

Li Pu-ch'ing, 'Chi-nan Ta-hsin Chuang i-chih shih-chüeh chien-pao'.

李步青　济南大辛庄遺址試掘簡报

Li Te-pao, 'Ho-nan Wei-ho chih-hung kung-ch'eng-chung-ti k'ao-ku tiao-ch'a chien-pao'.

李德寶　河南衛河滯洪工程中的考古調查簡報

GLOSSARY

Li Tung-fang, *Ch'un-Ch'iu Chan-Kuo P'ien* (*Chung-Kuo Li-shih T'ung-lun*).

黎東方　春秋戰國篇　中國歷史通論

Li Ya-nung, *Yin-tai She-hui Sheng-huo*.

李亞農　殷代社會生活

Li Yang-sung, 'Tui Wo-Kuo niang-chiu ch'i-yüan-ti t'an-t'ao'.

李仰松　对我国釀酒起源的探討

Li Yang-sung, Yen Wen-ming, 'Lo-yang Wang-wan i-chih fa-chüeh chien-pao'.

李仰松　严文明　洛阳王灣遺址发掘簡報

Li Yü-ch'un, 'Shan-hsi [Shensi] Hua-yin Yüeh-Chen Chan-Kuo ku-ch'eng k'an-ch'a-chi'.

李遇春　陝西華陰岳鎮戰國古城勘查記

Liang Ssŭ-yung, 'Hsiao-T'un, Lung-shan yü Yang-shao', *Kuo-li Chung-yang Yen-chiu-yüan Li-shih Yü-yen Yen-chiu-so Ch'ing-chu Ts'ai Yüan-p'ei Hsien-sheng Liu-shih-wu-sui Lun-wen Chi*.

梁思永　小屯龍山與仰韶　國立中央研究院歷史語言
研究所　慶祝蔡元培先生六十五歲論文集

Liang Ssŭ-yung, 'Hou-kang fa-chüeh hsiao-chi', *An-yang Fa-chüeh Pao-kao*.

梁思永　後岡發掘小記　安陽發掘報告

Liang Ssŭ-yung, 'Lung-shan Wen-hua – Chung-Kuo wen-ming-ti shih-ch'ien-ch'i-chih-i'.

梁思永　龍山文化——中國文明的史前期之一

Liang Ssŭ-yung, Kao Ch'ü-hsün, *Hou-chia Chuang*.

梁思永　高去尋　侯家莊

Liao Yung-min, 'Cheng-Chou Shih fa-hsien-ti i-ch'u Shang-tai chü-chu yü chu-tsao-t'ung-ch'i i-chih chien-chieh'.

廖永民　郑州市發現的一处商代居住与鑄造銅器遺址簡介

Lin Heng-li, 'P'ing Chang Kuang-chih "Shang-wang miao-hao hsin-k'ao"-chung-ti lun-cheng-fa'.

林衡立　評張光直"商王廟號新考"中的論證法

Ling Ch'un-sheng, 'Chung-Kuo tsu-miao-ti ch'i-yüan'.

凌純聲　中國祖廟的起源

Ling Chu'n-sheng, 'Pu-tz'ŭ-chung she-chih yen-chiu'.

凌純聲　卜辭中社之研究

Liu Chi-i, ' "Ao-tu" chih-i'.

刘启益　"隩都"质疑

Liu Chih-p'ing, Fu Hsi-nien, 'Lin-te Tien fu-yüan-ti ch'u-pu yen-chiu'.

刘致平　傅熹年　麟德殿复原的初步研究

Liu E, *T'ieh-yün Ts'ang-kuei*.

劉　鶚　鐵雲藏龜

Liu Hsiao-ch'un, 'I-chiu-wu-wu-nien-ch'iu An-yang Hsiao-T'un Yin-hsü-ti fa-chüeh'.

劉笑春　一九五五年秋安陽小屯殷墟的發掘

Liu Ju-lin, 'Lü-Shih-Ch'un-Ch'iu-chih fen-hsi', *Ku-Shih Pien*.

劉汝霖　呂氏春秋之分析　古史辨

Liu Pin-hsiung, 'Yin-Shang wang-shih shih-fen-tsu-chih shih-lun'.

劉斌雄　殷商王室十分組制試論

Liu Tung-ya, 'Ho-nan An-yang Hsüeh-chia Chuang Yin-tai i-chih, mu-tsang ho T'ang-mu fa-chüeh chien-pao'.

刘东亚　河南安阳薛家庄殷代遺址,墓葬和唐墓發掘簡报

Liu Wen-tien, *Chuang-tzŭ Pu-cheng*.

劉文典　莊子補正

Liu Yao, 'Ho-nan Chün-Hsien Ta-lai Tien shih-ch'ien i-chih'.

劉　燿　河南濬縣大賚店史前遺址

Liu Yao, 'Lung-shan Wen-hua yü Yang-shao Wen-hua-chih fen-hsi'.

劉　燿　龍山文化與仰韶文化之分析

Liu Yung-neng, ' "Miao-ti Kou yü San-li Ch'iao" wen-hua hsing-chih-ti chi-ko wen-t'i'.

柳用能　"庙底沟与三里桥"文化性質的几個問題

Lo Chen-yü, *Yin-hsü Shu-ch'i ch'ien-pien*.

羅振玉　殷虛書契前編

GLOSSARY

Lo Chen-yü, *Yin-hsü Shu-ch'i Ching-hua.*

羅振玉　殷虛書契菁華

Lo Ken-tse, *Kuan-tzŭ T'an-yüan.*

羅根澤　管子探源

Lü Chen-yü, *Chung-Kuo Cheng-chih Ssŭ-hsiang-shih.*

呂振羽　中國政治思想史

Lü Chen-yü, *Chung-Kuo She-hui Shih-kang.*

呂振羽　中國社會史綱

Ma Ch'eng-yüan, 'Man-t'an Chan-Kuo ch'ing-t'ung-ch'i-shang-ti hua-hsiang'.

馬承源　漫談战国青銅器上的画像

Ma Ch'üan, 'Cheng-Chou Shih Ming-kung Lu hsi-ts'e-ti Shang-tai i-ts'un'.

馬　全　郑州市銘功路西側的商代遺存

Ma Ch'üan, Mao Pao-liang, 'Cheng-Chou fa-hsien-ti chi-ko-shih-ch'i-ti ku-tai yao-chih'.

馬　全　毛宝亮　郑州發現的几个時期的古代窯址

Ma Te-chih, 'T'ang-tai Ch'ang-an Ch'eng k'ao-ku chi-lüeh'.

馬得志　唐代长安城考古紀略

Ma Te-chih, Chou Yung-chen, Chang Yün-p'eng, 'I-chiu-wu-san-nien An-yang Ta-ssŭ-k'ung Ts'un fa-chüeh pao-kao'.

馬得志　周永珍　張雲鵬　一九五三年安陽大司空村發掘報告

Mao Pao-liang, 'Cheng-Chou hsi-chiao Yang-shao wen-hua i-chih fa-chüeh chien-pao'.

毛寶亮　鄭州西郊仰韶文化遺址發掘簡報

Mao Tse-tung, *Chung-Kuo Ke-ming ho Chung-Kuo Kung-ch'an-tang.*

毛澤東　中國革命和中國共産黨

Mei Fu-ken, 'Hang-Chou Shui-t'ien Fan i-chih fa-chüeh pao-kao'.

梅福根　杭州水田畈遺址發掘报告

Meng Hao, 'Ho-pei Wu-an Hsien Wu-chi ku-ch'eng-chung-ti yao-chih'.

孟　浩　河北武安县午汲古城中的窯址

Meng Hao, Ch'en Hui, Liu Lai-ch'eng, 'Ho-pei Wu-an Wu-chi ku-ch'eng fa-chüeh-chi'.

孟　浩　陳　慧　劉來城　河北武安午汲古城發掘記

Ni Chen-kuei, 'Yen-Ch'eng ch'u-t'u-ti t'ung-ch'i'.

倪振逵　淹城出土的銅器

Pei-ching Ta-hsüeh, Ho-pei Sheng Wen-hua-chü Han-tan K'ao-ku Fa-chüeh-tui, '1957-nien Han-tan fa-chüeh chien-pao'.

北京大學, 河北省文化局邯鄲考古發掘隊 1957年邯鄲發掘簡報

P'ei Wen-chung, Chung-Kuo Shih-ch'ien-shih-ch'i-chih Yen-chiu.

裴文中　中國史前時期之研究

Shan-hsi Sheng Wen-wu Kuan-li Wei-yüan-hui, 'Shan-hsi Sheng Wen-kuan-hui Hou-ma Kung-tso-chan kung-tso-ti tsung-shou-huo'.

山西省文物管理委員會　山西省文管会侯馬工作站工作的总收獲

Shan-hsi [Shensi] Sheng Wen-wu Kuan-li Wei-yüan-hui, 'Ch'ang-an Chang-chia-p'o Ts'un Hsi-Chou i-chih-ti chung-yao fa-hsien'.

陝西省文物管理委員会　長安張家坡村西周遺址的重要發現

Shan-tung Sheng Wen-wu Kuan-li-ch'u, 'Shan-tung Lin-tzü Ch'i-ku-ch'eng shih-chüeh chien-pao'.

山東省文物管理处　山东临淄齐故城試掘簡报

Shang Ch'eng-tso, Yin-hsü Wen-tzü Lei-pien.

商承祚　殷虛文字類編

Shih Chang-ju, 'Chou-tu i-chi yü Ts'ai-tao i-ts'un'.

石璋如　周都遺跡與彩陶遺存

Shih Chang-ju, 'Hsiao-T'un C-ch'ü-ti mu-tsang-ch'ün'.

石璋如　小屯C區的墓葬群

Shih Chang-ju, Hsiao-T'un : I-chih-ti Fa-hsien yü Fa-chüeh : Chien-chu I-ts'un.

石璋如　小屯遺址的發現與發掘 建築遺存

Shih Chang-ju, 'Hsiao-T'un Yin-tai-ti chien-chu i-chi'.

石璋如　小屯殷代的建築遺蹟

Shih Chang-ju, 'Ho-nan An-yang Hou-Kang-ti Yin-mu'.

石璋如　河南安陽後岡的殷墓

Shih Chang-ju, 'Ku-pu yü kuei-pu t'an-yüan'.

石璋如　骨卜與龜卜探源

Shih Chang-ju, 'Kuan-chung k'ao-ku tiao-ch'a pao-kao'.

石璋如　關中考古調查報告

Shih Chang-ju, 'Yin-hsü fa-chüeh tui-yü Chung-Kuo ku-tai wen-hua-ti kung-hsien'.

石璋如　殷虛發掘對於中國古代文化的貢獻

Shih Chang-ju, 'Yin-hsü tsui-chin-chih chung-yao fa-hsien. Fu : Lun Hsiao-T'un ti-ts'eng'.

石璋如　殷墟最近之重要發現附論小屯地層

Shih Chang-ju, 'Yin-tai-ti chu-t'ung kung-i'.

石璋如　殷代的鑄銅工藝

Shih-Chang-ju, 'Yin-tai ti-shang-chien-chu fu-yüan-chih i-li'.

石璋如　殷代地上建築復原之一例

Shih Hsing-pang, 'Hsin-shih-ch'i shih-tai ts'un-lo i-chih-ti fa-hsien – Hsi-an Pan-p'o'.

石興邦　新石器時代村落遺址的發現──西安半坡

Shou T'ien, 'T'ai-yüan Kuan-she Hsin-shih-ch'i shih-tai i-chih-ti fa-hsien yü tsao-yü'.

壽　田　太原光社新石器時代遺址的發現与遭遇

Su Ping-chi, *Tou-chi T'ai Kou-tung-ch'ü Mu-tsang*.

蘇東琦　鬪雞臺溝東區墓葬

Su Ping-chi, Wu Ju-tso, 'Hsi-an fu-chin ku-wen-hua i-ts'un-ti lei-hsing ho fen-pu'.

苏東琦　吳汝柞　西安附近古文化遺存的類型和分佈

Sun Hai-po, *Chia-ku-wen Pien*.

孫海波　甲骨文編

Sun I-jang, *Ch'i-wen Chü-li*.

孫詒讓　契文舉例

Sun Tso-yün, 'Shuo "T'ien-wang Kuei" wei Wu-Wang mieh Shang i-ch'ien t'ung-ch'i'.

孙作云　説"天亡殷"为武王灭商以前銅器

Sun Tso-yün, 'Tsai lun "T'ien-wang Kuei" erh-san-shih'.

孫作云　再論 " 天亡殷 " 二三事

Sun Yao, *Ch'un-Ch'iu Shih-tai-chih Shih-tsu.*

孫　曜　春秋時代之世族

Ting Fu-pao, *Shuo-wen Chieh-tzŭ Ku-lin.*

丁福保　說文解字詁林

Ting Shan, *Chia-ku-wen so-chien Shih-tsu chi-ch'i Chih-tu.*

丁　山　甲骨文所見氏族及其制度

Ting Su, 'Hua-pei ti-hsing-shih yü Shang-Yin-ti li-shih'.

丁　驌　華北地形史與商殷的歷史

Ting Su, 'Lun Yin-wang-p'i shih-fa'.

丁　驌　論殷王妣諡法

Tjan Tjoe Som [Tseng Chu-sen], *Po-hu T'ung.*

曾珠森　白虎通

Tsang Li-ho, *Chung-Kuo Ku-chin Ti-ming Ta-tz'ŭ-tien.*

臧勵龢　中國古今地名大辭典

Tseng Chao-yü, Yin Huan-chang, 'Shih-lun Hu-shu wen-hua'.

曾昭燏　尹煥章　試論湖熟文化

Tsou Heng, 'Shih-lun Cheng-Chou hsin-fa-hsien-ti Yin-Shang wen-hua i-chih'.

鄒　衡　試論鄭州新發現的殷商文化遺址

Tung Hung, 'Cheng-Chou Pai-chia Chuang i-chih fa-chüeh chien-pao'.

東　紅　鄭州白家庄遺址發掘簡報

Tung Hung, 'Cheng-Chou Shih Jen-Min Kung-yüan ti-erh-shih-wu-hao Shang-tai mu-tsang ch'ing-li chien-pao'.

東　紅　鄭州市人民公園第二十五號商代墓葬清理簡報

Tung Tso-pin, 'An-yang Hou-chia Chuang ch'u-t'u-chih chia-ku wen-tzŭ'.

董作賓　安陽侯家莊出土之甲骨文字

Tung Tso-pin, 'Ch'eng-tzŭ Yai yü Lung-shan Chen', *Ch'eng-tzŭ Yai.*

董作賓　城子崖與龍山鎮　城子崖

Tung Tso-pin, *Chia-ku-hsüeh Wu-shih-nien.*

董作賓　甲骨學五十年

GLOSSARY

Tung Tso-pin, 'Chia-ku-wen tuan-tai yen-chiu-li', *Kuo-li Chung-yang Yen-chiu-yüan Li-shih Yü-yen Yen-chiu-so Ch'ing-chu Tsai Yüan-p'ei Hsien-sheng Liu-shih-wu-sui Lun-wen Chi.*

董作賓　甲骨文斷代研究例　國立中央研究院歷史語言研究所　慶祝蔡元培先生六十五歲論文集

Tung Tso-pin, 'Chung-Kuo shang-ku-shih nien-tai'.

董作賓　中國上古史年代

Tung Tso-pin, 'Chung-Kuo wen-tzŭ-ti ch'i-yüan'.

董作賓　中國文字的起原

Tung Tso-pin, *Hsiao T'un : Yin-hsü Wen-tzŭ.*

董作賓　小屯　殷虛文字

Tung Tso-pin, 'Kuan-yü ku-shih nien-tai-hsüeh-ti wen-t'i'.

董作賓　關於古史年代學的問題

Tung Tso-pin, 'T'an "T'an" '.

董作賓　譚譚

Tung Tso-pin, 'Tsai-t'an Yin-tai ch'i-hou'.

董作賓　再談殷代氣候

Tung Tso-pin, 'Wu-teng Chüeh tsai Yin-Shang'.

董作賓　五等爵在殷商

Tung Tso-pin, 'Wu-Wang fa Chou nien-yüeh-jih chin-kao'.

董作賓　武王伐紂年月日今考

Tung Tso-pin, 'Yin-hsü yen-ke'.

董作賓　殷墟沿革

Tung Tso-pin, *Yin Li P'u.*

董作賓　殷曆譜

Tung Tso-pin, 'Yin Li P'u hou-chi'.

董作賓　殷曆譜後記

Tung Tso-pin, 'Yin-tai-chih li-fa nung-yeh yü ch'i-hsiang'.

董作賓　殷代之曆法農業與氣象

Tung Tso-pin, 'Yin-tai li-chih-ti hsin-chiu liang-p'ai'.
董作賓　殷代禮制的新舊兩派

Tung Tso-pin, 'Yin-tai-ti niao-shu'.
董作賓　殷代的鳥書

T'ang Lan, 'Tsai chia-ku chin-wen-chung so-chien-ti i-chung i-ching i-shih-ti Chung-Kuo ku-tai wen-tzŭ'.
唐　蘭　在甲骨金文中所見的一種已經遺失的中國古代文字

T'ang Yün-ming, 'Hsing-T'ai Hsi-kuan-wai i-chih shih-chüeh'.
唐云明　邢台西关外遺址試掘

T'ang Yün-ming, 'Hsing-T'ai Nan-ta-kuo Ts'un Shang-tai i-chih t'an-chüeh chien-pao'.
唐云明　邢台南大郭村商代遺址探掘簡報

T'ang Yün-ming, 'Hsing-T'ai Ts'ao-yen Chuang i-chih fa-chüeh pao-kao'.
唐雲明　邢台曹演莊遺址發掘報告

T'ang Yün-ming, 'Hsing-T'ai Yin-kuo Ts'un Shang-tai i-chih chi Chan-Kuo mu-tsang shih-chüeh chien-pao'.
唐云明　邢台尹郭村商代遺址及战国墓葬試掘簡报

T'ang Yün-ming, 'K'ao-ku Tung-t'ai : Ho-pei Hsing-T'ai Tung-hsien-hsien Ts'un Shang-tai i-chih tiao-ch'a'.
唐云明　考古动态　河北邢台东先賢村商代遺址調查

T'ang Yün-ming, 'Lung-shan wen-hua yü Yin wen-hua t'ao-ch'i-chien-ti kuan-hsi'.
唐云明　龙山文化与殷文化陶器間的关系

[T'ang] Yün-ming, Lo P'ing, [Ch'eng] Ming-yüan, 'Hsing-T'ai Shang-tai i-chih-chung-ti t'ao-yao'.
[唐]云明　罗　平　[程]明远　邢台商代遺址中的陶窑

T'eng Ku, *Chung-Kuo I-shu Lun-ts'ung*.
滕　固　中國藝術論叢

T'ao Hsi-sheng, *Chung-Kuo She-hui-chih Shih-ti Fen-hsi*.
陶希聖　中國社會之史的分析

Ts'ui Shu, 'Chu-Ssŭ k'ao-hsin yü-lu', *Ts'ui Tung-pi I-shu*.
崔　述　洙泗考信餘錄　崔東壁遺書

GLOSSARY

Ts'ui Shu, 'Lun-Yü yü-shuo', *Ts'ui Tung-pi I-shu.*

崔　述　論語餘説　崔東壁遺書

Wang Chen-to, 'Ssŭ-nan chih-nan-chen yü lo-ching-p'an'.

王振鐸　司南指南針與羅經盤

Wang Ching, 'Hu-pei Hung-an Chin-p'en i-chih-ti t'an-chüeh'.

王　勁　湖北紅安金盆遺址的探掘

Wang Chung-shu, 'Han Ch'ang-an Ch'eng k'ao-ku kung-tso shou-huo hsü-chi'.

王仲殊　漢長安城考古工作收穫續記

Wang Chung-shu, 'Han Ch'ang-an Ch'eng k'ao-ku kung-tso-ti ch'u-pu shou-huo'.

王仲殊　漢長安城考古工作的初步收穫

Wang Han-yen, 'Chou-k'ou-tien Ch'ü Ts'ai-Chuang ku-ch'eng i-chih'.

王汉彦　周口店区蔡庄古城遺址

Wang Hsiang, *Fu-shih Yin-ch'i Lei-tsuan.*

王　襄　簠室殷契類纂

Wang Hsien-ch'ien, *Han-Shu Pu-chu.*

王先謙　漢書補注

Wang Kuo-wei, *Hai-ning Wang Ching-an Hsien-sheng I-shu.*

王國維　海寧王靜安先生遺書

Wang Kuo-wei, 'Ku-pen Chu-shu Chi-nien chi-chiao', *Hai-ning Wang Chung-ch'io Kung I-shu.*

王國維　古本竹書紀年輯校　海寧王忠慤公遺書

Wang Kuo-wei, *Kuan-T'ang Chi-Lin.*

王國維　觀堂集林

Wang Kuo-wei, 'Yin pu-tz'ŭ-chung so-chien hsien-kung hsien-wang k'ao', *Hai-ning Wang Chung-ch'io Kung I-shu.*

王國維　殷卜辭中所見先公先王考　海寧王忠慤公遺書

Wang Ming-jui, Chin Shih-hsin, 'Ho-nan Hsin-hsiang Lu-wang Fen Shang-tai i-chih fa-chüeh pao-kao'.

王明瑞　靳世信　河南新鄉潞王坟商代遺址發掘報告

Wang Pao-hsin, *T'ung-chih T'iao-i*.

王葆心　通志條議

Wang Po-hung, Chung Shao-lin, Chang Ch'ang-shou, '1955–57-nien Shan-hsi [Shensi] Ch'ang-an Feng-hsi fa-chüeh chien-pao'.

王伯洪　钟少林　張长寿　1955–57年陕西长安澧西发掘簡报

Wang Shih-jen, 'Han Ch'ang-an Ch'eng nan-chiao li-chih-chien-chu (Ta-t'u-men Ts'un i-chih) yüan-chuang-ti t'ui-ts'e'.

王世仁　汉长安城南郊礼制建筑(大土门村遺址)原状的推测

Wei Chü-hsien, *Chung-Kuo K'ao-ku-hsüeh-shih*.

衛聚賢　中國考古學史

Weng Wen-hao, 'Ku-tai kuan-kai kung-ch'eng fa-chan-shih-chih i-chieh', *Kuo-li Chung-yang Yen-chiu-yüan Li-shih Yü-yen Yen-chiu-so Ching-chu Ts'ai Yüan-p'ei Hsien-sheng Liu-shih-wu-sui Lun-wen Chi*.

翁文灝　古代灌溉工程發展史之一解　國立中央研究院
歷史語言研究所　慶祝蔡元培先生六十五歲論文集

Wu Gin-ding [Wu Chin-ting], 'P'ing-ling fang-ku chi'.

吳金鼎　平陵訪古記

Wu Ju-tso, Yang Chi-ch'ang, 'Kuan-yü "Miao-ti Kou yü San-li Ch'iao" i-shu-chung-ti chi-ko wen-t'i'.

吳汝祚　陽吉昌　关于"庙底沟与三里桥"一書中的几个問題

Yang Chi-ch'ang, 'Ho-nan Shan-Hsien Ch'i-li P'u Shang-tai i-chih-ti fa-chüeh'.

陽吉昌　河南陝縣七里鋪商代遺址的發掘

Yang Ch'i-ch'eng, 'Cheng-Chou Ti-5-wen-wu-ch'ü Ti-1-hsiao-ch'ü fa-chüeh chien-pao'.

楊啟成　鄭州第5文物区第1小区發掘簡報

Yang Chien-fang, 'An-hui Tiao-yü T'ai ch'u-t'u hsiao-mai nien-tai shang-ch'üeh'.

楊建芳　安徽釣魚台出土小麦年代商榷

GLOSSARY

Yang Chien-fang, 'P'ing "Miao-ti Kou yü San-li Ch'iao"'.

楊建芳 評"庙底沟与三里桥"

Yang Fu-tou, 'Hou-ma-hsi hsin-fa-hsien i-tso ku-ch'eng i-chih'.

楊富斗 侯馬西新發現一座古城遺址

Yang Fu-tou, 'K'ao-ku Tung-t'ai : Shan-hsi Hsiang-fen Hsien fa-hsien-ti liang-ch'u i-chih : 2 : Chao-k'ang-Chen-ti Tung-Chou ku-ch'eng-chih'.

楊富斗 考古动态 山西襄汾县发现的两处遺址 二 赵康鎮的东周古城址

Yang Tzŭ-fan, 'Chi-nan Ta-hsin Chuang Shang-tai i-chih k'an-ch'a chi-yao'.

楊子范 济南大辛庄商代遺址勘查紀要

Yao Nai, *Hsi-pao Hsüan Wen-chi*.

姚 鼐 惜抱軒文集

Yin Huan-chang, 'Pa-ko-yüeh-lai-ti Cheng-Chou wen-wu kung-tso kai-k'uang'.

尹煥章 八个月來的鄭州文物工作概況

Yin Huan-chang, Li Chung-i, 'Chiang-su Hsin-i Hsien San-li Tun ku-wen-hua i-chih ti-erh-tz'ŭ fa-chüeh chien-chieh'.

尹煥章 黎忠义 江蘇新沂縣三里墩古文化遺址第二次發掘簡介

Yin Ta, *Chung-Kuo Hsin-shih-ch'i Shih-tai*.

尹 達 中國新石器時代

Yin Ti-fei, 'Shih-lun "Ta-feng Kuei"-ti nien-tai'.

殷滌非 試論"大丰殷"的年代

Yu Ch'ing-han, 'K'ao-ku Tung-t'ai : Ho-nan Nan-yang Shih Shih-li Miao fa-hsien Shang-tai i-chih'.

游清汉 考古動態 河南南陽市十里廟發現商代遺址

Index

References to illustrations are in italic

Abẹokuta, 239
ablution
  facilities: Baluchistan, 231, 232, 233;
    Indus valley, 232
  practices, Islamic, 405
  purposes of terraces and spillways,
    296
Abydos, mortuary complex, 230
Academia Sinica, 3
Acarí, 238, 398
acropolis
  Athens, 309
  Copán, 260
  Indus valley, 232
  Zimbabwe, 397
Adams, Robert, 4, 262, 264-5, 266,
    269-70, 272, 274, 276-7, 278,
    279-80, 292, 293, 294, 295, 300,
    304, 313, 314, 317, 320, 324, 328,
    374-5, 376
administration
  of Chou state: bureaucracies of the
    Chan-Kuo, 118; oligarchic aristo-
    cracies of the Ch'un-Ch'iu, 117,
    118; propertyless strata, 118
  of Shang state, 56-7
administrative
  enclaves: An-yang, 37, 38; Cheng-
    Chou, 34, 35
  foundation, the city as, 176
  organization, in cities in realms of
    primary diffusion, 6
  staff: changes in personnel, 61;

extension of, 57-8; owning means
  of administration, 118; separated
  from means of administration, 118
structure, articulating with urban
  centers, 174
Aegean
  role of trade in urban origins, 288
  secondary diffusion in, 7
  secondary urban generation in, 9
  the question of compaction, 480
Afghanistan
  mother goddess cult, 232
  shrines, 326
afin(s)
  as sacred ceremonial enclaves, 240
  craftsmen of, 240
  defined, 238
  forms of, 239
  hierarchy of, 239
  inhabitants of, 240
  labor force for building, 261
  number of, 239
  plan of, 241, 243
  sanctity of, 238-9, 240
  site of, 238-9
  size of, 239-40
  visitors to, 240
age
  prestige and, 25, 325
  sets, transformation of, 249
agriculture, agricultural
  centralization of, and the rise of
    ceremonial centers, 267

INDEX

INDEX

INDEX

INDEX